THE MARXIAN LEGACY

By the same author

THE DEVELOPMENT OF THE MARXIAN DIALECTIC

SELECTED POLITICAL WRITINGS OF
ROSA LUXEMBURG (*editor*)

ESSAYS ON THE NEW WORKING CLASS
(*co-editor with Dean Savage*)

THE UNKNOWN DIMENSION: EUROPEAN MARXISM
SINCE LENIN (*co-editor with Karl Klare*)

THE MARXIAN LEGACY

Dick Howard

URIZEN BOOKS   NEW YORK

First published in the United States
by Urizen Books

ISBN 0-916354-95-4
ISBN 0-916354-96-2 pbk.

Printed in Great Britain

To Karl Klare

We do not face the world in doctrinaire fashion, declaring 'Here is the truth, kneel here!' ... We do not tell the world, 'Cease your struggles, they are stupid; we want to give you the true watchword of the struggle.' We merely show the world why it actually struggles; and consciousness is something that the world must acquire even if it does not want to.

Karl Marx, 1843

Contents

Preface

When Karl Klare and I decided in 1970 to edit the collection which appeared two years later as *The Unknown Dimension: European Marxism since Lenin*, we assumed that the political movements of the 1960s were in need of a theoretical self-understanding which would permit them to recognise their radical novelty as well as their place in the revolutionary tradition; and we assumed that Marxism provided the theoretical framework within which that self-understanding could be elaborated. Our assumption was mistaken. We began with the paradoxical claim that there were historical reasons sufficient to explain the devolution of orthodox Marxism, but also that the same History which explained Marxism's fate now showed the need for and possibility of a creative reappropriation of Marx's contribution. Further, we thought that the straightforward presentation of the work of a group of theorists who had remained committed to Marxism and struggled to confront its ambiguities without giving in to the pressures of orthodoxy would be seized upon by the political actors of the 1970s, permitting them to avoid the fall-back into dogmatism or the despair that is inevitable when a theoryless movement finds its path blocked and its radical intentions coopted by a constantly self-changing capitalist system. We wanted to offer a legacy purified of the ravages of History; and we thought that History had prepared the terrain for its reception. But the legacy is not a thing, nor even (in Lukács' famous phrase) a method; it is a *project*. Nor is the task to *give* a theory to a political movement; Marx's self-understanding in the passage which serves as the motto of this book is more accurate (as long as the 'must' does not imply Historical necessity).

I have tried here to articulate the problematic that emerges in the attempt to inherit from Marx through the interrogation of

eight seminal thinkers who themselves have confronted in their
own way the same problem. Each chapter was written with an
eye to the inheritance, and to the contemporary political scene.
The chapters are largely expository, and hopefully useful as
such. As I worked on each, it was clear that it could, perhaps
should, be expanded into a volume in its own right. Instead, in
the sinews of the reconstruction lay a developing theory which
constitutes the thrust of this book. I have of course had to omit
a number of figures who could well have found their place
here — Adorno, Benjamin, Goldmann, Gramsci, Korsch, Kosik,
Lefèbvre, Lukács and Marcuse come immediately to mind. Such
omission was inevitable; but it also serves to indicate that my
concern is not with portraiture, nor the history of ideas, but
with theory. More specifically: with political theory and its
ontological presuppositions.

A practical political intention accompanies the theoretical
concern. I feel on somewhat less certain ground here. Although
the theory that I am elaborating here attempts to define the
nature and limits of *the* political, from the standpoint of
practice and from that of theory, it is difficult to free oneself
from the old instincts. The book emerges from the *experience*
of the New Left in the United States and Western Europe in the
1960s. It is a part and reflection of my own search for
self-understanding. From the Civil Rights and Anti-War movements I developed a sort of phenomenological and existential
stance which rapidly crumbled on my arrival in France and
encounter with Marx. The two positions were quite suddenly
combined at the first General Assembly of the March 22nd
Movement, from which I emerged with the distinct impression
that 'Those doctrinaire French Marxists spoke English today!'
Returning home with the euphoria of May 1968 behind me, I
wrote *The Development of the Marxian Dialectic*; but put aside
the proposed continuation, which was to have been a study of
Capital. I turned instead to the history of the working-class
movement, with the intention of making available a perception
of a non-dogmatic, perhaps even 'phenomenological' tradition
which would fit with the attitude of the New Left, and
hopefully help it come to self-understanding. In addition to
editorial work with *Radical America* and *Telos*, this gave rise to
the *Selected Political Writings of Rosa Luxemburg* and *The
Unknown Dimension*. Meanwhile, the movement which was so
important to me was committing suicide, passionately and with
frightening intensity. Unable to remain apart, but incapable of
participating in the doctrinaire quarrels and frenzy of self-
flagellation that followed, the germs of the present volume

began to emerge.

One tentative title for this volume was 'In Search of Revolutionary Theory'. I wanted to know what a 'revolutionary' theory would be, what it could and couldn't do, and on what sort of premises it would rest. I was especially worried by the demands political engagement make on theory, and wanted to know in what the difference between practice and theory consists, since I took my theoretical work as having practical relevance. This is the problem that I began to elaborate in the essay which appears here as the introductory Chapter 1, 'The Theory and Practice of Dialectical Theory', which was written in 1972 for an informal conference organised with a number of friends on 'The Crisis in Marxism'. I wanted to be able to articulate my criticisms of the present bureaucratic and imperial society in a manner that reflected more than the pain and righteous indignation that I felt. But at the same time, I insisted on the independence of theory. The practice of the New Left had shown that the locus of political action was not the traditional liberal one, but that sphere of the everyday which is called civil society. But the disintegration of the New Left revealed that its discovery was not sufficient, or sufficiently elaborated, as I try to show in Chapter 2. The germs of the New Left's organizational suicide seem to have come from apparently opposite, yet in fact identical poles: the return of the political in its Marxian formulation, and the exacerbation of individualism justified vaguely by a political referent. The question of revolution turned into that of *the nature of the political*. What is the political, this noun that designates a verb, this theory that calls on a practice, this social form that depends on individual participation? The dual problem of the nature of revolutionary theory and of the political runs through the interpretation that is offered here.

My frequent use of the concept of 'the political' has been criticised by friends who find it either too vague or worse, a mystification of the practical dimension of social change. From the standpoint of traditional ontology, which will be seen to be that of Marxism as well, both accusations are justified. Marx's *project*, however, was to break with the traditional contemplative standpoint; he sought a mediation of theory and praxis, philosophy and the world, political and social change. Marx was seeking what Merleau-Ponty called a 'philosophy-non-philosophy', a stance that would privilege neither the subject nor the object. He saw History as incarnating the new ontology; but he was unable to remain with what he had uncovered, falling back on an explanatory, rationalising scheme that denies the historical either by privileging History as the telos of a liberated Humanity before which historical events are but accidents, or by turning for explanation to the structure of the 'objective' world in a breakdown theory of socialism's inevitability. Of course, Marx did not always revert to the traditional pattern, although this is the side of the legacy celebrated by Marxian orthodoxy. From the standpoint of the 'new ontology' that was Marx's project, as well as from that of revolutionary practice, the concept of 'the political' says precisely what it means: a noun/verb, theory/practice, social/individual is a *process*, an *experience*, whose completion or reduction would be its elimination or, in theoretical terms, the fall-back to the traditional ontology. Further sociological specification of the political depends on the specific social-historical formation in question; but such specification *is* necessary, for the political is not just any process, but rather designates a social institution without which no society could exist, and in terms of which different social formations can be analysed. In the present context, as the reader follows the movement from 'Within Marxism' to 'Using Marxism' to 'Criticizing Marxism', the fuller sense of this theoretical stance will emerge.

The title of this book is deliberately ambiguous. The book is a presentation of individuals' attempts to inherit from Marx. It is also an analysis of the problems confronting that attempt, as they are rooted in Marx himself *qua* theorist, and as they emerge in their practical translation. There is the further claim that the Marxian legacy consists in a new ontology, a new style of theory that consummates the rupture with the tradition that Marx began. And, from the standpoint of practical politics, the New Left (at least as I understand that experience) appears as the actual heir to and incarnation of the Marxian project. But what of my stance toward Marx himself? What about practice? I ask the second question before answering the first, because it is precisely from the standpoint of practice (including, in that awful term, the 'practice' of theory) that Marx's inability to carry through his radical project has (and has had) negative consequences, to the point that Castoriadis' assertion that it is 'the flesh of the world we combat' is more than justified. On the other hand, Marx is an epoch-making thinker; not only does every reading give new insight, but even more, whatever we may think of Marxian *orthodoxy* we cannot think without *Marx*. As to the problem of practice, which like the Marx-question runs throughout the book, I want only to stress again that the kind of activity one considers as 'revolutionary' depends on the notion of the political and the concomitant ontology adopted.

No recipes are forthcoming here; only the warning against 'Little Leninism' and the moralistic 'Sartre-complex'. Struggles continue in all the avenues and by-ways of our society; we participate from where we are, and as we can; and we recall the aphorism of Marx, which serves as our motto.

Publishing a book is more than the expression of a theory; and it is more than the articulation of the thoughts and experiences of a solitary individual. Rather than try to restate again the theses of this volume, which can only emerge gradually from the development of the text, it remains here to thank those who have contributed to its elaboration in more ways than even they would imagine.

The book is dedicated to Karl Klare, whose intellectual contribution is outweighed only by the personal support, kindness and friendship that we have shared over the years. To Karl's influence as a living presence of what the New Left has always been to me were added the intellectual contributions and friendship of Cornelius Castoriadis and Claude Lefort. From their work, and from our many discussions and disagreements, emerged the theoretical thrust of this book as a whole. Working with Andrew Arato and Jean Cohen, in study groups, on *Telos*, and on a forthcoming book on *Marxism as Critical Theory*, has been essential to my development. Separated by geography, the influence of the other editors of *Telos* was limited to occasional meetings and correspondence; but our common project, for which drafts of several of these chapters were written, has been a continual source of ideas and encouragement. Sandy Petrey has read drafts, and has offered help and criticism without which this book would look very different. The same is true of Hugh Silverman. Influential throughout in his own manner has been Professor Klaus Hartmann, with whom I studied at Texas, Bonn and Tübingen, and whose theoretical input — radically transformed — permeates this volume. Finally, John Winckler, who saw in a few of the early essays the material for a book, and who pushed me to complete it and then helped smooth it to a coherent whole, should be thanked for doing precisely what an editor should: seeing a project germinating, nourishing it, and seeing it through. The list could go on: discussions with Ernst Bloch were helpful in formulating the chapter on his work; similarly for Habermas, Castoriadis and Lefort. Rather than extend it, the list concludes with the most constant source of help, encouragement and support, Brigitte Howard.

Institutions too deserve thanks. During work on this volume, I was the recipient of grants from the National Endowment for the Humanities, the SUNY Research Foundation, and the Humboldt Stiftung. Chapter 2, on the New Left, was originally presented at a seminar of the Research Institute on International Change of Colombia University, and will be published, with a discussion, by Westview Press; it is reprinted here with permission. Chapter 3, on Rosa Luxemburg, was originally presented at the 1st International Meeting sponsored by the Istituto per lo Studio della Società Contemporanea in 1973; the English version published by *Telos* was an abbreviated version. Chapter 4, on Ernst Bloch, emerges from two *Festschrift* articles for Bloch's ninetieth birthday — one in French, the other in German: *Utopie-Marxisme selon E. Bloch*, and *Ernst Blochs Wirkung*. An earlier version of Chapter 7, on Sartre, was published in *Towards a New Marxism*, and another draft appeared in the journal *Cultural Hermeneutics*. Much of the chapter on Jürgen Habermas (Chapter 6) was published in the journal *Theory and Society*, and benefited from several suggestions by its editor, Alvin Gouldner. A version of the chapter on Claude Lefort (9) was published in an edited version in *Telos*. After an earlier draft essay on Castoriadis was rejected by *Telos*, an essay on him appeared as the introduction to a lengthy interview conducted by the APL of Caen; the present Chapter 10 has been extensively rewritten, taking into account his most recent work and lengthy discussions of the earlier material.

DICK HOWARD

Port Jefferson, N.Y.
August 1976

Part One
Introduction

1 The Theory and Practice of Dialectical Theory

The situation of radical theory is a paradoxical one. As theory, it presents analyses and assertions about the historically specific structures and social relations of the present. Its radical premise, on the other hand, is that the reality which it theorizes is contradictory, inhuman and in need of fundamental change. Moreover, if it is Marxian theory, its task is to discover *already* present in this self-contradictory givenness the mediations, the potential forces within the social relations which, once they become (class) conscious, will realize the social change with which they are pregnant. *As theory*, then, radical theory makes positive affirmations about a negative reality, and is consequently a 'critical theory'. As radical, however, it is not at first clear what function it plays, since the mediations are already present, though not active, and since the theory cannot be an external intervention of a voluntarist or moralist sort, for then it could not justify its analytic claims. On the other hand, if the theory has no contribution to make, one wonders what the potential world-changing forces are waiting for — why they don't get on the job.

What is the meaning of the Marxian injunction, in the 11th Thesis on Feuerbach, not simply to interpret but to change the world? On the surface, it suggests that we should not waste our time with theory, but rather get down to the serious business of world-changing practice. This in turn would imply that social contradictions on the strictly material level of physical existence and suffering lead to revolt and social change; and that consciousness of these contradictions springs directly from the material relations, unmediated by any theoretical or social-psychological circumstances. Theory would be a means, a weapon just like barricades or guns, at the service of instinctive practice. But. . . . The history of this century, in its suffering, war and repression, stands like the mocking statue of the Commander sneering at the mechanical materialist Don Juans. We cannot avoid the question: why has there *not* been a truly socialist revolution in this century?[1]

Reading the 11th Thesis as simply an option for practice is inadequate.[2] Closer to Marx's point is the Lukácsian interpretation. On the basis of an analysis of the problems confronting the classical German idealism in which Marx was formed and against which his own views developed, Lukács tries to show that it was his specific dialectical method which enabled Marx to solve the paradoxes and resolve the contradictions that plagued philosophers and social theorists. The Marxian dialectic differs from its idealist counterparts in that it breaks with the passive, contemplative attitude dependent on a pre-given world which it can know but not change.[3] In the place of the abstract observer — divine Logos, transcendental ego, constitutive subject, value-free scientist, or whatever — Marx sets the already involved, praxical participant in the social process. We are 'always-already-social'. The bird's-eye view, for which the world is a congeries of discrete objects interacting and reacting on one another, is replaced by the living participant for whom the web of objects is an invitation and a temptation, to act and react; the subject is part of the objective world, and the world itself becomes active, subjective. The danger that arises here, to which I shall return in the second part of this chapter, is the temptation to conflate theory and praxis, such that theory becomes only another form of social relations, losing its specificity as theory.[4] If this were done, theory would become superfluous. What is needed is already inherent in the paradox of social philosophy: theory which remains itself, but without remaining in splendid isolation. How is this possible?

I take the 11th Thesis as a methodological injuction which talks about the tasks of radical theory-building, and the nature of theory when seen from a dialectical perspective. What I propose to do here is to present the broad methodological lines that a dialectical analysis must follow, and then to reflect on the nature of a dialectical theory as theory, the type of information it gives, and its function as radical.

I   Dialectical Method as Critique

Let me insist from the outset that a radical philosophy is concerned with the social world. If there is such a thing as a 'dialectics of nature', it certainly cannot be understood in an Engelsian (or, indeed, Hegelian) sense where, for example, when water is heated beyond 212 degrees, quantity is said to change to quality, water to steam. We can consider nature as dialectical only if it is taken as a social category. The Engelsian dialectics of nature is a series of mechanical interactions perceptible to the non-situated and non-participant observer. Ultimately, it must treat nature as a thing, other and unchangeable; and therefore it will find itself confronted with the problem of the unknowable thing-in-itself.[5]

As a social and historical being within a socialized and historical world, the philosopher and his/her object are in a homogeneous medium. The philosopher is a socialized and historical product, actor and acted upon. We did not create the language we speak or the world in which we live. Our world and culture are the creation of humans past and present. Yet we use the language and world to our own personal and social ends, changing them and inscribing our presence in them. The objects we confront are themselves social and historical, created by past and present generations, inlaid with strata of meaning which we learn to reactivate and interpret in original ways, finding new sense in the old, and old sense in the new. The world is presented to us through social and historical mediations into which we were born but which we both preserve and alter by our action and passion. We and our world are defining and defined, individual and social, active agents and passive heirs. No transcendent god or ego can look down and take it all in; only we, in living, give and are given meaning. This is what Hegel meant when he insisted that the key to the dialectic is the notion of 'substance as subject'. It is also what Marx's Feuerbach critique aimed at establishing, and constitutes the basic position in terms of which philosophy functions as *critique.*

Of course, this supple reciprocity is not what appears to confront us in our daily lives on the soil of capitalism. There, the typical emotion is anxiety in the face of a seemingly self-regulating System; things and people threaten my identity and stand against me as Other; I feel empty, and try to fill out my person and give it permanence by buying and acquiring commodities. I become the centre of my universe, a world of things functioning according to their own laws which I can at best understand and use but never fundamentally alter. I become an object to myself, calculating how best I can 'spend' my scarce time, preserve myself and control the menace so as to acquire that empty calm called happiness. I do not create meanings in this world, but at best use the accepted value codes to carve out some sense of my person and place in the scheme of things. My passivity is continually solicited by the things around me: this year Chrysler is going to 'sell you peace of mind, so calm down, calm down'; Howard Johnson's motels provide me 'with a friend wherever you go'; *Time* magazine tells me that it is 'the last word in packaging the news'; and the seductive voice from the radio whispers huskily 'Fly me.' From 30,000 feet laser-guided 'smart' bombs are launched on a people struggling for their dignity and culture, while I inch along bumper to bumper on the super-expressway, pushing the buttons to get a better station, different commercials, only to hear them coming out of the music itself. In Sartre's terms, this is the situation of *serial* existence.

Henri Lefèbvre calls our social form 'the bureaucratic society of controlled consumption'.[6] Its tentacles reach out toward the smallest details of the most insignificant moment. Technological rationality, the quantification and calculation that has produced and is continually reproduced by industrial accumulating civilization has engendered its own justification and created its own meanings. But can this system close itself completely? Were it really a self-justificatory, self-referential, all-encompassing system which created us all in its image, then we wouldn't even be able to talk about it, to pin it down, to bitch about it; we wouldn't feel the anxiety of aloneness, search for identity, crave peace. Like the god presented in the 'free will' argument of the theologian, the system must allow a measure of freedom, if only so that we can recognize it and thus pray to it. But as some theologians also understood, because it must be recognized by us, it is, ultimately, dependent on us, on our belief, acceptance, and submission. This social system, like the god of yore, sets itself the contradictory and impossible task: it demands that the human being be obedient to it, recognize its authority and rights, at the same time that such absolute obedience would prevent it from functioning, since it demands recognition from *free* wills, not ones that are conditioned to believe.[7] The system demands that we feel the need for security, for how else would we keep buying, treat our work as a *means* to get newer and different things, blame ourselves and not it for our discomfort? But can this need be controlled?

It is logically impossible to conceive of a closed, self-recreating and self-perpetuating system. From the inside, it would not appear as a system. To conceive of it we would have to be outside of it — in which case it would not be closed. The continuation of the system, therefore, depends on our *active* acquiescence or internalization of its norms. Presuming, then, that we're not stupid (and excluding a historicist version of the original sin doctrine, which puts the blame on the Past, or on Nature), the question becomes: how is it possible for us to actively will our own unhappy subjugation?

The question is not how to conceive of some force breaking into the closed circle and liberating us (à la Marcuse . . . or à la Lin Piao). What we need to know is how it is possible for free beings to create their own slavery . . . for only then can they create their own liberation. Only on the assumption that it is such free beings who are responsible for the creation and perpetuation of bureaucratic capitalism can we even envision the possibility of liberation. A 'leninist' message of freedom, elaborated by bourgeois intellectuals, could not possibly touch the masses unless they were essentially free, though temporarily self-enslaved.

What must be accounted for is the *alienation* of the citizen in capitalist society which permits the thriving of a *reified* system in which the things and their impersonal laws rule supreme. How is it possible that the product dominate the producer, the object the subject?

Precisely that which prevents the system from being closed creates the possibility of alienation and reification: the fact that we are created by it and create it, are both subject and object, producer and product. The completion of the system would be its collapse; which is why Marcuse's notion of repressive desublimation in its varied forms of pseudo-freedom is so crucial to understanding the maintenance of capitalism, the failure of revolution. Even if we disagree with the details of Marcuse's argument, he has hit at the conceptual centre of the problem. On the other hand, as the system strives to maintain itself by reducing ever more the spaces for free activity, it must increase the alienation of the subject,— that is, make it even more object-like — and increase the fetishism by eliminating all traces of the human project from the objective world. It does so by increasingly abstracting from all human *quality*, reducing the world to the law-likeness of quantitative relations. At the same time, however, that it homogenizes for its own purposes, it renders all the more evident the commonality of our collective destiny.[8] This commonality is but the obverse side of the coin referred to at the beginning of this section — that insofar as the world is through and through a social world whose subjects are social subject-objects, and whose objects are social object-subjects, it is our common collective destiny to receive and create social meaning. And, to the common quantitative measure of the reified world, there corresponds on this obverse side a common qualitative measure: human praxis in its varied forms.

The social world (both essentially, and in its reified form) is a praxical world. By praxical (or praxis), I do not mean simply technique, activity of some sort or another governed by laws external to it. Praxical activity is self-regulated goal-oriented activity operating in terms of what Habermas calls an 'interest in freedom'. By freedom here is understood, in the sense of classical German Idealism, the autonomy of the moral subject acting in terms of self-given laws aiming at the overcoming of otherness, of heteronomy. Insofar as this moral subject is an actual, embodied social subject, its autonomy is not caprice (*Willkür*) but rather the social will acting within an historically given situation which it did not choose, and in which the activation of its autonomy is limited by the inherited forms. This is what Marx had in mind when he said that humankind does not begin any new work, but rather consciously completes that begun before its time. The past cannot be simply negated; my autonomy in relation to the world in which I find myself consists in my taking possession of it as mine, eliminating its reified dominance, changing my relation to it.

Insofar as we are embodied beings living in a world that is the collective creation of past and present humans, our activity will be governed, in part, by considerations external to ourselves. Though its common measure is praxis, our world is not transparent. If it were, these considerations would not be necessary; all would be for the best in the best of theory-less worlds, and the dream of the positivist or technocratic utopia would be realized. In fact, the world is shot through with opacity and irrationality, with objects and social relations which have outlived their times and yet remain to haunt the present. We need a concept like Sartre's 'practico-inert' or Merleau-Ponty's 'flesh' in order to account for that thick skin that remains and absorbs human intentionality and praxis long after its own subjective drives have left it. The Sartrean notion of the practico-inert, with its dualist construction, attempts to account for this intersubjective tissue which, in its separation from free praxis both incites and invites to action and at the same time is capable of absorbing it like a sponge, hiding from it its own meaning. Merleau-Ponty's flesh has a similar goal, but strives to avoid the dualism that vitiates the Sartrean concept. It is not important to enter into the nuances here, but rather to stress that this inter-world exists and acts, and that it must be taken into account when we attempt to present an historico-social account of the structure of our alienation and the possibilities of our self-liberation.

Our embodiment, and consequent rejection of either an idealism or a materialism in any simplistic sense, helps account for the possibility of alienation and reification. We are not pure minds, free essences, all-seeing egos. We make love, eat and defecate. Iron bars damned well do a prison make. It is precisely for this reason that we do much of what occupies our time and reveries. And it is precisely for this reason that the bourgeois social 'scientist' can predict our behaviour, that the Skinnerian can operantly condition us, that advertisements seduce us. But not always; not completely. The victory of total conditioning would at the same time be its loss. The bourgeois theorist dealing in the realm of appearances, juggling the surface presentations and searching for a quantitative ordering or pigeonholing, is incapable of providing an explanation for the phenomena manipulated. Theory becomes simply the mechanical reflection and descriptive ordering of a series of phenomena. If one manipulation fails, all that remains is to try another, and still another ... as long as the subjects let themselves be experimented on. More refined techniques of manipulation can be — and have been — developed. But this only prolongs the agony.[9]

That social practice which appears as other-determined, the result of necessity imposed by my bodily being-in-the-world, has to be understood as praxical as well as practical. Without the continual presence of praxis, alienation cannot be overcome. We can assert that in production there is an element of both, the former being called work and the latter labour. Labour would be action performed under external constraint (either of a personal master, or simply material necessity such as the technique an artist must acquire before he/she can create), while work would be self-definitional, teleological, creative.[10] The precondition of our liberation, then, is the liberation of work from labour, of praxis from constrained practice — *as far as that is possible.* (The last clause implies historical specificity, for work will always demand labour; what can be changed is the *relation* of the two operations.)

Thus understood, the task of philosophy (or theory) becomes an eminently moral one, social and engaged, which consists in uncovering the moments of praxis within a given social and historical structure. It provides the active subjects with that hermeneutic mirror which renders evident to them that which is implicit in their own lives. This evidence, which is nothing other than a socially specific autonomy as opposed to the unconscious heteronomy typical of the alienated world, renders them self-conscious, and thus autonomous social subjects. It does not, of course, eliminate the realm of necessity, nor does it alter the material infrastructure. What it does, as we shall see more clearly in Section II, is to create the conditions for the possibility of human self-affirmation, and hence for social change. It is not yet a politics, but it is the precondition for political action. And its insistence on the historical situatedness of its problems avoids the reproach of an abstract utopia.

In a word, what dialectical theory demands is not criticism but critique; not an ethical Ought but a mediated movement from heteronomy to autonomy. It is not a question of knowing what we Ought to do, but rather of understanding the stages or mediations by which we move from the inarticulate givenness of the present towards an autonomous opening to the future. We have to transcend the present, and not by imagination alone. We need a principle which has its foot, so to speak, in both the present and the future, the is and the ought; something which is not simply an ideal but actually a material force. Classical German Idealism sought such a principle, for example, in Schiller's *Spieltrieb*, in what Fichte first called Community and later called the Nation, in Hegel's Spirit and finally in Marx's Proletariat. The task of dialectical theory becomes the uncovering and unleashing of this principle of mediation in its concrete historical specificity.[11]

The fundamental principle on which this dialectical analysis operates is that every human practice is also a form of praxis, and that therefore social formations and activity must be understood in terms of the horizon towards which they are moving, their telos.[12] Without a principle of teleology, the analysis can only be positivist, static and descriptive; without such a principle, one remains at the level of appearance, society is atomized and immediacy reigns supreme. The teleological orientation demands that we think in terms of continually created and recreated relations, not fixed and permanent fluxes of atoms. It is an historical and dynamic approach, imaginative and active, not receptive and formal. The *telos* does not exist as a property or thingly aspect of the relations to be analyzed; it is their immanent *horizon*, their sense and their potential. It may be an unrealized potential[13] — indeed, it will be unrealized unless it is consciously acted upon, and the results of that action within human history will open up a new horizon. It is because each of us, in our daily lives, bumps up against something unexpected, unsatisfactory, incomplete, that we are jarred into recognizing that we tend to pass most of our lives unconsciously, happy in the world of appearances where we arrange our lives with more or less agility, like Plato's cave-dwellers. This is not a moral or intellectual weakness, for the fetishized commodity world is the world that we and our fellows inhabit. We can recognize that we are living in the shadow world of appearances only insofar as, being also praxical, we have some, perhaps vague and intuitive, knowledge of the possibilities that lie beyond. We needn't know more about them then that they are possibilities; in fact, they may not even exist — or perhaps if they do not exist now, they will come into existence when, acting as if they did exist, we confront the shadow world in such a way that our *telos* becomes a self-fulfilling prophecy. (This of course is only possible if objective mediations do already exist for us to set into action; otherwise, we would be striving to realize an abstract universal or an abstract utopia — and not a concrete one that is possible.)

The complex play by which praxis and practice combine in creating a world of objects and meanings that we continually reactivate consciously or unconsciously is of course affected by the control of power positions within the society. Whether the economic infrastructure is 'determinant in the last instance', as Engels would have it, is not the central issue. Indeed, we have to rethink the nature of the economic itself in praxical, dialectical terms. Marx's *Capital* is not an economics textbook. Subtitled a 'Critique of Political Economy', it makes sense only from a dialectical standpoint (which also prevents us from taking it as dogma, doctrine or timeless truth). In a letter to Lassalle (1857), Marx presents his task as 'a presentation of the system, and through the presentation a critique of that system'. *Capital* is precisely that paradoxical type of radical theory: a positive presentation of a negative or contradictory reality. By showing that the underlying structures of the capitalist economy are the product of a series of social relations, whose articulation he analyzes in a structure which parallels that of Hegel's *Logic*,[14] beginning with the most immediate relations of production (Hegel's Being), passing through the mediation of the circulation process (Hegel's Essence), on to a consideration of the system as a whole (Hegel's Concept), Marx pinpoints the play of social relations that make possible the continuation of the system.[15] The 'contradictions' of capitalism from a strictly economic point of view can be overcome, as Marx himself repeatedly shows.[16] The contradiction which cannot be overcome is that of the system's being fully systematic, of its complete subordination not just of the world economy (as Rosa Luxemburg thought), but of the human beings on whom it depends.[17]

The lesson of Marx's *Capital* for a dialectical theory is twofold. There is, first of all, the famous 'fetishism of commodities' discussion, which is central to the further development, and provides a model for the dialectical hermeneutic which dissolves the appearances, reducing their seeming fixity to a flux of interhuman relations. But, second, this is only possible because of the teleological orientation that enables Marx to go beneath, to uncover the contradictions in a system whose inhumanity is patent. Marx could have remained with a moral critique, as did many socialists at that time and since; he could have simply applied the material uncovered by bourgeois critics against the system, organizing opposition as a Proudhonian, Owenist or even Leninist. What he did do in *Capital*, however, was different; it was *theoretical*, not *political* (at least not in the common understanding of radical politics, centered around perceivable acts in a specific arena). He knew that he had to discover the underlying mediations, the forces that could lead the system to transcend itself. And these mediations only reveal themselves to the future-oriented praxical dialectic.

The dialectical theory which is conscious of its paradoxical insertion and the demands that this situation poses to it *remains a theory*. But it is a theory conscious that a successful interpretation of the social praxis and practice that weave the form and content of the historical present is only possible if it includes within its objects their horizon. The interpretation of the world is possible only for those who understand the need to change it by liberating its human possibilities, i.e., its human beings. Theory must therefore take account of praxis and its possibilities, but at the same time must itself remain theory. The theory must be oriented towards changing the world, but it itself cannot pretend to effectuate that change. It operates in terms of a teleology, not a causal analysis, and must take a possible future as operational in its analysis of the present. It was claimed above to have a moral, social and engaged function; yet it cannot be looked at as a means to some pre-given end, but rather must determine and justify its ends to itself. The relationship entailed here is similar to that of language to thought or poetry, where language is necessary to the project but not identical with it, nor merely a means to it, since the poem or thought does not exist except in the language used to express it. The subject who used the language to write a poem is not taking language as a tool or means, but rather needs the language itself to even entertain the poetic project, for which the language is then brought into play.

II The Importance of the *Difference*

In an early essay, Herbert Marcuse writes:

> When reason has been realized as the rational organization of mankind, philosophy is left without an object. For philosophy, to the extent that it has been, up to the present, more than an occupation or a discipline within the given division of labor, has always drawn its life from reason's not yet being reality. ('Philosophy and Critical Theory', in *Zeitschrift für Sozialforschung*, Bd 6, 1937, p. 632.)

The first insight of theory — and, incidentally, the condition for radical political practice which implies a break with routine — is that there is more to the world than what appears immediately, that the appearances are deficient in some way, and that they present themselves as they do because of forces which can be uncovered — or, in the case of radical practice, opened for change — by the critical use of reason. Philosophy, or theory, is thus based on the *difference* between appearance and reality, thought and being, the is and the ought, the signifier and the signified. This difference provides its motivation, defines the nature and limits of its interrogation. We can concretize the quest in Marcuse's terms as reason's searching the world in the attempt to reconcile itself with itself; or in Hegelian concept as a cosmic struggle for recognition by an Other which is like the subject; or in the language of the young Marx as the making philosophical of the world and the making worldly of philosophy; or simply as the everyday struggle of humans to live in a human world. The motivation of theory, in short, would be its own elimination.

We must be careful here. Is the goal to impose Reason on an uncooperative, dumb and passive world? Is it to change the world in such a way that the difference is eliminated and Reason no longer has an object? The error in both cases is not simply that of total systematicity but, correlatively, that Reason is treated as a thing, a system of doctrine, which is either to be applied to the world from without or which is nothing but the faithful reflection of the world's structure. Reason (or philosophy, or Theory) loses its specificity and is anthropologistically conflated with the other *things* existing in a monistic or one-dimensional universe. The result, in political translation, is in both cases a form of monolithic bureaucratism, a closed system in which orders come from the top and are imposed by whatever means necessary. While there have been historical examples of the attempt to realize this sort of systematicity,[18] they have always failed for precisely the reasons mentioned previously: namely, the inconsistency and impossibility of a closed social system, of the reduction of human subjectivity to dead passivity.

If this is the case, what sense does it make to argue that dialectical knowledge is governed by the inherent teleological possibilities of the social world, and that this knowledge is nothing but the self-understanding of its own object and the prelude to the object's self-realization? The teleology seems to demand an 'end of history', and the claim of the dialectic seems to be that we should let the world be what it can become, a becoming which does not call for our help. This seeming, however, omits the fact that we are part of that world; it is a contemplative, god's-eye view (the *pensée de survol* criticized by Merleau-Ponty). We need to look more closely, first at the nature of the social teleology; then at the kind of knowledge that the dialectic gives us, and its specificity as theory; and finally at the reasons for claiming that this theory, as theory, is inherently radical, that it is positive in its negativity, a critique which avoids the sterility of abstract criticism by continually recreating itself as it transcends itself.

The premise on which all theory rests is the *difference*. This implies that what is immediately given is not in itself complete and satisfactory, and it sets up the task of piercing beneath, uncovering the structure, relations and possibilities which present themselves as the conditions of the possibility of the object's appearing as it does. The task is both negative and positive, regressive and progressive, critical and reconstructive. Simply to begin implies that we have some notion of a truth-horizon, for otherwise the objects would overwhelm us with their sheer positivity, and we would remain passive spectators before a magic-lantern show. That we recognize the difference and commence the task supposes that the objects present themselves in relation to a truth or reality the explication of which is theory's goal.

The telos which must be supposed is the truth. In its nakedness, this statement is shockingly formal, slippery and empty. Concretely, the truth has many incarnations, is lived in many forms, all of which can be reduced to one basic structure: *social* autonomy. Note that I stress social here. The autonomy that is meant is not the immediate self-referential nature of a thing turned in on itself; that would be the empty formal immediacy of a monad. *Social* autonomy is that historically specific situation in which the social individual recognizes him/herself in a socially given other, such that the relation that is established is one of *mediated* homogeneity.[19] It is the social situation in which the rigidity of law-like social norms is overcome, the constraints of practice mastered, and social praxis let free in an infinite field of co-possibilities. The truth for a human being is not a state of affairs but an open expanse of playful development, where each achievement sets free new capacities and social variations.

As the horizon of social actions and social formations, the *telos* has no concrete incarnation outside of the historically specific moments in which individual and collective actions continually engender it. In a specific society, or in a given social relation, the same 'objective' formation may or may not be inscribed with the richness of teleological possibility. Actions, attitudes, institutions are contextual, and must be analyzed — dialectically — in their specificity. In a given historical configuration, for example, democracy may be simply a form by which those in power manipulate the masses in order to preserve their control; while at another juncture, democratic forms can serve to unleash desires and possibilities which lead precisely to the self-affirmation of the masses against the forms of socio-economic domination typical, say, of bureaucratic society. High culture may serve as an alibi in one social moment, while at another it may be the spur of revolt against a system whose quantitative norms impede the human goals articulated in culture. Sexuality, dope, and counter-culture may be progressive in one context, while in another they are the cop-out of resigned individualism.[20]

A dialectical analysis is no substitute for empirical investigation; its discoveries are limited and specific, continually to be begun anew. At the same time, however, the dialectical attitude inflects the style, form and execution of empirical study.[21] It warns us against the attitude which contemplates, orders and categorizes the objects of the world as if they were just so much dead matter; and it insists that we recognize our objects as social relations, themselves both objective and subjective. The manipulation of things is increasingly possible for our highly refined scientific techniques. But the very desire to manipulate things supposes that they could well be otherwise without the interference of the manipulator. It supposes that they have other possibilities, a horizon of openness, and, in the case of social relations, the stubbornness that is the greatness of the human animal.

The kind of knowledge that the dialectical analysis yields is obviously not that which the accepted paradigm of the natural sciences demands. It is the subject's knowledge of its, and the world's, possibilities. Thrust forward in its investigation by the difference, the subject is continually seeking to overcome the otherness of its world. We saw that in one sense the achievement of this quest would be the conflation of subject and object, theory and world. Indeed, insofar as the self-consciousness of the social subject involves consciousness of its social world — more specifically, involves the making subject-like of that social world, i.e., involves changing that world — then the self-consciousness which is social consciousness also carries with it the project of changing that world. But this project is self-annulling, and could only be achieved through the cancellation of the difference which made possible the original project. Absolute knowledge, like total dictatorship or total freedom, is possible only when all subjectivity — and hence, knowledge itself — is eliminated.

The knowledge yielded by the dialectical analysis preserves and respects the difference, existing only within or as that differential relation. Its goal is not possession of a thing but the self-understanding of a relationship. Here dialectic and dialogue converge.[22] Dialogue is only possible between two separate but equal subjects who respect their difference while striving to understand it. Dialectic is the means of that understanding and self-understanding in and of the dialogue. The dialectical dialogue takes place not only among humans, but also between them and their world (past and present) insofar as they, as social and worldly, and it, as impregnated with their meanings, projects and praxis, interact more or less consciously with one another. The model of the psychoanalytical dialogue, stressed by Habermas, Apel, Ricoeur and others, provides a useful analogy here.

In stressing the preservation of the difference, and in introducing the psychoanalytic model, I have obviously opened a hornet's nest, alluded to at the outset by the discussion of Marx's 'change the world'. If the difference is preserved, does this imply that we let things be as they are, drawing consolation from knowledge, as for example in Hegel's resigned 'Preface' to the *Philosophy of Right*, filled with phrases of reconciliation, refusing 'to construct a state as it ought to be', finding that 'there is less chill in the peace with the world which knowledge supplies', or envisaging philosophy's 'grey in grey' as not to be 'rejuvenated but only understood'? How can theory maintain itself apart from the world, and yet claim to be radical? And, how can theory affect praxis while remaining distinct from it?

The dialectical stance permits the rediscovery of a horizon of mediations whose material force can exert the physical change which makes possible the self-recognition and self-change towards a maximally free interaction of self-conscious social actors (persons *and* institutions). Theory does not come from outside the system; it is the system's self-consciousness of its own potential, and thus is itself a part of the system. It is historically and socially specific, not a once-and-for-all truth. Its immanence and specificity point to the fact that the object of theory (which is also its subject) is nothing other than daily life lived on the soil of the present. Within that daily life, theory must learn to distinguish the appearance from its horizon; it must understand the forces at work which create the disbalances that permit social movement, entail the growth of self-consciousness and, in fact, are the very condition of the possibility of the theory. In this sense, the locus of theory need not be the printed, or even the spoken, word. In our increasingly homogenized and reified world, we become more and more alike, share a common attitude towards the world and ourselves, an attitude determined or infected by the need of the social system, in all their contradictoriness. The awareness of the difference, the need for theory and the self-consciousness that arises with it, can be tripped off by various forms of praxical striving — exemplary actions of the few, the wildcat strike, the youth revolt against traditional values. What counts is that these triggers not be abstract utopias, off in the realm of phantasy; they must be concrete, rooted in daily life and recognizable to all of us because they spring from a common situation that lies all around us.

Not all praxis is theory; and not all theory is praxical. Nor should this be the case. Praxis that presents itself as, or is taken for a substitute for theory is blind, runs into dead ends, becomes habit or defensive spite, an excuse for the lazy and a denial of the difference. Theory that pretends to replace or even guide praxis is empty, pretentious and dogmatic. Nor is theory related to praxis, or vice versa, simply as the continual movement from one to the other, trial-and-error, redprint and execution. From a tactical point of view (in politics, or in arranging my own life), theory may be totally useless for the immediate tasks at hand, which are determined by an accidental conjunction of events.

Merleau-Ponty once entitled an essay on theory 'Everywhere and Nowhere'. This is the point, the paradox of radical theory from which we began. It has no specific object that would permit us to place it in an organigram of the tasks of society, next to say sociology or physics, above or below making love and listening to music. But, like ourselves, it is everywhere. It is critique; it is the opening of hidden horizons; it is the poetry which gives empirical prose its human meaning. We cannot reduce theory to, nor impose it on, practice. But without that awareness of the difference which is the condition of theory, our action is but dumb habit living in a world of pre-given meaning. In the project of daily life, simply in order to live and love, we do a kind of theory without being conscious of it. This is a first, and necessary, step; but it is not sufficient. Were we to know ourselves in what we do, we would acquire that self-consciousness and human feeling that is the condition of not just revolution but a human social world. Social self-consciousness is that positive built upon a negative typical of an open radical theory that continually transcends itself and realizes new possibilities for human relations.

2 The Future as Present: Theoretical and Political Implications

I Prelude ... and Fugue!

In retrospect, the incoherence of the New Left is astounding. Every shade of political and moral conviction united in single and multi-issue campaigns which brought to awareness the rent fibre of the American Joseph's many-coloured coat. In an immediate sense, it was not a vision of the future but a projection, an identification, that united the critics: identification with guerrilla movements — be they Castroist, Christian or Communist-Trotskyist; identification with Eastern European intellectuals and youth who dared speak out in the stifling world of total bureaucracy; identification with the Vietnamese, Chinese, North Koreans and even Albanians, as well as a projection on to the American Blacks, ethnic poor, technological and traditional working clases. Camus was as important as Marx, the Bible as 'On Contradiction', Nietzsche and Freud as Bakunin and Tolstoy. All this lived comfortably (for a time) with the attempt to restructure daily life, to build a counter-culture while at the same time fighting Imperialist-Capitalism as The Enemy.

Today the New Left is in shambles, from Czechloslovakia to the Third World, to our own. We wonder what in fact it was. Dropping out, returning to God or gods, to the earth or the drug-dazed sky? (Or, too often, crushed by the bureaucratic state, be it FBI, CIA, or USSR!) It is difficult to conceive of the Marches on Washington, the solidarity of building occupations, the intensity of the minute. When Leonard Woodcock calls his UAW troops to Washington, it seems as incoherent as Ford's economic experts — though perhaps more traditional. The New Left rose like a meteor, burned itself out, ecstatic. What happened? What traces remain? What did it mean? Benign neglect has replaced the Civil Rights Movement; Allende is dead and the only 'progressive' regimes in the Third World are military; the war has temporarily ended in S.E. Asia, but the Middle Eastern situation has worsened; the invasion of Czechloslovakia confirmed the most dour anti-communists; and the Lin Piao escapade coupled with Nixon's visit demystified China. Unless you're a believer in the Breakdown Theory — which the New Left never was — it's certainly not comforting to read the economic statistics for the U.S. today.

Because it rose so quickly and catalyzed so many hopes; and because it died so pitifully and seemed to leave nothing in its place — the New Left presents an enigma, rich in suggestions for the interpreter. The following remarks should be read under a series of *caveats*: (1) They do not claim descriptive completeness, nor is each illustration or suggestion coupled with a stock of references; each of us will certainly be able to provide our own. (2) The description that is offered is conceptual and historical at once, trying to make clear *post festum* the choices that were often made quite unconsciously. My goal is to offer a *framework* for a general interpretation. The guiding thread is that the New Left was neither 'necessary' in some causal sense, nor 'accidental' in an existential-irrationalist world. It represents our society's own self-interpretation. (3) This implies a kind of reflexive sociology to whose presuppositions I can only allude in this essentially descriptive account. This over-general approach seems to have the virtue of proposing discussion, not blocking it off with 'facts'. Hence, I shall be less concerned with what the New Left said and/or envisioned than with what it did and the meaning of its activity for our understanding of our present situation. (4) I will be starting from the premises of Marx, adapting his method to the present, and then using the structure of that present — including the lesson of the New Left — to criticize Marx. This does not lessen the importance of Marx; nor should it be interpreted within a Manichaean friend/foe context. I write as a participant, reflecting on the New Left experience as my own, concerned with the spirit more than the letter; and attempting here to learn something about myself and my society as well as the meaning of my — of our — work in the present.

II Problems of Definition and of Method

If anything is clear, it is that the New Left was hardly a unified phenomenon. The term may be one of those 'sponges' ridiculed by C. Wright Mills. On the other hand, it has its usefulness. It forces us to look beneath the empirical to the structural conditions which the category reflects and defines, however inadequately. It demands that we analyze in such a way that the unity and sense of our object emerge in the analysis itself. We cannot fly above our object, assuming that it has already been defined; we are looking for the *new*, and hence our method must permit to appear.

It is not generally helpful for an historian to speak of a 'New' Left practice in opposition to the 'Old'. If we were to think of the Old Left as characterized by the Leninist 'party of a new type', for example, this labelling of the New Left would prove deceptive. After all, anti-Leninists of the non-Social Democratic type were strong enough to lead Lenin to write 'Left-Wing Communism: An Infantile Disease'; to give Stalin reason to defile and disfigure the person and work of Rosa Luxemburg: and to be partially at the root of the sacrifice of Spain to Franco and his minions — to mention but three cases that come immediately to mind. In this sense, the 'New' Left is an old phenomenon.

Nor is it historically useful to distinguish a New Left from an Old Left theory of capitalism and its revolutionary potential. From the moral and liberalist utopia of the Port Huron Statement to the radical rhetoric of the Weatherpeople, Progressive Labor and assorted company, the path was back to Marxism — but if the first time was tragedy, this time was a farce as well. Encountering practical and theoretical problems — to be discussed in a moment — much of the New Left took the facile path back to 'science', a kind of compensation for the 'sins' of its moralistic past and a way of countering its academic enemies on their own terrain. The Marxism that was adopted was mostly of the crudest sort, mechanical in its sociology, metaphysical in its ideology. It is not surprising that, even within its own frame of reference, it made no really fruitful contributions here. As opposed to this, if we think beyond the context of the United States, the German SDS, Sozial Demokratische Studentenbund for example, was probably the most scholarly political movement in recent memory, basing its new tactics and style precisely on a rereading of Marx.[1] The same was true at least partially elsewhere, from France to Czechoslovakia.

If we try to use the criterion of 'vision of the future' as a *differentia specifica*, we get only a bit further from the historical stance. If anything characterized the New Left *as an everyday practice*, it was its denial of a vision of the future, its insistence on living today in the everyday, incarnating the new social relations in the here and now. The 'old' idea of sacrifice for the future, making the revolution for one's grandchildren, or awaiting the maturation of the contradictions, was ridiculed. This was perhaps one reason for the New Left's anti-Leninism. It certainly had something to do with the youthfulness of most of the participants; but youth is not a sufficient explanation, any more than is psychology, for a political practice.

The question of vision immediately entails that of ideology. Marxism itself of course emerged from the discovery of the function of ideology, first as a mask of the real (critique of religion) and then as the structure of the real itself (critique of capitalism). Marxists like to talk about 'scientific socialism', to distinguish themselves from 'utopians' of various orders. This is certainly consistent with Marx insofar as what really galled the Founder was not the goals of the utopians, but that their theory and practice hurt, not helped, the good cause.[2] But the Marxists, from Engels on, also tended to make 'scientific socialism' an ideology — now in the sense that it was not just a refutation of disguised and misguided positions, nor solely a guide to practice; it was also to be an ideology in the explicitly 'religious', faith-giving, sense. Ideology justified the sacrifices and trials here in the capitalist present; and — however vaguely — promised the socialist future.[3]

If the Old Left had a vision of the future and an ideology — in the double sense — the New Left's immediacy and concern with the everyday today acquires a structural importance. Certainly, New Leftists threw around the term ideology; and periodically were convinced that one was needed. Its lack, however, speaks loudly. Marx *discovered* ideology as a structure of the real; he did not run around accusing others of being subjectively ideologists — as his continual writing of 'Critiques' indicates. He did not oppose a true to a false ideology, nor a 'really real' revealed by science to a false representation of it. He turned to the structure of the real in order to read its sense as ideology.[4] The everyday practice of the New Left is consistent with Marx's theoretical practice as ideology-critique: making the world speak the contradictory structures and imperatives which present themselves as fixed, permanent and natural. Neither moral criticism based on values externally derived or justified, nor scientific comparison with a true and a false, a good and a bad society: Marx's theory and the New Left's practice aim, as Marx put it enigmatically in 1843, at 'bringing those petrified relations to dancing by singing before them their own melody'.

My methodological premise, therefore, will be that of Marx's ideology-critique. To relate the expression to the expressed, signifier to signified, in a unitary structure; to try to read the New Left as a phenomenon without prejudicing the analysis by pretending either to know the real or to know what the real ought to be. It is not a question of judging. Accepting its disparateness, refusing to privilege the 'subjective' or the 'objective', the attempt will be to see what the New Left has to tell us about our society and the kind of revolutionary project it engenders.

III Intellectual Roots

While all the New Lefts can be understood as oriented by and around Marxism, the salient features reside in the ways in which they deviate from the model. Since the movement in the United States was the least affected by Marxism in its formative stage, these 'deviant' sources expressed themselves most purely and profoundly here and are a reason to concentrate on the U.S.

There is a further reason to concentrate on the United States as typical. The New Left existed as a 'movement', which affected far more persons than those who were organizationally affiliated with it. Its open structure permitted many to feel themselves a part of the movement, to empathize with it and to learn from it. Particularly important to all the New Lefts were the vast protest movements that grew up in the U.S. — first the Civil Rights Movement, then the University Reform and Free Speech Movements, and finally the movement sparked by opposition to the Vietnam War. Most striking in this *movement-character* is that the moral stance predominated over the strategic revolutionary orientation. The lack of organization of these multifaceted movements typified also, to a large degree, the revolutionaries whose causes they supported. Particularly in the case of Vietnam, the role of *revolutionary will*, individual courage and willingness to be sacrificed, were impressive. It was inevitable that a certain *voluntarism* characterize the intellectual, organizational, political and tactical stance of the New Left.[5]

This voluntarism, which typified the climate in which the New Left functioned, coloured its choice of theorists. In the U.S. — though nowhere else to my knowledge — the Camus of *The Rebel* played a crucial role. Where he was replaced by Sartre, it was certainly not the Sartre of 'The Communists and the Peace', nor the author of the *Critique de la raison dialec-*

tique (finally translated after fifteen years!). Of course, the existentialist tradition opened on to the Anarchists on the one hand, and the holy, mystical and self-sacrificing populists on the other. Moral issues, such as those portrayed in Camus' play 'The Just Assassins', dominated the discussion of means/ ends — rather than the concern with strategy and tactics, the organizational question, social structure, the proletariat, and the like. When historical issues — from the Russian terrorists to the classical anarchists — arose, they were treated as part of the existential present. There was no historical consciousness, as the metaphors and images chosen by New Left writers indicate.

This existential voluntarism helps us to understand the two areas where the New Left in the U.S. developed its own theoretical contribution. Psychology became important. The often quite astute structural criticisms of capitalism raised, for example, in *Walden II*, made no impact: Skinner was the goat; Rogers, Fromm and an areopagitica of pop psychologists became the common currency. Freud was not taken seriously; at best, one borrowed some rhetoric from 'Civilisation and its Discontents'. Wilhelm Reich came into his own only later; and even where he did it was his more idealistic side that dominated over the heavy mechanism of his 'dialectical materialism'. It was in this context too that Marx made his first entry as the theorist of an ill-defined 'alienation' stripped of its original connection to the structure of proletarian labour, closer to a Heideggerian fundamental ontology than to a concrete sociology. Overlaid as it was with an existential voluntarism, this psychology could immediately and easily adapt itself to the drug culture. At the same time, however, as it fled beyond, the stress also turned to the *critique of everyday life*. This theme, central to the New Left, will be treated in more detail below. For now, it is important to recognize that the turn to the (right-wing) libertarianism of a Szasz, to psychiatric liberation movements, and most importantly to the small group — fundamental to the rise of the Woman's Movement, whose importance cannot be overstated — stemmed from an intellectual — often, seemingly, an anti-intellectual — stance which was not arbitrary. The 'getting into your own head' arose from a movement of social concern whose models of revolutionary voluntarism were consciously movements for social change. Fanon struggled with Camus; the reform of everyday life with the flight to drugs; social change with personal salvation.

The second intellectual contribution of the New Left lay, paradoxically, in the domain of the very history which the voluntarism tended to neglect. Significantly, it was not History with a capital H that was interesting; it was the existential history of the everyday. This was typical of most of the movements. However, the United States was again unique in its choice of object. Where the Germans, for example, chose to unearth forgotten episodes and movements of their revolutionary history — the various oppositional groups during the Weimar period in particular, or the Opposition within Russia — the turn in the United States was to local history. There were of course the 'revisionist' radical historians of the W. A. Williams school and *Studies on the Left*, whose intellectual role was crucial in the debunking of myths, from the Open Door through the Progressive era down to the origins of the Cold War; there were fundamental studies like those of Green or Snow on the way we were mystified about China; and there were important attempts to revivify the specific American revolutionary tradition, from the Wobblies through the great strike movements which marked the advent of the United States as a world capitalist power. But far more important were the pathbreaking works on the structure of daily life — from the slave plantation to the northern city, from the gangs of the mid-nineteenth century to the relation of work and community in the twentieth. This concern with the existential and everyday, which owed so much to the work of E. P. Thompson, showed the juxtaposition of political activity with intellectual practice — and most significantly, it was conducted (for the most part) in an a-Marxist, often a-theoretical or agnostic vein. The 'anti-intellectual' stance of the New Left was not, therefore, a rejection of thought and analysis, but a putting into question of a kind of Enlightenment rationality whose 'dialectic' Adorno and Horkheimer had exposed years before in a little-known volume.

In short, the 'intellectual roots' of the New Left were largely a rejection of the traditional, rationalist views; they were part of a political practice, a social regrouping, and a personal will and moralism. None of this is the stuff of which 'ideologies' are made, at least not politically effective ones. This was to present a problem — not a problem that arose from the material itself, nor even one that emerged necessarily from practice. The attempt was very American; very much in *our* tradition of natural law.[6] [7]

Although the Vietnamese were a model of voluntarism, they also claimed to be Marxists; so did the Chinese; and so did many participants in the movement, feeling the need for science, the passion to *make* — not just *live* — the revolution. Marxism entered — a mysterious doctrine, sanctified, accompanied by a priesthood, sects and holy books. It was a disaster; a weapon in the hands of potential leaders, a cudgel to beat the individualist, and a theory for a non-theoretical movement. Of course, it was a deformed Marxism; and of course, there was much to be learned from Marx. But it came from the outside — as Lenin and Kautsky might have wished — and it was not natural. The guilty adopted it, learned its rhetoric and style ... or slunk away. Defining the movement atomized it; single issues became just that. The height of absurdity was reached at a California conference bringing together the black and white movements to 'fight fascism': the fundamental text was Dimitrov's Speech on Fascism to the 7th Congress of the 3rd International in 1935!

IV   Social Roots

In retrospect, the introduction of Marxism as ideology into the New Left helps to clarify a fundamental feature of its development. One can look at the history of the American SDS (Students for Democratic Society) as the *search for the revolutionary subject*. Not consciously at first, but ever more so, an essentially student, largely 'middle-class' group attempted to shake its guilt-feeling by identifying its actions with those of the classic oppressed groups. First it was civil rights, then the liberal-labour coalition within the Democratic Party, then the various Third World peoples, and finally — and fully incoherently — a 'proletariat' defined in terms of a combination of Imperialism theory and Marxian orthodoxy. The history of the New Left can thus be conceived as a history of self-denial, with the resultant loss of its own originality.[7]

Marxism as ideology is not the same as a Marxian analysis of contemporary social relations. From the latter perspective, for purposes of simplification, it might be argued that three events symbolize the changed social relations from which the New Left emerged. There was the post-1956 face-lifting in Russia, whose importance is manifest not only or simply in the open 'revisionism' and power politics revealed in the Sino-Soviet split but, more importantly, in the consecration and open emergence of the bureaucracy as a new class operating in a new social formation.[8] Second, there was De Gaulle's assumption of power through a playing off of the landed and colonial capitalists against the modernizers in order to end the Algerian war and open France to a new, state-dominated capitalism.[9] Finally, there was the Kennedy tax-cut, whose counter-position to Hooverian fiscal orthodoxy marked a 'fiscal revolution', and symbolized a new conception of the relation of society and the state.[10] These three symbols, notwithstanding archaic remnants such as the Berlin Wall, Castro's revolution, or Sputnik, consecrate a change that restructured the globe.[11]

Broadly speaking — though the Russian case is somewhat different — the historical struggle of the working class had resulted in the paradoxical success crowned by integration into a system of countervailing powers sharing a common interest in 'delivery of the goods'. This class struggle operated not only through the formal mechanism of the strike; it was not always a conscious 'class' struggle, and certainly not led by a Party, but rather was the everyday guerrilla warfare of production relations. In Marxian terms, it forced the capitalists to increase the production of relative surplus-value, i.e. to introduce technological advances on an ever-greater scale; and at the same time, the increased intensity of labour was achieved through a variety of technical and socio-psychological means. Its results were manifold. More skills were demanded of labour-power, which meant increasing the length and quality of education; which was also necessary to prevent youthful (and other) unemployment due to the decreasing number of productive jobs; which in turn meant that since more and more goods were produced, an ever-greater sales force of parasites was necessary, credit purchasing became the rule, and the role of the unemployed and underemployed, as well as the ethnically underprivileged, increased; which meant in turn the increased responsibility of the state in the sphere of scientific innovation, labour training, investment credits, and social legitimation, which in turn restructured the colonial-imperial system and changed the relations of the 'capitalist' and 'communist' worlds. With all this arose a series of 'objective' and 'subjective' contradictions — between state and private capital, skilled educated labour and routine tasks, demand for worker participation and need to make every minute count, client and state, production and distribution, etc., as well as the tension between work and leisure, formal democracy and actual powerlessness, scientific rationalization and creative experience, education and job training, etc.

One could go on describing features; and one could debate the degree to which they are *really* differences that make a difference. The New Left's existence — though not necessarily its self-understanding — suggests a mode of analysis. Capitalism is a mode of social relations predicated on the production of surplus-value profit. It doesn't matter what is produced, nor how it is produced; to make a profit producing shoes or bibles is equivalent. Whether you accept the labour theory of value and its implications, or chose to reason commonsensically from the standpoint of the individual capitalist, the implication is that the worker is crucial to the endeavour. If the worker will work more for less — longer hours or more intensively — the capitalist profits. The result is a class struggle, which manifests itself in a series of adaptations in the productive process. From being a crafts-person, whose personal skills or training are central. to production, the worker becomes simply a cog. This is the classical proletariat, trained on the job, immediately replaceable, and fully dominated. Its situation is explosive; and is de-fused only through the formation of unions which defend its most immediate interests. Able only to 'cash in', as it were, on the crisis of the thirties and the War, this proletariat found itself restructured by the pressure that it itself put on the capitalist. Production processes changed, new technology was introduced, group dynamics were restructured. A 'new working class' emerged. Not that the 'old' one was eliminated or its situation altered; simply, it was no longer the vanguard, the locus of the most advanced forms of struggle, the seat of felt contradiction and the source of an impulse toward the *positive* restructuring of society. The 'new working class' is an ill-defined, hermeneutic device, not an empirical statistic. The suggestion is that capitalism develops new needs, and that its reply to them points to a new structure.[1][2] The point is not Veblen's, Burnham's or Galbraith's — to mention only those. It is not a new permutation of an old set of relations, social goals and norms. It is that *capitalism as a total experience changes*: its imperatives are different, its social relations modeled after a new principle, its norms in flux.

The suggestion is that capitalism has changed (as has the Russian system). We can begin to account for that change in terms of the class struggle and the profit-imperative. But this means that, once it accounts for the new, the old theory, self-destructs, so to speak. The experience of the New Left witnesses this. What was fundamental to capitalism has disappeared: the free labour market, the establishment among fully independent partners of free contracts, and the domination of production over consumption.[1][3] Not that the contradictions on which it was based have disappeared, or become less crying or cruel — to the contrary. The point, however, is that the logic of the present social conflicts is determined differently — by thy logic of *bureaucratic rationality*. Such a logic is of course not foreign to classical capitalism. Weber saw its implications very early. But Weber did not go far enough in his analysis of it, and studied it in its own terms: though he knew and discussed the role of the political in its institution, Weber did not see that this rationality is the ultimate result not of the logic of the entrepreneur, still less of the Protestant spirit, but rather of precisely the politics of the class struggle. In a favourite Marxian metaphor: 'its victory is at the same time its loss'. Better: its transformation. The phenomenon of the New Left pushes us to analyze this transformation.

V Tactics, Themes and Practice

The New Left considered itself a *movement*. Save in the phase of its ideological phantasies, it never saw itself as the expression of the proletariat; and certainly it never claimed to be a political party in any traditional sense. Its success as a movement, and its failure once it sought to limit and define itself, testify to the correctness of this self-understanding. Given its intellectual nature and sociological insertion, it could not have been anything else. The smoothed-over capitalism whose conflicts have shifted does not permit a frontal attack: it offends everyone, but not in the same manner. A new series of issues open; but they open in series, in seriality, and their unity becomes a problem. The unification which — eventually — poses the question of the nature of the social totality did push toward Marxism as the immediately available explanation. That didn't work. It could, and did, lead to other approaches on the level of social theory. On the level of practice, the movement form made possible a unification of the differences, however unstable and fragile.

The themes around which New Left practice centered are well known. From civil rights and anti-war through community organization, women's and gay rights, to the drug culture and student power — they can be unified around the concerns with *daily life*, and the *autonomy* of the *person*. These were lived, felt issues which demanded immediate responses. They could be communicated, it seemed, through the counter- and the mass-media. The speed at which the movement-as-feeling or attitude spread testifies to the society's ripeness. It witnesses the homogenization that resulted, covering the differences while making them all the more explosive. If the theories of the Frankfurt School, or Marcuse's writings, appeared to express the New Left, it was because of a — perhaps old-fashioned in its Frankfurt formulation — recognition of the ever-present need for autonomy in all spheres of daily life.

If we ask why these themes could take as they did, the above sociological description, guided by the practice of the New Left, provides a key. Bureaucratic capitalism, Marcuse's one-dimensional society, Adorno and Horkheimer's 'dialectic of enlightenment', point to a common structure, a unity in difference: *a modernity which hides from itself its own origins*—in a manner analogous to the way Marx's ideology critique in *Capital* points to the role of the fetishism of commodities. The tactics of the New Left are significant in this regard: from Berkeley to Berlin, from Warsaw to Washington and Paris to Prague, the tactic was the deed, the confrontation, the direct action. The goal was to unmask the power relations hidden by the apparently smoothly functioning machine. *The tactic unmasked the power lurking beneath bureaucratically rationalized social relations, uncovering the new structure of domination in its most intimate resting place: daily life.* This tactic was not just the result of a philosophical or moral existentialism, nor the practice of desperados and outsiders; it was sociologically rooted, and points to the core social structure. That the New Left was able to discover this makes its experience all the more important.

The tactics, themes and practice of the New Left reflect a further aspect of the present social structure: its use of the immediate, the here-and-now, the pseudo-personal to cover over the root *historical* structure and *origins* of the system. 'In no epoch has one talked so much,' writes Claude Lefort.[14] Everything is present, open, available — from the ski-vacation of 'our' president to the local porn shop; from the starvation in the Sahal to the napalm in Vietnam or the Neareast; from *Psychology Today* to the *Intellectual Digest*. The everyday is trivialized and thus stolen; domination is rationalized in our scientific belief systems. God is dead because we don't need her any more; we are our own gods — and hence all the more vulnerable. One can leap forward into a new whose novelty is already structurally old, vain and predictable like the changing of fashion; or one can turn for anchorage to an ideal derived from the dead past. The system has conjured the risk of change by making change its principle. It seems to have created a closed world, a system, with no outside — Hegelianism with feedback loops.

Drawing this lesson, implicitly, the New Left committed suicide. It was incapable of imagining its own insertion or role, and fell back on the old models. It moved backward, groping for certainty and denying itself.

This need not have been. The stress on the immediate, on experience, on the personal and the communal, implicitly posed

a forward-reaching demand: that of self-management in all
spheres of life, self-activity and self-representation. *This lesson
burst forth in May 1968!* No one started it; no one planned it;
no one consciously wanted it. Yet it spread like a prairie fire:
l'imagination au pouvoir! Sure, it was crushed and de Gaulle
re-elected; but that doesn't make it the less important. February
to October 1917 — if we want to remember those dates — was
an extended learning process; revolutionary consciousness is not
achieved overnight. The old is tenacious, the new fragile.

As an organized, self-identified movement, the New Left is
dead. Its practice and its themes are still with us, in communi-
ties, groups and issues. If we turn now to some aspects of its
vision, the implications of its life-style-as-practice, we will be
able better to understand our present and its possibilities.

VI   Implications and Questions

From its intellectual roots to its themes, tactics and practice,
the New Left represented a *critique of the political.* Not just a
critique of politics, politicians and the irrationality of their
imperatives; the New Left rejected the political as a form of
mystification — an imaginary community floating in the clouds,
as the young Marx puts it. The New Left critique of representative democracy is far more than a critique of the political from
within its bounds and premises (as is, for example, the 'marxian'
debunking of formal democracy). It is the critique of a mode of
life, a form of self- and social perception. The implication is
that it is in *daily life*, in 'civil society', to use the consecrated
term, that change must occur.

It is worth noting, however, that the a-political politics of the
New Left is a *rediscovery of the path of the Young Marx*, from
the critique of the Hegelian state through the discovery of the
proletariat and the phenomenon of alienated labor. As Marx
looked back at the French Revolution, so the New Left — when
it looked back at all — saw that the revolution must not only
destroy the political bonds that limit and narrow, but must
revolutionize the sphere of personal interest and egoism. It
would seem that the New Left could have followed Marx (in
'On the Jewish Question') in citing Rousseau:

> Whoever dares to undertake the founding of a nation must
> feel himself capable of changing so to speak human nature
> and transforming each individual, who is in himself a com-
> plete but isolated whole, into a part of something greater

than himself from which he somehow derives his life and existence, substituting a limited and moral existence for physical and independent existence. Man must be deprived of his own powers and given alien powers which he cannot use without the aid of others. (*Social Contract*, Book II, Chapter II)

What emerges from the critique of the political as the constant theme and tension is, paradoxically, the *politicization of daily life*, the over-determination of every activity with a political sense, the denial of the private and the individual. As a sociological critique of contemporary bureaucratic capitalism, this stress is rich in potential. It discovered and uncovered a manifold of experience heretofore unthematized and ignored; society and socialization were experienced as a unified process, each the horizon of the other and each the critique of the other.

There was an unbearable tension in this turn to civil society and its politicization. Not simply the tension with the individualistic, existential and anarchic roots of a movement based on moral will; the Rousseauian stress on 'transforming the individual' implies a deprivation of one's 'own powers', which is hardly consistant with the New Left's original impulses. Yet the internal logic of its approach drove the New Left towards Rousseau — towards Lenin and a certain Marx as well — creating a tension which would become a rupture. Activism, spontaneism, immediacy and the lack of taboos, along with more overtly negative phenomena like anti-intellectualising, drugs, and the continual strain of becoming an individual through the collective, fitted together so long as development and success did not demand reflection and analysis. With the first failures, as the movement slowed down, the poles began to separate. Society had been conceived as the relation of one to one; the future society would be one of dyadic communication; and the properly social was felt as 'alienation'. At the same time, however, experience pointed to the role of the *totality*. Not simply that community organizers found that you can't create 'socialism in one community', or that each inside issue group found itself forced to go beyond its issue by its very successes — the demand for totalization appeared in the very immediacy of civil society, of daily life and immediate experience.

The *politicization of daily life* which appeared so apparent and effective a perspective implicity implied the *destruction of everyday life*. Concern with the individual and the everyday led to the totality; but the route back remained barred. The particular and the universal were conflated and collapsed, each losing what was specific to it. The psychological effects were of course disastrous. But more important here, the image of the political changed. It was through this door that a Marxian orthodoxy implicitly mediated by Lukács re-entered. For all its sublety in analyzing the phenomenon of reification in the daily existence of the proletariat, Lukács' attempt led of necessity not simply to an *ouvrièrisme* but directly to the Leninist Party as possessor and incarnation of the totality. Though most did not read Lukács, their logic followed, or recreated, his — and returned to the old politics. Those who remained with the original impulse of the New Left encountered another set of problems.

The politicization of daily life is an attempt to remove the mystery, to render society transparent to itself, to end history in the present. This position is of course the identitical obverse of the orthodox, which removes the mystery through its science, understands the present in terms of a necessary future, and sacrifices the present to that future. Making the totality, the political, present in the immediacy of daily life permitted a critique of that everyday experience, and guided attempts to restructure it in terms of what Trent Schroyer has called 'utopian enclosures'. From food co-ops to day-care centres, from small-grouping to ethnicity, the attempt was to transform the single issues into total social solutions through the transformation of the individual experience. As a form of critique-in-action, this led to an important reconsideration of the nature and role of *power* in society and social relations. At the same time, it opened a critique of the *technological rationality* of strategic action which structures our society. Here, Marcuse, Habermas and the Frankfurt School struck the theoretical chord.

While the experiments still continue, their internal logic poses problems. On the one hand, the above considerations of the social roots of the New Left suggest that in the blabbermouth society, critique of this sort is precisely *essential* to the *masking* of the social divisions. The turn to the immediate, the small group and closed community naturally (not socially or politically) defined, conceals as well as reveals. It may be a personal necessity, but precisely the stress on immediacy turns it inward and limits its thrust. The identical opposite, which stresses the totality's presence in the immediate, is in fact dealing with a representation of the totality which it attempts to incarnate through the creation of what Claude Lefort calls 'a new social type: the militant'. If you must always incarnate the totality in the everyday, you *become* it, denying your particularity and your experience — and the totality is in fact lost. The quest for the totality in the immediate, whether through the dyadic group, individual consciousness, or the representational imagination of the militant, tends towards a new form of totalitarianism — which, to its credit, most of the New Left conscientiously attempted to avoid — but only at the cost of either the incoherence of its projects or the psychological integrity of its members.

The politicization of daily life is not, however, a wholly negative phenomenon: it points forward — to a redefinition of revolution and to a rethinking of the nature of society and its political structure. Explicitly, the New Left stressed and harped on two central themes, without which the notion of socialist revolution is a contradiction in terms: *the end of the division of manual and mental labour, and the notion of self-management.* The striving for the immediacy of dyadic communication — whatever criticism it calls forth from one standpoint — recognizes that the element of power and domination in personal relations must be eliminated. Power and domination are exercised daily in a society structured in terms of the exacerbation of the division of labour; not consciously, but of necessity, our languages are different, our self-conceptions limited, our horizons blocked, and sub- and super-ordination distort communication. This *is* ideology as the structure of our bureaucratic society. It can only be overcome with the elimination of the structured divisions which affect the individual to the core, and are crystallized in that division of manual and mental labour. At the same time, the notion of self-management becomes central; it is the issue of control and power, but also that of personal relations. Self-management — *not only in production but in all spheres of life* — is the central theme of the New Left, and essential to its vision; but the vision is not one of a future which teleologically affects practice in the present, it is a vision which bureaucratic capitalism itself calls forth, as it increasingly socializes society, making all dependent on each, and yet dividing them at work and in leisure. Self-management and the end of the division of manual and mental labour as the goal of a revolution are already inscribed as demands in our present while they are still denied in the everyday. This is why the New Left's tactics of immediate action and provocation met with such success. Where the success turned sour, it seems, was when the question of totalization emerged and, as such, either separated revolution from present activities (the Leninist view) or distorted the present by over-determining it (the group *as* future).

From this perspective, the New Left opens on to a *changed sociology of contemporary society*, and a *critique of Marxism*. Not simply a critique of the simplified and vulgarized Marx of the apologists. It is obvious enough that capitalism has changed; indeed, Marx himself can account for these changes. What is more important is that the New Left is a critique in action of *Marx as the last Hegelian*, of *Marx the rationalist*. Of course, there is the myth of the proletariat as the Subject-Object of History, an inverted materialist form of the Hegelian *Geist* or, seen politically, his bureaucracy. Of greater import is the critique in action of Marx's linear view of History, of History as the Progress of Humanity towards its Self-Realization through the elimination of Otherness. Capitalism is not necessarily the antechamber to the socialist reconciliation; nor is it doomed to collapse through its own inner 'logic'. The class struggle will not come to fruition when 'X' millions are unemployed, any more than revolution can be organized as a societal *coup d'état*. The increased role of the state, not simply as collective capitalist but as distributor of legitimation through its relation to its clients, throws into question the absolutizing of the infrastructure, which is inherent in the orthodox analysis. Human relations are certainly not independent of their material substratum; but the latter is not to be taken in isolation, as the 'really real' on which all else sits. Marx's analysis of *laissez-faire* competitive capitalism is limited to a specific case where the universe of meaning of the society is structured around accelerated reproduction through a free market — including the labour market. Such was not the case in pre-capitalist societies; and it is true today only in the vaguest manner. Marx spoke of four constitutive elements of human being: production, consciousness, language and community. The latter three appear ever more central as liberal capitalism veers towards bureaucratic capitalism. The result is the re-emergence of daily life as a sphere of contestation, and the need for a renewal of sociological analysis. Marx was perhaps not so much wrong as he was misunderstood — though the misunderstandings are inherent in the scientized self-understanding he had of his own work.

The most pressing problem which emerges from the consideration of the New Left's vision is the changing role of the political. The move to civil society as the place of the political has been seen to be paradoxical and insufficient — or worse, to contain the seeds of a new totalitarianism. The old politics, on the other hand, is all the more bankrupt in that even its formal legitimacy hinged on the now-surpassed structure of liberal capitalism. At a first level, the New Left can be seen to reopen the domain of the political as it has traditionally been conceived since the Greeks *invented* democracy: as the dimension in which the *good life in the City* is elaborated. Politics is neither science nor technique; the politician is neither planner nor administrator. The slogan of 'participatory democracy' takes on its full sense here. Politics is not the sum and substance, the totality, of everyday life; it is and must remain different. At the same time, it cannot be isolated in its difference, either determining directly daily life from on high or being the simple addition or representation of the atoms which compose the social. It is the locus of Power, *the place where society represents itself to itself*; but at the same time that it is constitutive of the form of the society, it is constituted by and dependent on the society itself. Neither identical with, nor separate from the society, the political is not for that reason simply nothing: it is a *process* which is unending — and whose end could mark only the advent of a totalitarianism — in which the society and its members seek to define and structure their relations. In its concern with the good life of the citizens, it is universal; in its dependence on and relation to the individuals, it is particular and open to change.

What then would revolution mean from a New Left perspective? *L'imagination au pouvoir* is not a slogan but an analysis! — a programme. Power is not to be occupied; to think that one could — or should — seek to seize the reins of state is to be the victim of an illusion. Being on the axis of the demand to occupy the place of power, revolutionary activity becomes a question of adequate means to a given end, a technological equation neglecting the human material one wants to serve, and denying oneself one's own particularity. Through its experiments, however successful or however incoherent, the New Left points to the dimension of the political process in which the good life is put into question and developed. The forms of language, consciousness and community take precedence over any unilateral determination of society by production and reproduction. They are the universals in terms of which the particulars structure their relations. In today's bureaucratic capitalism, the question of rationality, and with it, that of legitimation, is the locus of political debate and practice. This cannot be 'seized' or 'occupied'. But it is nonetheless the centre from which the manifold variety of empirical struggles, from the traditional workplace to the community and the classroom, spread. These latter have, and will continue to have, a surface ressemblance to those predicted by the orthodox theory. But they find themselves in another context, and wear a different meaning. To treat them in the old manner would be to neglect the change, and to return to the time-worn patter.

The implications of this 'revolutionary politics' for the New Left theory are first of all found in its critique of the 'Old Left'. The Old Left politics — despite some glimmerings found in Marx — are caught within the bourgeois system of representation. Power is conceived as a *place* to be occupied; society is seen in economic metaphors; practice is taken to be the production of an object. The goals are determined through a means—ends rationality; and success is defined in terms of an adequation of theory and practice, ends and means, plan and realization. *It is this rationality which the New Left has put into question.* History is not a linear process, an empty objective space within which we move, guided by a teleological vision of the Good. The visual metaphor is destroyed; Cartesian rationalism with its 'clear and distinct' ideas and causal thinking falls by the wayside, not to be replaced by an irrationalist existentialism or some qualitative physics. The *process* of the political is archetypal: it points to the implications of the particular in the universal, and vice versa; to the inseparability of subject and object, thought and reality, mind and body; and most importantly, it signals to us the danger of thinking that we could somehow possess the truth or totality as a thing to be held and caressed in our hands.

The New Left foundered because it was unable to recognize and realize both its own sociological insertion and the implications of its critical project. It fell for the image of having (or being) the totality: either returning to an orthodoxy of Marxism-Leninism, or turning inward to the ideology of dyadic immediacy. To founder is not, however, to fail. The New Left may be dead as an *organized* movement — but then it never really lived as such. It lives on in all its contradictoriness because the structure of bureaucratic capitalism based on the division of society forces the emergence not only of traditional revolts, but of new ones as well. If the New Left has anything to teach us, or itself to learn from its own experience, it is the dangers of objectivized 'success'. Perhaps the 'failure' was inherent in the project; not because the project was wrongheadedly conceived, but because it can only structure itself in terms of the redefined political. The future of the New Left — its own, and the one it (however implicitly) conceived — is still with us in a project which was not engendered in the heads of the theorists, but structured into our society itself.

No explicit tactic or theory emerges from the New Left. Yet

whatever we do, and however we conceive ourselves, the structures that the New Left revealed, the imaginative tactics it applied, and its openness to experiment and self-criticism, cannot help but be of influence. This is no small tribute to its vision.

Part Two
Within Marxism

3 Theory, the Theorist and Revolutionary Practice: Rosa Luxemburg

> No coarser insult, no baser defamation, can be thrown against the workers than the remark 'Theoretical controversies are only for intellectuals. (*Social Reform or Revolution?*)

The question to be addressed here is not that of the adequacy of this or that particular theory in accounting for, or acting on, a given context of social relations. I am not concerned whether, for example, the theory expressed in *The Accumulation of Capital* is adequate to account either for the conditions of the period in which it was formulated, or for our present conditions; nor, *a fortiori*, am I concerned with whether that theory conforms to the ediface of Marx's *Capital*. To judge a theory in terms of its adequacy implies a latent conservatism and positivism; theory is treated as a statement of 'facts' about a world that itself is taken as pre-given and fixed. Such an approach implies a dualism — on the one side, the theory; on the other side, the 'facts' which it is to reflect — which makes it fundamentally undialectical. Moreover, the point, after all, is not to understand a given positive world, but to change it! And this implies a very different notion of theory.

Moreover, my question goes beyond the person and activity of Rosa Luxemburg. Through her person and activity, I want to look at a problem that affects our understanding of Marxism, and our own self-perception as theorists who are also revolutionaries: namely, *the relation of theory and practice*. For Rosa Luxemburg this was no problem even in the darkest hour: 'Marxist theory gave to the working class of the whole world a compass by which to fix its tactics from hour to hour in its journey toward the one unchanging goal.' (p. 325, *The Junius Pamphlet*)[1] Today, after the (however temporary) setbacks of the working class in the West, after the excesses, stupidities and crimes committed in the name of Marxism, after the so-called successes of revolution where Marxism least expected them — we can no longer be so sanguine as Rosa Luxemburg. And as theorists, we know too that Marxism itself contains profound ambiguities: we know that there is a latent positivism in the thought of Marx himself, we know how Engels tended to 'naturalize' the dialectic, how the Second International assimilated an evolutionary Darwinian element into its doctrine, how the Third International was able to continually change its line to fit national need and convenience while always justifying itself in terms of Marx citations, etc. We have seen Marxism loose its critical thrust and become what Oskar Negt calls a 'science of legitimation'. And, on the other hand, we have seen those who have attempted to maintain the razor-edge of dialectical criticism fall victim to bourgeois pop-culture, practical dispair, or insular theorizing.

We are living a crisis of Marxism; and a crisis of Marxists! The effects of this crisis on our theory and our practice have been disastrous — whether in the form of an exacerbated Third Worldism culminating in phenomena like the Weatherpeople, Baader-Meinhof, etc., or in the neo-populist return to the factories in search of a somehow redeeming contact with the 'real' working class, or in the form of theoretical doubt, sterility and/or eclecticism. With the bonds of theory and practice burst asunder, theory becomes dogma and practice becomes blind activism.

In this context it is opportune to re-examine the legacy of Rosa Luxemburg. Not as a precious heirloom, placed on the mantelpiece to be admired but not touched; not as a political, or theoretical, 'third way' between alternatives that, for whatever reasons, we don't like — for Rosa Luxemburg is neither a spectacle to be observed, nor the mouthpiece of a new dogma that will give us that dull certitude of which we feel in need. It is not a question of Luxemburg or Lenin, spontaneity or organization, mass or party; nor is it a question of 'competing' theories of imperialism, the national question, the peasantry or the role of formal democracy and it is certainly not our task to judge the 'authenticity' of her — or any other — 'Marxism'. We cannot approach the question in terms of 'if only her advice on this or that had been taken', for such an attitude is of interest only for parlour discussion and bad novels. Our concern is with our present and the tasks it poses; we turn to history not to salvage some 'pure' thinker or some unblemished 'truth' ignored or misunderstood by its contemporaries, but rather with the understanding that, in however distorted a form, it too is part of our present, that we must reflect on it in order to understand better what is to be done.

The appeal today of Rosa Luxemburg to a heteroclite group of left-inclined activists and theorists in opposition to the dominant tendencies within the official international Communist movement is understandable, and yet there is something quite paradoxical about it. There is of course the critique of revisionism and opportunism in theory and in practice, the stress on spontaneity and self-formation of consciousness, the early recognition of Kautskyian dogmatism and of the increasing bureaucratization of the SPD, the shrill outcry against the Social Chauvinism of the national parties and the recognition of the role of imperialist capitalism as forcing an internationalist and anti-war strategy on the world proletariat, the avid defence of the councils form as the crucial element in the coming revolution; and, to be sure, there is the critique of Lenin's views on the party. All of these, interpreted in one or another manner, give more than enough grounds for adopting the label of Luxemburg. And yet, there is another side which should be less pleasant for those who latch on to a label in their rush to be more radical than Thou. Luxemburg was a dogmatist (in a sense to which we shall return). For example, she is satisfied that she has refuted Bernstein when she 'shows that, in its essence, in its bases, opportunist practice is irreconcilable with Marxism.' (p. 130, *Social Reform or Revolution?*) She accepts Marxism as 'the specific mode of thought of the rising class conscious proletariat', (p. 127, *SR or R?*) and never doubts its truth despite the series of defeats which she, and the proletariat, suffered. Or, to give another example, she was a 'legalist' when it came to construing Party or International decisions, advocating expulsions, justifying her position on the mass strike in terms of 'the true essence of the Jena resolution . . .', and, on the International scene, proposing the reconstruction of an International which would have a control over the national parties not essentially different from what came to pass with the construction of the Third International. Or, concerning her position with regard to Leninism, one must recall not only the 'non-democratic' manner in which she functioned in the Polish SDKPiL, but also, within her critique of Lenin, the option for a control from the top within the *German* party, to whom the Lenin-critique was actually addressed.

In Sections I and II of the following, I want to look at the two sides of Luxemburg's activity in order to delineate and explicate their logic. In I, 'Revolutionary Practice and its Theory', my concern is to bring out Luxemburg's attitude, as theorist, to the ongoing struggles of the class and the different forms that they took. To make her position clear, it will be necessary to make reference to the theoretical work of Marx. In II, 'The Theorist and her Practice', I will look at the implications of Luxemburg's practice as theoretician and revolutionary, in order to show the problems and paradoxes which the theoretician-as-revolutionary must confront. In III, 'Revolutionary Theory', the attempt will be made to draw some conclusions with reference to theory itself. What is it about a theory that makes it revolutionary?

I Revolutionary Practice and its Theory

> Only the working class, through its own activity, can make the word flesh. (*Was will der Spartakusbund?*)

Marxian theory has always had a somewhat ambiguous (or, charitably interpreted, dialectical) relation to revolutionary practice. Marxism claims to be the theory of the working class. This notion, however, can be interpreted in two senses, whose consequences are radically different. On the one hand, it can mean that Marxism is the working class's theory; that it is the theory which the working class adopts, accepts, and uses as a guide to its action. On the other hand, it can mean that Marxism is the expression in theory of the actual practice of the working class; which means that practice implicitly contains its own theory, which is expressed in Marxism in such a way that the class can recognize itself in the theory, understand what it in fact is doing *as a class*, and draw the implications of that activity. The distinction, in other words, is that between a theory *for* practice and a theory *of* practice.

The distinction between the two interpretations is often blurred. Gramsci, who tends to be a representative of the latter tendency, nonetheless speaks of the need for Marxism as an ideology to help the proletariat maintain its faith in the struggle at those times when the revolutionary tide is out. Lenin, who tends to be a representative of the former tendency, achieves his greatest moments precisely when he breaks with the received doctrine and opens new paths based on his empathetic understanding of the masses and their capacities at a given moment. Indeed, there is an ambiguity in the work of Marx himself. *Capital* is an attempt to integrate a rigorously scientific or deductive economic model with a theory of the class struggle as the basis of the various forms taken by the capitalist production process. We see the first of these moments, for example, in

Marx's discussion of the move from cooperation, division of labour and manufacturing, to machinery and modern industry; or in the 'law' of the tendency of the rate of profit to fall. But in both cases, the second moment immediately intervenes, in the first case when Marx's discussion points to the role of capitalist reaction to working-class struggle as leading to the introduction of new methods for the production of relative surplus-value; and in the second, when the chapter on countervailing tendencies points to the level of the class struggle as a central variable of the rate of profit. The same ambiguity runs through many of Marx's conjunctual political analyses. For example, the Paris Commune is first condemned on theoretical grounds, then enthusiastically accepted and integrated into the theoretical conception of the nature of proletarian revolution, and then once again brutally criticized, on theoretical grounds, in some of the later letters.

This Marxian ambiguity appears in Rosa Luxemburg's practice as a revolutionary theoretician. Mention has already been made of her belief that revisionism could be refuted once its incompatibility with Marxian theory had been shown. She could of course claim efficacy for this approach insofar as, within the dualistic confines of the Erfurt Programme, her opponents insisted that their position was compatible with Marxism. But the notion of a theory *for* practice enters at a second, theoretically more interesting, level in her discussion of the dialectic of the 'final goal'. This needs to be looked at in some detail, before going on to see how the element of the theory *of* practice figures in her work.

In *Social Reform or Revolution?* we read statements like these: 'It is the final goal alone that constitutes the spirit and content of our socialist struggle which turns it into a class struggle.' (p. 39) 'The final goal of socialism is the only decisive factor distinguishing the Social Democratic movement from bourgeois democracy and bourgeois radicalism, the only factor transforming the entire labor movement from a vain attempt to repair the capitalist order into a class struggle *against* this order . . .' (p. 53) How are we to interpret these assertions? On a first level, they are of course replies to the political implications of Bernstein's famous assertion that 'the movement is everything, the final goal is nothing.' A further, somewhat lengthy, assertion in the same text goes further, however:

The secret of Marx's theory of value, of his analysis of money, his theory of capital, his theory of the rate of profit, and consequently of the whole existing economic system is — the transistory nature of the capitalist economy, its collapse, thus — and this is only another aspect of the same phenomenon — the final goal, socialism. And precisely because, *a priori*, Marx looked at capitalism from the socialist's viewpoint . . . he was enabled to decipher the hieroglyphics of capitalist economy. (p. 101)

What worries Rosa Luxemburg, as *revolutionary* theorist, in the Bernsteinian position — and even more, in its translation in the pragmatic horse-trading of the opportunist politicians, for example in Schippel's military policy — is its *empiricism*. In effect, for the empiricist the facts are precisely what is out there, before my eyes, in all its gross ugly reality. The empiricist with a heart — i.e., the humanist — confronted with this reality desires to smooth the rough edges, efface the ugliness, make peace. The empiricist standpoint is that of the vulgar economist, the Benthamite continually attacked by Marx as having the mentality of the small shopkeeper who can only see things from the individual point of view, never that of the class or social totality. The essential connectedness of things is lost to the empiricist, for whom all relatedness is accidental and external. The political result of empiricism is that strikes, electoral action, demonstrations, etc., are not in themselves revolutionary; they are either a moral reaction to evil or a defensive reaction to oppression, which the "socialist" politician can use as means or pawns in the political game. But if there is no essential connection among the various activities undertaken by the working class, then a fundamental insight of Marx is lost — namely, that capital and labour form a conflictual pair such that each affects and depends on the other. Luxemburg's point here, as Lukács correctly perceived, is that there is no such thing as a 'fact'. The 'facts' only make sense in their interrelatedness, in their totality — in this case, in the context of the inherently contradictory and doomed capitalist system; hence, in the context of the ongoing revolution.

While agreeing with Luxemburg's political and epistemological critique of empiricism and its consequences, we should note a problem here. One is somewhat taken aback by her use of the term *a priori* when referring to Marx's theoretical standpoint in *Capital*. Is it really an *a priori*? If so, the argument takes on an ideological character, posing the technological question: 'What signification must I give to the "facts" in order that they fit into the theoretical and practical structures that I want to develop?' — and the theory becomes a theory *for* practice, no longer a theory *of* it. That is, if, as Luxemburg suggests, what differentiates socialism from bourgeois democracy and bourgeois radicalism is nothing but this *a priori* belief in the final goal, then one is at a loss to explain the patient and detailed research of Marx writing *Capital*; *Capital* becomes a construction! If Marxism starts from the assumption of the necessity of revolution, then it is a viciously circular theory, not totally unlike Christian doctrines of 'original sin'.

Rosa Luxemburg has unconsciously pointed to an ambiguity in Marx himself. In the Marxian philosophy of history there often appears a latent neo-enlightenment or Hegelian belief in the external progressiveness of history as it moves towards a final reconciliation. Whether latent or actual, this tendency was theorized — ideologized is a better term — by the Second International. To a degree, their argument makes sense. If we recognize the vanity of a hyper-empiricism, we ask ourselves how we are to make sense of the present. Certainly, the present is historical; but that simply implies variation. Something more is necessary: a directionality, a positive goal, an end to (pre-) history. If, then, history has a direction, all those stages which have not yet reached the 'end' are imbued with a kind of negative valence; a dialectic ensues between the present-as-not-yet-future, and the future-to-which-the-present-tends. In a present pregnant with the future, we can avoid the symmetrical errors of opportunism-revisionism and ethical utopianism.

It can be argued that this tendency — which reifies history into a mechanistic process unrolling with predetermined necessity — is in fact overcome in the works of Marx and Luxemburg. For the present purpose, it suffices to note its presence, even if only latent. Without the qualifications to which I will refer below, it would be a mystification of the actual process of revolution, and would have as a logical consequence a kind of technology of revolution, a means-ends doctrine deducing from the putative inevitability of the revolution a series of techniques to hasten the 'birth-pains'. Its upshot would be the equation of socialism with nationalization and planning, and the neglect of the human relations that are central to socialism's content.

Luxemburg's practical experience of the day-to-day political struggles served to insulate her against the abstractions of theory. Luxemburg refers to 'two reefs' between which the proletariat must chart its course: 'abandonment of the mass character or abandonment of the final goal; the fall back to sectarianism or the fall into bourgeois reformism; anarchism or opportunism.' (p. 142, *Militia and Militarism*; p. 304, *Organizational Questions of Russian Social Democracy*) The same approach occurs repeatedly in her work; the theorist as revolutionary seems to have the task, as theorist, of maintaining at all times the tension between the present and the possible future, avoiding the temptations of the immediate as well as the dreams of a Beyond, leaning now to one side then to the other in order to maintain that *difference* which is the space within which the movement can develop. Here, one only need refer to the brilliant critiques of the Blanquist temptation — in *In Memory of the Proletariat Party*, in the *Mass Strike* essay, or in *Our Program and the Political Situation* — and the concomitant stress on the nature and role of the *transitional programme* to see how she avoids the temptation of reifying the historical process. In her analysis of the Polish *Proletariat* Party — a model of Marxian historical analysis — she writes that what 'separates the Social Democratic position from those of other movements is . . . its conception of the relationship between the immediate tasks of socialism and its final goals'. (p. 179) She then presents a detailed analysis of the programmatic statements of the Party, comparing them with the Blanquist attitude of the *Narodnaya Volya*, and with the programmatic sections of the *Communist Manifesto*. Her conclusion is that 'The ABC's of socialism teach that the socialist order is not some sort of poetic ideal society, thought out in advance, which may be reached by various paths in various more or less imaginative ways. Rather, socialism is simply the historical tendency of the class struggle of the proletariat in the capitalist society against the class rule of the bourgeoisie.' (p. 201)[2] It is the developing struggle and the tension created by the opposition of classes, not a poetic, ethical or technological necessity, that makes socialism appear as the *sense* of the actual class activity of the proletariat.

History is the history of the class struggle; and certainly before 4 August 1914, Luxemburg never doubted that that class struggle would end as Marx had predicted. But the immediate tasks of practical politics had to be dealt with; and Luxemburg's manner of dealing with them is innovative and rich with lessons. Faithful to Marx, she asserts that:

> Man does not make history of his own volition. But he makes it nonetheless. In its action the proletariat is dependent upon the given degree of ripeness of social development. But social development does not take place apart from the proletariat. The proletariat is its driving force and its cause as well as its product and its effect. The action of the proletariat is itself a co-determining part of history. (p. 333, *The Junius Pamphlet*)

The upshot of this is fundamental not only for the theory of history — which must lose any character of predetermined necessity, lose its external and mechanistic character, and become that *experience* of choice and creation that we live daily — but also for political practice. It means that *class consciousness* becomes the central focus and locus of revolutionary activity.

Luxemburg notes a fundamental paradox constitutive of the class struggle. She sees that 'the proletarian army is first recruited in the struggle itself', but yet that 'only in the struggle does it become aware of the objectives of the struggle.' (p. 289, *Organizational Questions of Russian Social Democracy*) This 'dialectical contradiction' (ibid.) cannot be resolved via the Leninist-Kautskyian class-consciousness from the outside approach. That is a *technology*; it supposes a knowledge of a predetermined historical necessity to be taught by the knowledgeable to the unknowing, and preserves the relations of subordination. Luxemburg insists that 'the masses can only form this [revolutionary] will in a constant struggle against the existing order, only within its framework.' (p. 131, *Social Reform or Revolution?*) Concretely, this means that

> the solution to this apparent paradox lies in the dialectical process of the class struggle of the proletariat fighting for democratic conditions in the state and at the same time organizing itself and gaining class consciousness. Because it gains this class consciousness and organizes itself in the course of the struggle, it achieves a democratization of the bourgeois state and, in the measure that it itself ripens, makes the bourgeois state ripe for a socialist revolution. (p. 180—1, *In Memory of the Proletariat Party*)

It must be stressed that this is not simply a psychological process, a kind of additive learning by the accumulation of bits of experience; the position only makes sense when we recognize that the conditions in which the proletariat begins the struggle are conditions of which it is the co-creator, and each new phase of the struggle forces new conditions which modify the proletariat objectively as well as subjectively. Thus, despite all her work in economics and her rigid insistence on the centrality of the breakdown theory, when it comes to practical politics and its theory, Luxemburg insists — vehemently in the *Anti-Kritik*, for example[3] — that economics alone will not bring socialism. History is richer, more complex and more human than that.

As a theorist *of* the class struggle, for whom the development of revolutionary class consciousness becomes the central variable, Luxemburg implicitly throws into question any dogmatism of the 'final goal', and with it any linear view of the evolution from capitalism to socialism. This could be richly illustrated from any of her works, particularly the *Mass Strike*.

> Each new rising and new victory of the political struggle simultaneously changes itself into a powerful impetus for the economic struggle by expanding the external possibilities of the latter, increasing the inner drive of the workers to better their situation and increasing their desire to struggle. After every foaming wave of political action a fructifying deposit remains behind from which a thousand stalks of economic struggle shoot forth. And vice versa. The ceaseless state of economic war of the workers with capital keeps alive the fighting energy at every political pause. It forms, so to speak, the ever fresh reservoir of the strength of the proletarian class, out of which the political struggle continually renews its strength. And, at the same time, it at all times leads the untiring economic boring action of the proletariat, now here, now there, to individual sharp conflicts out of which, unexpectedly, political conflicts on a large scale explode.
>
> In a word: the economic struggle is that which leads the political struggle from one nodal point to another; the political struggle is that which periodically fertilizes the soil for the economic struggle. Cause and effect here continually change places . . . And their unity is precisely the mass strike. (p. 241, *Mass Strike, Party and Trade Unions*)

The mass strike, which is a class action taking place over time, alters the very conditions which engendered it, at the same time that the new conditions which it creates bring it forth again in a different form. The economic continues and develops the political, the political does the same for the economic; and both affect and are affected by the drives *and desires* of the proletariat. It is interesting that nowhere in the Mass Strike essay does Rosa Luxemburg present an 'economic' analysis in the strict sense of the term; nowhere does she talk, for example, of the role of French capital, of the unequal regional development, or of the class composition of the Russian state. In effect, she shows the inner connection of a series of economic and political struggles over a period of nearly a decade; yet she gives no 'cause' and shows no external 'necessity' for this development, and repeatedly insists that 'the mass strike cannot be propagated.' Indeed, if 'Marxism' is taken to be a theory which explains capitalist society on the basis of its contradictory economic infrastructure which necessarily engenders crisis and revolution — and this is, at least in part, the interpretation Luxemburg gives in *Social Reform or Revolution?* — then it is questionable how 'Marxist' Luxemburg's mass strike theory is.

The mass strike theory is the theorization *of* proletarian practice. The interplay of the economic and political struggles that Luxemburg theorizes makes sense only when we realize that both aspects of the struggle are the *results* of proletarian practice. In effect, the proletariat has seized the role of social subjectivity; and the Other which it confronts is not some eternally fixed form — 'capital', the bourgeoisie,' the state', or what-have-you — but rather is nothing but the result and incarnation of its own previous action. Instead of passively undergoing the capitalist accumulation process which 'science' analyzes in its creative class possibilities. When Luxemburg talks of the mass strike as the 'unity' of the political and economic struggles, we have to understand this unification as depending not on some sort of 'objective' factors, but as incarnated in the practice of the active class subject. The mass strike is the *sense* of the movement of *differentiation* between the political and the economic.

Luxemburg's activity during the 1918—19 revolution in Germany reinforces this interpretation, while pointing to the question that has to be addressed in the next section of our interpretation, namely the role of the theorist within the revolutionary process. Her position — outvoted at the founding Congress of the KPD (Spartakus) — was based on the recognition that abstract theorization based on models of what ought to be is useless, and that the theorist must confront the actual practice of the movement, theorizing it in order to show its strengths and weaknesses, possibilities and limits. The positions of the ultra-left, which carried the Congress, made her nuanced analysis of the next tasks of the revolution appear moderate and unappreciative of the tempo inaugurated by 1917; indeed, her speech was greeted, the stenographic minutes report, by 'weak applause'. The opposition to Luxemburg's analysis was based partly on the impact of the Russian success, and the lessons that the German revolutionaries thought they could draw from what they knew of Leninism. Luxemburg had already replied to this sort of criticism, pointing out that the Leninist view of the party won't bring socialism because 'it is not based on the immediate class consciousness of the working masses.' (p. 288, *Organizational Questions of Russian Social Democracy*) Rather,

it transforms even the members of the revolutionary group 'into
pure implements of a predetermined will lying outside their
own field of activity — into tools of a central committee.' (p.
289, ibid.) It makes the 'mass of comrades' into 'a mass
incapable of judging, whose essential virtue becomes "discipline," that is obedience to duty.' (p. 264, ibid.) While these
criticisms of Leninism are certainly valid in the abstract, it is
important to recognize that Luxemburg's argument is based in
the specific conception of socialism as a process whose nuances
have been traced above, and that each specific situation demands a concrete analysis whose task is to reveal its possibilities
and its limits.

In *'Our Program and the Political Situation'*, Luxemburg
stresses the difference between bourgeois and socialist revolutions: in the former, 'it sufficed to overthrow that official
power at the center and to replace a dozen or so persons in
authority,' whereas 'we have to work from beneath, and this
corresponds to the mass character of our revolution.' (p. 407,
Our Program and the Political Situation) What had taken place
on 9 November was, in this sense, a bourgeois revolution,
despite its formal incarnation in the workers' and soldiers'
Councils.

> It was characteristic of the first period of the revolution . . .
> that the revolution remained exclusively political. We must
> be fully conscious of this. This explains the uncertain
> character, the inadequacy, the half-heartedness, the aimless-
> ness of this revolution. The struggle for socialism has to be
> fought out by the masses, by the masses alone, breast to
> breast against capitalism, in every factory, by every prolet-
> arian against his employer. Only then will it be a socialist
> revolution. (396, ibid.)

The limits of the situation were clearly the unripeness of the
masses; the possibilities were those created by the very action of
the masses, action which had changed the meaning and reality
of their situation, and changed them as well. The dialectic of
praxis and its sedimentations that she had pointed to in
analyzing the mass strike would have to play its role here. She
proposed participation in the vote for a National Assembly,
agreeing with Paul Levi's speech which asserted this as a prime
task while admitting that of course it would not 'make' the
revolution. Against the activism of the ultra-left — typified by
Gelwitzki's 'Ten men on the street are worth more than a
thousand votes' — she spoke of a 'long revolution', of the

proletariat's maturation process through a series of struggles, and she criticized the gross alternative of 'guns or parliament', demanding a 'more refined, dialectical choice'.

Luxemburg's position did not carry the Congress; and two weeks later, she and Liebknecht were dead, in the ruins of the revolution. Her last article, 'Order Reigns in Berlin', proposes again a theorization *of* the struggle; no recipes for future success, but only possibilities and limits are proposed. The limits were partly conjunctural — the need to combat the Ebert-Scheidemann-Noske regime — but mainly concerned the limited development of class consciousness. The possibilities are shown by the spontaneous creativity of the Berlin masses, 'the people's instinctive recognition that . . . the counter-revolution would not rest with the defeat it had suffered, but rather would be bent on a general test of strength.' (p. 412, *Order Reigns in Berlin*) She insists on the fact 'that from the very beginning the moral victory was on the side of the "street".' (Ibid.) The stress on the moral character of the struggle, on the *possibility* that the people recognize that they themselves must take charge of their own liberation, and on the historical character of that struggle as creating meaning and opening possibilities in the present — this strain runs throughout Luxemburg's life. Socialism remained for her an objective necessity; yet in the crucial theoretical moments, in the theorization *of* revolutionary practice, it was the conscious, subjective, moral element that came to the fore. Reflecting on the defeat of 1919, she wrote:

> The leadership failed. But the leadership can and must be created anew by the masses and out of the masses. The masses are the crucial factor; they are the rock on which the ultimate victory of the revolution will be built. The masses were up to the task. They fashioned this 'defeat' into a part of those historical defeats which constitute the pride and power of international socialism. And that is why this 'defeat' is the seed of the future triumph. (p. 415, ibid.)

Here, as throughout, the theorist gives no recipes and offers no tactics; she strives to understand, to express and to crystallize the sense of the actual struggles. Yet she is the same theorist who taught economics at the Party School, who wrote *The Accumulation of Capital*; the same person who on countless occasions analyzed the international politico-economic conjuncture in a variety of widely-read party newspapers and journals; and she is the self-professed orthodox Marxist, defender of the Theory against internal critiques as well as against bourgeois attempts to weaken it through expropriation. How do both sides of this picture hold together?

We began this part of the discussion with the motto 'only the working class, through its own activity, can make the word flesh.' The formulation is typical. On the one hand, there is the ethical phraseology coupled with the stress on autonomous self-activity of the proletariat. On the other hand, there is that enigmatic 'word', which seems to be pre-given and foreordained. If the Word is already immanent and awaiting only History for its realization, there is present here the danger of the theory *for* practice and the seeds of a dogmatism. If, however, we understand with Luxemburg the revolution as a process, as the totality and sense of the struggle signified by the Mass Strike and based ultimately on the dialectic of class consciousness and its objective sedimentations, then the Word takes on the sense of an open self-creation. Then we can avoid the danger of technological recipes for revolution, and describe our task with Rosa Luxemburg:

> The essence of socialist society consists in the fact that the great laboring mass ceases to be a dominated mass, but rather, makes the entire political and economic life its own life and gives that life a conscious, free and autonomous direction. (p. 368, *What Does the Spartakus League Want?*)

The Word is not that of the theorist, but that of practice. What then is the role and task of the theorist?

II   The Theorist and her Practice

> The element of spontaneity plays such a prominent role in the mass strikes in Russia not because the Russian proletariat is 'unschooled' but because revolutions allow no one to play school-master to them. (*Mass Strike . . .*)

Rosa Luxemburg was a party-person. One recalls her angry letter to Henriette Roland-Holst concerning the decision of the left of the Dutch Social Democracy to split from the turgidly opportunistic Centre and form a new, truly left, party. Even if they were theoretically correct, she argued, separation from the 'party of the working class', however corrupted it may be, is suicide. A split would be a separation from the life-blood of socialism; it would be to privilege purity at the cost of participation in the inevitable revolution. The Beautiful Soul, entrenched in its purity at the cost of being unable to put that purity into practice, is not Marxist. More important than any question of efficacy — though the fate of the Dutch Left, and countless other pure doctrines, is certainly instructive — is the basic notion of revolutionary theory as a theory *of* practice, whose implications are that if one separates oneself from the masses, then one's theory will become an ideology, become sterile and be unable to evolve with the evolution of the mass struggle itself. In however corrupted a form, the Party represents that focus wherein the forms of struggle find their expression, their reflection, and from which they are reflected back to the masses who can thus become conscious of the wealth of possibilities implied in their own actions.

There is an ambiguity in this view of the party which, as we shall see, corresponds to an ambiguity in the role of theory itself as well as to an ambiguity in the theorist's own social insertion. On a factual level, we know that Rosa Luxemburg's activity within the Polish SDKPiL did not correspond to her view of the function of the German Party; and we know that, after serious doubts and hesitations, she left the SPD to join the newly formed Communist Party of Germany (Spartakus). We can offer conjunctural explanations for both of these activities; and this is sufficient for the present purposes. What is more striking for us is that she insists that the Party is necessary, but *not* as a tactical tool for the seizure of power! This is clear in her critique of the Leninist technology of revolution, and in her analysis of the German revolution of 1918—19. In the latter, she points to the political onset of the revolution, shows its insufficiency, and insists that the next stage must be the economic combat in which, 'breast to breast', each proletarian becomes aware of his/her task, becomes conscious of the situation and its demands. Decrees, the seizure of central power, programmatic statements are not enough. 'The masses must learn to use power by using power.' (p. 406, *Our Program and the Political Situation*) It seems, in effect, that the Party's task is precisely *to avoid the temptation of seizing power*, the political temptation; it must, as she puts it in the Mass Strike essay:

> give the slogans, the direction of the struggle; . . . organize the *tactics* of the political struggle in such a way that in every phase and in every moment of the struggle the whole sum of the available and already released active power of the proletariat will be realized and find expression in the battle-stance of the party; . . . see that the resoluteness and acuteness of the tactics of Social Democracy never fall below the level of

the actual relation of forces but rather rise above it. (p. 247,
Mass Strike, Party and Trade Unions)

The Party, in other words, depends on the level of struggle of
the masses for the formulation of tactics; *and* at the same time,
the Party must 'rise above' the actual level of struggle. How can
it do both? This is the question of Theory, and the challenge for
the radical theorist.

The same problem is posed somewhat differently in the final
section of the *Mass Strike* essay. Discussing the relation Party—
Trade Unions, Luxemburg insists that it is the Party which is
responsible for the growth of the Unions insofar as the Party,
by spreading what we must call the 'ideology' of Social
Democracy, sensibilizes the masses to their situation. She rejects
the Trade Unionists' argument that their numerical strength
indicates that they and their ideology of compromise should
dominate the movement. The movement is more than its
organizational forms, and the Party, as the 'spirit' of the
movement, transcends its organized mass, and is more than just
its organized kernel centred in offices and official functions.
But, if this is the case, one has to ask why Rosa Luxemburg put
so much stress on the 'legislative' function of the Party
Congress, as if she expected this yearly 'assembly of buddhists
and bonzes' to create correct tactics that all must follow. The
only explanation seems to be that she saw the Party and its
decisions as not simply representing (i.e., theorizing) ongoing
practice, but also as guiding it, as pushing it forward, giving it a
sense of mission and totality. This, however, is an ideological
function and supposes a certain — linear — theory of History.

This ambiguous attitude runs throughout the activity of Rosa
Luxemburg. Look at the apparent contradictions on nearly
every major issue: On the one hand, she insists that parliamentary and trade union struggles are not the way to socialist
revolution, showing their one-sided defensive character rooted
within the game-rules of the capitalist system; on the other
hand, she argues that without parliamentary democracy and
without free trade unions and their struggles, a socialist revolution would not be possible for there would be no political
room for the proletariat to develop its consciousness and no
economic space to free itself from the immediate pressure of
the struggle for existence within a society of wage slavery. She
argues that bourgeois democracy is an empty hull, a formality
which veils the class domination of the bourgeoisie; but insists
that without this formality there would be no possibility for the
proletariat to organize and recognize itself as a class; and

moreover, she attempts to demonstrate that in the age of imperialism the only party which must objectively support democracy is that of the proletariat. She insists repeatedly and vigorously that without the economic necessity of the break-down of capitalism there are no objective grounds for the socialist revolution, but argues just as emphatically that it is only the class-conscious proletariat which, by its own efforts and through its own self-educative experience, can make the system tumble. In her last political struggle, she opposed a hyper-activist politics in favour of a 'long revolution' based on electoral as well as economic struggles; yet she supported the majority decision, laying down her life in the abortive actions that followed, and justifying this not as a 'mistake' but as a necessary step in the historical development of the proletariat.

In each of these decisions — and one should point to others, for this theorist of proletarian spontaneity was also probably the only Marxist of her time to understand the importance of a transitional programme, to whose necessity she returned time and again; this convinced internationalist did not hesitate to oppose 'Marx' on the national question; this 'bloody Rosa' did not hesitate to criticize what she saw as excesses in the Russian Revolution — in each case the first pole of the opposition seems to represent a theoretical position based on the ideology of Marxism and valid for capitalism in general; while the counter-position, which she actually adopted in the fire of action, is a modification of that theory based on what is in fact its basis: i.e., based on the action of the proletariat as inflecting the social-political configuration that is capitalism. The orthodox Marxist that she was is responsible for both poles: the ideology itself must be defended against the opportunistic incursions of those too short-sighted to see the basic necessities to which the fundamental contradiction capital/labour points; and at the same time, the revolutionary kernel of the theory — that class consciousness, achieved in the struggle within the existing order, is the *sine qua non* of its elimination — must be maintained open. The revolutionary Marxist theorist, in other words, is both *a conservative and a visionary*. Both must be maintained, for the theory without vision becomes a dead weight on the practice of which it was once the expression — i.e., becomes an ideology; and vision without analytic content becomes a utopian and baseless wish, a groundless existential acti-vism — i.e., also an ideology.

The practice of Rosa Luxemburg as theorist is a remarkable attempt to maintain both poles of this dialectic of revolutionary theory. For example, in the debate with Bernstein, her defence

of economic orthodoxy suddenly gives way when confronted
with Bernstein's challenge: what if, suddenly, the power fell
into the hands of the proletariat? Her reply is that 'the idea of a
"premature" conquest of political power ... [is] a political
absurdity, derived from a mechanical conception of social
development, and positing for the victory of the class struggle a
time fixed *outside* and *independent of* the class struggle.' (p.
123, *SR or R?*) That is, Bernstein's question supposes an
ideological view of a History unrolling independent of precisely
the forces that constitute it; it supposes that the theorist is in a
position external to the class struggle, able to see the totality of
history and its necessities *from outside.* Yet, immediately
following this defence of a theoretical position situated within
and partaking of the class struggle, she returns to the defence of
economic orthodoxy, maintaining the necessity of the breakdown theory in purely economic (i.e., external) terms. The
point is that the two go together, that neither alone is sufficient
and that each influences the other. One could demonstrate in
detail — whether in her Polish work, in her analyses of the
situation in France, or her practical and theoretical attempts to
demonstrate the necessity and prevent the onset of the World
War — this two-sidedness of Luxemburg's practical theoretical
work. If one looks at her speech, *Our Program and the Political
Situation*, one is first of all struck by the fact that she felt the
need to introduce a resolution against the counter-revolutionary
activities of the SPD government with regard to the Russian
situation, and the care with which she documents these inter-
ventions. This care for socialist legalism is transferred to the
plane of actual considerations with the return to the Erfurt
Program, which she attempts to interpret in the spirit of the
ongoing revolutionary activity, with the manifest aim of linking
the activities of the new Party to the tradition of Marxism. At
the same time, however, one sees the visionary side in the stress
on, and recognition of, the new creative form taken on by the
mass activity: the workers' and soldiers' councils. Both poles are
there, as always.

Yet, what is striking in the practical activity of this revolutionary theorist is that *she was a failure.* On *every* central
issue — from the revisionist-opportunist debates, through the
mass strike, the question of militarism and imperialism, the
attitude to adopt towards the war, the tactics to be followed by
the KPD in 1918–19 — she was refuted. She was refuted on
other issues as well — the parliamentary tactic to be followed,
the nature and function of the Party, the role of the trade
unions, the status of the International. What is important in

these refutations is that she was never beaten by other arguments, but rather refuted by the facts, the events; *refuted by History*. For a Marxist, this is of course the most damning refutation of all!

There is a further pecularity in Rosa Luxemburg's practice as a theorist. *She was a dogmatist*, in the sense already alluded to. She never put Marxism into question, never doubted its teachings for a moment. We know that hers was a creative Marxism, following the spirit and not the letter, open to new developments, as a theory *of* practice must be. Yet the result of this was *only* that she was *a dogmatist eternally in opposition*. This is paradoxical; for if I am correct in asserting that she captured the spirit of the movement in her theorization, then the practice of the revolutionary theorist, and the revolutionary theory itself, is cast into doubt by Luxemburg's fate.

Several explanations could be advanced. We might say, as with Fidel Castro's famous speech, that 'history will absolve her.' That, however, implies a linear view of history, seen from a divine or transcendental viewpoint, where progress takes place continually until such time as it eventually reaches its — i.e., our — imputed goal. But to say that a Marxist is 'ahead of her time' is to say that she was in fact incorrect in her analyses; for what distinguishes Marxism from the run-of-the-mill utopians is that it claims to discover the future within the present. The linear view of history, as already mentioned, separates History from the class struggle which constitutes it; it is ideological.

We might say that her analyses, her perceptions of the ongoing and innovative reality, were incorrect either because of a too dogmatic adherence to the Theory, or because of an overly optimistic interpretation of the reality. We might say that she chose the wrong points of intervention, that for example she should have broken with the SPD as early as 1907—8, or that she should have tried to build a stronger oppositional base within the party, instead of confining herself to journalism, the Party School, and agitational speech-making. We might say that she gave too great credence to the spontaneity of the masses, and consequently did not take care to prevent them from falling victim to the deceptions of the leadership; that she should have followed Lenin's tactics and used organizational measures to maintain the purity of the Party. We might advance a variant of Michels' oligarchy thesis to explain why a theory that is the theorization of the practice *of* a vanguard can not, for *a priori* reasons, become the reigning position within a mass democratic Party. We could add details concerning the manipulation by the party leadership, with which Michels' discussion of the SPD is rich. (Indeed, Luxemburg seems to see something similar to Michels' analysis in the sociological remarks in the last section of the Mass Strike essay.) We might go on and suggest, with A. Rosenberg, that she ought to have known, as did Lenin in July 1917, when to beat a tactical retreat in order then to choose the right moment for a comeback; or we could refer to Hannah Arendt's interpretation, that she was ultimately a romantic and a moralist, not a Marxist at all.

There are thus many possible explanations of Luxemburg's practice as a theorist, and its destiny. None is in itself convincing, for each is obliged to introduce external and contingent factors. At best, one says that if Luxemburg was defeated, and if there were contradictions in her position, the source of this lies in the historical terrain on which she stood. The contradictions in her work would thus be due to the immaturity of capitalism and the consequent immaturity of the proletarian movement; her 'defeats' would be seen as only temporary, and the advance of the capitalist contradictions will show the long-term fruitfulness of her position. In other words, one asserts that Luxemburg had the correct theory, but that when she *applied* this theory to the reality of her times, a distortion emerged because of an inadequacy in the reality itself. The implication of this is that we need to extract, through a Marxist 'inversion' of Biblical hermeneutics, the correct theory (or method, if one prefers Lukács' notion) and to apply this revolutionary philosopher's stone to turn the leaden present into a golden future. This, however, neglects a fundamental point, common to the dialectics of Marx and Hegel: that dialectical theory (or method) cannot be separated from its content. In other words, this solution falls back behind the advances of Hegel and Marx; it implies a kind of Kantian dualism of form and matter, and a resultant dialectic of the bad infinite 'resolved' by the eternal ethical striving of practical Reason. In effect, whenever a defeat occurs it can be blamed on one or the other side of the interacting terms, whose interaction is external precisely insofar as neither is affected by its contact with the other, for each has its own 'truth-criteria' internal to itself. This separation implies an external, linear view of History, and divides precisely what Marxism strives to unite: theory and practice. We have, therefore, to ask why a true Marxist — and the above arguments have implied that Luxemburg was faithful to the best elements in Marx himself — was powerless to relate as a revolutionary to the actual practice of her time? And, if the Marxist theory, as theorization of proletarian practice, is unable to command the allegiance of the masses and to effect social change, then perhaps there is something wrong with the theory itself?

It might be suggested that the assertion of Luxemburg's 'failure' is a kind of pragmatic judgement itself situated outside of the history in which her work was forged. It would seem that the verdict 'failure' was arrived at by superimposing her theory and her practice on an ever-flowing History which was the material base on which her work functioned. This would give her theory and her practice a closed, positive, and ultimately ideological character, instead of presenting it as an open, interrogative theory *of* practice. Indeed, the motto with which we began this part — that no one can play school-master to the revolutionary proletariat — suggests that our criticism has violated one of her own central precepts. In order to clarify this problem, the next part will have to look at the ambiguities of revolutionary theory itself by returning to the question that was posed but not answered in this second part: how is it possible for the theory to be a theory *of* the actual practice of the proletariat, and at the same time to *rise above* that practice?

III Revolutionary Theory

> Far more important, however, than what is written in a
> program is the way in which it is interpreted in action.
> (*Our Program and the Political Situation*)

The essential variable in the theoretical and practical work of Rosa Luxemburg is class consciousness. It is no doubt for this reason that today, when capitalism has revealed itself as a total system seemingly capable of absorbing its economic, social and political contradictions, we find her work a congenial source of reflection on our own problems. In a way, this is ironic; for she was too orthodox, too dogmatic and too much an optimist to have sensed the problems posed by the advent of a scientized, bureaucratic capitalism as we know it. She is not concerned with the mechanisms of individual or mass psychology, with problems like reification, alienation or false consciousness. Yet she has been, and is, a source of fruitful reflection on just these problems.

In asserting that class consciousness is the essential component, the *sine qua non* of any revolutionary movement, Luxemburg is certainly no different from many other Marxists. What is distinctive is her analysis of it — or better, the fact that she never makes it into the *object* of her theorizing, but rather shows its actual appearance as the reflection *and* critical self-reflection of the open possibilities that proletarian action has created. This central 'ingredient' is never thematized, is always present on the margins, emerging and taking form only to be carried onward and reappear in a different guise; it is not a thing but the *sense* and *meaning*, the *unity* and *totality* of the class struggle. It is not external, the product of a theory or the property of the Party; it is the condition of the possibility of the struggle and the product of that same struggle. We can fix the elements that play a role in determining the present status of class consciousness, talking about the material conditions which determine the forms of consciousness. But this cannot be understood as a cause-effect relation, empirically determined. We know, for example, that the same conditions can give rise to very different forms of consciousness and activity; we know, for example, that the inflationary wave we are presently living is given a different human, lived-significance from what appears in the official statistics. What is crucial is that the material conditions can only affect the class precisely insofar as the class itself is willing to be affected, i.e., *gives a significance to these conditions.*

As we read Luxemburg's articles analyzing the events of her time, and as we vicariously follow her courses on political economy at the Party School, what gives her work a character that is more than just good analysis and 'correct' interpretation is her ability to continually put her finger on the dynamic, the *possibilities*, the sense and radical *signification*, the *openness* of the situation she is describing. Of course, much of what she 'predicted' did not come to pass. But, as already observed, this 'failure' cannot be judged from the transcendent standpoint of a History that has now closed off the possibilities and shown an erroneous judgement. Her task was not to present *'the'* necessary path to follow, to *'prove'* the correctness of her view inductively and/or deductively; it was rather to reveal the sense of a situation, to point to its central feature: its openness. When we judge her a 'failure', we treat her practical political work as a closed thing with only one possible signification; and therewith we fall back into a view of a linear and mechanically unrolling history. History as lived is precisely the openness of interrogation; and Luxemburg's task as practical theoretician was to focus on this openness, on the possible class-consciousness with which the situation is rich.

It would be an oversimplification to assert that since class consciousness is the central variable of the revolutionary process, the task of the theorist is to act always in such a way as to raise the level of that consciousness. For that supposes that we know what class consciousness is; it implies that class consciousness is a thing, and that it grows, somehow, by the addition of little bits of information received from outside itself; and it makes theory into a kind of tool or weapon, preparing the ground for the famous practice of 'substitutionism' whereby the Party as the possessor of the theory substitutes itself for the masses, whose 'correct' consciousness it claims to be. Of course, class consciousness is not indeterminate either; and we have already mentioned (in Section I) the correctness of Lukács' epistemological appropriation of Luxemburg's use of the notion of the necessity of the 'final goal' of socialism. But Luxemburg also avoids the trap of an external, linear conception of history, which would contain a fixed view of the nature of socialist consciousness. Thus, we find her speaking with confidence and sanguinuity of the need for the proletariat to accede to power several times, each time losing it, before it finally learns to establish its new society. (p. 123, *Social Reform or Revolution?*) And we are struck by her continual return to the historical 'failures' of the movement — lost strikes and revolts, 1848, 1891, the history of May Day, etc. — as being a necessary component in the growth of class consciousness. She does not present a pseudo-materialist explanation of these 'failures', *refusing to explain them away*; instead, and the difference is crucial, she gives them a positive significance because of the new dimensions that they open.

Yet, we are still confronted with the problem of theory's being at once a theory *of* the actual movement and at the same time '*rising above*' it. In effect, this is a false problem once we escape from the external, linear view of History and recognize that our theory is part and parcel of history itself. Theory cannot be simply a static reflection of the present, nor an external construct that serves as guide. The reason for this is that the central variable determining the historical process is not fixed but in-determinant, open, changing and creating new significations. *Theory is not and cannot be a system* — at least not if it is revolutionary theory. And indeed, in what sense can we say that Rosa Luxemburg 'had' a theory? Certainly, she accepted Marxism, and even attempted to present a theoretical correction of it in *The Accumulation of Capital.* But in her practice, and in the relation of her theory to practice, she never attempted to elaborate a series of positive and determined formulae that could be followed. For example, is the Mass Strike essay the presentation of a theory? Certainly not in the traditional sense; yet as engaged Marxists we talk about it as such. Why?

If we look again at the theory of the Mass Strike, what is central is the shifting forms taken by class consciousness, expressing itself now politically, now economically, now in minor movements or in quiescence, now in major flare-ups whose cause seems minor in comparison with the enormity of the class's oppression. Moreover, the Mass Strike movement that culminated in the Revolution of 1905 is seen to have its roots in activity in different geographical regions over a period of nearly a decade. The 'Mass Strike' itself, Luxemburg explicitly notes, is a *concept*, a totalization, the unity of a variety of actions. The historical actors did not consciously sense themselves a part of this movement whose unity the theorist presents; they did not follow directives in moving their struggle from one plane to another, one region or issue to another. *Yet the Mass Strike is there.* It is the historical *sense* of proletarian struggle, not consciously appended to the individual actions but their latent signification and *meaning*. The theory gives an empirical accounting *of* the events, and thus is a theory *of* the activity; and at the same time it '*rises above*' insofar as it unifies and designates the *possibility* that has been opened.

What is the process of revolution, and on what does it depend? Ultimately, on a free space, on a vacuum that is created and felt in the power relations that have hitherto held the proletariat in bonds. The opening of this space is not the result of theory or of class consciousness in the sense that they would function like a kind of archimedean point or can-opener. Obviously, there are real events and material conditions which play a role. But when we begin to analyze these events and material conditions, we find that they could play their role only because of their lived, human *significance*. And it is through this notion of *significance* that theory finds its role as *rising above*. It rises above insofar as it is the integrated *sense and possibility* of the present whose theory it is. It is this not simply as theory, but as lived experience, insists Rosa Luxemburg, noting that 'in the storm of the revolutionary period, the proletarian is transformed from a provident family man demanding support into a "revolutionary romantic" for whom the highest good, namely life — not to speak of material well-being — has little value in comparison with the ideals of the struggle'. (pp. 246—7, *Mass Strike*) The sense and possibility, inherent in the movement and theorized by the revolutionary, are the *difference* which makes all the difference in revolutionary action.

The notion of the 'two reefs' between which revolutionary

practice must continually navigate can be extended to the paradoxes of revolutionary theory. As a theory of practice within capitalist society, it must remain affixed to its material base; yet at the same time it must 'rise above' and dwell in the realm of sense, of the difference, of the possible. It must hold together the poles: alone, the first makes history into a mythology, and itself becomes either a shameless empiricism or a technology which treats humans as objects; while the second alone runs the danger of falling into moral utopias, vague hopes or empty ethical demands. The implication of the motto with which we began this Section is that the stress should *not* be placed on the mystifying adjectives 'proletarian' or 'revolutionary', but rather, when we are concerned with theory, they should be applied to specify the particular kind of theory for which we aim — binding rigour with openness, critique with self-critique, and necessity which points to possibility. The duality to which I have pointed in the theoretical and practical activity of Rosa Luxemburg is not something that the famous *Aufhebung* can take care of in some magical manner. Rather, it is constitutive of the project itself. It must be understood; and it cannot be changed by any simplification of whatever sort.

4 Marxism and Concrete Philosophy: Ernst Bloch

Banality too is counter-revolution against Marxism itself.
(*Das Prinzip Hoffnung*, p. 322)

To situate Bloch, to speak of his Marxism: this supposes that we move beyond the history of ideas in order to enter into the concerns and choices of a real movement aiming at changing the world. We find ourselves before the double difficulty of trying to understand a thinker who has always been an actor in this movement for the past seventy years, and at the same time trying to cast some light on this movement itself which flees from any totalising comprehension. And there is a supplementary complication: Bloch considers himself a *philosopher*, but a Marxist philosopher for whom the *Aufhebung* of philosophy proposed by Marx would be only the elimination of the *bad*, contemplative philosophy of the past, not the destruction of philosophy itself. This means that we cannot use the facts of history as if they could somehow explain a movement of action or thought; we must try to philosophise with the philosopher-Marxist, trying to illuminate his contribution as it was and as it remains.

Bloch is willing to grant that Marx has not been the 'Theologian of the Revolution', instilling in it that warmth, hope and dynamics that Bloch analysed in his study of Thomas Muenzer; willing to grant that Marx did not thematise his dialectical theory of superstructures, of revolution or even of class consciousness; and even to admit that Marx accepted from the pen of Engels — and his own — formulae which make the Fathers of Marxism responsible for the sins of their descendants. He nonetheless maintains with insistence that only from a faithful Marxist perspective will one be able to understand and change the world, here and now. This bothers the philosopher,

Marxist or not. One finds side-by-side in Bloch a fidelity without shame, a complete engagement and an enthusiasm without limits; and one finds too the pen of the poet, the imagination, culture and subtlety of a philosopher of the great period of German Idealism, as well as the passion, vision and sense for detail of a living man determined to sup on the marrow of the everyday. Bloch is too orthodox and too heterodox to enter into our received categories: too engaged in the struggles and the intellectual life of his time, and too much a systematic and rigorous philosopher. Faithful supporter, even champion, of the communism of the Third International, he nonetheless remained critical on the level of theory when it seemed necessary to him — a position which earned him critiques from the right as well as from the left.[1] We too may want to criticize him for his defence of and obedience to Stalin, for his naïveté towards East Germany, or for his unabashed defence of the Moscow Trials; we may want to point out the evident divergence between his radically critical theory and his conformist orthodox practice: nonetheless, one cannot help but be caught up in the rhythm of his 'experimental' thought which has doggedly pursued itself through all of the manifestations of humanity, from the smallest and nearly banal events to the most monumental of the classics.

The work of Bloch poses the question of the intellectual, of the philosopher who wants to and must participate in the struggles of his time. Bloch was one of those young intellectuals seeking their way during the period in which the preparations of the World War were painfully evident. A friend of the Expressionists, participant in the Salon of Max Weber, friend of the polyvalent philosopher-sociologist Georg Simmel (at whose home he first met a young Hungarian, Georg von Lukács, whose friend and inseparable collaborator he was to remain for more than a decade), Bloch was a pacifist who preferred exile in Switzerland to Germany at war. Like so many others, he was thrown into a turmoil by the Revolution of 1917 — the 'Novum', as he was to call it in his later systematic language. Returning to Germany after the abdication of the Emperor, he took part in the revolutionary struggles which continued until 1923. During this agitated period, he wrote the *Spirit of Utopia* (1918, revised edition, 1923), *Thomas Muenzer as Theologian of the Revolution* (1921), and a collection of essays, *Through the Desert* (1923). That year marked the end of an epoch: Soviet Russia lived, but in isolation; the revolutionary wave had been stopped before the gates of Warsaw; while its counterpart in Germany was soon to be replaced by the Brown Plague, and the

Weimar Republic presented itself as the symbol of a new order infected by the sins of its birth.

This was also the year in which the question of the communist intellectual was most immediately and acutely posed with the appearance — and condemnation — of Lukács' *History and Class Consciousness* and Korsch's *Marxism and Philosophy*. The parallel but opposed destiny of these two great innovators in the tradition of Hegelian Marxism poses a choice with which we still live: Lukács renounced certain of his key ideas in order to remain faithful to the party and 'thus' to the Revolution, whereas Korsch remained faithful to his position, becoming rapidly isolated and without influence on his times. The third great 'Hegelian Marxist' is Ernst Bloch, who never joined the Party, and whose less directly political style and concerns at least partially spared him from the attacks and polemics of the new orthodoxy. Does Bloch's way offer an adequate model? While the answer is, I think, negative, the question itself is ill-posed. We must make our own way. But what Bloch does offer, and what we shall see to be a central category in his work, is the notion of an *active inheritance*. Our task is to assume that heritage.

In the following remarks, I want first of all to set forth the basic principles or axes around which Bloch's work revolves, in order then to set contrast it with the position of a superficially similar approach which begins from the same philosophical forebears — that of the Frankfurt School's director, Max Horkheimer — and finally to ask again the question of our heritage from Bloch. More specifically: (1) Bloch's review of Lukács' *History and Class Consciousness* illuminates the specificity of his own position within the spectrum of Marxism. The historical theory of the proletariat as subject/object indentical is conceptualised by Lukács in such a manner as to demand the smooth transition to a Leninist and ultimately Stalinist obedience. This need not have been the case, as the implications drawn by Bloch point out. (2) Already in 1924, Bloch was aware of the threat posed by the Fascist movement. Rather than offer an analysis based on the traditional economic categories and a simplified notion of class consciousness, Bloch attempted to apply the categories that he had developed through his own reflection and experience. The results open up the implications of his theoretical stance. (3) Bloch's analyses were never translated into practice. He himself became the more obedient politically to the Moscow orientation, finally assuming a professorship — his first — in Leipzig, East Germany, after the war, and leaving neither after 1953, nor 1956, but only with the erection of the Berlin Wall. The politics of his theory force one to ask whether a 'critical theory' such as that proposed by Max Horkheimer and the Institute for Social Research might offer a better alternative. (4) While the comparison with Horkheimer will point to the greater richness and subtlety of Bloch's approach, this is not a solution nor a reason to adopt the Blochian stance. Applying Bloch to Bloch, we can and must pose the question of our own heritage.

I Bases of Bloch's Dialectics: Actuality and Utopia

The long and lyrical review of Lukács' *History and Class Consciousness* which Bloch published in 1923 under the significant title, 'Actuality and Utopia', must be taken all the more seriously as the two had been inseparable friends for more than a decade. Indeed, Bloch remarked to me one day that his *Spirit of Utopia* was as much indebted to Lukács' collaboration as was *History and Class Consciousness* to his own.[2] In that atmosphere charged with despair, passion and revolt, where there stood side-by-side a Social Democratic Party incapable of imagining itself other than as it was and a revolt of the human imagination represented as much by Expressionism as by the many varieties of irrationalism that flourished, Bloch and Lukács were tied together by a culture based on the German Idealism of Kant-Goethe-Hegel, and by a desire to *do something* so that the world could be changed. It is thus not surprising that the first three pages of the review speak in a lyrical but sober voice of that world which is unable to understand itself, losing its senses in a frenetic activism. Nor is it surprising that the next ten pages are a staccato reconstruction of Lukács' essential contributions: the analysis of the crisis in terms of reification; second nature; the lack of a conception of the totality which is responsible for a situation where the world seems to run of its own momentum towards a crisis whose coming one can see but against which one is powerless; Lukács' attempt to think through that crisis in terms of the philosophical problem of the Thing-in-itself, where the quantification of life which emerges from specialisation and the division of labour is seen to hide a qualitative base without which the ties between the partial systems would be lost; the diagnostic of contemporary forms of art and morality as sometimes rich but failed attempts to reply to that loss of the totality; and finally, the return to Hegel and Marx in order to think history in its creativity as the basis of the totality which mediates the individual consciousness and the everyday experience.

Bloch reproduces the path of *History and Class Consciousness* in his own manner, his own language, and articulated
around his own preoccupations. The theory of the Party
developed by Lukács does not bother him, despite the fact that
Lukács would soon be led to abandon much of what Bloch
finds important in his analysis precisely because of that theory.
Nonetheless, from the beginning of the review, Bloch predicts
the problems which Lukács' book will encounter. He speaks of
the 'Russians for example, who act philosophically but think
like uncultured dogs . . .'³ Though they 'are infinitely different
from the Revisionists, . . . they are nonetheless in nearly the
same manner separated from the philosophical heritage, and
many of them will say that Marx did not stand Hegel on his feet
in order that Lukács once again stand Marx on his head.'⁴ The
bourgeoisie too will misunderstand the return to the fundamental problem of German Idealism — the subject/object problem — just as they have always done with their best products.

In Bloch's reading, the key to Lukács' theory is that 'The
instant [Augenblick], which for all others is a conceptual
embarassment, is here raised to the moment of decision, the
penetration [Durchblick] into the totality.'⁵ Lukács' analysis
of the fetishism of commodities which shows that the proletariat as commodity is an object whose self-knowledge is at the
same time the critique of bourgeois society in its totality is seen
to turn around a dialectically open conception of the Now
[*Jetzt*] : 'In this manner we are finally capable of grasping the
Now in which we stand.'⁶ This Now is not that of Hegel,
standing impoverished and abstract before the single consciousness about to undertake the journey of its education into the
Absolute. The Now is intersubjective and actively mediated by a
we-subject. Lukács' analyses of the structure of capitalism as
well as of the paradoxes of German Idealism open on to a
concrete task: revolution as the repossession of man and nature
through the elimination of alienation. Theory implies praxis:
'As soon as the accompanying concept, itself dialectical, is
capable of grasping the present, recognizing in it those tendencies from whose opposition it can *create* the future, then the
present is *its* present, the moment of deepest and most ampli-
fied mediation, the moment of decision, the birth of the new.'⁷
What Bloch is presenting is a theory of *constitution*; the Now is
mediated, constituted, by the we-subject which can only seize
itself precisely in its act of constitution and as its act of
constitution. The fixed, reified static presence is exploded; the
Now is the new, the utopia which is actual.

Bloch's review does not deal directly with the political

analyses offered by Lukács, but his criticism is only rendered
the more telling through the opposition of what he reads in
Lukács' book and the latter's political reality. He notes that
Lukács tends towards a 'sociological homogenization' which
reduces history to a single dimension and a linear structure. But
no more than the Now, history is not simply a total social
formation closed on to itself, with its own sense waiting to be
seized by the preceiving consciousness. History is a 'polyrhythmic formation'[8] which includes the artistic, the religious, the
metaphysical as well as the social-economic. Lukács' reduction
loses the dianoetical element. The implications of this reduction
appear especially in Lukács' treatment of nature. When Bloch
points out that 'its subject, which here could create the
surpassing of Nature as its own reality, has not yet come ... is
not yet discovered',[9] he is implicitly criticising the political
programme of *History and Class Consciousness*. The argument
appears a bit more directly when Bloch writes that 'Socially, an
adequation can be achieved economically more easily than
legally or morally, and specifically the spiritual [*das Geistige*]
can follow another, more devious force, or can take its path
more slowly.'[10] Lukács' reduction was motivated by the necessity of eliminating both bourgeois positivism and the moralistic
dualism that results from it. But his solution carries the
drawback that the leap, the constitution of the actuality of
utopia in the present, gives way to a conceptual mythology
based on the subject/object identical incarnated in the Party.

The corrective proposed by Bloch is significant in its warning
and in its further implications, which emerge in his analysis of
fascism. Lukács moves too quickly; closure replaces openness;
solutions take the place of problems demanding analysis, choice
and action. Bloch suggests that we need '*the weighing down of
the totality through the concept of the sphere*'.[11] This notion
would be adequate to the mediated and multi-levelled conception of the Now which Bloch proposed. 'The sphere', he
writes is 'the expression of different subject/object levels
posited in the process itself, ... which expresses and dissemi-
nates itself temporally in the process and also spatially in the
positing of the sphere.'[12] In this manner, Lukács would have
been able not only to seize the Now in its processuality, but
would have avoided the reduction which impedes the leap into
the new. 'Only one level higher in the Now,' exhorts Bloch, 'and
beside, above the proletariat appears the obscure mystery of the
lived instant [*Dunkel des gelebten Augenblick*], the actuality
generally [*überhaupt*] hidden in it, victorious against all abstraction which is removed from the subject.'[13] Had he carried

through his analysis, Lukács would have been led to the *'unconstructible question [unkonstruierbare Frage]* ... Respect for the secret of the We which in reality is undiscovered not only for us but thus also for itself; the secret which is the secret of the world.'[14] Posed in this manner, actuality and utopia would appear together, as Bloch's title suggests; they would be co-constitutive of each other. This, perhaps, is what Marx meant when he suggested that until now the world has merely possessed in a dream what it needs to consciously demand in reality.

Bloch's interpretation of Lukács indicates, perhaps without really intending to do so, the two senses or tendencies contained in *History and Class Consciousness*; and at the same time, we witness the appearance of the difference which will continue to grow between the positions of the two friends. The chasm between the conception of theory on the part of the two appears most strikingly in the Hegel interpretations which the two published after the Second World War. In *Der junge Hegel*, Lukács attempts to paint a nearly marxist Hegel, limited only by the socio-economic and political conditions of the Germany of his time; whereas in *Subjekt-Objekt*, Bloch's goal is to illuminate the heritage of Hegel through a sustained reflection on the tensions which are contained and uneasily maintained within the system of the greatest of the German Idealists. Where Lukács attempts to justify Hegel within the framework of a doctrine which he is said to have anticipated but been unable to realise, Bloch can never accept the idea of a complete and finished doctrine which would *give* reality in its sheer positivity to the theorist who applies the method. For this reason, Bloch attempts to demonstrate the wealth of the Hegelian reflection through an analysis of the systematic and mature works, while Lukács concentrates on the early critique of the positivity of institutions and the studies of political economy which lead to the *Phenomenology of Spirit*. Where Lukács' study is continuous, systematic and well-rounded, Bloch's disconcerts, leaps, doubles back on itself only to stride forward precisely into that Now, the spheric totality opening to and opened by a We-Subject. Lukács' analysis is perhaps useful to the student or general reader wanting to know who Hegel was, and why he could have been so important to Marx; Bloch's attempt is not so much to present Hegel as to use him to confront the world, guided by that 'one-sidedness ... which makes one point sharply at the goal.'[15] Of course, living in Leipzig in the DDR, Bloch the Communist identifies this goal with Marxism and even with its Stalinist form. But what he brings out in Hegel by this means is precisely that unity of a concrete philosophy and a grasp of the totality, stressing for example that 'attention to instances in the sense that no detail is *a priori* designated as inessential is unavoidable for concrete philosophizing.'[16] For Bloch, 'Actuality is *nominalism, not conceptual realism*; but a nominalism the entirety of whose moments and details are held together by the *unity of the objective real-intention*, founded by the *utopian unity of the goal*.'[17] It is precisely this sense that Bloch had noted as well in Walter Benjamin, speaking of his 'sense for the incidental', and adding that 'Benjamin had that which so unbelievably lacked in Lukács . . .'[18] Thus, to conclude with a significant anecdote, Bloch tells the story that once when he and Benjamin joined Lukács in Capri at the beginning of the 1930s, they began to discuss the impression that a fairy tale makes on the young listener. After a long discussion in which Lukács did not speak, Bloch asked him what he thought of the matter: the reply was stereotypical — it depends on the social conditions of the hearer, the author, etc., etc. They did not meet again!

The contrast of Bloch and Lukács which emerges here points to the ambiguity of the heritage of Hegelian-Marxism. In contrast to Korsch, Bloch and Lukács remain with the party of the proletariat, refusing what they take to be the isolated purity and abstract moralism of a truth with no objective referent. Both also justify their fidelity in terms of Fascism-as-the-Enemy. And yet, in spite of his claim that much of his work during this period was 'aesopian', Lukács never again rose to the passion and concrete openness which Bloch found in *History and Class Consciousness*. Bloch's fidelity was of a different stuff: to the Now, the spherical totality, the unconstructible question. Yet a fidelity it was, often to the detriment of its own desires. Thus, the analysis of Fascism contained in the *Heritage of This Time*, to which we now turn, includes much that is questionable in its specific cultural analyses — even while the underlying direction, on which we shall concentrate, is rigorous and concrete. The danger to be avoided is the temptation — to which Lukács succumbed — to conflate the theoretical analysis with the concrete reality in such a way as to close both and thus prohibit that qualitative leap to the new, to socialism. While aiming to open the real through its mediated structures, the high degree of conceptual abstraction of the Hegelian-Marxists tends, when pursued as if it were itself a form of praxis changing the real, to fall victim to the crude practicalities which that reality imposes on it.

II Confrontation with Fascism and Development of the Dialectic

Not only was 1923 the date of the appearance of the books of
Lukács and Korsch, and that of the final failure of the German
Revolution; it was also the date of the Munich Putsch by Hitler.
Never accepted by the Left or the Right, Weimar was seeking to
establish and maintain itself; infected by a formal democracy
which was daily contradicted by the social conditions, it would
live out its life for another ten years, before handing over the
power legally to Hitler. What to do? How to understand what
lay ahead? Bloch hated the timid bourgeoisie, be it Centrist or
Social Democratic; and its predicament was no surprise to him.
He supported the Communists, but without joining them. He
would say later, after Hitler's ascension, that everything they
did was correct — simply that they neglected the essential. This
may sound naïve, even contradictory; yet Bloch was not a
politician but a revolutionary and philosopher for whom the
analysis of reality and action in the everyday were what
counted. With a small group of friends — Benjamin, Adorno,
Kracauer, Weill and Brecht — he attempted to illuminate that
polyrhythmic and spherical Now where the totality in its
futurity opened itself. While most of the writings contained in
the *Heritage* concern the arts, culture, philosophy, and the
everyday, the political lesson was drawn in a short essay,
'Noncontemporaneity and the Obligation to its Dialectics'.

Bloch begins his analysis from orthodox economic premises:

> As opposed to the proletariat, the middle class does not in
> general participate directly in production but enters it only
> with intermediary activities, with such a distance from social
> causality that an alogical space can build itself unhindered, a
> space in which wishes and romanticisms, primal drives and
> mythicisms come onto the stage.[19]

What holds for these middle classes holds, *mutatis mutandis*, for
the peasantry. That 'alogical space' is not nothing; its contents
must be analysed. The concrete articulations of that 'polyrhythmic formation' which is history as lived in the present must be
studied. The economic analysis is only a beginning, which must
be gone beyond.

Bloch begins from a political evidence: 'Were misery to hit
only contemporaneous men, even if they were from different
positions, backgrounds and consciousnesses, it could not drive
them to march in such different directions, especially not so far

backwards.'[20] Proletarianisation, impoverishment and the heavy cloud of uncertainty for their future might be expected to drive the middle strata and even the peasantry to the Communists, or at least to the Social Democrats. If this did not occur, argues Bloch, it is because, though they tend to become commodities like everything else in the reified world of capital, there remain *real remnants of a past which is still present* to which they can actively relate their situation. It is not simply a false consciousness, or the effects of capitalist or fascist propaganda which drives these people. Particularly in Germany, where the bourgeois revolution waited until 1918 for its consummation, and where therefore capitalism was overdetermined by modes of production and consciousness which were never really submitted to the levelling of the commodity world of capitalism, these remnants could play a role. Driven, hounded, threatened, these strata reach actively for anchorage at the port closest to what they perceive as home.

In Marx's analysis of the contradictions of capitalism, the antagonism between the forces and the relations of production is the key to revolutionary upheaval. The revolutionary project of the proletariat is inscribed in the conditions of capitalism. Its activity is determined by its everyday experience of the limits, artificiality and irrationality imposed on its free activity. What it seeks, therefore, is a future already present but yet dependent for its actualisation on its own conscious revolutionary activity. The contradiction described in this manner is what Bloch calls a *contemporary contradiction.* There are, however, other contradictions which make themselves felt within the social totality: these Bloch treats as *non-contemporary contradictions.* These latter are part of the polyrhythmic Now, structures of the sphere which is the present as history. Marx himself recognized the existence of such non-contemporary contradictions, for example in the Introduction to *The German Ideology* where he talks of the existence of other modes of production alongside the dominant one; or in the *18th Brumaire*, where he subtly analyses the behaviour of the peasantry in terms of their remembrance of the French Revolution and their role in the Napoleonic empire. Bloch's task is to thematise these contradictions in terms of the Now mediated by a We-Subject.

Strata such as the peasantry, the petite-bourgeoisie or their petty-bureaucrat descendants live their present in the mode of the past, and their future through the mirror of capitalism with its exploitation and rationalisation of human relations. Something is wrong; but they don't know what, and aren't able to change their lives. Their ideals — duty, honour, *Bildung* — are no longer accepted; their idols — the house, land, the people or nation — have been crushed under the leaden foot of capitalism. They live a diffuse *ressentiment* which is incapable of giving itself a name, crystallizing itself or comprehending itself. Such a *ressentiment*, which Bloch calls 'dammed-up rage' [*gestaute Wut*] is a *subjectively non-contemporary contradiction*. It is not a sort of 'false consciousness', insists Bloch, for 'to it corresponds the *objective* non-contemporary contradiction as the continued effectiveness of older, no matter how thwarted, relations and forms of production, as well as older superstructures. The *objective* non-contemporary is what is far from and foreign to the present; it includes the *declining remnants* as well as, above all, the *unutilized past* which has not yet been capitalistically "*aufgehoben*".'[21] These objectively non-contemporary contradictions are not due to the specific circumstances of German capitalism alone; they point to an incompleteness inherent in the structure of capitalism itself. In Bloch's ontology, their existence plays a crucial structural role permitting the possibility of a critical-utopian philosophy.

The two forms of non-contemporary contradictions can be used by capital to turn the rebellion, *ressentiment* and discontent of the concerned strata toward other goals and activities. This must be taken into consideration by the proletarian strategy and tactics. In theorising the problem, Bloch's suggestion is that we take seriously and articulate the futurity contained in *every* form of contradiction. In the case of the contemporary contradiction, as we have seen, there is a future already present but repressed by the capitalist relations. This future-present is the leap which is revolution. In the case of the non-contemporary contradictions, what is crucial is that the 'unutilized past' was not eliminated precisely because it was never realised in its own time.

> They are thus *ab ovo* contradictions of unfulfilled intentions, divisions with the past itself: not simply in the present, as the divisions of the contemporary contradictions, but equally running throughout the entirety of history; so that here hidden contradictions, namely the still unutilized contents of intention, themselves in this case join in the rebellion.[22]

The Now is thus full with a future-present *and* with a future-always-already present. Their unification in a revolutionary movement would be the justification of Marx's well-known assertion that the proletarian revolution will be the last revolution, the repossession in reality of what we have until now possessed only in a dream.

This analysis implies a politics. Bloch insists that it is only the contemporary contradiction, the proletarian struggle against the domination of capital, which can animate the non-contemporary contradictions.

> Even the possible full ripening of the specifically unutilized elements of this past can never on its own leap to a quality which we do not already know from the past. To such a leap, an alliance which frees the still *possible future* from the *past* by positing both in the present would be the best help.[23]

The proletarian struggle animates the non-contemporary contradictions positively and negatively; it awakens the *ressentiment*, and at the same time has the potential to join with it in a common struggle. In order to correctly understand the multiple antagonisms tearing at the social fibre, one must recognise that even the contemporary contradictions, at least in part, are driven and activated by the same content as the non-contemporary ones: what lacks in the Now from the point of view of non-contemporaneity is at least in part the same as what the proletariat is seeking in the present. What is positive, creating the future in the struggle of the proletariat, is nothing but what has never yet been realised in the past: full human being, non-alienated labour — in short, paradise on earth. 'In a word, in the last analysis, in the revolt of the proletarian and reified negativity there is also the material of a contradiction which rebels from wholly non-released "productive forces", intentional contents of an *always still non-contemporary sort.*'[24] The principal contradiction in the present remains of course that between the forces and relations of production, between proletariat and capital; and the struggle must be conducted under the hegemony of the proletariat. But at the same time, in that Now where the We-Subject breaks into a spherical, polyrhythmic history, the dialectic of the struggle must include all of the contradictions which comprehend and compose the totality. To have neglected this was the root of the Communist Party's inability to mount a coherent counter-movement to Hitler's brown-shirts.

The analysis of the contemporary and non-contemporary forms of contradiction is found in a collection of essays, *Heritage of This Time*, published in 1935. The reader is struck by the fact that it is not only from the past and in the ideological sphere that Bloch finds his heritage. Through the modern — Kracauer's analysis of the newly developing stratum of employees in offices, the philosophy of Bergson, modern physics or Brecht's theatre — Bloch also attempts to reap his harvest. In this, he separates again from Lukács, for whom the heritage would only be the attempt to take over the conquests of the radical bourgeoisie in order to put them, *immediately*, at the service of the proletariat.[25] Bloch's suggestion is that 'The foundation of the non-contemporary contradiction is the unfulfilled fairy tale of the good old times, the unresolved myth of the mysterious old being or of nature; one finds here and there not just a past which, from the standpoint of the class, still lives, but also a past which has not been materially realized.'[26] To inherit, for Bloch, is thus not to receive from the past; it is rather to *pay the debts* of the past in order to receive the present. As long as the past remains as a debt, the present will never be free.

This notion of heritage poses the problem of Marxism, and that of Marx himself. On this score, Bloch is chary — more so than he need be. His contribution to the *Expressionismusdebatte*, for example, is a scintillating refutation of the platitudes to which an unexamined, narrow and insensitive orthodoxy in Marxism can lead. Although he never makes it explicit, Bloch's own analysis of the expressionist phenomenon is only possible on the basis of *his* specific inheritence from Marx. That is, Bloch uses Marx, but as if Marx were Bloch, as if there were no legacy to be actively struggled for and to be further developed and realised, but simply the direct transmission of a given intuition of truth. Here, as so often, Bloch's orthodoxy gets the better of him. To be sure, he criticises the 'all too great progress from utopia to science' within the Marxist tradition and suggests that to Marxism's 'Critique of Pure Reason' a 'Critique of Practical Reason' must be added. But he never takes up the question of what we might call a 'negative' inheritance which the Marxists have received from Marx. At best, he explains it by explaining it away, through the kind of sociological homogenisation that he had criticised in Lukács. It is here that the attempt by Max Horkheimer to develop a 'critical theory' which would be based precisely on Marx's legacy without at the same time becoming a scriptural repitition applied immediately takes on its full importance. Beginning with an intra-theoretical reinterpretation of Marxism as a critical theory, Horkheimer (along with Adorno, in the *Dialectic of Enlightenment*) ends with a pessimistic-critical stance towards the basic principles of Marx's theory itself. Indeed, the return to Schopenhauer and to a conservative religiosity on the part of the later Horkheimer is grounded in just this reconstruc-

tion of Marxism as a critical theory. It is to this critical theory
and its problems that we have now to turn in order to bring out
more clearly the implications of the Blochian approach.

III   Bloch *v*. Frankfurt: Dialectics of Labour and Futurity

The idea of Marxism as a critical theory, neither contemplative
philosophy nor sheer empirical description, is of course the
guiding thread of Marx's own work — as the continual use of
the term 'critique' in his titles or subtitles indicates. At the same
time, however, not only Engels, and Marx's Second International successors, but Marx himself, were tempted by the lure
of science, so strong at the end of the nineteenth century.
Marx's praise for the Russian reviewer of *Capital* (in the second
edition of *Capital*) is but one example among many; his
collaboration on and acceptance of Engels' *Anti-Duehring* is
another. From here it is but a short step to the flatness and
flabbiness of a Kautsky, or to the pragmatic genius of Lenin's
means-ends rationality. The praxis-oriented dialectical interpretation of history gives way to a theory of science in which there
is no room for the complex-explosive structure of the everyday.
The dualism of subject/object is reintroduced; the making of
history falls on the side of the object, while theory becomes the
clear — and decisive — vision.

The early Frankfurt School revolted against this devolution
of Marxism. Although he was the close friend of two of the
School's most original collaborators — T. W. Adorno and W.
Benjamin — Bloch never shared the style nor the goals of the
School, as defined by its director, Max Horkheimer. Thus,
though we might relate Bloch to Adorno or Benjamin —
recalling themes from Adorno such as 'exact phantasy,' 'non-
intentional truth', or the use of 'historical images' such as the
'bourgeois interior' as a key to Kierkegaard; or recalling Benjamin's monumental and unfinished study of the Paris of the
nineteenth century, which was to be constructed entirely of
what its author called 'dialectical images' — this incursion into
the intellectual history of ideas would take us away from our
main task. To that end, consideration of Max Horkheimer will
prove more useful.

Horkheimer attempts to restore to Marxism its nature as a
critical theory whose analysis of the present is at once a part of
that multivalent present and an actor in the process of changing
it. Where 'traditional theory' is produced by the theorist
separated from the object and attempting to manipulate it for

goals which have strictly nothing to do with the object itself,
critical theory breaks that separation in finding in its object
itself a direction, a future, a sense which escapes the comprehension of the object itself. This is what Marx did in *Capital*, it
is claimed; and this is the task to be picked up again today. The
critical theorist must be able to account for the directions and
the structure of theory from the material side of the object. The
old goal of the autonomy of thought is replaced by the
recognition of its imbrication in the object. Of crucial importance in this venture are the mediations between the material
and the psychological, to which the Frankfurt School proposed
to devote its energies. The pages of its journal, the *Zeitschrift
für Sozialforschung*, abound with theoretical-cultural analyses
of such phenomena as the family, mass culture, bourgeois
culture, literature and the arts with their implications and
tensions, as well as with reconsiderations of the past of
'traditional theory'. While they are often fascinating as cultural
and intellectual history, revealing the tensions between a
thinker and his epoch, as well as strains within an individual
development, these analyses are disappointing in one fundamental aspect: it is never clear *who* is doing the analysis, how he/she
came to the point of posing *these* questions, and how he/she is
practically implicated in the object being analysed. Horkheimer
shows an awareness of this problem. Yet the best he can offer
are vague references to the 'imagination' of the critical theorist,
his/her 'phantasy', or even 'engagement'. Horkheimer insists
that the truth of the analyses can only be demonstrated after the
revolution which they call for and seek. But while this is
perhaps consistent with his programme, it is no more adequate
than the historicist position which argues that the growth of
capitalism which socialises the world of production permits the
theorist to at least comprehend the totality for, at last, that
totality is itself realised by the efforts, and behind the back, of
capital itself.

Bloch's approach to these same problems is most clearly
indicated in his lengthy interpretation of the 'Theses on Feurer-
bach' in *The Principle of Hope*. Central to Marx's achievement
is that the traditional contemplative view is replaced by concrete *labour* as the basis of our understanding of the world.
Historically, it is only with capitalism where, for reasons of
ideological legitimation, the ruling class is led to emphasise the
role of labour such that not simply an ethics of labour but also
a *logos* of labour becomes central to the self-understanding and
project of the human species. Of course, the entrepreneur and
the ideology of his class portray labour in a form which is

ideological, passive and contemplative. Nonetheless, a rupture is introduced, from which the tensions and progress of German Idealism emerge. It is in this sense as well that Marxian materialism is radically different, for example, from that of Democritus who, because of his contemplative approach, is closer to a Plato than to a Marx. For Marx — who, from this point of view, is nothing but the *Aufhebung* of German Idealism — labour is conceived as a real relation between subject and object such that, on the one hand, the idea of an immediate givenness has no longer any sense, since every givenness is mediated by and is the result of human labour; and, on the other hand, the priority of being over consciousness is understood only in the sense that working on an object does not in any way eliminate the object, but rather marks it, opens it, mediates it. This explains the ontological source of the always present non-contemporary contradictions.

This theory of labour is totally lacking in Horkheimer. True, a large part of Horkheimer's approach depends on his insistence that there exists an independent Nature which cannot be reduced to thought. But his theory of 'mimesis' does not pose the mediations, even the psychological ones, that would be needed for concretisation.[27] Lacking a theory of labour, Horkheimer's philosophical anthropology — like that of Feuerbach before him — is incapable of understanding and working out its relation to the philosophical heritage. With Feuerbach, it is through the critique of that heritage — a critique which permits the emergence of the 'true' by denouncing the 'false' — that a 'true humanism' is elaborated. With Horkheimer, one encounters at first a brilliant series of antinomical analyses of past and present tendencies in theory, and then finally a pessimism which gives way to a reactionary politics and a sceptical theory. Thus, in the *Dialectic of Enlightenment* (with Adorno) as well as in *The Eclipse of Reason*, Horkheimer develops his critical analysis precisely in terms of that Reason which, for traditional philosophy — for example, in Kant's philosophy of history — constituted the hope for the humanisation of the world, but which has gone astray and become a rationalisation used in the service of domination. The problem is not that Horkheimer neglects the socio-economic base of that degeneration, nor that his analyses are superficial or uninteresting; but rather, that his critical programme, his engagement, and the praxis of theory disappear without a trace, giving place first to an apocalypticism expressed in his 'Authoritarian State' essay of 1942, and then to the flat reactionary pessimism. The active heritage to whose need and nature Bloch pointed is neglected. At best, Horkheimer draws from his pessimism a lingering regret for the conquests of bourgeois individualism which, he suggests, was capable of saving itself from the reification of both Reason and social relations.

In order to inherit from the tradition, including that aspect of it which by and for socio-political reasons has been suppressed,[28] thought must be conceptualised according to the model of the mediation of the subject/object by labour within precisely that polyrhythmic formation which is history. Horkheimer's attempt to inherit from the 'critical theory' of Marx tries to take seriously the degeneration of Marxism at the hands of the epigone; that is its virtue. But because his conception of reason is alternatively based on the traditional Enlightenment view, or at best on the engagement of the imagination and phantasy of the critical theorist, Horkheimer's attempt at critique from within the Marxian movement falls flat and ultimately inverts itself. He has missed the fundamental point: correlative to the sociological levelling of Lukács, one could argue that with Horkheimer there is a levelling either in terms of a flattened-out Reason, or at best a flight from those implications to a phantasy which, ungrounded in concrete activity, tires after a while and seeks a secure niche from which criticism (but not action) can be undertaken. Because he never gets to the core of Marxism — the theory of labour — his account of the degeneration of the heritage is external and flawed.

A comparison of Bloch's sketches from the history of philosophy with those of Horkheimer shows that Bloch's theory is articulated by different concerns. Of course, both treat the role of the social-historical conditions in the formation of a thought; and both characterise that thought in terms of its internal contradictions and tensions. Simply: with Bloch, this is structured in terms of a futurity which one is led to see as active in the non-contemporary thought. This is not a futurity for which the theorist wishes or phantasises. The point is to demonstrate its internality to the chain of thought in question. There has been too much change in the world, from the conquest of Rome to Genghis Kahn to the modern barbarians. 'But *salutary* change, not to speak of achieving the *Kingdom of Freedom*, comes about only through salutary knowledge, comes with ever more precisely controlled necessity.'[29] This knowledge is no more a technical knowledge than it is that of contemplative philosophy. In interpreting the 11th 'Thesis on Feuerbach', Bloch insists on the task which it poses to philosophy: 'The final perspective of changing the world which Marx sought to formulate is illuminated here. Its idea — the knowledge-conscience of every praxis in which is reflected the Totum which is still afar — doubtless demands just as much innovation in philosophy as it creates the resurrection of nature.'[30] The innovation in philosophy and the resurrection of nature: both are structured in terms of the arguments that have been developed here, through the polyrhythmic Now, manifesting the remnants of a not-yet resolved task, and mediated by the concrete labour of the plurality of social beings. Present, these elements are only active if we are capable of taking them into our possession.

Horkheimer's phantasy remains external to its object, un-mediated by it, and at best grounded by that search for individual autonomy which was the goal of the classical German idealists. Bloch, on the other hand, insists on taking a position. In his major work, *The Principle of Hope*, Bloch does not spare the reader, citing various polemics of Marx against the 'true socialists' whose self-satisfaction given by a vague sentiment of love for humanity is pilloried as impractical, useless and even harmful. For Bloch, the modern equivalents of the 'true socialists' cannot even refer to this sentimentalism: their 'love' is seen as only a mask for an anti-communism which dares not reveal its true face. Bloch insists: 'Without choosing a party in love, without a very concrete pole of hatred, there can be no true love; without the *party standpoint* in the revolutionary class struggle, there is only an idealism turned backwards instead of praxis aiming forward.'[31] Such a standpoint is precisely the one taken by Bloch at the time of the Moscow Trials. Such positions trouble the reader who has accepted the engagement with Bloch's thought as well as his/her own political engagement. One could suggest with Oskar Negt[32] that compared with the purity of the Frankfurt School, Bloch's engagement points to the other concretely possible position. Condemning the com-munists as well as the fascists, the Frankfurters found them-selves isolated, adopting an apolitical politics after the war coupled with an often uncritical acceptance of the methods of American social science. This, however, is still no justification of Bloch. It simply points out that it is not sufficient to look at his politics as if his actions were to be understood in isolation from their time; and it suggests that it is not enough to say that a theory which leads to *that* is not worth examining in greater depth.

IV   The Problem of our Heritage

The paradox we have encountered is that the concrete philosopher who is so aware of the nuances which structure the Now finds himself opting for a political practice which is not simply disappointing or naive, but one which disturbs us precisely because it fails to recognise what seem to us — perhaps with hindsight — patent realities. Bloch's goal is a unification of reason and hope, the human and the natural, the dream and reality. The project is made the more complicated by the fact that each pole is itself double and incomplete. Reason, humanity and the dream: each is determined by what it has been, but each has been that only by virtue of a 'not yet' (*Noch-Nicht*) which drags it, pulls it, works on it. And, by the mediation of concrete phantasy whose model is labour, hope, nature and reality are also doubly dynamic and incomplete. To seek this unification is not to return to the quest for that philosophy of identity which was the summit of German Idealism. The point is that it is only through this unification that each element can become fully what it potentially is already. Bloch's interpretation of the 11th Feuerbach Thesis spoke of the 'resurrection of nature'. The point is not that nature will become identical with humanity, nor that humanity will explain itself and its destiny when it understands nature. There is an 'intentionality' which is specific to the object itself (which was recognised, before Benjamin and Adorno, by those philosophers who are treated by Bloch as the 'Left Aristotleans'). The violation of this objective intentionality is precisely the foundation of all alienation.

From this point of view, Bloch's theory is related to a long mystical tradition whose influence on Hegel and German Idealism was considerable. This point is argued in Jürgen Habermas' essay, 'A Marxist Schelling', in which Bloch's 'Philosophy of Nature' serves as the fulcrum for the exposition and critique. Nature for Bloch is not something which has always been; its essence is not something in the past (*ein Gewesenes*) to which one could return, but is rather out there, on the horizon, not-yet. The utopian dimension is anchored in nature itself which, mediated by thought and/or labour, gives a presentiment of the new, of what has not yet been. To bring out the specificity of Bloch's approach, Habermas compares utopian thought with speculative thought, insisting that Bloch opens a third alternative. Utopian thought considers its analyses as refutable, but does not expect that reality will offer a definitive proof of them insofar as praxis always goes further than the anticipating theory. Speculation, on the other hand, wants to continue its philosophical quest, looking to reality only for the proof, never for the refutation. Bloch's position is the unification of the two attitudes: 'The guarantee of salvation falls away, but the anticipation of salvation preserves certainty for itself, saying: it will work thusly or not at all, all or nothing will be achieved, the finally fulfilled hope according to the anticipated images of fulfilment — or chaos'.[33] This is the teleology of the Not-Yet. It depends ultimately for its validity on an ontology; but one which is consistent with Marx's project (though not necessarily that of the Marxists).

This approach to nature and its potentialities, which is central to the Blochian position, leads to a hard critique of technology as we know it. Whereas Marx had the tendency to view technology as a neutral factor, Bloch sees clearly — as does the Frankfurt School, though from a different theoretical base, as we have seen — that our civilisation is based on a domination of nature which cannot help but turn back against us, deflecting our aims, needs and hopes. The 'resurrection of nature' for which Bloch calls and which would be achieved by socialism, would permit a 'co-productivity' of man and nature. Similarly in the sphere of art: where Adorno, for example, sees the truth of art revealing itself in the contradiction which it bears, arguing that this intrinsic contradiction illuminates the real itself, Bloch insists on the utopian dimension which must be actively inherited. The point is neither despair, nor the return to a paradise which we once possessed but somehow lost. Bloch's concern is with the completion of what throughout human and natural history has been seeking its expression and realisation without having the power or mediations that would permit such a completion. This is the New, even the new in nature; always active as a force, it has never existed as such. Permitting it to name itself, to recognise itself for what it is, the philosopher becomes truly that Socratic midwife of which the tradition spoke but could not conceive because its attention was turned backwards, to what was and not towards what has not yet been. The philosophical concern with essences, *das Gewesene*, 'what has beome', must be transformed.

Despite the often brilliant results to which this standpoint leads particular analyses, when it is given a political translation it appears to pose problems. The analysis of Habermas is penetrating here. His suggestion is that: 'A utopia which understands the dialectic of its own realisation in a utopian manner is in fact not so concrete as it pretends to be.'[34] He adds elsewhere that it is striking that Bloch concentrates on deciphering theories of law rather than actual legal structures, theories of the state rather than the state itself.[35] The problem is that a theory which is concentrated on the Not-Yet, the utopian in the present, remains a prisoner of that reality which it seeks to surpass. We have of course known of this problem since Hegel. But in his effort to protect Marxism against a vulgar utilitarianism or pragmatism, Bloch goes too far, says Habermas. in insisting on the need for philosophy, he neglects the other side of the critical intention that guided Marx. His theory lends itself to concrete research only with great difficulty. Based on that fundamental idea that the transition to socialism is not the result of a linear progress but rather of a qualitative leap, and stressing the importance of the historical and spherical Now at the same time that he seeks to philosophically ground our understanding of it, Bloch finally loses the historical-empirical side of Marxism. In seeking to inherit actively here and now the New, Bloch's theory has the paradoxal result of losing the everyday in which it is to be based. Thus, concludes Habermas, however concrete it may seem, Bloch's theory remains abstract and speculative in the last analysis.

Habermas' critique neglects a fundamental point which underlies the entire Blochian edifice. Bloch offers a double account of the origins of that critical phantasy which inhabits not only the few who are its theorists, but which is in fact possible and often actual in the many. The analysis of the temporality of contradiction which is the manifest source of that phantasy is itself grounded in the temporality of the Now; and this latter is ontologically structured by the concept of the Not-Yet. Bloch's stress on the 'obscure mystery of the lived instant', on the sphericality of the Now, and on the 'unconstructible question' is not just poetry or speculative mysticism. It is a claim about what theory can do; its tasks and its insertion. Bloch is not the philosopher of identity so abhorred by Horkheimer and the Frankfurters; but he is also not the apostle of progressive linear history. His is the paradoxical task of an *open system*, an *Experimentum Mundi*, as the title of his latest systematic presentation (1975) calls it. This is a paradoxical task; but the only one open to us. The world is not clear, translucent, opening its meanings to the casual glance. It is thick, multivalent and clear-obscure; it itself poses the task of the inheritance. What can be resurrected is not what was but rather only that which was Not-Yet. Critique is not negation but anticipation.

What we inherit from Bloch is no more than what he too sought to inherit. He gives us, in a sense, nothing. At best, we can learn from his errors. But as we work with him, as we learn to see the tradition through his eyes, and as we watch him function in his own present, we acquire perhaps something more important: the desire to inherit, to pay the debt of the past and redeem it. What we learn from Bloch, as we seek after his legacy, is that it is no accident that we are driven from politics to philosophy and then back again. The oscillation will go on; neither pole can be abandoned, for in a sense neither is possible without the other. Bloch's utopia is not abstract, nor is it the project of the political thinker separated from or guiding the proletariat. In a sense that is only apparently paradoxical, Bloch's politics is an accidental result of his political thought. The paradox is only apparent for, in the last analysis, Bloch's philosophy is his politics; the philosophy of the Not-Yet, of the polyrhythmic and spherical Now, itself designates a politics, demands the practice of inheritance, and offers the guidelines for practical analysis. In this conception of the unity of philosophy and politics we, Bloch's heirs, can recognise the very motives which drive us, to praxis and to theory. As in the many unforgettable vignettes in his own work, Bloch too is brought into our present.

Part Three
Using Marxism

5 Towards a Critical Theory: Max Horkheimer

In trying to render more explicit the concrete philosophy of Ernst Bloch, and the creative manner in which he appropriates Marx, I set his position on the relation of concrete phantasy, labour and the futurity of the present which is to be actively inherited in contrast with the Critical Theory of Max Horkheimer. Since my concern was with Bloch, I didn't treat the nuances in Horkheimer's text. That choice was necessary for purposes of exposition. Yet Horkheimer's position is more subtle and rich than my counterposition could portray, particularly in the earlier elaborations of the notion of Critical Theory which, through the self-declared 'dictatorship of the director', was to determine the research programme of the Institute for Social Research.[1] Though my counterposition retains its validity, I want to take up here Horkheimer's own programme in order to illustrate its approach to our still present task of inheriting from the Marxian program; and at the same time, to point to the nature of what can be inherited as it manifests itself in the dizzying zenith of Horkheimer's revolutionary zeal, the 1942 essay on the 'Authoritarian State', after which the path to pessimism and away from revolutionary goals became increasingly and painfully evident.[2]

There was a strong temptation to entitle this chapter with a question: 'Marxism as Critical Theory and/or Critical Theory as Marxism?' In Horkheimer's early writing it often becomes apparent that 'Critical Theory' is used simply as a code word for Marxism. This may have been occasioned by the desire to legitimate his discourse within the academic establishment. More importantly, it gave him a double freedom of which he continually made use: the freedom to redefine and go beyond the narrow and, in his own term, 'economistic', reading of Marxism which made Marxism rest on an economic analysis while this economic analysis was itself interpreted in a manner which limited its implications for social theory; and the political freedom to stand against the Party as well as the explicit conjunctural behaviour of the proletariat at any given moment. The choice of Critical Theory as a trademark carried the further advantage that by replacing an already established and consecrated doctrine and its accompanying practice with a still-to-be-elaborated theory, the intellectual was given a role and function permitting independent analysis and decision, and demanding that new domains and methods of research be opened. Without Marx's contribution, Critical Theory would not have been possible; but the implicit goal seems to have been that the child be the father of the man. This renders Critical Theory still contemporary.

This chapter might also have been entitled 'Away from Critical Theory'. Or, at the least, the problem could have been to trace the movement by which Horkheimer was led not simply to reject Marxism but also to the adoption of positions which — importantly — are formally consistent with his Critical Theory, but turn out in practice to have been simply reactionary. The 1970 Speech, 'Critical Theory Yesterday and Today', illustrates the paradoxical stance which Horkheimer found himself adopting. After criticising Marx on grounds of economic-theoretical prediction, Horkheimer suggests that Marxists don't understand the connection between equality and justice, and that while the former may be achieved, its acquisition comes at the cost of justice and freedom. As a result, the 'new' Critical Theory takes as its task not the making of revolution but opposition to the 'new terrorism' that has emerged; and for its positive programme it wants to support those elements of Western liberalism which protect the autonomy of the individual and human culture. The 'new' Critical Theory also stresses two lessons from theology: the doctrine of original sin, which stresses the impossibility of full happiness, as well as the fact that our present culture is the result of a miserable and cruel past, the guilt for which we all bear; and the Old Testament prohibition on the portrayal of God, which translates into the injunction that we can't know the True and the Good — only Stalins and Hitlers make that claim. There is of course evil to be combated, admits Horkheimer; but 'Hunger is not in the least the worst of these; worse is the fear of force. And it is certainly one of the tasks of Critical Theory to speak this out.'[3] More concretely, Horkheimer attacks the German students' demonstration against the visit of the Shah of Iran to Berlin, arguing that Germans can do nothing about Iranian conditions, and should have directed their attention against what goes on in German prisons, for example. Yet it was precisely this demonstration, and the police violence against it, which led to the changed consciousness that manifested itself in the birth of a New Left which, significantly, took many of its theoretical insights and critical tools from the 'old' Critical Theory.

Horkheimer's political stances in the 1960s ring reactionary, and yet they cannot be written off, or taken as the direct expression of Critical Theory. The student activists he criticised developed their politics precisely by unveiling and protesting against that hidden force and subtle violence which glues together bureaucratic society. They wanted to find new ways of struggling against the effects of the 'Affirmative Culture' (Marcuse) that Critical Theory had begun to unmask; in their actions they sought to go beyond the atomisation and passivity imposed by bureaucratic society seeking to preserve its domination. They adopted the totality perspective and historical point of view that Critical Theory had stressed; theirs was a critique in action of domination, of the repression of the sensual, and of the authoritarian family and socialisation process which Critical Theory had deciphered in the 1930s. At the same time, however, there is no denying that the movement took directions which turned against its members' own intentions; and these make one look again at the theoretical basis of Horkheimer's criticisms. One tendency which emerged as the Movement changed direction was precisely the 'portrayal of God' and the demand for immediate and full happiness. The result was that the Movement turned either to pessimism or to a dogmatic Marxism of one or another variety. This is not to say that Horkheimer was right, and that his suggestions ought to have been followed but only that the Critical Theory might have served the Movement in its self-understanding as well as in its analysis of contemporary society, and that by restricting it to the latter, the Movement misunderstood the basic thrust of the theory. This was made difficult by Horkheimer's own political statements — which, we shall see, are not inconsistent with the theory he elaborated — but insofar as his analysis often seemed congenial to the Movement as it advanced, one has to push back today to try to find the *source* of the distortion, which does not lie simply in the cynicism of a bitter old man whose infamous condemnation of the pill as destroying human love has been justly ridiculed, though not always understood. In form, Horkheimer's most reactionary statements seem consistent with Critical Theory — as in the case of the pill, where in effect the increased sexual freedom that is granted comes at the

price of increased exploitation of the Other as mere body and
not his/her being treated as a full person. The superficial
similarity in the structure of the argument only hides a deeper
ambiguity in Horkheimer's programme for Critical Theory.

I   The Agenda

Although Horkheimer did not shy away from stating the
revolutionary goals of Critical Theory, the immediate tasks he
assigned to it were defined by the double crisis of Marxian and
bourgeois theory. Verbally, he appeared more concerned with
the crisis of bourgeois science, while in practice the work
undertaken and the perspectives from which it emerged were
Marxist. The analysis of bourgeois science itself was conducted
in Marxian terms. Science was seen as defined and limited by its
role in the capitalist division of labour, which restricts it to
empirical fact gathering and prevents it from putting itself in
the service of human needs. This is not the fault of individuals,
but emerged when empirical science's once progressive function
changed. Concentration on the empirical served the rising
bourgeoisie quite well; but its tendency is to be both a-historical
and unaware of the totality perspective, such that the empirical
researcher cannot distinguish what is essential from what is
merely accidental.

> To the method which is oriented towards being and not
> towards becoming corresponds the view of the given social
> form as a mechanism of self-repeating processes which, of
> course, can be disturbed for a shorter or longer period but
> which in no way demands any other scientific attitude than,
> for example, the explanation of a complicated machine.[4]

The result of this attitude and social insertion is that although
the scientists and even philosophers are aware of the crisis, they
are unable to discover its causes. They are blinded because, as
part of society, science is involved in a double contradiction: in
theory, each step of research has epistemological grounds, but
yet the first posing of the problem cannot account for itself;
moreover, even if it recognises its social insertion and dependence, this science is unable to develop a theory of that society
in its contradictions and its becoming. Thus, concludes Horkheimer, the crisis of science and the crisis of society are part of
one problem. If science is to advance beyond the limits which
express themselves in its form and content, its methods and

materials, and right down into the individual details of its work, a theory of present-day society is necessary.

Horkheimer is even more explicit about his revolutionary goals in the provocative essay 'On the Problem of Prediction in the Social Sciences' (1933). Science needs to be able to predict; the element of futurity is essential to it. But for the social sciences, prediction clearly depends on the social conditions concerning which the prediction is offered, and not on the cleverness or subtlety of the theorist. Duprat had suggested the distinction between *prévision* and *prédiction*, where the prevision is expressed as an abstract law or tendency as opposed to the prediction of facts or events. But a law is expressed in the form 'if x then y'; and this means, says Horkheimer, that if we can show, for example, that market economies necessarily develop both monopolistic and crisis-filled results, and if we can establish that we live in a market society, then we can predict the impossibility of ameliorating these conditions. This, however, is still not enough; historical prediction is a risky business precisely because, despite Vico, men still do not make their own history, or at least do not make it as they would chose. Yet such uncertain conditions need not last; planning is indeed possible, and the more planning is introduced the more accurate will be prediction. Thus, concludes Horkheimer, prediction will become fully possible only in a free society: 'For the true human freedom is neither that of being unconditioned nor that of mere caprice, but it is identical with the mastery of nature within and without us through rational decisions.'[5] Therefore, the task of science and that of politics come together: 'the effort of the sociologists to come to accurate prediction is translated into the political effort towards the realization of a rational society.'[6] The next step is to formulate this coincidence into a research and political programme.

In the Inaugural Lecture, on 'The Present Situation of Social Philosophy and the Tasks of an Institute for Social Research', delivered on assuming the directorship of the Institute, Horkheimer sets out the perspectives in which he intends to direct his research group. The project of a social philosophy emerges in the development of German Idealism from Kant to Hegel. The Kantian project grounded the forms of social existence — state, law, religion, economy — in the individual as constitutive agent. Even though Kant did not confuse the constitutive individual with the empirical one, he was unable to move beyond the analysis in terms of the abstract opposition of autonomy/heteronomy. Fichte developed the analysis of the split between the individual and the social, but the resolution of the problem had to await Hegel's attention to the 'labour of history' for an answer.

> With Hegel idealism thus becomes social philosophy in its essential parts: the philosophical understanding of the collective whole in which we live and which gives the basis for the creations of absolute culture is at the same time now the knowledge of the sense of our own being in its true value and content.[7]

Horkheimer stresses that while Hegel's idealism argues in terms of a logic of Spirit, it also takes account of the role of individual interests, drives and passions. This is most clear in the *Philosophy of Right* with its detailed economic analyses, and in the Introduction to the *Philosophy of History* with its image of history as the 'slaughterbench'. Yet Spirit triumphs, transfiguring the individual and its particularity while achieving reconciliation. The death of this Hegelian reconciliation was, however, not long in coming; the progress of science, technology and industry implied that the *need for philosophical mediation* such as Hegel had offered *was no longer felt*;[8] the effects of social action appeared directly, achieving the desired results immediately. But again, history moved onward, and the immediate success began to appear as naked exploitation; Hegel's archenemy Schopenhauer celebrated the triumph of his pessimism as the senselessness of society became too evident. With this, however, the need for social philosophy was born anew, for the contradiction between the individual and the social whole was not to be bridged. Passing through the efforts of Cohen, Scheler, Hartman, Reinach and Heidegger, Horkheimer's conclusion is:

> If speaking in slogans is permitted, one could assert that today social philosophy encounters the longing for a new sense (*Sinngebung*) of a life which is restricted in its individual search for happiness. Social philosophy appears as a part of the philosophical and religious efforts to reinsert the hopeless individual existence into the womb or, to speak with Sombart, into the 'golden ground' of meaningful totalities.[9]

This 'new sense' cannot be given, nor can the conditions which engender the longing be analysed, by those irrationalist approaches which leave the empirical entirely for unities like the Soul or the *Volk*. Nor can the Kantian individualism be renewed. Theory has thus come full circle; but in its travails, it has acquired criteria of validity and methods of research; and it knows that even at its most empirical, the Hegelian project is not adequate to the task posed today.

Horkheimer stresses the need for empirical research, but insists that the lesson of the critique of positivism is not that science free itself from philosophy, but rather that it consciously integrate an adequate conception of philosophy into its research. He proposes for the Institute that,

> on the basis of actually present philosophical questions, investigations are to be organized in which philosophers, sociologists, economists, historians and psychologists come together in a lasting work community and do together what in other regions is done by a single person in a laboratory, what all true researchers have always done: namely, following through their philosophical questions which aim at the greatest with the most precise scientific methods; reformulating and making more precise the questions in the course of the work; inventing new methods; and yet not losing sight of the universal. No yes-or-no answers to the philosophical questions emerge in this manner, but rather these questions themselves are dialectically brought into the empirical scientific process; that is, their answer lies in the progress of factual knowledge which affects their form itself.[10]

Philosophy cannot be separated from concrete research, as if philosophy took care of the big problems, giving sense to the empirical materials and integrating them into a totality. That would leave research with the chaos of specialisation where the projects chosen and the methods applied are arbitrary (or socially pre-formed); and the materials delivered by such fragmented research would be unsatisfactory because, after all, the research itself forms the facts and implicitly gives them a sense, whether it is aware of this or not. At the same time, were the separation instituted, philosophy itself would lose its relevance, remaining separate and caught up in its 'universal' problems, unable to deal with the specificity of the particular.

Horkheimer gives an example of the type of problem with which he wants the Institute to deal, and the methods he proposes to apply:

> the question of the interrelations between the economic life of society, the psychological development of the individual and the changes in the cultural sphere in the narrower sense, to which not only the so-called spiritual contents of science,

art and religion belong, but also law, customs, modes, public opinion, sport, forms of leisure and life style, etc. The intention of investigating the relations among these three processes is nothing but a formulation in a manner adequate to the methods at our disposal and the status of our knowledge of the old question of the interrelation of particular existence and universal reason, of reality and idea, life and spirit, now posed in terms of the new constellation of the problem.[11]

The research is to be centred at first around a study of the qualified workers and employees in Germany; it is then to be expanded to other countries as well. Horkheimer lists seven methodological tools that are to be applied. Published statistics, reports of organisations and political groups are to be evaluated. This is to be done in the context of a continual examination of the total economic situation. A psychological and sociological study of the press and belletristic literature is to be undertaken, evaluating not only the literature but its effects on the members of the group. Questionnaire techniques are to be used, not as an end in themselves, but to keep close contact with the life situations of those studied, and also to check assertions and ideas developed through the use of other tools. Critical reports (*Sachverständigengutachten*), especially from persons with practical knowledge of the group or situation, are to be used. Non-book documents are to be gathered and evaluated, especially through the Institute's branch office in Geneva where the Archives of the International Labour Bureau are located. All of this is to be the subject of continual evaluation, comparison with new and old publications on the subject, and further revision.

In the Inaugural Lecture, Horkheimer does not deal explicitly with Marxism; in fact, in rendering homage to his predecessor, Gruenberg, he suggests that whereas in the latter's Inaugural statement stress had been laid on the fact that no research is unaccompanied by a *Weltanschauung* (in Gruenberg's case, by Marxism), the new direction is to be 'the unchangeable will to serve truth without any hesitation'.[12] Yet, the definition of this first research project was clearly proposed by perceived lacks in the Marxian theory. In the Forward to the first volume of the Institute's journal, the *Zeitschrift für Sozialforschung*, Horkheimer makes this motivation even more clear. He proposes that a crucial problem for social research and theory is the development of a social psychology which would be adequate to the needs of history. This task, which Erich Fromm was to assume in the Institute's first years, and which found an empirical and theoretical expression in the *Studies on Authority and the Family* (1936), was one which circumstances forced upon Marxism. To this theoretical task was added the practical concern that it be adequate to the needs of the present historical moment. This concern with the present-as-history means, continues Horkheimer, that the studies presented in the journal will often have a 'hypothetical character'. Further, 'Much will show itself to have been false, but the expectation of future correction cannot hinder the research from applying the means of the different sciences to the problem of present society and its contradictions in order to conceptualise in a manner adequate to present knowledge those processes which are important for the functioning and changing of social life.'[13] Horkheimer speaks out explicitly for social change. Yet, the Foreword continues that 'The obligations to scientific criteria divide social research methodologically from politics.'[14] He admits that science is historically conditioned, that knowledge is not free from the attitudes of the knower, and that it is not an end in itself and without consequence. Nonetheless, Horkheimer insists on the theoretical criteria. This insistence suggests that he intends to elaborate a specific kind of theory, which will have a precise social function. It was only in 1937, in the article 'Traditional and Critical Theory', and in its Afterword — as well as in Herbert Marcuse's 'Philosophy and Critical Theory' which appeared with Horkheimer's After-word — that this was spelt out.

II A New Type of Theory

In the Foreword to the *Zeitschrift*, Horkheimer suggested a further reason demanding the unification of empirical research into a social philosophy: 'the presupposition that under the chaotic surface of events a structure of active forces can be recognized which is accessible to concepts.'[15] This presupposition, to whose rationale Horkheimer frequently returns, guarantees against the disciplinary fragmentation occasioned by the capitalist division of labour which affects the sciences as well. The suggestion is that there is a totality with which social theory is concerned; and that this totality is an active one, structuring the 'chaotic' appearances though not bringing them yet to their full rationality. Active as a structure, these forces must be brought to their explicitness by the theorist, who therefore cannot be simply a receptive observer cataloguing and ordering the 'facts', but must make an active contribution. Traditional philosophical approaches have always recognised this difference between appearance and essence. Hence, to make only this assertion is to criticise the specialisation of one type of research, but it is not yet enough to elaborate a new theory type.

This first observation implies that the traditional separation between the subject and the object of investigation cannot be maintained. The hypothetical formulation which seeks confirmation by testing and subsumption of the particular under the universal is thrown into question by the assertion that the 'facts' are part of an active totality, but one which has not completely penetrated them. The 'clear and distinct ideas', to which the model of mathematical deduction is applied, are a fiction. The contribution of the theorist, who looks beyond the immediate givenness, changes the notion of necessity and theory of causality with which the traditional sciences worked. The incompleteness of the effects of the 'structure of active forces' means that the objects with which theory deals are not only incomplete, but also that they are changing and hence historical.[16] With the surpassing of the traditional dualisms of subject/object, knowledge/known, universal/particular are eliminated the hypostatisation of theory and 'fact', and the accompanying dream of a complete and self-contained theory. With the opening of theory comes the demand that the contribution of the theorist be examined.

Horkheimer's analysis depends heavily on Lukács' reconstruction of the history of German Idealism from Kant to Hegel/Marx. In the era of the rising bourgeoisie, the task of the theorist could be well accomplished by empirical and positive theorising. Social reality was in advance of its own theory, which functioned as a regressive ideology; the theorist had merely to call things by their name and to argue for an adequation of institutions to reality. But as the reality began to show its negative social consequences, theory's function shifted, and the totality approach became imperative, the contemplative dualism had to be overcome. Kant's recognition of the new situation was vitiated by his conception of the individual constitutive subject; he could affect the required synthesis only by having recourse to the transcendental schematism, an 'art hidden in the depths of the human soul', or (in the third *Critique*) with the notion of genius. Fichte's development of the Kantian notion of practical reason, and Schelling's *Naturphilosophie* found their culmination in Hegel. Reading back the Hegelian resolution and its Marxian translation onto the

Kantian formulation, one can make the double assertion that the subject comes actively to the world equipped with a set of categories which, themselves, are formed and developed by and in the engagement with that same world. However, this *double preformation* of the subject by the object and the object by the subject would tend toward a harmonistic view unless it is possible to show how the theory can transcend the present from which it emerges.

Horkheimer rejects the Marx-Lukács analysis of the proletariat as the source of a truth or standpoint which transcends its immediate situation, while retaining their insight that this transcendence toward the standpoint of a realised totality is a necessary ingredient of a critical theory. In its place, he adopts from Marx the priority of the economic, though in an enlarged sense, as being precisely that 'structure of active forces' underlying the chaos of appearances to which he referred in the Foreword. Marx had already expressed Horkheimer's fundamental insight aphoristically: 'Reason has always existed, but not always in a rational form'. For Horkheimer, production always contains a planned component, a social reason, however limited and narrow. Once the role of social reproduction in the formation of the 'facts' of the world, as well as in the structuring of the subject, is granted the first step towards grounding a critical theory has been made. Production is not completely rational, nor does it function to satisfy human needs; but from an analysis of the tensions, contradictions and historical development that it undergoes, a notion of reason adequate to the demands of the totality and open towards the future can be developed. By extension, insofar as the traditional theory is shaped and determined by the demands of the productive division of labour, the critical theory can and does make use of its results by means of interpretative analyses. A political consequence which emerges already here is that where the traditional theory aims at making the machine run more smoothly, the critical theory which recognises that the machine is only incompletely rational does not attempt to make it function better, aiming instead at its replacement. But, it must be added, the double social preformation implies that politics is not the act either of the individual or of the theory on a world which stands outside of it and on which it can act because its theory indicates points of leverage; such a position only recreates the dualism, and is typical of the bourgeois entrepreneur studying the laws of the economy to use them for his/her own benefit. The political consequences of this for the Leninist theory of the Party are of course devastating.

The primacy of the economic is interpreted by Horkheimer with Marx and against the Marxists, although this frame of reference is never really made explicit in the programmatic statements. For Critical Theory, human beings as 'the producers of their entire historical form of life are the object'.[17] This gives to the economic priority an extension whose importance Horkheimer repeatedly stresses. At the same time, he never puts into question the essential laws that Marx's economic theory (in the narrow sense) had established. Returning to the research project outlined in the Inaugural Lecture, the essay 'Traditional and Critical Theory' poses the question of the significance of the shift to large-scale capitalism as it manifests itself in the juridical, political and ideological spheres. Juridical owners no longer direct their factories, even though the laws of property remain the same; and the managers extend their control even to the political sphere. The entrepreneurial capitalists lose their dominant and active cultural role as well as their moral authority. Ideologies of 'great men' arise, along with the distinction between parasitical and productive capitalists. This, however, implies a questioning of the laws of property, since the productive persons ought to be rewarded. The result, says Horkheimer, lays the bases for fascism, whose economic roots are undeniable but not understandable unless the economic is taken in an expanded sense. Critical Theory — by which Horkheimer clearly means Marxism here — does not fall for the illusions; it knows that society is still based on property and profit, and it never took the juridical and cultural forms as anything but appearance in the first place. The sources of profit and the methods of its extraction remain the same. But, continues Horkheimer, with the elimination of any real content to which the law corresponds, and with the economic concentration completed by the authoritarian state, the old ideology disappears. Ideology and culture are now the direct reflection of the productive base. In liberal capitalism there were positive mediations present. Good character, critical individual judgement and a general cultivation were economic necessities; but they also became part of individual behaviour, preserving independence. This relative independence has disappeared; mass belief patterns are directly inculcated, people are atomised and are thus more dependent on the economic than ever before because the previous *mediating agencies* are absent. Thus, while the economic analysis retains its validity, the task of Critical Theory changes, for *it is now the only mediator on the scene.*

Critical Theory rests on the primacy of the economic, but 'it would be mechanical, not dialectical thought to judge also the forms of the future only in economic terms.'[18] From the standpoint of the totality, the economic is more than what presents itself in strictly economic terms. It is not simply a question of putting the economy in the service of the people, for such a position forgets the preformation of human beings by the process of social reproduction and treats them instead as if they were independent, isolated atoms. The enlarged conception of the economic developed by Critical Theory led directly to the concern with the process of socialisation whose analysis was begun in the *Studies on Authority and the Family*. It led also to the analysis of culture in the broadest sense, as well as to a reconsideration of the traditional problems of philosophy, where it sought not new resolutions but rather the elucidation of the constitutive tensions in a position. This stance carried political implications as well. The Russian model came in for repeated (though usually implicit) criticisms; as did the 'economistic' practice of the Marxist parties. This posed in turn the problem of Critical Theory's own political insertion which, in its most general sense, was to be that of restoring the mediations which the changed economic scene had eliminated.

The broadened analysis of the economic specifies Critical Theory's nature even further once the source of its critical insights is interrogated. The suggestion is that Critical Theory attaches itself to the reason which is present in but unrealised by the historical process of social reproduction. If it is asked to prove its analyses, Critical Theory cannot appeal to traditional methods. Where theory in feudal times was based on categorical judgements ('this is the case, it cannot be changed'), and where bourgeois theory is expressed in hypothetical or disjunctive judgements ('if x then y'; 'either this or that'), Critical Theory makes its assertions as 'existential judgements'.[19] The kind of proof which could be offered in this case can only appear when the future is made present through a praxis based on the existential judgement. This is because Critical Theory cannot work in terms of the schema of a subject analysing an object; from the standpoint of the enlarged conception of the economic and the double preformation it implies, one must recognise that the existential judgements of the subject do indeed affect the object: Critical Theory is co-constitutive of the change which its existential judgements seek. More important still, the theory's 'interest in freedom' is constitutive of its object as well; it co-determines the 'facts' of experience which the theory integrates. The existential judgement, interest in freedom, or interest in the future turn out in the end to have been that which permitted the Critical Theorist to recognise the still incomplete humanity and rationality which are said to be inherent in the process of social reproduction.

Although Critical Theory now appears to be caught in a tautology, further reflection permits another step forward towards its delimitation. The assertion that the existential interest in freedom and the future determines the research project and style of results of Critical Theory was justified by an appeal to the enlarged conception of the economic; but this latter could only be pointed to because of the existential interest. The problem appears even more vexing when Horkheimer finds himself appealing to the 'concrete phantasy' of the theorist in this context. The Critical Theory is 'constructive' once it has established its first premises, from which develops further materials to be integrated into its structure.[20] The edifice that Critical Theory erects in this manner now shows two further peculiarities distinguishing it from traditional theorising. The double preformation of subject and object implies that the theorist is involved in and affected by the theorising; or more accurately if more paradoxically: that the object of Critical Theory is the critical theorist. In Horkheimer's words, the difference between traditional and critical theory is 'not so much a difference of objects as a difference of subjects'.[21] The existential interest is therefore not the establishment of a final position from which all else is judged; it is but the necessary starting-point, which is itself modified by the very act of choice. The Critical Theory is thus essentially *historical.* The tautology is only apparent; there is a circle only if the two terms are taken as pregiven and permanent, if the futurity and interest are denied on the basis of an ontology of substance.

What emerges here is that Critical Theory is not a set of statements or hypotheses, but rather an *attitude* or a form of *praxis.* If it is separated from the world from which it emerges, or if the choice is made into doctrine, Critical Theory returns to the problems that vitiated the traditional approach. From this point of view, Horkheimer's adherence to the Marxian economic analysis as giving the true underpinnings of the capitalist economy is surprising. Its implications will be discussed below. For now, Horkheimer's political consistency with the stance of his theory needs be stressed. He refuses the argument that one should put oneself in the service of the proletariat, pointing out that if that class were in immediate possession of the truth, theory would be useless, or at best just like the traditional theory, simply registering facts. The task of the intellectual is rigorous criticism:

> The intellectual who only announces with open-mouthed awe
> the creativity of the proletariat, and finds his satisfaction in
> adapting to it while transfiguring it, does not see that any
> swerving of theoretical effort which he allows through the
> passivity of his own thought, as well as any avoiding of the
> temporary opposition to which his own thought could bring
> him, only makes these masses blinder and weaker than they
> need be.[22]

More important still, 'his own thought belongs in this
development as a critical, forward-driving element.'[23] Professional optimism only prevents one from understanding the
temporary defeats in the struggle. This does not mean that
Critical Theory formally joins with the party of the proletariat;
indeed, Horkheimer insists that the existence of the proletariat
is no guarantee of the eventual success of Critical Theory's
goals:

> There are no universal criteria for Critical Theory as a whole
> . . . Just as little does there exist a social class on whose
> assentment one could base oneself . . . Critical Theory . . . has
> no specific instance standing for it save the interest which is
> connected with it in the elimination of social injustice.[24]

In the 'Afterword' to 'Traditional and Critical Theory', this
position seems to give rise to a certain optimism:

> But if its concepts which emerge from the social movement
> ring futile because not much more stands behind them than
> their persecutors, the truth will none the less come forth; for
> the goal of a rational society which, granted, today appears
> present only in phantasy, is truly inherent in every man.[25]

This faith in the emergence of truth does not mean that struggle
is unnecessary, nor that its result will be victory, wiping away
the tears and sweat of the past. The passage cited above which
denies the centrality of the proletariat continues: 'Bringing this
negative formulation to an abstract expression: it is but the
material content of the idealistic concept of Reason.'

III   Excursus: Herbert Marcuse on the Philosophical Genesis of Critical Theory

In the issue of the *Zeitschrift* which followed the publication of Horkheimer's essay, there appeared a two-part article, 'Philosophy and Critical Theory', announced under the joint names of Horkheimer and Herbert Marcuse. In fact, the two contributions were distinguished by author, and to a certain degree by approach. Where Horkheimer's 'Afterword' developed his arguments for Critical Theory more directly through an analysis of the tasks of the social sciences, using Marx without explicit reference, Marcuse works within the problematic of philosophy, showing where Marxism and the project of a Critical Theory emerge, and how their function must necessarily change. A brief discussion of Marcuse's argument will help make clear the problematic and project of Critical Theory.

Marxism emerged from the peculiar German situation in the 1830s when the claims of philosophy were more advanced than the contemporary social conditions which, in Marx's phrase, were 'beneath the level of history'. When the philosophical critique discovered the economic base on which social conditions rest, philosophy lost its specific function; all of humanity's ultimate questions and desires had to be posed in economic terms. 'Economic' did not imply simply concern with production, any more than materialism meant simply the primacy of matter. Materialism, in Marcuse's analysis, implies first of all that the concern for human happiness motivates the analysis; and second, that this happiness can only be achieved through social change. This correlates to the philosophical adequacy of the economic concepts; i.e., to their being articulated in terms of the social totality structured by the still unfulfilled demand for happiness. Economic materialism thus took over the traditional claims of philosophy which, 'to the extent that it is more than a speciality within the given division of labour, has always lived from this: that Reason was not yet reality.'[27] By Reason, Marcuse understands:

> Philosophy wanted to investigate the ultimate and most universal grounds of Being. Under the name Reason it thought out the idea of a specific being in which all the decisive oppositions (between subject and object, essence and appearance, thought and Being) are unified. Coupled with this idea was the conviction that beings are not immediately already rational, but must first be brought to reason. Reason

must present the highest possibility of man and of beings. Both belong together.[28]

In this sense, philosophy is always idealism, subsuming being under thought; but at the same time, insists Marcuse, philosophy also becomes critical philosophy. Whatever does not satisfy the demands of Reason is to be criticised. This critical task was internalised by bourgeois philosophy and, to a degree, by bourgeois society, such that Reason and freedom were identified. The problem, however, was that this critical Reason quickly became mere subjective freedom, most explicitly in Kant's ethics, where the practical effect of an action counts for nothing as concerns its ethical validity. Nonetheless, this was not just an ideology; it really was idealistic, insists Marcuse: although it could not satisfy its expectations in bourgeois society it nonetheless preserved a domain of freedom, opposition and protest.[29] Here too, differently than in the Marxian perspective, philosophy came to an end; Reason was internalised by the individual and manifested in social behaviour. But here too, as it becomes apparent that social conditions limit the exercise of Reason, bourgeois philosophy-as-behaviour must turn to social theory in order to understand itself and be consistent with its own demands.

Marxian economics-as-philosophy and bourgeois behaviour-as-philosophy are turned to the social world, looking for a change that does not come; from their disappointment emerges a critical theory, a return to the concerns of philosophy but now in spheres that go beyond the traditional concerns. In its new domain, philosophy-as-critical-theory maintains the goals of freedom and Reason in terms of which it poses its tasks, constructs its programme beyond the narrow boundaries of the economistic view. It is aided in this by the fact that there are real struggles for freedom continually engaged which make the demand for the happiness and Reason which are not-yet into a *concrete mediation* and not just an abstract utopia. Philosophy is thus part of the struggle, but *as philosophy*, preserving its rigour and maintaining its demands. This is the importance of the contributions to the *Zeitschrift* which deal with topics like truth and verification, rationalism and irrationalism, the role of logic, metaphysics and positivism, and the concept of essence. More than sociology is entailed in this effort. Examining philosophical problems, the task is to find that content which goes beyond the social limitations of its formation to uncover the tensions and limits which are constitutive of the problem. As Marcuse put it in 'The Concept of Essence', since so much of 'men's real struggles and desires went into the metaphysical quest for an ultimate unity, truth and universality of Being', the critical theoretical analysis will have social implications.[30] The point is to seek the philosophical truth which 'is only truth insofar as it is not the truth about the actual society. Precisely because it is not this truth, because it transcends this actuality, it can become a concern of critical theory.'[31] The point is not to do a sociological analysis relating theory and material conditions; that would be to neglect the truth inherent in past struggles and constitutive of past philosophies as Marcuse had defined it lies precisely in the maintenance of the idealist perspective.

As with Horkheimer, Marcuse attributes to the critical theorist a 'phantasy' which is necessary for the critical project. This phantasy had already been ingredient in philosophy, for example in Aristotle or Kant. Marcuse does not explain its origins, but simply insists that it is not the caprice of the fool for it is part of a social process which continually shows it its limits. More important, that which the phantasy shows is more central than any collection of facts, for it is clear that the facts have a sense only in terms of the goal which structures them. By holding out the philosophical goal, the proposed analysis permits and demands a continual process of self-criticism. The implications which Marcuse draws from this position in his writings of this period would take us too far afield here.

Marcuse concludes his essay with the suggestive observation that we have returned to the situation of the 1830s as Marx confronted it: theory is beyond the social conditions of the time, which are 'beneath the level of history'. The Critical Theory must make conscious the possibilities which the philosophical acquisitions of struggle bear within them; it must show the presence of the unfulfilled tasks. Significantly, however, Marcuse makes no proposal for Critical Theory analogous to Marx's move to the economic as a new foundation and formulation of those unfinished works which it preserves. Horkheimer's Critical Theory seemed to imply a new stance for philosophy, a kind of philosophy-as-critique-in-experience, which would preclude a quest like that of Marx, since once it was formulated any such new theory would become separated, a traditional theory neglecting the subject which is in fact its object. Both Horkheimer and Marcuse seem to take for granted the continued validity of Marxian economics, in order to work at its interstices, correcting its excesses and filling in its incompletenesses. The question is: is this a sufficient delimitation of the tasks of a Critical Theory? Horkheimer's

'Authoritarian State' (1942) needs to be examined before an answer can be proposed.

IV Political Implications

From his American exile, after the *Zeitschrift* had finally begun to publish in English before closing up shop altogether, Horkheimer drew together the political strands of Critical Theory in a passionate essay published in a privately printed volume dedicated to the memory of Walter Benjamin. The familiar motifs return here, rendered more explicit by the political framework into which they are thrown. The painful problem of Critical Theory's place, role, justification and contribution, as well as the source of the existential judgements, interest in the future and critical phantasy, is historically and theoretically specified in a manner that one would hardly have expected from the professor's pen. 'Authoritarian State' is one of those peaks to which the theorist sometimes ascends, rising up in anger, hope and yet sober lucidity to achieve a formulation whose tensile strength can never be reconstructed. The tension cannot be maintained, the fragile structure splinters, and for the remainder of a life's activity the theorist picks up the pieces, with a greater or lesser constancy and creativity. The optimism based on Reason, Truth and Freedom which marked the first formulations of Critical Theory is combined in 'Authoritarian State' with its identical opposite, a pessimism so total and unremitting that hope can clothe itself only in the apocalypse. In this unification of opposites whose tension pervades every paragraph, *Critical Theory as attitude* reaches its culmination. Horkheimer's work from this point on is increasingly dominated by the pessimistic lucidity; but with the tension weakening at each successive formulation, until the writings of the last years which are but a pale shadow, a formalised Critical Theory establishing itself as a tradition.

'Authoritarian State' begins significantly by pointing out that the Marxian predictions have come true: machines have made work but not the worker superfluous; the bourgeoisie is decimated and dependent — 'The Eldorado of bourgeois existence, the sphere of circulation, is liquidated';[32] the state has become the Total Capitalist, while exploitation continues: this is the *society* of the authoritarian state. The result was supposed to be the creation of conditions for the breakdown and revolution; but neither has come, and the authoritarian state's elimination of the market gives capitalist domination new breathing space, while planned production nourishes the masses better in order, in its turn, to be better nourished by them. The forces of revolution have not manifested themselves; workers' organisations have been integrated into the state. The situation in Russia offers no more hope: 'The most fully developed kind of authoritarian state, which has freed itself from any dependence on private capital, is integral Etatism or state socialism.'[33] Granted, as opposed to the 'mixed form' which is fascism, the Russian situation is better, says Horkheimer. 'But the producers, to whom capital legally belongs, remain wage laborers, proletarians no matter how much is done for them.'[34] The roots of this authoritarian development lie at the beginnings of the bourgeois era: Robespierre's France began a kind of welfare state centralism, with parliament maintained simply to register laws edicted by the Jacobins, and the spirit of the masses heated by 'brotherhood and denunciation'.[35] The anti-Church measures were taken not for their own sake but because the state wanted to control the Church: 'The "sans-culotte Jesus" announces the Nordic Christ.'[36] Thermidor was only a temporary halt; the secret negotiations between Lassalle and Bismarck are symbolic of the tendencies of the present.

The decline of the revolutionary movement, indeed its contribution to the erection of the authoritarian state, is the most disturbing aspect of the new situation. Horkheimer gives two accounts of the lack of revolutionary opposition. The bureaucratisation of the movement is explained through a version of Michels' 'iron law of oligarchy'. Like Michels, Horkheimer describes the pressures on the movement as it becomes a mass organisation: the need to maintain itself leads to caution; the seeking after system-immanent rewards like increased wages which will maintain the members' adherence; the leaders' becoming experts who are increasingly specialised and necessary; the growth of collusion between the workers' representatives and capital; and the pervasive and impersonal influence of capitalist rationality within the ranks of the movement. Opposition to the leaders' betrayal is forced, if it succeeds, to maintain itself through the same means. While Horkheimer sees this as the result[37] of a change in the mode of capitalist production, he gives a further explanation which cuts deeper. In a telling passage, he writes scornfully: 'If phantasy freed itself at all from the soil of factuality, it put in the place of the present state apparatus the bureaucracy of the party and unions, in the place of the profit principle the Plan of the functionaries. Even utopia was filled with disciplinary rules.'[38] People were conceived of as objects; in the best of cases, their

own objects. 'So far as the proletarian opposition in the Weimar
Republic did not die as a sect, it fell to the spirit of
administration.'[39] In short, 'The revolutionary movement was
the negative reflection of the conditions that it attacked.'[40]
The logic of this development and its causes was to become a
major concern of the later Institute analyses, into which,
however, we cannot delve here.

Although Horkheimer's first reaction to these conditions is to
fall back on the optimism guaranteed by the Marxian theory, he
is too lucid to remain with it in the face of the evidence. While
it certainly matters to the individual whether Bolshevism,
Reformism or Fascism is in the saddle, the bureaucratic
domination remains; a radical overthrow is necessary. Its
possibility is defended first in the terms from which the essay
began: state capitalism is the creator of the conditions of the
final proletarian revolution. The authoritarian-bureaucratic state
is in fact inefficient. The strength of bureaucratic domination is
declining with the loss of legitimation. Not only that 'obedience
is not productive',[41] but also bureaucracy brings about petty
struggles among the bureaucratic departments, which are
complicated by the continued presence of anarchy on the world
market. The authoritarian state is forced to resort to police
methods, permanent mobilisation, use of racial prejudice, and
the generalisation of propaganda. Internationally, there will
come to exist 'Two friend-enemy blocs of states with changing
composition [who] will dominate the world, offering along
with the fascio better rations to their followers on the backs of
the half-colonial and colonial masses, and finding in their
reciprocal threat to each other new grounds for an arms race.'[42]
Horkheimer verbally retains the Marxian position:

> That the rationality of domination is already weakening
> when the authoritarian state takes over is the true ground of
> its identity with terrorism, and also of Engels' theory that the
> prehistory of mankind ends with it.[43]

But the meaning of Engels' assertion is transformed in the
further argument, once Horkheimer admits not only the
inadequacy of the Russian model, but also the possibility — too
often demonstrated in history — of regressions in social freedom. Engels' position must be interpreted at the social level:
state capitalism has created the capacities which would permit
its members in fact to take the direction of society; and the
delegitimation process has made possible a recognition that a
new form of social relations must replace the domination which

reaches its highest and most visible point in the authoritarian state. Horkheimer points to the form of the councils which emerged spontaneously in 1871 and 1905 as an example of the innovation of which the masses are capable *when they will it.* However, 'The possibility today is no less than the doubt.'[44] There are no guarantees, structural or rational; the revolution rests on the *will* of the revolutionaries. Can it free itself from the logic of capitalism? And how?

At this point, Marxism comes under a heavy double-fronted attack. With the primacy accorded to the revolutionary will comes the recognition that one source of the bureaucratic spirit which so easily became a part of the authoritarian state is precisely the kind of theory which Marxism offered.

> Truth which is experienced as property changes into its opposite; it opens itself to the relativism whose critical thrust is based on the same ideal of security as the absolute philosophy.[45] Critical Theory is of a very different sort.[46]

Relativism as well as traditional philosophy suppose a notion of truth which is precisely the one against which Critical Theory had erected itself. The practical consequences of this style are that political realism manifested by the bureaucratic leadership of the revolutionary movement. Horkheimer points to the results in a telling passage: 'Although the later course of history has confirmed the Girondists against the Montagnards, Luther against Münzer, humanity was not betrayed by the premature undertakings of the revolutionaries, but through the mature wisdom of the realists.'[47] His temper boiling, Horkheimer ripostes: 'for the revolutionary, the world has always been ripe enough.'[48] Yet Marx based his theory on a linear, formalistic and logical conception of history as passing through necessary stages. Borrowed from Hegel, the political translation of this theoretical attitude was the revolution as midwife of history. This is nothing but a bourgeois attitude. On Marx's own authority, the politics of St Simon and Comte, from whom Horkheimer cites telling passages, are taken over by Bebel and the German Marxists. The result is that 'the revolution is brought down to the level of mere progress.'[49] With this linear conception of history translated from Hegel into 'materialist' terms goes a positivist rationalism which wants to realise in history the identity of the Ideal and the Real, but whose practical result is the tendency of the authoritarian state toward universal exploitation.

Horkheimer elaborates his own stance through the critique of the forms and logic of the domination exemplified in the authoritarian state. He rejects the 'practical' question: what will you do with the power once you have it? The question itself supposes that domination over labour and other humans will continue. The goal of revolution is precisely to overcome this structure and its logic. 'The forms of free association do not close themselves off into a system.'[50] The logic of the closed system, typical of traditional theory, is an expression of that need for security which Horkheimer had found expressed in the Marxian theory and those who cleave to it. 'Without the feeling of being with a large party, an all-honored leader, world history, or at least the unerring theory, their socialism doesn't function.'[51] If 'dialectic is not identical with development', but is based precisely on the *leap*, then the rational can never be completely deduced, the security never really won.

It is for this reason that the Marxian science consists in the critique of bourgeois economics and not the projection of a socialist one: Marx left that to Bebel. Marx himself explained reality through its ideology: through the development of classical economics he discovered the secret of the economy. The discussion concerns Smith and Ricardo; but the accused is the society.[52]

Ideology is never the perfect reflection of the social conditions from which it springs; and the Critical Theory could only guarantee necessity at the cost of losing the *will* whose action is constitutive of the conditions it attacks. The revolution has no material or logical necessity; its claim cannot be to avenge the wrong that has been done to it by setting itself up as a new ruling class. The revolutionary situation and action as elaborated by Critical Theory would prohibit this establishment of a new form of domination.

Horkheimer is aware that his position sounds like one of those utopias whose vanity Marx so frequently criticised; but in the changed situation he has described, this is the only choice. He agrees with Marx that if theory and its realisation are not thought together the result is but an abstraction. However, the social conditions he has analysed seem to justify a new role for the *utopian mediation*. The atomisation of society means that each atom is like the others; and the destruction of the traditional mediations means that *the Word* carries more weight. Not the Word as propaganda or rhetoric, insists Horkheimer;

that would be just a replay of the existing society. What the word speaks is 'what everyone knows and yet forbids himself from knowing ...'[53] The Word speaks through thought; through the Critical Theory which seeks to restore the sense of the past struggles and hopes. The atomisation and demystification of the tradition has banished even the thought of freedom, the hope for utopia; in this way, the authoritarian state ensures its continued domination. Yet precisely this abuse renders the Word more powerful: "The powerless expression in a totalitarian state is more threatening than the most impressive demonstration by a party under Wilhelm II.'[54] It is not for nothing that the authoritarian state bans its philosophers; nor in return is it for nothing that Horkheimer insisted that the *Zeitschrift* continue to publish in German while in exile. Human phantasy, the desire for freedom, must be rekindled:

> Thought itself is already a sign of resistance, the effort not to let oneself be deceived. Thought is not simply against orders and obedience, but rather puts them in relation to the actualization of freedom. This relation is endangered. Sociological and psychological concepts are too superficial to express what has happened to the revolutionaries in the last decades; the goal (*Intention*) of freedom is damaged, and without it neither knowledge nor solidarity, nor a correct relation between group and leaders is possible.[55]

It is not without significance for his future development that Horkheimer would expect that the rekindling of the spirit of freedom and the desire for utopia would be coupled, finally, with the rebirth of a revolutionary movement which would find the 'correct relation between group and leaders'. Nonetheless, in the actual context, he doesn't project any further what this relation could be. His concluding sentence returns to the radical stance which Critical Theory adopts through the path of the almost desperate search of this essay. The suggestion that one should try to work within the system, bettering conditions as much as one can, is rejected coldly. Such a proposal implies that history follows a schema of gradual progress; and implicitly suggests that one consider people just as does the capitalist. Yet, concludes Horkheimer: 'As long as world history goes in its logical path, it does not fulfil its human nature (*Bestimmung*).'[56]

Horkheimer leaves us on this apocalyptic note; he leaves us as well with the uncertainty whether it is hope or despair that animates him. He leaves stubborn in the task he has given himself, perhaps implying that we too are to adopt this 'refusal to be deceived'. As we rethink the structure of his essay, the schema of the 'negation of the negation' remains as a leitmotif. The authoritarian state is the summit of negativity, the reformulation of Marx's description of the proletariat as the nothing that is to be all, now extended beyond the industrial work situation. But that is precisely the Hegelianism which comes in for such severe criticism in 'Authoritarian State'. This would explain the maintenance of the 'group and leaders' problem, as well as of the Marxian economics and its ultimate (though not explicitly asserted here) expectation of the breakdown, Bebel's 'great Kladderadatsch'. In this sense, Critical Theory would be simply an elaboration within Marxism. Yet the stance appears to imply more; the repeated demand for Critical Theory as a *mediation* is given socio-political substance in this essay, suggesting that Horkheimer's theory is more than Marxian 'science'.

V The Independence of Critical Theory

The path traced by Critical Theory moves away from an empirical research programme aimed at filling the gaps left in Marxian theory towards the elaboration of a radically new type of theory. But the path was never travelled through to the end; the traces of Marxism remained present both in the theoretical assumptions and in the political consequences. The inability to finally articulate and maintain a specific stance for Critical Theory was responsible for the deception and ultimately pessimism which marked the next three decades of Horkheimer's life.[57] If we recall for a moment the earlier comparison with Ernst Bloch, it is only with qualifications that the claim can be maintained that Horkheimer was unable to ground his critical categories because he never took seriously Marx's theory of labour as the ground of that phantasy and existential choice which found and direct the interest in freedom in its concrete manifestations. Horkheimer does indeed stress that it is the planful, rational element in the produced human world which makes it accessible to, and demands the use of, reason. He does not, however, develop this theory any further; and from the stance of 'Authoritarian State', he would certainly have to say that the 'reason' and 'planning' manifest in the productive system are still forms of rationality-as-domination. The hope for prediction expressed in 1932 now appears caught within a traditional attitude toward theory. It was for this reason that Herbert Marcuse's effort to ground Critical Theory in the history of philosophy was discussed. But despite the essential theoretical difference between Horkheimer and the Blochian position,[58] what is more striking in the present context is that beneath the very different political stances which each adopted lies a common conception of the nature, tasks and possibilities of theory. Indeed, it seems to have been their inability to recognise and maintain the independent and innovative positions that they staked out which was responsible for the fact that both opted for political positions with which we disagree.

Radicalising Marx's project and correctly criticising those elements in it which are the result of Marx's scientific and rationalistic prejudices, Horkheimer elaborates a Critical Theory which is in constant contact with the social structures and actions which is seeks not only to understand but to change. Critical Theory is set apart from its traditional counterpart specifically by its historical nature, in the sense that *as its own object it can never fixate itself, never become a theory standing apart from, flying above or contemplating its object.* It is this character — and not, as so often claimed, the assertion that Nature will always remain Other — which is responsible for the rejection of the identity theory of philosophical rationalism. With the rejection of the identity theory and the historical insertion comes the 'critical' nature of the theory; and at the same time, its political thrust. The phantasy, futurity, and existential judgement are grounded in this structure of the theory itself. Because Horkheimer never drew these conclusions, he found himself appealing to an always-inherent sense of freedom which he supposed present in all individuals. The term 'freedom' is not the most apt, however, to describe what he is seeking; it is loaded with metaphysical overtones which must be deciphered. It wodld be better to elaborate the notion of freedom from the structural character of Critical Theory — for in effect, what Horkheimer is describing as the task of the theorist is nothing but the elaboration of the notion of human *praxis.*[59]

Because Critical Theory *is* a praxis, it must always be transformed against its will into traditional theory: becoming an hypothesis, a slogan or even a political programme. This is not the betrayal of the theorist. Critical Theory is consciously structured by the expectation of this development, for it is always critical of itself since it is its own object. Praxis has the same structure, though not always the same reflexivity as Critical Theory. When I act, my action becomes an object, affecting the world and yet taken up by the other praxeis in the world and transformed away from what I originally intended. But my action or praxis is not a discrete action, undertaken with a clearly delimited goal in mind (although I may think that I have such a project). Praxis emerges within the world, coming to its self-understanding only in 'the thick' of it, and continually to be begun anew. When Horkheimer's essays are read from this point of view, the apparent meanderings, doubling back on themselves and reformulating the problem,[60] as well as his political indecision, take on their full sense. In the world of bureaucratic domination described in 'Authoritarian State' a Critical Theory must be a *mediator*, but of a specific type. It incites to the empirical research that was so important to the Institute, but it can never become a traditionally formulated theory. *Critical Theory cannot be taught or formulated; it can only be done!*

6 From Critical Theory towards Political Theory: Jürgen Habermas

The goals Max Horkheimer had set out for the Institute for Social Research, and indeed the Frankfurt University chair in Philosophy and Social Science that had been created for the Institute, were taken over in the 1960s by Jürgen Habermas. Faithful to the *attitude* of critical theory, Habermas' still developing work has been driven between two seemingly opposed, but in fact mutually dependent, poles: the concretisation of Critical Theory as a research programme and method capable of confronting and incorporating academic and administrative social science; and the theoretical and practical political concerns that are bound up with the Marxian heritage of Critical Theory. By actively inheriting this tension, Habermas has been able to rethink many of the important issues which blocked the development of Marxism. At the same time, however, he has been attacked politically by others who also claim to be inheriting from Marx. This is not the place to adjudicate the testamentary case. It will prove more useful to ask why the issue has been raised at all — or, to put it in its classical philosophical form: whether we have before us a *quid facti* or a *quid juris*. What is Habermas' position, and how is it justified?

Even before he left Frankfurt in 1971 for the Max Planck Institute in Starnberg, where he has established his own research unit, Habermas' approach to the politics and theoretical elaboration of Critical Theory was hotly debated. Having been a supporter of the early student movement, he became critical of its actionistic tendencies which gave rise either to an anti-intellectualism or to its identical obverse, a dogmatism closed off from concrete social and political analysis. The theoretical work on which he concentrated during this period proposed an alternative in the political sphere. Building on the insights of his predecessors into the changed role of science in contemporary capitalism, and on the pessimistic analysis of reason in the *Dialectic of Enlightenment*, Habermas undertook the interconnected analyses of the 'logic of the social sciences' (1967), the irrational and decisionistic manner in which this logic played itself out in social and political policy making, and finally the philosophical presuppositions which made possible the travesty of reason in a society of domination while simultaneously permitting a critique of that logic. This latter panel of his triptych, published as *Knowledge and Human Interests* (1968), entailed a re-examination of Marxism's theoretical foundations. Particularly important to this reclaiming of the Marxian project was the distinction between the logic of labour and inter-action — the former being seen as the monological and purposively rational action of an individual subject on an external world, whereas the latter is structured as the dialogical interaction of human subjects making discursive truth claims. This distinction permits Habermas to avoid the problems that we have seen Bloch and Horkheimer attempt to confront. At the same time, however, this *philosophical* step carries with it *political* implications to which Habermas' first major publication from Starnberg,[1] *Legitimation Problems of Late Capitalism*, addresses itself. It is from an examination of this volume that we will be able to evaluate Habermas' contribution, and the problems which it poses.

Legitimationsprobleme has three parts. The notion of a crisis is elaborated descriptively through the methods appropriated from systems theory. There is a difference between an organism, which can be immediately distinguished from its environment and whose crisis is one of physical life or death, and a society, where the assertion of a crisis must be based on a *theory* which allows for making this distinction; otherwise, there would be no way of knowing whether social change is just a form of system adaptation or learning. Therefore Habermas attempts to sketch the principles of a theory of social evolution and to illustrate its function in differentiating the forms of human sociality. This theory of social evolution turns out, although Habermas does not use the term, to be based on the sphere of the political as that *process* by which the social formation asserts its own identity.[2] The second part of the book attempts to confront and clarify the implications of the various possible analyses of late capitalist crisis. The goal here is to make plausible Habermas' contention that the need for legitimation is the central systematic problem, which late capitalism can only overcome by changing its class structure or by a radical change in the heritage of traditional cultural needs and motivations. The third section of the book questions whether capitalism can in fact effectuate this latter sort of change (since, by definition, it cannot change from a class to a classless society and remain capitalism). Habermas applies his 'universal pragmatic' or 'praxeology' to try to show why this change has not taken place. The result of this contention becomes a political practice of Enlightenment.

I   What is Late Capitalism?

In his 1957 analysis of the central debates within contemporary Marxist theory, and in his 1960 study 'Between Philosophy and Science: Marxism as Critique', both of which appear in the volume *Theorie und Praxis*, Habermas recognises and begins the thematisation of the modern phenomena which go counter to the predictions of Marxian analysis. The political and theoretical analyses which appeared in the volumes *Student und Politik* (1961; co-authored with, among others, L. v. Friedeburg, former Education Minister in Hessen), *Strukturwandel der Öffentlichkeit* (1962), and *Theorie und Praxis* (1963) do not follow up the structural critiques of capitalist change, but rather attempt to elaborate the notion of a radical politics that is not dependent on objective economic crisis as a condition of its success. In the second phase of his work, marked by confrontations with positivist theory and ideology, Habermas' attention returns to the problem of social structure and of elaborating a methodology capable of meeting the requirements of a critical theory as Marx originally defined it. The methodological questions were posed in the volumes *Zur Logik der Sozialwissenschaften* (1967) and *Erkenntnis und Interesse* (1968), while the structural and political problems emerge particularly in the collection *Technik und Wissenschaft als 'Ideologie'*, where the role of science, science policy and state intervention come to the fore. The debate with the systems theoretical social theory of Niklas Luhmann in *Theorie der Gesellschaft oder Sozialtechnologie* (1971), taken up again in *Legitimationsprobleme*, points up the fact that the methodological analysis, the structural description and the political practice appropriate to contemporary society are all intimately tied together. The new Introduction to *Theorie und Praxis* (1971) sums up with the assertion that:

All of these studies of the empirical relation of science,

politics and public opinion in late capitalist societies must remain unsatisfactory as long as the serious starting points for a theory of late capitalism are hardly worked out.[3]

Legitimationsprobleme is thus the culmination of fifteen years of experience and reflexion; Habermas' other works will prove useful in analysing it.

The term 'late capitalism' is awkward.[4] Descriptively, it points to the increased role of organisation through the intervention of the state in all areas of life. This occurs because of a high degree of capitalist concentration, multinational corporate activity and an ever more controlled and manipulated market. The increasingly restricted private sphere and the minimisation of the market as a form of social distribution imply a change in the class stratification which creates a variety of new forms of social behaviour. The increased application of science and technology changes the work process and affects the profit and investment choices of the giant corporations, as well as the options for government spending. Mechanised farming and greater urbanisation create new social problems that take on a political expression outside of the traditional scheme of party democracy. Mass media and the theoretically equal chance of all for education affect the socialisation process and role conceptions. Scarcity is no longer immediately physical (at least in the developed capitalist countries — with some exceptions which, however, seem incapable of self-organisation); it is nature itself, and a meaning for social existence which have become the scarce resources. What is needed here is not a description of the changes, but a theoretical guideline to make sense of and differentiate this complex of phenomena.

Habermas proposes a systems theoretical approach articulated in terms of the question of crisis. There are three potential sources of crisis: the economic, the political, and the socio-cultural. And these crises can manifest themselves in four forms: as system crises of the economic or of the rationality of administration, and as identity or social crises in the form of legitimation or motivation failures. What is described at this level of abstraction is the systems theoretical structure of *any* social system. Differentiation can be achieved if it is possible to distinguish a 'social organisational principle' analogous to the Marxian notion of a 'social formation' (p. 18)[5] which presents the terms which assure the system's *identity*. Such principles

determine the learning capacity and thus the level of development of a society first with regard to the forces of

> production and their system of interpretation which assures
> identity, and thus also limits the possible growth of steering
> capacity. (p. 30)

In this manner, an empirically based theory can be articulated
which will eliminate the contingency of the choice of a
theoretical standpoint. To do this, systems theory is not
sufficient.

> Without a theory of social evolution on which I could base
> myself, the organisational principles can not yet even be
> abstractly grasped but at best indictively illustrated and
> explained with reference to the institutional domain which
> for each level of development has the functional primacy
> (system of kinship, political system, economic system). (p.
> 31—32)

A fully developed theory of evolution would then give more
precise indications than those which Habermas presents in this
volume. But even without it, the reflection on the need to
complete the systems theoretical analysis by moving from the
realm of the investigator's contingent choice is sufficient for
Habermas to argue that it is *crises of identity* which will shed
light on the central components of a social system. Correlatively, this means that the systems crises in the economic and
administrative spheres cannot be interpreted as the motivating
force for the collapse of a society, *unless* that society's form of
self-identity is assured by these systems, as was the case
respectively for the period of liberal market capitalism and
feudalism.

Habermas' analysis of late capitalism sequentially develops
the four possible forms of crisis. His basic assumption is that of
a fundamental economic contradiction which Marx articulated
as the 'law of the tendency of the rate of profit to fall'.[6] Once
this 'law' is given, the economic sphere can only solve its
problems by recourse to the state administrative sphere.
Historically, this recourse seems at least temporarily to have
been successful. The relative lack of economic crises can be
explained through the state's having enlarged the limits of the
basic economic laws, even while these nevertheless remain
ultimately operational. Or, alternatively, the state can be seen as
the planning agent for 'united monopoly capital'. Habermas
argues that neither is in fact the case, but rather that the state
has a limited functional freedom insofar as its intervention has
changed the rules of the economic game. From this follows the
possible *rationality* crisis, emerging either because of the

conflict of opposed individual capitalist interests that can limit the state's freedom, or because the state, to do its economic job, has to create structures — transportation, housing, education, business subventions of various sorts, etc. — which are not functional to the system as a whole. In both cases, new demands are imposed on the state to *legitimate* its activity. It can deal with these either by attempting to buy off potential protest (building hospitals, schools, etc.) or by creating its own ideology to assure allegiance. In the former case, problems of a fiscal nature emerge; and in addition, there ensues the politicisation of life in areas previously thought of as a-political. In the latter case, the problems of *motivation* emerge; that is, the question of the degree to which the state can create an ideology that changes the accepted and traditional forms of social-political life.

The definition of late capitalism that emerges from this systems-theoretical description has two central features. The adjective 'late' can be used insofar as it is demonstrated that the system has used each of the four types of crisis-prevention available to it. Habermas' position here is taken from Claus Offe, who writes:

> There is no recognizable dimension in which *new* mechanisms for the self-perpetuation of the capitalist system (which are at the same time compatible with its continued existence! — which of course doesn't affect thermonuclear wars) could be found and applied. What remains is the variation and refinement of the triad of usual self-adaptive mechanisms which at least to some degree have been applied in all developed capitalist systems, and on the other hand, namely in the case of their insufficiency, either the historically unproductive or the productive-revolutionary breakdown of the basic structure of capitalism.[7]

Secondly, the inability of the system level to function alone for its self-regulation implies the centrality of legitimation and motivation crises as the distinctive features defining the identity of late capitalism. The form that these take, however, needs further clarification.[8]

All social systems have had legitimation problems which they have resolved in different ways. Primitive societies are organised around either a system of kinship or of religion whose permanence preserves the social order and provides a truth-referent for practical questions. Pre-capitalist Western societies generally evolved a politico-religious legitimation process in which the forms of social and personal interactions were infused with an external sense. Liberal market capitalism was able to claim legitimation in terms of the principles of democracy and equal opportunity in the market. Empirical observation of contemporary society seems to indicate that this form of legitimation has lost its attractiveness; the question is to what degree this is simply an appearance, or to what degree it can be systematically explained. Habermas' proposal is to look first at the general notion of legitimation, manifested both in the political (hence, system) plane and in the socio-cultural (hence, identity) plane. To reveal the socio-cultural, he needs a theory of societal individuation, i.e., of the way in which the individual personality is shaped by culture and society.

The necessity of state intervention in late capitalism gives rise to political legitimation problems. These, says Habermas, can be dealt with through the use of two state resources: value and sense (p. 104). To the degree to which the state does function as the ideal Total-Capitalist, it must be democratic, earn the allegiance of its members through the appearance of participation and responsiveness. This means that the present tendency towards increasing participation at all levels — from urban planning to academic reform, from local political initiatives on specific issues to citizen representatives on business boards— must be furthered so that even those who are structurally penalised by the maintenance of the class-based system feel that they have a voice in their destiny. This implies that

> Because the activity of the state follows the declared goal of directing the system by avoiding crises, and thus the class relation has lost its unpolitical form, the class structure *must* be affirmed in struggles for the administratively mediated division of the social productive growth. (p. 76)

In prosperous times, the state can buy allegiance through tax-rebates, model cities, urban subsidies and so on. But when a crisis appears on the horizon, when unemployment and inflation begin to rise, the state needs to be able to act with the support of the citizens in order, for example, to increase taxes, give aid to depressed areas or impose wage-price restrictions. But precisely at this moment its fiscal resources will come under pressure such that compensatory action is more difficult. At the same time, confidence in the state will have fallen, reducing the parameters within which it can act. What it can no longer buy with value, it must purchase with sense. But here, too, it will have undermined its own sphere of activity. The state's functions in helping the system to avoid crisis are not simply economic. It intervenes as a market-substitute to keep demand and profit high; and where weaknesses occur it may fund infrastructural improvements and the like. It becomes involved in the educational system, and takes over the funding of science and its transformation into technologies. Moreover, it attempts to compensate for the dysfunctional results of capitalist accumulation by taking over ecological costs, helping failing industries, giving aid to agriculture, or supporting reformist trade unions. All of these functions are ultimately *use-value oriented.* The activity of the state cannot, therefore, be hidden in a cloak of neutrality. Its embeddedness in a class society means that the state must produce legitimation for itself; it must develop an ideology to assure allegiance where its structural bias has been unveiled.

The problems of political legitimation thus ultimately depend on the ability of the state to provide a meaningful basis for the activities of the individual. It is here that the motivational crisis appears. Habermas writes:

> I speak of a motivation crisis when the socio-cultural system so changes that its output is dysfunctional for the state and for the system of social labor. (p. 106)

Habermas is often unclear as to whether the motivation crisis arises because of a change in this socio-cultural system, as in the above passage, or whether it occurs when the economic and political systems change so that the current motivational structure becomes dysfunctional. Motivation is not the same as legitimation; it is based on a logic of normative structures and images of the world which, Habermas insists, have their own logic independent of the political and the economic.[9] The empirical questions are whether they have changed, or become dysfunctional, and what that means.

Habermas looks at four elements of motivational structure: (1) the non-regenerability of the tradition; (2) the way social structure has undermined the principle of individual effort; (3) normative structures which emerge from post-autonomous art and emerging communicative morality destroy the motivational patterns of privatism; and (4) the fact that the tradition is nonetheless necessary. The discussion is often unclear, but one can see where this theory must take him. The first and third elements point to precisely the manipulability of motivations. Habermas notes the scientisation of the professions; the expansion of service industries which makes commodities of what previously were interpersonal relations; the increased role of political administration in all life areas; the commercialisation of culture and politics; and the scientisation and psychologisation of child-rearing. He points to the role of science in destroying any image of the totality, replacing it with fads based on partial evidence (e.g., ethology, not to speak of astrology, etc.); to the dilemma of modern art which, having lost the promise of happiness it once held, has reacted to its increasing 'commodification' by turning inward to an obscurity that protects its independence, but also makes it less meaningful to most people; and to the relativisation of ethics, or their identification with positive law. On the other hand, the second and fourth points indicate the non-manipulability of norms, and point in the direction of Habermas' theory of social evolution based on a universal pragmatics. Thus, while the old parallel of effort and gratification assured by a supposedly equal market has been replaced by what are in principle equal chances for education, its effect has been over-qualification, unrewarding work, meaningless jobs and increased free time that one doesn't know how to use. More importantly, regarding the fourth point, Habermas leans on the Döbert-Nunner analysis of adolescent crisis as a typical manifestation of the problems of assimilating the new norms of late capitalism.[10] The young radicals and alienated youth of Kenniston are seen as a necessary result of this system because it does not permit the normal, communicative, assimilation of social roles.

The role of motivational crises is neither final cause nor basis for the other forms; the book's title, *Legitimation Problems*, indicates that it is these forms that are at the nub of the issue. A basis in motivation would ultimately make the analyses of the other three crisis manifestations irrelevant; it would psychologise, or ontologise away the problem. Habermas gives two reasons why motivation is not the foundation of his analysis. First, it must itself be analysed in its own logic; this is the task of the theory of social evolution. Second, motivation is based on norms which are universal. They are not the product of individual action, but rather are responsible for its production. The individual only becomes a particular individual insofar as she/he individuates her/himself in regard to a pre-given institutional-normative framework. The norms in question in the theory of motivational crisis are responsible for the 'production' of the kind of persons who are confronted by a social system seeking to preserve itself. In this sense, it is the legitimation crisis which is central. Legitimation has the property of being defined *both* by the parameter of the system integrative mechanisms of the economic and the political, *and* by the normative-institutional structure that institutes motivational forms. This dual structure explains both the centrality of legitimation problems, and why they become the object of a *critical theory of society.*

II Marxism and Critical Theory

Crisis manifestations in late capitalism differ fundamentally from those of the liberal capitalism described by Marx; and so too must the critical social theory which analyses them.[11] This accounts for Habermas' reformulation of critical theory as an Historical Materialism which would realise what he sees as Marx's goal, while being at the same time capable of dealing with more than liberal capitalist market society. Liberal capitalism was peculiar in that its economic system crises were also identity or social crises. The free market structured not simply production, but also the social and institutional distribution of power through the 'free' market for labour and through mediating the dual nature of the commodity. Marx's decision to write *Capital* as a critical, i.e., revolutionary theory of capitalist *society* depended on this phenomenon. Habermas formulates the requirements of a theory of Historical Materialism as follows:

> Historical Materialism seeks an explanation of social evolution which is so comprehensive that it covers not only the process by which the theory itself develops but also the context in which it is applied. The theory gives the conditions under which a self-reflexion of the history of the species has become objectively possible; and at the same time it names the addressee who, with the help of the theory, can enlighten itself concerning itself and its potentially emancipatory role in the process of history.[12]

As long as the liberal economy ran smoothly, it legitimated the social inequality which resulted from free exchange on the market. Crises are its 'practical ideology critique' (p. 47), affecting not only the system integration, but also questioning social integration as well. The interdependence of system and social integration means that economic analysis is immediately translatable into social terms; thus, says Habermas, Marx 'is the author of the *18th Brumaire* as well as *Capital*.' (p. 49)

The central role of legitimation as an *independent* manifestation of crisis in Habermas' analysis of late capitalism is not surprising given his earlier work; and given his theoretical aims, it is the only choice.[13] Habermas began his confrontation with Marxism in the wake of the Frankfurt School's increasing recognition that the modern form of the Critique of Political Economy had to be a Critique of Instrumental Reason. But, as Albrecht Wellmer notes, the Frankfurt critique was still bound to Marx's basic position in one fundamental sense: the pessimism expressed, for example, in *The Dialectic of the Enlightenment* was based on a concept of human labour which, as it expands its conquest of outer nature, increasingly subjects its own inner nature to the same tendency. Reification becomes a property of the individual subject as well as of the social world. This, however, entails either automatic economic catastrophe (as Lukács' theory had to articulate the collapse of capitalism), or an apocalypse, which could as well be barbarism as socialism. Habermas saw this problem first politically; he attempted to circumvent it by returning to a reconsideration of Marx's notion of productive labour.

Briefly,[14] Habermas rejected Marx's famous assertion in the *1844 Manuscripts* that what is positive in Hegel's *Phenomenology* is that Hegel 'grasps the nature of labor, and conceives objective man (true, because real man) as the result of his own labor'. Not only does he reject this in Hegel;[15] Habermas insists that Marx himself conflated two phenomena which he had originally distinguished: the forces and relations of production. These two, and their sources, *labour* and *social interaction*, obey different criteria of rationality. The former is monological, goal-oriented activity for whose purposive rationality content is irrelevant. The latter is the symbolically mediated form of human relations in which the other is not a thing or object but another subject with whom I enter into dialogical human relations; its rationality is communicative or emancipatory, and its content counts.[16] In present terms, the former is system, the latter social integration.

The difference between the rationality of instrumental action (labour) and that of communicative (institutional) action provides a guiding thread. It is communicative-institutional activity that constitutes the normative social structures within which we live with and speak to others. These structures must be accounted for. Habermas began his explanation in his debate with N. Luhmann,[17] for whom norms are defined simply as the structure of reciprocal expectations of role-bearers within a society. Such norms, however, are perfectly arbitrary; they have no cognitive basis or truth-reference on which to rest their justification. Habermas argued that norms are in the structure of the speech situation which must make the counterfactual assumption that the competent speaker/hearer is fully capable of understanding and communicating. Speech supposes a universality that can be attained both concerning *what* is spoken of, and with regard to the situation of the *speaker* her/himself. This universal or norm is counterfactual; it is nonetheless activated with our first words, is the universal quality of speaking beings, for without it communication, however distorted, would not be possible.[18] This means that a first stage of Habermas' argument is reached. *Critical theory can be redefined.* The critical theorist makes the counterfactual assumption and then asks; what would each member of a society think *if* he or she were completely aware of the situation, free and able to verbalise the occluded aspects of social life, and could ask whether his or her empirical interests were or were not universalisable? From this counterfactual question it becomes possible to show both the functional necessity for the system to legitimate itself ideologically, and, at the same time, to indicate the possible forms of critique of that ideology.[19]

Thus far, the argument claims to be following and developing the logic of Marxian class analysis, which showed that the particular interest of the proletariat demands its universalisation in a classless society. But there is a difficulty. There is, first of all, the philosophical problem of the creation of a universal through the action of the particular individuals. Habermas perceives and returns to this problem. He criticises the notion of normativity proposed by analytical philosophy for its non-cognitive nature. This is the reason why legitimation, not motivation, is central. The model of contractualism with its image of partners defining a contract is inadequate to account for universality. The correctness of human behaviour and the truth of our activity is not determined by our adaptation to a predetermined external world. Monological subjectivity can never achieve the universality of a norm or a true analysis. The norms which govern our intersubjective activity must exist *before* the speaking subjects which actualise them.[20] Atomized individuals in a presocial situation would be incapable of coming together to make a sort of social contract claiming universal validity. Habermas takes up this theoretical problem in his chapter on 'The End of the Individual' (pp. 162—78), where he recognises that without universal norms, world-images etc., the individual cannot achieve his specific individuality; meaning comes only from society and only within the parameters which it, as more-than-individual, defines. But the question that Habermas poses in this discussion is not that of the nature of these norms and the specific differences among them — the norms of private law, familial relations, the ethics of business, and the obligations and duties of the citizen. Habermas is concerned, rather, whether the individual as traditionally conceived still exists today. This shifting of accents is important. A social theory which is formulated on the basis of an *undifferentiated universal*, of the sort Habermas' universal speech situation proposes, demands concretisation.[21]

This 'philosophical' problem has plagued Marxian theory *and* practice. In the 1843 'Critique of Hegel's Philosophy of the State', Marx attempts to solve it by pointing to the need for universal democratic voting rights. Each individual citizen, he asserts, would participate 'individually-as-all'; the legislator would be my representative in the same way that the shoemaker represents my needs. This merely political solution appears unsatisfactory to Marx, and in the essay 'On the Jewish Question', which marks his turn to civil society as primary, he cites Rousseau to the effect that whoever would build a new and just state must change the nature of its members. The error of the French Revolution, insists Marx, was that it changed the political structures without changing the egoistic and competitive civil society on which it rested. It is this insight that led Marx to the study of political economy. The problem of the relation of the state to civil society, of the universal and the particular, will be solved when the nature of civil society is changed so that the particularity of the economic subjects is eliminated and each relates to the other as universal. This is the basis of the notion of the 'withering away of the state'.

As a theoretical solution, Marx's position is inadequate. The suggestion is that under changed conditions and relations of production, the vast system of interdependence established by the capitalist division of labour, but occluded by the egoistical and profit-oriented forms of capitalist domination, would become conscious. Production would be production for universal needs according to a plan established by all for the good of all. This, however, supposes that it is possible for someone — either the philosopher or the planner(s) — to stand *outside of* the actual historical process, to see its directions and to orient its effort. But the entire thrust of Marx's dialectical critique is to refute such a philosophical stance; idealism is precisely that attitude which believes that it can abstract itself from the social and historical conditions of its time. This theoretical error has *practical* consequences when it is suggested that the 'class consciousness' which would be the universalising of the particular individuals in a socialist situation can actually be incorporated in some body, say the party. This is the theoretical source of the *party-myth*.

Another theoretical approach to the same problem is that of Sartre's *Critique de la raison dialectique*. Sartre does not make the mistake of moving to a position outside of the actual process. He begins with the existential individual in its here and now; and he refuses to leave it. The individual relates to the world and to others by totalising them in an ongoing project. This process of continual totalisation by which social structures — couples, triples, series, groups, institutions etc. — are formed is continually in danger. It is menaced on the one hand by the risk of dissolution: the group of which I feel myself a part may change as a result of the action of another member, or of an outside force: suddenly, I no longer feel myself a part of it and sink back into my individuality. On the other hand, there is the threat of reification: the group may become a super-subject, and I its servant; the party or state becomes the active force and I, in order to achieve my goal, must subordinate myself to its means-ends rationality. In both cases, the attempt to move from the individual to the group or intersubjective level is unsuccessful. Sartre's solution to the problem of the universalisation of the particular is to declare it impossible: from the inside, I can never go beyond myself; temporary totalisations in the course of (revolutionary) action are possible, but only as temporary. 'The dictatorship of the proletariat', concludes Sartre, 'is itself an absurd idea'.

The dictatorship of the proletariat as that class which, because it is nothing and has nothing to impose on any other class, and because it alone can establish a state which will wither away, is central to the Marxian project. *In practice*, two solutions exist, both indicated in Lenin's *State and Revolution*. The first is the idea of the workers' councils, the soviets. The *process* of revolution will effect a change in human nature of the sort that no amount of theoretical study or participation under conditions of capitalist domination could effect. Every cook will be able to govern because in the *praxis* of the revolution the cooks will have recognised the role of the universal, and will have transcended their narrow interests as cooks. Lenin's presentation of this alternative is brief and unsatisfactory; it has been developed further by the Council Communists, whose insistence on a simple two-class model of society renders their discussion ultimately abstract and analytically deforming. The problem here, once again, is that a universal interest is *supposed* as existing; but as existing outside of, independent of, the actual process. The councils form of government is indeed perhaps the only revolutionary alternative; but the question of whether it can achieve the universalisation of the existential particular is open to question.

The other solution to the problem of the universal and the particular, which Lenin tried to put into practice, is more mechanical. One sees it in Lenin's admiration for the achievements of the 'modern factory', and in his image of a socialist society functioning like 'the post office'. Lenin speaks of the role of the party after the revolution as inculcating 'new habits' into the working class, as educating them to be good communists, etc. He follows Engels' suggestion that the withering of the state will come about because the government over men will be replaced by the administration of things. Here, however, social theory gives way to natural science with its myth of thy observer as outside of the process. The implication is that there is *a* specific form of socialist behaviour, and *a* specific way in which society can be *objectively* run. These absolutes are known by the party, which has the 'revolutionary' task of imposing them on the workingclass. The universalisation that thus occurs is in fact a levelling, a *depoliticisation* precisely of the kind that took place in Russia, where politics was raised to the possession of the Party.

The point of this excursus is that Habermas correctly sees the *constitutive* and *unavoidable* nature of the problem. It will not do to ignore the political, arguing that the level of civil society and interpersonal relations is its 'real' base. Habermas' stress on the role of the universal — in the form of the norms without which individuation would not occur, and in the form of the truth-reference without which practical activity would be only the meaningless, anomic activity of a Brownian movement — addresses the central *political* problem. He thus helps us to avoid the *reductionism* that follows from an overly simplified and instrumental reading of Marx. He does so by restoring to its integral place the role of the political in Marxian and revolutionary theory. The adequacy of his solution is another question, to which I will return.

There is a further problem. Which interests are universalisable? Habermas recognises that not all are, and suggests a model for *justifiable compromise* when (a) the two sides are equal, *and* (b) the interest in question is not universalisable (p. 154). In fact, however, this suggestion is quickly abandoned; the general demand for universalisation dominates the theoretical development. Indeed, in an essay written after *Legitimation*

Problems,[22] Habermas writes that 'Compromises are the results of clever acting and negotiation, not of discourses'. But how can this demand for universalisation be maintained? Habermas goes through a variety of possibilities.[23] None is satisfactory. We could make anthropological assumptions about the nature of the species, but no one knows what human needs in fact are. We could apply a universal, objectivist philosophy of history like that of Marx, but that supposes a teleology and makes assumptions about the class divisions in order to effect its proof. We could talk about the normative state of a system, but we don't know what that is, and we can't distinguish accidental from systematic omissions. We could compare the claim and reality of a system, but again we don't know whether the contradiction is systematic or accidental. We could analyse legal codes to see who is excluded from what, but no system organizes itself totally by written laws. We could look at destabilising demands which the system unintentionally calls forth, but again, what is accidental and what is necessary? Comparison with other systems also gives only contingent results. Habermas thus opts for an 'advocatory model' (p. 161). This does not imply arbitrarily choosing a group or class to defend:

> The advocatory role of critical social theory would rather consist in a substitute [*stellvertretende*] simulated discourse between the groups that are divided by an articulated or at least virtual opposition of interests in order to find universalizable and at the same time repressed interests. (p. 161)

These interests would then be the object of empirical research.[24]

Habermas develops the basis for his advocatory model in the final two chapters of *Legitimation Problems*. In the first of these he continues his debate with Luhmann, who replaces subject by system with the consequence that democratic decision-making is viewed as only uselessly increasing the complexity of the system whose concern is simply its own self-regulation and preservation. Habermas provides a quasi-empirical critique of Luhmann's position through the example of planning, which shows that the model of democratic planning is at least as good as that of administrative non-participative planning; and that it has the additional benefit of allowing the development of a practical rationality that goes beyond the purposive-rational administrative form (p. 189). If the role of norms and individual reason is eliminated, Habermas concludes, then no crisis theory is possible. As a result, we must make this assumption. Critical theory *can* fail in a society which has so changed the role of the individual or of rationality and discursively universal norms, that only self-regulating systems and sub-systems exist. But this possibility of failure is better than prejudging reality (as does Luhmann), in such a way that from the beginning the individual is removed from the scene.

The argument against Luhmann in defense of the advocatory model is passionate but weak in one crucial sense. The option for the individual as the basis of a social theory clashes with the need for universal norms. Habermas vacillates. We have already seen one instance of his handling this problem. He returns to it in his concluding chapter, 'Partiality for Reason' (*Parteilichkeit für Vernunft*), noting first that you can't ask people to be reasonable, for that would be asking the constituents to constitute that which in turn constitutes them. Reason must already exist if we are to make a reasonable argument for being reasonable. Second, if there is a choice as to who is to be reasonable, the state (Luhmann) or the people (Habermas), then one has already made rationality the property of one particular group, and hence stripped it of its universality. As a result of these arguments, however, Habermas returns to the 'old European idea of human worth' which provides a basis for action within a social system that is increasingly taking its own course. Such an idea is the idea of the Enlightenment, which Habermas proudly assumes as our only choice. We will return to the problem posed by this choice.

In the present context, the difficulty is using a systems theoretical standpoint while at the same time insisting on the role of the active individual. Habermas' claim is that it is wrong to treat society as constituted by some non-social subject, as in traditional transcendental philosophy. It must be socially constituted, but at the same time its constitutors must be already social. The systems theoretical standpoint which Habermas wants to adopt must start precisely from this already constituted society in order to see its contradictory tendencies. Thus despite his recognition of the problem of the universal and the particular (the social and the individual), Habermas wants to retain both.[25] Two further points raised by Habermas' colleagues at Starnberg need be mentioned here. U. Rödel points out that this systems theoretical standpoint is ultimately that of the capitalist; it ignores the fact that the function of political intervention by the state is not simply arbitrary, but rather the result of class struggle.[26] In the same vein, Claus Offe asserts that a systems theoretical analysis is useful for seeing the problems of the capitalist state, but *from its point of view.* Moreover, in an essay which attempts to demonstrate the class nature of late capitalism, Offe finds himself forced to opt for an actionism which asserts that 'Revolutionary theory can thus always be constructed only as the self-explanation of a practical movement that is already in process.'[27] Habermas reacts vehemently to this assertion at the close of *Legitimation Problems.* If praxis can only be justified after the fact, then, he says, nothing differentiates one praxis from any other, including that of the fascists. Habermas claims to have shown that the reconstruction of norms of omission, of selection and latency within the functioning of late capitalism provides reasons for asserting the class nature of that society; and that his notion of the universalisability of interests provides the justification of radical praxis. In order for this to be shown, however, we must return to his theory of evolution. It is this theory that will have to explain the central position given to legitimation crises and account for the systematic ambiguity that we have seen between the levels of the universal and the particular, the social and the individual. (Anticipating: it will also have to account for the political as well — a task that is implicit throughout Habermas' work, but in fact never articulated.)

III Historical Materialism and Theory of Evolution

Habermas suggests that Luhmann's systems theoretical strategy provides a 'paradigm'[28] for the analysis of *one* dimension of the problem of social evolution; but the two other dimensions in the structure of the species' self-reproduction need to be treated independently of this paradigm. We saw that the organisational principles of human society are articulated in the dimensions of: the productive forces, which through science and technology continually extend the boundaries of the available world; organisational forms of human societal interaction, which govern the self-maintenance of the given society; and emancipatory learning, which is concretised in the form of the critique of ideologies and the demand for rational legitimation. According to Habermas' reading (which Luhmann, in replying, rejects, not entirely convincingly), Luhmann's interpretation makes the second dimension, organisation, the central determinant of the evolution of society. Insofar as a system maintains itself, it does so by increasing its internal complexity, and hence, steering capacity, while decreasing the complexity of its environment. The most efficient form of increased internal complexity is the differentiation of sub-systems which can take over the burden from society. Social evolution is seen in the degree to which the administrative system is differentiated from, and able to control, the society. Systems theory, as a method of administration, is thus a theory which is also a practice — but an ideological one, says Habermas. Leaving aside the theoretical problems of systems theory,[29] and the reduction of the three components of human social reproduction into one, Luhmann's position omits the role of legitimation, *the truth-relatedness of practical activity* which for Habermas is crucial to any critical social theory. Luhmann's notion of 'legitimation through procedure' (the title of one of his books), ultimately returns to a decisionism whose only foundation is its self-consistent functionality, i.e., it floats above the society and individuals it is supposed to steer.

Habermas rejects Luhmann's reduction of social relations to one level which can then be studied in its functionality. Consistent with his revised Historical Materialism, he wants a differentiated model of society in which each level corresponds to a specific type of truth claim. Instrumental activity, social interaction and human emancipation require different meta-theoretical frameworks; if they are reduced to one, the possibility of human individuation and praxis are lost, the social cement cracks. In his earlier work, Habermas saw History as the horizon which constitutes the boundary within which praxis moves. In Baier's summary.

> History is not a theme for dialectical sociology for its own sake, but as a condition of praxis, to be understood as a hermeneutic philosophy of History from a practical standpoint . . . in order to formulate a theory of how praxis is possible by the mediation of History.[30]

In *Erkenntnis und Interesse* (1968), Habermas connected the three forms of truth-oriented activity to three cognitive interests, and attempted to show epistemologically the need for and limits of each. The thrust of that book was to show that insofar as these cognitive interests are socially embedded, it is social theory which provides the final foundation for epistemology. This concretised the mediation by History (whose capitalisation here indicates its indefinite referent); and the suggestion that the grounds of theory must be at once its truth-reference *and* a social theory point to the need for a theory of social evolution which will enable social theory to avoid the contingent embeddedness in brute factuality. To avoid the relativism and the contingency of a merely social referent (which could change at any time), and to avoid the a-historicality of a fixed notion of truth outside the sphere of human relations, Habermas had to move beyond the position of *Erkenntnis und Interesse* where the question of the validity of social norms and the truth of metatheoretical statements is concerned.[31]

The development of a theory of evolution is not a substitute for a theory of History, let alone for a concrete analysis. A first reading of Habermas' preliminary sketch of social evolution in *Legitimation Problems*[32] can be misleading; there is the tendency to view this as an ontologisation which covers over the sources and forms of the transition between the evolutionary levels. But the point here is that the theory of social evolution is necessary precisely *to make possible* a human social praxis which is *not contingent* but rather truth-oriented and open to discursive questioning. If there were no such theory, human history could not be written or *theorised*, for it would only be random events with no claim to truth or normativity and no place for the actors to confront themselves and their tradition in a dialogue which asks for reasons. That a critical theory of social evolution which is oriented towards the questions of normativity and truth is possible would itself have to be understood as a conquest of human evolution, suggests Habermas; it would be the theoretical equivalent of Engels' 'leap from necessity to freedom'. At the same time, he warns, one should not confuse the particular knowledge with the conditions of its universalisation, individual freedom with its social form, any more than one can immediately transfer the liberating process of psychoanalysis to the social plane.[33] That is, Habermas again recognises the problem of the universal and the particular.

Albrecht Wellmer suggests that the theory Habermas needs would be 'the phantastic demand to develop a materialist version of [Hegel's] "Phenomenology of Mind".'[34] This seems to me misleading. Hegel's *Phenomenology* deals with *appearing* knowledge, and is to the last contingent. What is demanded would be more like the *Logic*, of which Hegel says in the Foreword to the Second Edition:

In that it deals with the thought determinations which over all penetrate our mind in an instinct-like and unconscious manner, and themselves remain unattended to because they enter into language as well, the science of logic will be the reconstruction of those determinations which are separated out by reflexion and fixed by it as subjective external forms in their matter and content.[35]

Hegel is reacting in these passages to a position which he says is concerned 'only with the correctness of knowledge, not with its truth',[36] i.e., a position like that of his own *Phenomenology*. This is essential to the present stage of Habermas' work, namely: its insistence on Truth as that which is fundamental to, and erroneously neglected by, social theory.

In recent re-evaluations of *Theorie und Praxis* and *Erkenntnis und Interesse*, Habermas has attempted to indicate the place of the theory of evolution within his earlier work. He establishes a categorial distinction between: constitution and validity; categorial meaning and discursive verification; life-related communication and discourse; praxis and theory. In each pair of categories, the first refers to the tasks of a critical theory while the second belongs to the domain of a theory of social evolution. The first refers to the constitution of a life-world; it makes up the categorial meanings which provide the content of a statement. The second refers to the truth claim constituted by the intersubjective element in the performative aspect of the speech act. That such-and-such is the case, and that such-and-such is true are two different types of claim. The first can be immediately verified once we agree on the objective frame of reference or measurement (the cognitive interests which constitute the domain of such-and-such); the second demands an intersubjective and mediate verification through the discourse of all potential participants — that is, it must be universalisable in the sense that we have already discussed. The first claim, that such-and-such is the case, is not. The first type of claim is particular and is bound to a monological action context; the second concerns the reconstruction of universal and anonymous systems of rules within the context of a discourse removed from practical imperatives. Each of these represents a form of self-reflexion, but the first is modelled on the (a-symmetrical) relation of analyst/analysand, which is particular, where the second is the reconstruction of 'know-how', the intuitive rules that all must follow. The self-reflexion achieved by the former will therefore have practical consequences, whereas the universality of the latter promises only the transcendental foundation of species-activity. This reconstruction is to be the sought after theory of evolution, *itself grounded by and grounding Habermas' 'Universal Pragmatics'*.

In the same context, Habermas has recently redefined his

notion of cognitive interests. This is useful, since it demonstrates clearly that he is not moving in a circle or drawing
distinctions without a difference. He suggests that the mediation of the two types of theoretical self-reflection (i.e.,
critical theory and reconstruction as particular and universal) is
found in the notion of interest, which is their 'latent nexus'.[37]
The cognitive interests are neither ideology-critical, nor based in
a psychology or sociology of knowledge: 'they are invariant.'[38]
Moreover, despite some misleading formulations, he insists that
they cannot be directly deduced from the imperatives of
life-praxis, for that would make them contingent.[39] Rather,
they are said to be 'deeply rooted anthropological' forms
against which we 'collide'.[40] This does not, however, imply a
naturalism, as Theunissen and Rohrmoser have argued. Though
Habermas does admit that he is unclear as to whether these
interests are 'transcendental' in a strict sense, or 'empirical', i.e.,
based on a theory of social evolution which demands the
incorporation of, among other things, the still unclear theories
of ethology. Even in the latter case, however, they would not
have the contingency which would vitiate their validity-claims
because the question of contingency and necessity makes no
sense when it is applied to the species as a whole.[41] The same
notion is formulated two years later, in the Postscript to
Erkenntnis und Interesse:[42]

As long as cognitive interests can be identified and analysed
through reflexion upon the logic of inquiry in the natural and
cultural sciences, they can legitimately claim a transcendental
status. They assume an 'empirical' status as soon as they are
being analyzed as the result of natural history — analyzed,
that is, in terms of a cognitive anthropology, as it were. I put
'empirical' in quotation marks, for a theory of evolution
which is expected to explain historically the emergent
characteristics of a socio-cultural form of life (in other words,
the constituent elements of social systems) cannot itself be
developed within the transcendental framework of objectiv-
ating science.

The ability to treat the 'empirical' is crucial to Habermas'
reconstruction of Historical Materialism. The theory of evolution will be able to do so only if its reconstruction of the
universal and anonymous rule systems can articulate that 'latent
nexus' which binds it to an action-oriented critical theory.
Habermas sees the key element in the fact that the roots of the
cognitive interests 'result from the imperatives of the socio-

cultural life form bound up with work and language'.[43] This
assertion does not contradict his insistence that the interests are
not derived from the imperatives of life praxis; it coincides with
the 'anthropological' and 'species' character he is stressing
insofar as *homo sapiens* is *at once* a working *and* a speaking
animal. The reformulated Historical Materialism is thus based
on cognitive interests which are *at the same time* what is to be
reconstructed in its evolutionary universality *and* what in its
particularity makes possible the situated critical theory that is
ultimately grounded in them. The theory is thus doubly
reflexive in the sense demanded; the open problem at this point
is who is to be the 'addressees' to realise it.

The parallel of Habermas' project with Hegel's *Logic* does not
of course mean that both have the same conception of truth.
On the contrary, Habermas' discursive theory of truth based in
the consensus concerning validity, arising in a situation of
undistorted and equal speaking, makes the paradoxical claim
that the truth *both* exists as a universal (hence, is not
constituted but constitutive) and yet that it depends on the
particular individual subjects for its factual validity. For this to
be the case, it seems that if Habermas' theory is not to be
idealist in a caricatural sense, his theory of evolution must be
somehow *projective* in a sense that includes an 'empirical'
referent. Again, his own statements are unclear. Stressing the
importance of reflexive theory as reconstructive, he asserts that
'therefore the claim to be acting dialectically with insight is
senseless. It rests on a category mistake.'[44] But in the very next
paragraph, he suggests that indeed we can make a counterfactual assumption — of precisely the sort on which his reformulation of critical theory in *Legitimation Problems* is
based — and act in terms of it. This counterfactual assumption
and the action based on it would be a practical ideology
critique, stripping the blinders from the eyes of the participants.
If, in Albrecht Wellmer's phrase, 'The entirety of past history is
the history of distorted communication,'[45] it would follow that
undistorted communication in each of the evolutionary spheres
is the universal which founds the evolution of the species, *and*
that it is the task of the particulars to achieve what they must
always already posit in the forms of their practical life. Thus
Habermas concludes his political discussion in the new Introduction to *Theorie und Praxis*, 'in a process of enlightenment
there are only participants.'[46]

IV The Tasks of Philosophy and the Question of the Political

The theoretical ground of Habermas' position is the notion of truth or validity whose translation into a critical theory takes the form of legitimation. Both depend on language, whose theoretical articulation presupposes a situation of undistorted communication, which is always counterfactually assumed. This is to be the basis of Habermas' still to be worked out 'universal pragmatic' or 'praxeology'. To avoid misunderstanding, it must be stressed that language here will have to be analysed in the context of the 'empirical' theory of evolution. This means that where Luhmann's systems theoretical account of evolution made one element primary — the political steering system — Habermas argues for the priority of Truth — an independent category with an ontologically different status — as the foundation of all three evolutionary domains. Thereafter, the formulation of his argument is similar to Luhmann's. In the domain of the productive forces, truth results in the reduction of the complexity of external nature; in the domain of social interaction, it becomes the increasing differentiation of subsystems that guarantees to the individual a greater freedom and larger social possibilities for adaptation to a variety of roles; and in the domain of emancipatory learning, it permits that critique of ideologies which makes possible the continued learning process that maintains the flexibility of the other two aspects. Insofar as Habermas' notion of truth is articulated as the form of social discourse, emancipatory learning cannot be defined (as does Luhmann), in terms of system complexity, but rather as a function of ideology-critique and self-reflexive activity.[47] Thus it defines the goal of present political tasks and locates where the system of late capitalism's actual weaknesses must find their crucial manifestation. In other words, this concluding step to the argument justifies the structure of the entire theory, giving the *non-contingent* grounds that Habermas needed in order to escape the problems posed to empirical research into the structures of late capitalism. And it justifies the politics of enlightenment. We must now look at some of the implications and problems of this theoretical project.

One might ask with what justification Habermas lays claim to the heritage of the philosophical-anthropological notion of truth as interpreted within his model of undistorted communication. And from the 'Marxist' standpoint, it might also be asked why this claim to appropriate 'bourgeois' notions is so important. Habermas' paper, 'The Role of Philosophy in Marxism', presented in August 1973 at the meetings of the journal *Praxis* in Korcula, Yugoslavia, provides the first stages of an answer. He discusses three problem areas that affect philosophy: (1) the changed nature and role of bourgeois culture in late capitalism; (2) the domination of scientistic assumptions, and the reactions this sets off; and (3) the positive tasks of philosophy. In the first case, he points to the contradiction to which we have already made reference, namely: that the motivational kernel of culture is functionally altered and yet remains present as a dysfunctional element. The results are revolts by those who — whether youth, artists, or simply those raised in traditional moral patterns — cannot tolerate the cynicism of a Vietnam or Chile, urban-renewal-cum-removal, 'benign neglect', etc. Most, however, adopt the cynicism of scientism, sometimes mitigated by a form of 'analytic' philosophy. The reaction of philosophy to this takes three equally inadequate forms: (*a*) either a relativism, or what Habermas calls a 'complementary philosophy' (*Komplementär-philosophie*) which claims that although science is all-powerful, there are nonetheless 'existential' domains of particularity with which it cannot deal. This tendency, from Jaspers to Kola-kowski, reduces philosophy to a *Weltanschauung*, denying philosophy's vital claim to truth and universality. (*b*) There is the renewal of a Heideggerian 'ontology' which seeks to revive a tradition and ignores all that happened in between. The example of Heidegger's technology-critique indicates the dead-end to which this position leads. (*c*) There is the renewal of *diamat* in the Russian sense. While this view attempts to reflect the social totality, to orient action in terms of truth, it makes the fatal — idealistic — assumption that it *has* this truth, and ends by dogmatically fitting science to it. Rejecting these alternatives, Habermas poses three tasks for Marxist philosophy. It must develop a theory which uses the advances of the social and natural sciences without falling into their positivist tendency. It must defend reason as the demand for truth both in science and in the practical questions of life. And it must demystify the appearance of objectivity which the thought and institutions of late capitalism have assumed by showing their connectedness with the human project of seeking and creating the good, and hence true, life. That this may not sound like a revolutionary break with the past, Habermas admits: 'Whoever would eliminate philosophy sets aside an element of the bourgeois world whose heritage we cannot ignore without harming science itself'. More important are his concluding passages, which take up again the problem of the universal and the particular. As the unity of theoretical and practical reason, philosophy is the medium or universal in terms of which the identity of society and its members are formed without the risk of falling into particularistic identities. Philosophy, in a word, must be adequate to the tasks of reconstructive as well as critical social theory.

Social theory based on (discursive) truth standards is intended first of all to be a reconstruction, a self-reflection which has no practical consequences other than enlightenment or clarity concerning that which we already are and do. This latter, however, is the foundation of a critical self-reflection on the *particular* form in which we live and act; mediated by the anthropological cognitive interests, it is the basis of a critical theory. In Habermas' work it seems to function in three, inadequately differentiated senses. (1) Because of its universal character it is a critique of all particular structures.[48] (2) Its universal structure can be interpreted as a theory along the lines of psychoanalysis. As a reconstruction, the social theory functions like the Freudian meta-psychology. This means that it is used to set off the a-symmetrical discourse between the theorist-as-already-knowing-and-obliged-to-teach, and the social persons whose communicative relations are socially prevented from being what in fact they as members of the species indeed are. Like psychoanalysis, the acknowledgement of the validity of the theory would take place in the context of open discussion by those whose life situation it attempts to explain.[49] (3) Finally, it could be interpreted as the task of 'all as individuals', as Marx phrased it in the 'Critique of Hegel's Philosophy of the State'. That is, the reconstruction of the evolutionary history of the species can be seen as depending finally on the individual members of that species for its realization. Here, however, the problem of the universal and the particular again emerges. To try to solve this by the notion of 'universalisable' interests, as Habermas does, seems to be a return to a Humean notion of the universal. The interests said to be 'universalisable' are not the cognitive interests which ground the theory as reconstruction separated from the life context; the interests dealt with here are those of you and me, and they are bound to the particularity of our situations. Unless, of course, a claim such as Marx's for the proletariat could be established!

Does the situating of social theory within a universal, non-contingent history of the species help solve the problem? This is Habermas' proposal. It would give non-contingent grounds for the expectation that the ideology-critical, enlightenment-oriented activity of the theorist would have political results. But why should this be the case? Habermas argues through a *via negativa* when he confronts the criticisms of his former assistant, O. Negt: that is, he attempts to show that his is the only option available.

In his defence against the criticisms of Negt, whose position begins from similar premises,[50] Habermas puts himself in the Enlightenment tradition. He poses the question of the organisation which institutionalises the process of continual critical self- and social-reflexion. With the development of the Communist party type of organisation, he sees a new step in the 'history of the species', where the naturally emerging discursive problem solving methods become specifically reflexive:

> With this type of organization something very remarkable is institutionalized: outwards, against the class enemy, strategic activity and political struggle; inwards, in relation to the mass of wage laborers, organization of enlightenment, discursive initiation of processes of self-reflexion. The vanguard of the proletariat must master both: the critique of the weapons and the weapon of the critique.[51]

The party organisation would be the mediator between the self-reflexion of the proletariat and the practical political struggle. Interestingly, Habermas says nothing here about why Marx thought it was the proletariat and not some other class, stratum — or the species in general — that was *capable* of this form of self-reflection. He says only that those who have the power want to keep it by acting strategically and not discursively, in their particular interest and not in the universalisable manner of rational theory. Hence, they are in a situation where distorted communication would not permit them, even if they subjectively wanted it, an insight into the universal interests. This is Habermas' reinterpretation of Lukács' argument for the universality of the proletariat, but without the socio-economic underpinning. To make his case stick, Habermas would need a theory explaining the 'institutionalisation' to which the above passage makes reference.

Habermas further views the revolutionary organisation as having three *distinct* tasks: the development of theories; the organisation of enlightenment in which the theories are used and tested as to their ability to start a process of reflection in given groups; and the choice of strategy and tactics in the political struggle. Giving these roles to only one institution, the Party, has blurred the necessary distinctions among them. Habermas illustrates his point through a critique of Lukács' position in *History and Class Consciousness*, and concludes:

The only advantage of which Marx could legitimately have assured a proletariat acting in solidarity would have been this: that only a class which constitutes itself as such with the aid of a true critique is in a position to clarify in practical discourses how one should act rationally in the political sphere . . .[52]

To do more than this is to subordinate the class *and* theory to the Party. In such a case, theory is not truth-oriented at all, for since the party is a unity, it is not capable of interaction among many independent opinions in free discourse. A practice in which the Party becomes the independent bearer of truth initiates actions for the masses who are then supposed to learn *post hoc* that their interests coincide with those of the enlightened Party. This, however, violates the premise that individuals are capable of learning freely and together how their own particular interests relate to one another and to the universalisable interests. Finally, such a strategy, which is 'freed' from the need for self-reflection by the participants, ultimately results in a kind of Stalinism, for which theory becomes, in Negt's apt phrase, a 'science of legitimation'.[53] Translated with reference to the contemporary practice of the student movement that Negt defends with its ideas of provocation and exemplary action to uncover the hidden repression beneath the smooth surface of the status quo, Habermas' critique is that this uses people without giving them the chance to build a discursive opinion about their situation.[54]

Habermas' criticisms of the (Leninist) Party-form of political activity are generally well-taken; but his own position remains fastened to an individualism which seems to suggest that only face-to-face interaction can institute the process of social change. He recognises the need for institutionalising this form of discursive confrontation, for example in the following:

I do not want to hold that a sufficient realization of the demands that we must place on discourse is *a priori* impossible. The limitations which we have considered can either be compensated through institutional arrangements or at least neutralized in their effects on the declared goal through an equal division of the chance of excercising speech acts.[55]

But at the same time, as we saw in his disagreement with Offe's 'actionism', and as he repeats in the debate with Negt, Habermas admits that there are situations in which we *must* act.

Indeed, the contemporary phenomenon which seems to have driven him to the reflections we have been examining is the revolt of those strata of society who have begun the demand for freedom *now*. How does Habermas' philosophically inspired politics of enlightenment apply to this situation? What is *political* activity for this type of *social* theory?

V   The Political: Action or Institution?

Late capitalism differs from liberal capitalism particularly in the expanded role of the state, whose effect is to politicise areas of life which heretofore were the province of private interaction. Whether it is wages, child-rearing, health care or urban policy, state action eliminates the appearance of naturalness from decisions; it thus creates a demand or need on the part of those affected to participate (or at least to think they are participating!). Habermas' approach is based on the work of Claus Offe, who combines Marxist political sympathies with a systems theoretical analysis of the nature and function of the state. The following is typical of Offe's procedure when trying to establish the class nature of the present state:

> In the following reflections, the attempt is undertaken (1) to conceptualise the domination organised in the state as a selective, event-producing system of rules, as a 'process of sorting out'. Then we must (2) deduce the kind of selectivity which would demonstrate the class character of the domination by the state: which *specific* selections must a state apparatus perform in order to function as a capitalist state? Finally, (3) the methodological problems which appear in the *empirical determination* of selectivity must be studied: by what empirically demonstrable criteria can the presence and effectiveness of the specific selectivity by means of which a structural complementarity between state activity and the dominant class interests come into being be demonstrated.[56]

As in the case of Luhmann, the state becomes a 'sub-system' *of society* to which specific complexity-reducing functions are delegated. Thus, Offe insists that the state must be called the 'state apparatus' in order to avoid the implication that it could function as an independent subject.[57] This is consistent with the idea of a state *in* capitalist society (Miliband). On this view, then, the political becomes whatever 'is made into an object of administrative activity'.[58]

Once again, the problem with the systems theoretical approach is that it *reduces* all phenomena to one level: society. A counter-example, Hegel's *Philosophy of Right*, points to a different attitude toward the political. In his discussion of 'civil society', Hegel devotes a long section[59] to what he calls 'The Police and the Corporations'. Neither term should be understood in its contemporary meaning. The function of these two institutions of *civil society* in Hegel's analysis is that of the welfare state of today! With this discussion, Hegel brings to a close the analysis of civil society, the sphere of atomistic particularity, and leads into that of the state proper, i.e., the sphere of the political, or the universal as concrete. Though Marx criticised at length the hypostatisation he found in Hegel's discussion of the state, it is also important to see that, particularly in his own concrete analyses such as the *Eighteenth Brumaire*, Marx recognised the existence of a sphere of the political which was *not* the same as the 'state apparatus' destined for destruction. It was precisely this, and not the day-to-day *administrative* role of the state apparatus, that Marx dealt with in his analyses of the Paris Commune as well. Marx's *political* analyses are remarkable for the recognition that politics is something *more and other* than economics or the control of state administration. Thus, while systems theoretical analysis may be empirically adequate to certain tasks, as Offe himself admits, it indicates only the structural problems. It does not itself point beyond them. Habermas realises that a critical theory must do this.

The problem is that the political must be concretely universal — or at least, in Habermas' terms, universalisable — in relation to the sphere of individual and social particularity. It is for this reason that Habermas (and Offe) see the question of *legitimation* as the crucial point for an analysis of late capitalism. There is no need to repeat how Habermas confronts the problem of the constitution of a universal, which itself must pre-exist in order for the individuals together to constitute it. The structure of his argument rests on the possibility of establishing a theory of evolution of the sort he proposes, and is a reply to an objection by B. Willms.[60] Willms argues that Habermas is, in the final analysis, a 'bourgeois' thinker who has not understood the dialectic of universal and particular. Habermas' subjects are said to be those of the rising bourgeoisie confronting what Marx referred to as the feudal 'democracy of unfreedom' with the demand for freedom of opinion and the right to constitute society as a universal that emerges from their own particular needs (e.g., the social contract, bourgeois legal theory, etc.). Moreover, Habermas' notion of discourse as the solution to problems of truth and validity is said to be modelled precisely on the market principle of that bourgeois society. The suggestiveness of these criticisms is undermined not only by Habermas' theoretical arguments with which we have already dealt; it is also a misunderstanding of Habermas' notion of an ideology-critical reappropriation of 'bourgeois' ideas to confuse form and content as Willms does. The discussion of the 'End of the Individual' in *Legitimation Problems*, to which reference has already been made, is an attempt to retrieve what is essential in 'bourgeois individualism' through a critique of both those theories that announce the disappearance of this bourgeois individualism on the one hand, and those which assert its surface presence in order to pander to it as a consumer on the other. The question is not that of opting for the individual *qua* atomised particular, as Willms seems to suggest, but of dealing with the *content* of the individual. Habermas realises that he can do so only by reference to the universal, i.e., in the last analysis the quality of the *political* that constitutes the individual precisely in her/his act of constituting it.

The problem is to concretise the universality of the political. This poses the further problem of the revolutionary subject and the form of its institutions. Willms has seen both problems, but his suggestions are often confused. He insists that Habermas is unable to account for positive institutional forms because of his fundamental distinction between work and interaction and their respective forms of rationality. Institutions would have to be forms of alienation in which the individual interactions would be subordinated to a form of purposive-rationality. As already cited, Habermas understands this distinction as a *meta-theoretical* statement, not a concrete distinction in actual life-praxis. As such, Habermas would have to accept institutionalisation in both the work and interaction aspects of social evolution. Willms suggests that positive institutional forms demand a unitary conception of rationality, such as in the Hegelian or Marxian theories. While Habermas rejects this in its concrete form, he does not deny the validity of the theory. When Willms suggests that the Marxian party is a positive institution, it is difficult to see what he means — unless it is Habermas' description cited above, to whose problems we have already pointed. Habermas argues that only in terms of the *meta-theoretical* distinctions he has offered is it possible to develop an *affirmative* theory of political institutions as a constitutive universal constituted by the particular subjects. To describe Habermas' position as nominalist-individualist, *a priori* rejecting institutions as a form of alienation, is not adequate. Whether, in the end, Habermas' position is adequate to the task is another question (to which we will return); in any event, he does see the problem.

More serious is Willms' suggestion that Habermas' use of language as the fundamental paradigm for the realised relation of universal and particular implies a form of 'systematic depoliticisation' because its over-general form does not permit any differentiated content. Together with Willms' objection to Habermas' 'bourgeois' individualistic subject, this points to the problem that Habermas' theory is so formally undifferentiated that it cannot avoid precisely the problems to which bourgeois political theory and practice have fallen victim. The 'linguistic universal', or even its critical theoretical translation into an 'ideal speech situation' does not seem to provide grounds for institutional differentiation. Habermas speaks of the positive institutional achievements, which he explains from his theoretical standpoint:

In social evolution such institutionalizations of regionally specific partial discourses show conquests rich in results which must be explained by a theory of social development ... Dramatic examples are the institutionalization of discourses in which the claim to validity of mythic and religious interpretations of the world can be systematically put into question and checked: we understand this as the beginning of philosophy in classical Athens. Further, the institutionalization of discourse in which the validity claims of professionally inherited, technically useful profane knowledge can be systematically put into question and checked: we understand this as the beginning of the modern empirical sciences, of course with precedents in Antiquity and the end of the Middle Ages. Finally, the institutionalization of discourses in which the claims to validity of practical questions and political decisions *should* be continually put into question and checked: this in England of the 19th century, then on the continent and in the USA, with precedents in the northern Italian cities of the Renaissance, led to the birth of a bourgeois public and with it the representative form of government — bourgeois democracy. These are very rough examples, and certainly only examples. Today the traditional models of socialization which had been previously anchored naturally in the cultural tradition have been set free by the psychologization of child-rearing and the educational-politics of curriculum planning, and through a process of 'scientificization' have been made accessible to general practical discourse. Similar is the case of literature and the production of art: the 'affirmative' bourgeois culture, separated from life-practice and affirming the transcendence of the beautiful is in a process of dissolution.[61]

The notion of 'institutionalization' here is at once stretched to the point of distortion and limited to a specific and specifically vague form. Institutions seem on the one hand to be a general achievement of culture which become part of the 'motivation' system, while on the other hand, they are limited to forms of collective individual behaviour expressed through discursive questioning. Yet, when we ordinarily talk of institutional questions, we refer to such things as the constitutional division of powers, the domain of private and public law, the family, forms of corporate enterprise, etc. A theory like Hegel's can account for the relations between these different areas so that each belongs to a specific ontological region. The result is that the individual who is a member of a family is therefore not *only* defined by her/his being a member of a family. Habermas' illustration of the universality of the 'ideal speech situation' does not seem to allow such a differentiation. He would no doubt reply that turning to language is the recognition of a *languaging-situation*, and that the ideal speech situation is not simply a relation of pure free spirits but that of physical human beings in a complex world. He rejects a purely hermeneutic analysis of the Gadamerian sort, but only because it does not critically demystify the distorted and distorting structures of the tradition which is constitutive of individuality; and his proposal is still only that of the ideal speech situation and the assertion that 'The enlightenment, which effectuates a radical *Verstehen*, is always political.'[62]

The problem of institutions is linked with that of the revolutionary subject. This latter is raised, but left vague, by Willms. Habermas' theory of evolution which gives him the theoretical basis for his description of the politics of enlightenment as well as for the empirical centrality of legitimation crises, treats the *evolution of the species*. He could, of course, refer to Marx, for whom 'species life' was the goal of revolutionary action which in a specific historical period is anchored in the proletariat as revolutionary subject acting in the name of universalisable interests. However, institutions are also a problem in Marx: not only those to be introduced after the successful revolution, but even those responsible for the revolution. The history of the transmutations of the Communist party-form both as member and opponent of its own society bears this out. Nonetheless, one can begin to discuss specifically proletarian forms of organisation, as distinct from those of other sectors of society,[63] but not organisations or institutions of the entire species. We need a principle of differentiation and articulation. Habermas recognises and analyses a variety of diverse sectorial struggles, from students to housewives, users of public transportation to victims of urban removal, traditional workers to frustrated engineers. For all, the model of the enlightenment is proposed as a solution.[64] But the solution is still an individual *act* despite the rejection of Offe's and Negt's actionism. The distinction between a reconstructive and a critical theory, developed in the form of a 'universal pragmatics' might take us further.

The difficulty with Habermas' theory rests in his inability to demonstrate the articulation of his universal discourse in institutional structures, and in his option for a systems theoretical analysis. In both cases, the specific *difference*, the sense that makes the political, is lost. Habermas makes a virtue of necessity by repeatedly insisting on the limits of theory, the need for empirical study and (sometimes) for non-theoretically grounded action. For example:

> Against many sectarian efforts, it should be pointed out today that in late capitalism the change of the structures of the general educational system is possibly more important for the organisation of enlightenment that fruitless cadre school-ing or the building of powerless parties. I mean by this only that: these are empirical questions which should not be prejudged.[65]

My point is not that a theory must at every moment tell us what to do. But theory ought *at least* to be able to discuss more than the merry-go-round of continual enlightenment. The chances of organisational forms like workers' councils, communes or parties are more than empirical questions. They are theoretical *and* historical problems; ultimately both of these dimensions are lost to the systems theoretical approach, despite Habermas' attempts to salvage it with the addition of a universal pragmatic based on his communication theory of society.

Habermas' theory is ultimately unsatisfactory for the para-doxical reason that he does not consistently develop those theoretical insights that first impelled him to elaborate his theory. He has seen the crucial problem of the universal and the particular as central to a political theory, and articulated it theoretically and empirically in his demonstration of the centrality of the legitimation problem. He recognised the need for a politics that goes beyond middle-class monotony as well as self-proclaimed left-wing monological practice. Most importantly, he has demonstrated that questions of truth and validity cannot be excluded from social and political theory. The theorising of political praxis as enlightenment is a necessary component, but only a component, of the response to the *structures* of late capitalism. Unless the undifferentiated universal of an ideal speech situation can be concretised through the application of a theory of evolution, Habermas' work will remain only as a challenge. That theory of evolution, however, will have to incorporate a reconsideration of the ontological premises inherited by Habermas' critical theory if it is to account for the concrete relations of individual and institution. Habermas' stress on a theory that leaves room for, and demands, empirical verification makes one eagerly await the further development of his work.

7 The Rationality of the Dialectic: Jean-Paul Sartre

The rupture that was May 1968 threw into question not only the functional machine of modernising French capitalism; the spontaneous creativity that it revealed was also so much sand in the smoothly oiled machinery of orthodox Communist practice and Marxist theory. Neither the Gaullist victory at the polls in June, nor the later near-success of the Socialist-Communist electoral challenge can deceive anyone: the spectre of May has replaced that 'spectre of communism' that Marx depicted in the *Communist Manifesto*. The New Left spectre has not achieved an institutional identity, and this makes it all the more dangerous to the established order, while at the same time preserving its explosive force. The discovery and self-discovery of May was in fact a rediscovery of that unfinished work and elemental hope that Ernst Bloch shows to be not just the driving force, but as well the *arché* and *logos* of revolution. If we use an historical analogy, it could be suggested that the bourgeois revolutions, followed by bitter proletarian struggles, achieved but one of the three emblems that adorned the banners of 1789 — equality; and that May 1968 incarnated the forms of liberty and fraternity that remain to be realised. This was expressed most emphatically in Cohn-Bendit's iconoclastic: 'Tu fais la révolution pour toi', and in the explicit stress on the role of pleasure and desire in the festive atmosphere of fraternisation and communality that made the revolt into a positive affirmation. Underground, surfacing only in occasional and punctual actions, the spectre of May, like that 'old mole' whose image captured the imagination of poets and philosophers alike, is digging away and undermining the structure of bureaucratised capitalist daily life.

The relation of the new spectre and the old remains to be established. One model that appears useful in seeking this articulation is Jean-Paul Sartre's attempt to articulate the relation of his existentialism to Marxist theory and Communist practice. On the one hand, the pseudonymous Epistemon's *Ces idées qui ont ébranlé la France* is certainly correct in pointing out that Sartre's *Critique de la raison dialectique* provides an abstract, but accurate, account of the structure of action followed during May. On the other hand, Sartre himself has insisted that it was only after May that he was able to see clearly how those ideas of freedom and morality expressed in his early work could find their political articulation.[1] Despite the eclipse of Sartre's influence in France (where, for example, the *Critique* is hardly discussed, and the three volumes on Flaubert, *L'Idiot de la famille*, seem to have found few readers), his existential phenomenology and his gifted pen make him the representative of a temptation that demands analysis. His quixotic personality adds to his appeal. He knows that his name, not himself, is an institution which can be used; and he lends it freely — signing appeals, writing prefaces, presiding over the Russell Tribunal, taking the direction of the forbidden Maoist newspaper or demanding to visit Andreas Baader in his West German incarceration, for example. And the person who preserves himself while lending his name has the gift of analysing himself as a typical nobody living in the banal everyday, universalising thereby in his phenomenological vignettes or his literature an Everyman as existential hero.

The Sartrean position is a particular kind of temptation, for the intellectual. There is a certain self-deprecation and even anti-intellectualism in Sartre's highly conceptual analyses which reflect the frustrations of the thinker who would see his ideas translated into action. At first, one applauds Sartre's unstinting support for the Good Cause, agreeing when he asserts, for example:

> But if I consider the entirety of the conditions that are necessary for man to be, I tell myself that the only thing to do is to underline, to show the value of and to support with all my power that which, in particular social and political situations, can bring about a society of free men. If one does not do that, one accepts that man is nothing but shit.[2]

But this minimisation of the task of the intellectual goes against precisely what Sartre claims to have learned from May: that the 'old intellectual' style, which consisted in opposing the universal claims of Man to the injustice of particular situations, must be replaced. The 'new intellectual' in whom Sartre says he recognises the demands of his earlier philosophy is part and parcel of the ongoing political movement; her/his engagement in the movement fulfills what Sartre proposed in *Being and Nothingness*: 'there is only the point of view of *engaged* knowledge. That is to say that knowledge and action are only two abstract moments of an original and concrete relation.'[3] No more than the earlier existentialist, the new intellectual should not find her/himself in the position of only following the ongoing movement, ratifying the events which have already begun. The pathos of Sartre's self-understanding, and the reality of his political practice — not simply the already mentioned cases of name-lending, but also others, which are more objectionable, particularly his support for the Communist Party in the 1950s — put into question the fundamentals of his position.

Though the moral theory which was to accompany the existential ontology of *Being and Nothingness* was never published, Sartre now finds that the existence of a New Left practice permits his return to that project. Taking a concrete act of revolt — a worker refusing to accept the racist remarks of his foreman — Sartre argues that 'we are dealing here with freedom, because ... there is no particular situation which by itself would suffice to determine a revolt.'[4] The rupture with the chain of everyday acceptance and passivity — the worker has surely been treated in a racist manner before — implies that a new element has intervened, beyond the facts and beyond falsely inculcated social values. This new element, freedom, entails the invention of true values; the act of revolt is a moral affirmation. Generalising to other revolts, for example those of students against authority, or workers against bureaucracy, Sartre insists:

The philosopher who would express in words the nature of that freedom would permit them to become more profoundly conscious of their situation. From such a position, the maoists [who, for Sartre, at least at that time, represent the New Left] have come to pose anew the question of morality; or rather, no, they haven't posed it, they undertake practical actions which always have a relation to morality. It will be the task of the philosopher of the maoist society to define morality in terms of freedom.[5]

But there are two distinct positions in this passage: the philosopher who expresses in words what people are doing; and the activists whose practice creates the situation in which the philosopher can recognise the free, moral task. Sartre's Maoist interlocutor here, Pierre Victor, picks up this problem at two different points. 'What still bothers me in your position, Sartre, is that freedom is the same at the beginning and at the end.'[6] Sartre's weak reply is left lying, to be picked up again later when Victor insists that, in practice, there must be a development and articulation of the forms of freedom. Yet, Sartre's reply confirms the earlier objection: 'one is free or one is not free.'[7] Sartre's freedom has no depth, no tradition, no ability to reflect on itself and to learn.

The appeal of Sartre's theory is that it seems to give each of us a specific task, one that we can each accomplish on our own while at the same time furthering the revolution. He envisages revolution 'not as a movement for the overthrow of one power by another', but rather as 'a long movement of liberation from power'.[8] He hammers away mercilessly at the Communist Party as an institutional form which stifles revolution:

> An institution is a demand which addresses itself to abstract and atomized individuals whereas a true *praxis* can only exist in concrete assemblies. If a revolutionary party must exist today, it should have the least possible ressemblance to an institution, and it should contest all institutionality — outside itself, but first of all within itself. What must be developed in people is not the respect for a supposed revolutionary *order*, but rather the spirit of revolt against all order.[9]

The goal is a society consisting of only fully human and open encounters. But whereas the ontology of *Being and Nothingness* could only pose this as the goal of authenticity, Sartre now thinks he sees the path to its concretion:

> In order that a true social concord be established, a man must exist entirely for his neighbor, who must exist entirely for him. This is not realizable today, but I think that it will be realizable when the change in economic, cultural and affective relations between men will have been accomplished, first of all by the suppression of material scarcity which is, in my opinion — as I showed in the *Critique de la raison dialectique* — the basis of all the past and present antagonisms between men.[10]

Sartre's vacillation here should be noted. The elimination of scarcity — whose concrete definition, we shall see, is itself a problem — is not a task for our freedom, at least not until that freedom is situated. Once it is situated, however, it is also limited and hence dependent. Freedom then consists in support- ing the Good Cause. But how is one to know what in fact is the Good Cause? A social theory which accounts for the structures of freedom — and of unfreedom, of alienation — is necessary.[11] Given Sartre's insistence on the engagement of the knowing subject, this theory will have to be, in Habermas' terms, *at once* a reconstructive and a critical theory. Is this possible? Can the moral theory of freedom be combined with a social theory such that political practice is explained? Will Sartre be providing a political theory that is based in morality, and serving to explain a moral theory based in politics, as in orthodox Marxism?

I   The Necessity of a Critique of Dialectical Reason

The title of Sartre's systematic social theory suggests its multiple goals, and points to the kind of theory offered. Sartre offers a running criticism of what has passed for dialectical Reason in the 'Marxist-Leninist' tradition. A major negative ground for that criticism comes from the delimitation of the boundaries of the domain of validity of dialectical Reason. The positive ground and theoretical contribution is an ontological presentation of the conditions of the possibility of dialectical Reason itself. The parallel with Kant's task is obvious,[12] and Sartre plays still another register when he suggests that his theory is a 'Prolegomenon to any future Anthropology' (p. 153).[13] From here it is but a step to the particular 'existential- ist' problematic of *Being and Nothingness*, which Sartre is reclaiming here within the context of a critical confrontation with and refounding of Marxism. He does not renounce his past, but recognises its limits: existentialism is only an 'ideology' within Marxism, which in turn is 'the philosophy of our time' (p. 29). As long as capitalism remains, Marxism cannot be surpassed — a peculiar assertion from the philosophy of free- dom, whose explanation will show the fundamental philosophi- cal dualism with which Sartre is working.

Sartre's encounter with Marxism in theory and in practice has been marked by skirmishes, friendly reunions, misunderstand- ings and verbal violence. From the 1946 polemic 'Materialism and Revolution' to the founding of the RDR as a Third Force in post-war politics; to the amicable reunion during the Korean War and the series of articles on 'The Communists and the Peace' (which cost him the friendship of Merleau-Ponty); to a new split over the Hungarian invasion and the Polish liberalisation of 1956 (the first part of the *Critique* was written for a Polish journal in 1957); and finally to a 'new leftist' opposition to France's colonial war in Algeria, to which the *Critique* forms the theoretical pendant.

For all his inconsistencies, Sartre has nonetheless been remarkably persistent in the pursuit that led him to the *Critique*. Three problems from *Being and Nothingness* plagued him: (1) the problem of the 'we-subject'. In the 1943 book, Sartre can deal with the 'we-object' — i.e., several discrete individuals who are recognised by an Other as a unity even though they are not acting in concert — but cannot explain how there can exist a plurality of social subjects harmoniously conjoined, since each *pour-soi* (subject) can only objectify (i.e., negate) the being of every other *pour-soi*, and therefore remains caught in a world of its own reifications. (2) The problem of matter. The unforgettable descriptions of *Nausea* as well as the analysis of *Being and Nothingness* point to matter as something 'opaque' or 'massive' which interferes with the transparency of the *pour-soi*. Matter is sheer facticity to be manipulated and used by the negating activity of the *pour-soi*. It plays no positive role as a mediator between the subjectivities which inhabit the social world, with the result that Sartre risks falling back to a kind of Cartesian dualism of 'thinking' and 'extended' substance. (3) Correlatively to these two problems, Sartre is unable to cope with the concrete historical experience which is central to the Marxist problematic. That a theory of history (and not just the notion of human historicity or 'project') is necessary was evident to Sartre; however, *Being and Nothingness* does not provide satisfactory tools.

Sartre's confrontation with Marxism is enriched by his recognition of the major theoretical flaws of the orthodox version of the doctrine. These are flayed mercilessly in the 1946 'Materialism and Revolution', and discussed more sympathetically in the 1957 essay on 'Questions of Method', which is printed as the first part of the *Critique*.[14] Particularly important for the development of his theory is Sartre's criticism of the so-called 'dialectics of nature', and his attack on the analytical and reductionist epistemology of crude materialism.

Sartre's concern is ontology. As a result, his reaction to the pretensions of 'scientific' Marxism is a criticism of the foundations of its epistemology. Insofar as his ontology is anthropological, Sartre wants to show the human project and human responsibility which underlie the structure of the social world. To deal with a phenomenon like colonialism, for example, it is necessary to do more than identify and label a certain sociological process. Labelling not only reveals but also conceals the specificity of the experience. The 'thing' is not just out there; it is a result, the product of a specific *praxis*[1][5] of specific individuals.

> The lifeless movement of appearance that economic Reason can study is only intelligible in relation to the anti-dialectical system of super-exploitation. But this latter in its turn is not intelligible if one doesn't begin by seeing in it the product of human labor which forged and which does not cease to control it. (p. 683)

The objectivist fallacy which separates the subject from the observed object, purging radically the latter of any trace of human subjectivity and human projects must be avoided.

The danger facing an epistemological materialism is that theoretical intelligibility will be sacrificed before the quantitative altar of positive science. The condition of dialectical intelligibility is the homogeneity, the self-recognition or reflection of the interacting poles. With everything human eliminated from the world it is *a fortiori* impossible for that world to be intelligible. At best quantitative science permits the exterior presentation of a totalisation which is frozen into a totality. Sartre rejects such a materialist reductionism.

> . . . if one had to reduce the relations of practical multiplicities to simple contradictory determinations which are produced, simultaneously or not, by the development of a process; if one had, for example, to consider that the proletariat is the future destroyer of the bourgeoisie by virtue of the simple fact that the progressive decrease of variable capital and the increase of fixed capital, by increasing the productivity of the worker and reducing the buying power of the working class as a whole, will produce, passing from crisis to crisis, the economic catastrophe from which the bourgeoisie will not escape, then one ultimately reduces man to the pure anti-dialectical moment of the practico-inert. (p. 731)

The anti-dialectic or practico-inert (i.e., the material and cultural world) is not sheer inert facticity, with no depth and only one meaning. Rather, it '. . . is only intelligible because we produce it ourselves. . . . In a word, if in human history the mode of production is the infrastructure of every society, this is the case because work is the infrastructure of the practico-inert (and of the mode of production. . .).' (p. 671)

The problem can be seen in the works of Marx and Engels. When they attempt a genetic account of the origins of alienation in *The German Ideology*, they begin with the primitive division of labour and explain the succeeding developments in terms of permutations and combinations of this original 'historical' circumstance. Their move to this genetic account followed on what seemed to be the failure of Marx's *1844 Manuscripts*, namely the circular deduction of private property from alienated labour and of alienated labour from private property. Yet, for Sartre, the earlier analysis was in fact on the right track, basing itself on a dialectical understanding of the interpenetration of the individual and the social. The genetic account presents a pseudo-history in which a mechanical machinery originating in nature determines the fate of humankind. Not only is human *praxis* mechanised; there is a theoretical problem as well. If the division of labour is natural, as Marx and Engels claim, and if its extension will ultimately extend its negative effects to the point at which the negation will be negated, then we are faced with the problem of the *origin of negativity*.[16] The dialectic needs negativity, without which there is no movement, no project, no present stage to surpass — indeed, without which there is not even a human world. The genetic account becomes mechanistic determinism, the human actor is left out, and socialism is reduced to an inert reorganization of thingly relations.

Engels' theory of the 'dialectics of nature' makes an analogous mistake. Here too the source of negativity is occluded and naturalised. The Engelsian position falls back into a dualism of subject and object: the scientific investigator is presented as a neutral observer contemplating the activity of a world of objects to which he/she does not belong. These supposedly neutral observations are then tested in experiments whose chief epistemological characteristic is that by isolating the elements to be studied one recreates the atomistic world which the subject-object dichotomy presupposes. All subjectivity is stripped from the supposedly dialectical nature, which is then fitted to a pre-formed mould, the trinity of 'dialectical laws'. 'But', objects Sartre, 'in the historical and social world . . . there is *truly* a dialectical reason; in transporting this law into the 'natural' world, in engraving it there by force, Engels takes its rationality from it; it is no longer a question of a dialectic which man makes in making himself, and which, reciprocally, makes man, but of a contingent law of which one can only say: *this is how it is*, and not otherwise' (p. 126). Because it cannot justify itself and must borrow a schema from another domain, the 'dialectics of nature' is irrational.

The orthodoxies that Sartre criticises as irrational are not simply to be abandoned. They themselves must be understood, dialectically, as the product of a certain kind of human activity. The reasoning of the quanto-maniac, the economist Marxist, or the bourgeois sociologist is not simply the wrongheadedness of some individuals; it is a partial (in both senses of the term) approach to the Truth which must be understood and used. As noted above, these modes of thought typically conflate totality and totalisation. When a totalisation, a process, is treated as an already made totality, the human element is inevitably lost. In a totality all is fixed and finished; men and women are dead objects isolated from one another and from the observer who is contemplating them. They become things, objects without will and feeling, incapable of projects or *praxis*. And the observer is but a passive Other contemplating the world. How is this possible?

II The Foundations of the Dialectic

Dialectical rationality is *reflexive* — not reflective or contemplative. It depends on the homogeneity and reciprocity of Self and Other, Subject and Object — though strictly speaking these polarised terms are not applicable, since the dualism on which they are based is the condition and premise of analytical thought. Sartre describes his dialectical project this way:

> In a certain sense . . . man undergoes the dialectic as though it were a foreign power; in another sense, he *makes* it. And if dialectical Reason is to be the Reason of History, then that contradiction must itself be lived dialectically. This means that man undergoes the dialectic in as much as he makes it, and that he makes it in as much as he undergoes it. Moreover, it is necessary to understand that Man does not exist: there are only persons, who define themselves entirely by the society to which they belong and the historical movement which carries them. If we do not want the dialectic to again become a divine law, a metaphysical fate, then the dialectic must come *from individuals* and not from who-knows-which super-individual ensembles. In other words, we encounter this new contradiction: the dialectic is a law of totalization which makes for the existence of collectives, societies, history — that is, realities which impose themselves on individuals; but at the same time the dialectic must be the product of millions

of individual acts. Thus, we will have to show how it can be at once a *result* (without being a passive means) and a *totalizing force* (without being a transcendent fate); how it can at each instant realize the unity of the dispersive pulsing movement and that of integration. (p. 131)

The dialectic is intelligible only insofar as the individuals who constitute it are themselves dialectically constituted; and vice-versa, the individuals in their social and historical milieu are dialectically constituted only insofar as this milieu is itself dialectical. Neither pole can be taken alone, for each is the condition of the intelligibility of the other: this is the structure of reflexivity.

If we reflect on society in its historical context, we find that we cannot understand the collective structures that society gives itself without the constitutive acts of the many individuals; but at the same time, we cannot understand the individual constitutive acts unless we understand their societal context. If this dialectical circularity is not to imply a relativism, it will be necessary to discover the formal, *a priori*, structures which govern the relationship between the individual constitutive acts and the plural social structures they constitute, and which in turn reconstitute them. That is, writes Sartre, 'if it exists, the dialectic can only be the totalization of the concrete totalizations produced by a multiplicity of totalizing singularities. This is what I call the dialectical *nominalism*' (p. 132). (Sartre should have added here that the 'totalizing singularities' are themselves totalised. That he omits this aspect in his dialectical nominalism will be part of the grounds of the critical comments to be made after discussing the *Critique*.) The task of the first volume of the *Critique of Dialectical Reason* is to move from the most simple and abstract[17] structures through the stages of totalisation and re-totalisation, finally reaching the concrete historically given society in all its complexity and richness as the *result* of a continual ascent of intelligibility in which each later, more complex structure is comprehended as grounded by previously established principles. Once this formal, *a priori* task is completed, the second volume[18] would have to show that these structures permit an intelligible understanding of history.

Sartre's project, then, is one of *transcendental social philosophy*, and can be seen as an attempt to found and complete Marx's 1843 *Critique of Hegel's Philosophy of the State*. Marx's critique, it will be recalled, attacks the inversion of subject and object which permits Hegel to treat social categories as subjects of which the actual individuals are the determined predicates.

For Marx this is a mystification which is unintelligible because the dialectical circularity is broken and Spirit, not the people, determines the social categories. Sartre's task is to reconstruct, beginning from the individual, the increasingly concrete determinations of human society and its history.

Sartre's project is *transcendental* in that it attempts to articulate a categorial structure based on a principle of which each successive development can be seen as a *principiatum*; each moment must have its intelligibility in a ground of which it is the grounded. The dialectical circularity, with its comprehension of the interpenetration of the terms as totalisations and not fixed totalities, permits the ascent to ever-more complex structures without falling back into an 'atomism of the second degree' (p. 152) insofar as the principle itself — as opposed to the Hegelian Spirit, which is present only in an incomplete form in each category, and whose incompleteness motivates the ascent to higher concretions — is modified and enriched at each stage of development because of the reciprocal mediation of principle and *principiatum*.[19] In other words, from a methodological point of view, Sartre's transcendental edifice is a philosophical departure; the introduction of a *real ground* (the human being, as we shall see) which interacts with and is modified by experience but still remains ontologically what it was, avoids the static analysis of traditional philosophy and, at the same time, as already noted, modifies the (analytic) notion of a fixed and unchanging Truth known by a contemplating neutral subject in favour of a dialectical philosophy of intelligibility. This permits the formulation of a theory which is both reconstructive and critical.

Sartre's transcendental-real ground is the immediate, 'abstract' human individual and its *praxis*:

> The critical experiment will begin from the immediate, that is, from the individual in his abstract *praxis*, in order to rediscover through more and more profound conditionings the totality of his practical relations with others, and by the same means, the structures of the diverse practical multiplicities, and, through the contradictions and struggles of these multiplicities, to come to the absolutely concrete: historical man. (p. 143)

For the dialectical movement to begin, this individual and the as yet undifferentiated and inhuman world in which the individual finds itself must interact. It is in fact this interaction, as ontological, that defines the starting point. Because it does not pretend to be a 'natural history' of humankind but rather a self-consciously ontological ground, and because the nominalism is in fact a *relation*, Sartre's position avoids the problem that vitiates *The German Ideology*. The initial position is an ontological relation in which *praxis* and the world, as yet undifferentiated, give each other meaning *via* a totalising interaction in which each mediates the other.

The first totalising structure is based on *need*: 'Need is the negation of the negation in so far as that it reveals itself as a *lack* in the interior of the organism; it is positivity in so far as that by means of it the organic totality tends to conserve itself *as it is* . . .' (p. 166). That is, the organic being, man, depends on the inorganic world which is external to it and which it must internalise in order to survive. In this process of internalisation, the organic must externalise itself in order to appropriate inorganic nature. The organic thus gives unity and sense to the brute factuality of the inorganic world, which becomes a thing-to-be-consumed. Simultaneously, the organic being opens itself to the world and its risks: 'The organism makes itself inert (man *weighs* on the lever, etc.) in order to transform the surrounding inertia' (p. 174). The process is thus circular, dialectical: 'Man is "mediated" by things in exactly the same measure as things are "mediated" by man' (p. 165). Man externalises his internal relation to the external world, and in so doing negates its exteriority; man becomes a being-in-the-world, and the world becomes a being-for-man.

There is, however, a 'contingent and ineluctable' fact about the external world, which is crucial for the development of the theory: *scarcity* (p. 168). The internal relation to the world in terms of need structures the world by externalising itself and acting on the world; but it cannot alter the brute fact of scarcity (or, at least, has not yet done so; with the end of scarcity would come the end of what Marx called 'pre-history', and at that stage the dialectical theory — that of Sartre, or of Marx — would no longer be applicable).[20] Due to the dialectical reciprocity, the factual existence of scarcity is internalised (as scarcity of food or raw materials; at a higher level, scarcity of time, clients or even fresh air: scarcity itself is dialectical, modified by the complexity of the societal totalisation process). The internalisation of scarcity introduces negativity (*le néant*) into the notion of the human subject in a dialectically intelligible manner, as opposed to the more phenomenological-descriptive approach of *Being and Nothingness*, and permits Sartre to develop the notion of *praxis*-as-project, and to explain how the future acts as a negativity which affects the present as a facticity-to-be-totalised.

The dialectic of material scarcity appears to permit Sartre to go beyond the negative understanding of matter as brute Otherness (as portrayed in *Being and Nothingness*) to a positive appreciation of its role in the development of historical society. Matter becomes the condition or mediation which creates the possibility of social relations. 'In effect, as the univocal relation of each and of all to matter, scarcity finally becomes the objective and social structure of the material environment, and thus, in return, designates with its inert finger each individual as a factor and victim of scarcity' (p. 207). The social relations thus established are seen by Sartre as antagonistic: 'In pure reciprocity, the Other-than-me *is also the same as me.* In reciprocity *modified by scarcity,* the same appears to us as the anti-man inasmuch as *this same man* appears as radically Other (that is, as carrying the threat of death for us)' (pp. 207–8). This threatening Other — which I may become at any time for any Other — is the 'Excess Third'. In that each can become the Excess Third, negativity and conflict enter human affairs not, as in *The German Ideology*, because of the division of labour, class divisions and the like; Sartre's account has ontological precedence over such a pseudo-historical description which is caught up in an infinite and non-dialectical (historical) regress.

In the social world, each individual as individual works upon matter, attempts to appropriate it (negate it and form it) in terms of an individual project which gives sense to the world. Though our projects may be different or similar, they are inscribed in one and the same material world, which accepts them as the wax does the seal: passively. But though it is the 'inert memory of all' (p. 200), and thus that in which our common history is inscribed, matter also mediates our projects in precisely the measure that our projects mediate it. Consequently, it is not passive at all: it is *actively passive.* Every 'material' advance of civilisation has its effect on the daily lives of men and women. The TV, the private automobile, the paperback book, the MacDonald's hamburger — they affect us in ways that our personal projects never intended; and they do it as an active passivity.

The active passivity of matter is paradoxical; its actions seem to be the result of the *praxis* of everyone and no one. Each of our individual projects is absorbed in its materiality, and is reflected back at us as through a kaleidoscope. Matter becomes a 'counter-finality', an 'anti-*praxis*', a '*praxis* without an author' (p. 235). Sartre gives two examples (borrowed from Engels, and from Adam Smith and Marx). Chinese farmers eking out a bare living on a small plot of land each decide individually that they can grow more food if they cut down the trees on their plots in order to have a greater arable surface. The result of this *praxis*, however, turns against them *all*, though it was willed by *no one*, in the form of giant floods which occur on the treeless land. Or, if we look at the influx of gold into seventeenth century Spain we see each individual forming the project of personal enrichment, importing gold from the colonies, with the result: inflation, lowered domestic productivity, outflow of gold to foreign middlemen, and finally the decline and impoverishment of the entire nation — willed by no one, yet produced by all.

Because of its paradoxical nature, its lack of univocal signification, Sartre speaks of matter as *practico-inert*. The etymology of the term indicates its dialectical origin: it is the product of plural individual *praxis*, but in the inertia of exteriority it has lost the translucidity of that *praxis*. The active passivity of the practico-inert is at the root of *alienation*. Insofar as our products escape from the project for which they were intended, dominating us their makers, each of us is caught up in a machinery that we did not will but cannot escape. Each of us becomes Other: each is determined by the project of the Other, just as each determines the project of the Other. 'In a word,' writes Sartre, 'otherness comes to things from men and returns from things to men in the form of atomisation . . .' (p. 246). The practico-inert, then, is not simply any thing: it is a frozen *praxis*-as-Other produced by each individual in its isolated project (as Other of each Other), and which in turn reinforces the otherness of each as Other. It is not a 'thing' in the positivist sense: the practico-inert encompasses the domain of what Hegel calls 'objective Spirit' and Marxists call 'superstructures': art, language, history, the state — all of the structures formed by and forming social pluralities.

The practico-inert is a dialectical permutation of the ontological principle of man-as-*praxis*. Its intelligibility has its source in the interaction of men and matter in a world of scarcity. What is important is that while the tool, the machine and the other manifold products of collective individual *praxis* (including, it must be stressed, language and other cultural artifacts) can be understood as practico-inert — as products and producers, inhuman and human at once — *so can men*. Insofar as our human being is defined, even partially, by the non-human, we are not the free *praxis* of the ontological principle on which dialectical intelligibility is built. Yet, this definition of the human by the inhuman Other does not violate the principle of intelligibility; it does not mean the loss of the project of human self-reclamation. On the contrary, it marks an important progress.[21] The analysis will become more complex as it becomes more concrete; and the task remains that which Sartre stressed at the end of 'Search for a Method': 'Anthropology will not merit its name unless it substitutes for the study of human objects the study of the different processes of becoming an object' (p. 107).

III The Dialectic of the Social World

In the world of the practico-inert, the social collectivity exists in a condition of *seriality*. Parallel to the active passivity of the practico-inert, the serial individual lives as a *passive activity*, determined by the object (the Other) which totalises (i.e., gives sense to) the series. In an elevator, for example, or waiting for a bus, the plurality of persons is (passively) defined as a kind of unity by its object (riding-the-elevator, waiting-for-the-bus). Each is there as the result of an individual project (going to work, seeing a client or friend); yet their unity comes not from their individual projects but from the external object. From the point of view of each, each Other (on the elevator, in the bus) is interchangeable; no internal, interpersonal community is established; each recognises itself as defined by Otherness (the coming-of-the-bus, the riding-in-the-elevator) which totalises. This is a situation of *powerlessness*: the object which defines us is absolutely Other; the persons with whom we form a serial unity are interchangeable, faceless Others; we ourselves feel de-personalised and de-humanised by the knowledge that for each of the other Others we are yet another Other, replaceable by any other of them: '. . . each is identical to the Other inasmuch as he is made, by the Others, an Other acting on the Others. The formal and universal structure of otherness (*altérité*) is the *rationality of the series*' (p. 314).

In the serial relation, I can affect the Other only insofar as I treat myself as Other (just as, in order to affect the material world, individual *praxis* must externalise itself and expose itself). Since we are replaceable one by the Other, I act as I would want the Other to act, I do what I think the ideal Other would do. I fear becoming the 'Excess Third', and refuse to take risks, keep my own counsel, fear the Others and fear myself as Other. Sartre illustrates the functioning of serial rationality with examples such as the market place (pp. 328ff.), public opinion (pp. 338ff.) and racism (pp. 345ff.). He could have added to his list the failures of that political practice that couches itself in radical rhetoric only to act 'rationally', that is, in terms of what the serial Others are thought to think. Serial rationality cannot transcend the serial relation. As serial, I size up the 'objective situation' (that is, the practico-inert which determines the unity of the serial collective), and I gauge my actions in terms of its demands. My projects become its projects; they become projects of the Other, of the Thing, and therewith we are all determined by the Otherness of that thing called the system.[22] Our mutual Otherness determines us as belonging to the serial unity determined by an external Thing; but the totality that we form is a collective as always Other, a dead totality and not a living totalisation.

Take, for example, the classroom. We enter at the appointed time, sit in identical seats firmly riveted to the floor to prevent any but a linear arrangement with all heads facing the teacher. We take this class because 'one' should take it: either it is interesting, or useful, or required. We pay attention, take detailed notes (alongside our doodles), and look alert: to the teacher we are all Other, mutually interchangeable; and we compete for scarce goods (controlled by the teacher): high grades. When one of us is questioned in class, or when we have to produce written work, we don't come together to aid one another, but compete: each is afraid of becoming an Excess Third (receiving a low grade); and we know that this is how students are supposed to behave. We ask few questions, hazard few original ideas, since 'one' is supposed to fit in, to receive and not give ideas, to acquire an Education like everyone else. What interpersonal and group relations we have spring from sources other than the classroom, for there we are a seriality defined by the Thing whose bidding we have internalised. The serial unity is a *lateral* relation of Other to Other. Yet it appears that the individual is acting freely when, for example, the exteriority is internalised in the (successful) attempt to make good grades — and Sartre's point is that this is precisely the case! What the dialectical analysis must show is the *intelligibility* of actions which seem to go against the possibility of human liberation; its task is not to compare what is with what ought to be — that is the idealist or utopian stance — but rather to explain consistently the structures of what is. If a person who obeyed the dictates of the Thing were irrevocably alienated, the possibilities of human liberation would be eliminated. By showing the dialectical rationality of such alienated serial behaviour, Sartre at the same time shows the possibility of social liberation.

The transition from the all-pervasive serial plurality to the *group*, the next stage in Sartre's categorial development, has the same dialectical intelligibility as the previous moments. 'The group is defined by its enterprise and by the constant movement of integration which attempts to purify its *praxis* by attempting to suppress in it all the forms of inertia; the [serial] collective is defined *by its being*, that is, inasmuch as it makes all *praxis* into a simple *hexis*' (p. 307). The group differs from the series in that the basic structure of the latter is the lateral relation of Otherness, whereas the group is founded on Sameness. The group is the active attempt to escape from determination by the Other (thing or person) and to create a self-determining social plurality — a *we-subject*. Because it is an *active* self-foundation, Sartre speaks of the group-in-fusion or of a totalisation-in-progress in order clearly to demarcate the active group from the passive seriality, the we-subject from the we-object. Hence, the unresolved problem of *Being and Nothingness* finds its solution.

The events of the French Revolution, to which Sartre often returns, can be used as an illustration of the transition from the seriality to the group. The Paris population in the days before July 14 was a mixed bunch, in effect united only by geographical location, the fact of poverty and discontent: in a word, a seriality. As the situation worsened, rumours flew (transmitted from Other to Other, reflecting a fear of the Other: the state-power); demonstrations took place and the people armed themselves (still in a serial context: each reacting to the menace of the Other, each seeing in the neighbour's actions the determination of what one should do). Thus the seriality, by the very inertial force of its actions, created the possibility of its own regroupment as a self-determining active group. What was needed for the fusion to occur was (1) a menace from the outside (the possibility of negation, death, for the collectivity and each individual as being potentially an Excess Third); and (2) a 'totalising Third'.[23] The external menace was the Bastille, in whose shadow they lived day in and day out; it was not just a prison but a fortress from which the government could bombard the quarter, menacing each Other in the populace. In the days of protests, as the population began to arm itself, the level of discontent rose, feeding upon itself; the temperature of the crowd, as Sartre puts it metaphorically, rises. Then, suddenly, someone (*anyone!*) galvanises the crowd: "*A la Bastille!*" Everyone runs, suddenly totalised by the voice of someone, anyone, one who is of the crowd and has understood the danger that threatens. The heterogeneous crowd fuses into a group, acting together for a common cause. Its organisation is still determined by an external force (the-Bastille-as-a-menace-to-us-all), and is a means to overcome it. But at the same time, within the group-as-means, otherness is overcome. 'It is not that I am myself in the Other; it is that *in praxis* there is no *Other*, there are only *me's* (p. 420). The structure of social otherness is replaced by a fusion of the Same: belonging to the active, fusing group makes each individual the Same (mediation by the group), and the action of each Third (and anyone can be or become the totalizing Third: each action is called forth by some, any, catalyst) mediates between the group and myself as Third.[24] The action here is not the active passivity of the serial individual, for it is now belonging to the group which defines all as the Same and which determines their action as homogeneous, not determined by external heterogeneity. The Bastille is taken!

The group, however, was defined as a *means* towards an external goal, the negation of the menace that weighed over the group-in-fusion. Once the menace is overcome, the Bastille taken, the activity consummated and the group fused, then what? The mode of existence of the group changes when, on the Sunday following the seizure of the Bastille, with no action having intervened, individuals return to that half-destroyed fortress, showing it to their families and children, and pointing out what 'we' did. The group is no longer a fusion but a passivity. The heat of the action has passed, there is no longer any unifying force, and the fall back to seriality threatens. The Bastille becomes a monument, the symbols of a group that was, where *spectators* come to gape (among them, yesterday's activists). To hold the group together a new fear, a new threat from outside, and a new totalising Third are needed. This may occur if, for example, the rumour[25] spreads that the royalists are coming from Versailles, and the group decides that the threat to all is a threat to each as the Same, and maintains its organisation and awareness. But the mobilisation will only last so long: fear becomes a habit, pain is dulled, and seriality again threatens. To maintain itself the group needs a 'practical invention', the Oath (pp. 439—40). Each individual as the Same swears on its life and person that the group and the we-subject it constitutes take precedence over all else. The Oath represents a form of negation or 'alienation' of freedom, but a negation that is freely and consciously willed insofar as the individual makes itself into a *group-object*. I define my being as the being of the Same; I limit my freedom to the freedom of the group so that, in that we all act this way, we can count each upon the Other, and can be certain that this 'practical invention' has (artificially) created the fear-reaction needed for the preservation of the group. The group now takes itself not simply as a means towards the negation (destruction) of an external menace to each Other-as-the-Same, but rather as an end in itself, worthy of preservation. Written in the blood of each, the Oath permits the preservation of the group *and* the differentiation of functions within it (bound by the discipline of the oath, the group can send spies and infiltrators, form a fifth column or deploy its reserves in such a way that the enemy will not realise its strength).

The Oath institutes the 'Fraternity-Terror', which itself will provide the ground for a theory of institutions. Sartre again illustrates this category through the French Revolution. The Oath is only a spiritual force and cannot maintain the coherence and unity of the group. 'The oath is a free attempt to substitute the fear of all for the fear of oneself and of the Other in and by each inasmuch as it suddenly reactualises violence as an intelligible move beyond the individual alienation by the common liberty' (p. 450). That is, if after taking the Oath you let the Other (the Enemy) appeal to you as Other-than-us, the group to whom you swore to remain the Same — and for whatever reasons you do so: fear for the ultimate victory of our group, desire to gain material wealth and comfort, fear for your family, etc. — then it is our duty, to you and to ourselves as a group, to eliminate you. And this violence that we do to you is 'a practical relation of *love* among the lynchers' (p. 455). It affirms to you that, to the very last, we still consider you as one of us; and at the same time it proves to us that we still exist as a coherent group. In a word, purges are necessary to maintain the group.[26]

The paradoxical institutionalisation of the group is a necessity whose structure results from the ontological foundation of the group. The action of the group is the action of a *constituted dialectic* whose foundation is the *constitutive dialectic* of individual *praxis*. The constituted dialectic is not, Sartre insists again and again, some kind of hyperorganism or collective unconscious which would function like the *praxis* of a super-individual.[27] This is the crucial point, for the group is thus seen to be a functional but inherently instable unity:

> born to dissolve the series in the living synthesis of a community, it is blocked in its spatio-temporal development by the insurpassable status of the organic individual, and finds its being outside itself in the passive determinations of the inorganic exteriority that it tried to suppress in itself. It

formed against alienation, which substitutes the field of the practico-inert for the free practical field of the individual. But no more than does the individual, it does not escape from the practico-inert, and through it, falls back into serial passivity. (pp. 635—6)

The group, 'the practical organism [,] is the unifying unity of the unification' operated by the constitutive individuals (p. 431). The constitutive individuals are the rock-bottom foundation of Sartre's 'dialectical nominalism' and their existential freedom can never be totalised from without.

The group does not have the existence of an object; it *is* not, but is a perpetual *becoming* or fusion, constituted by the multiplicity of individual totalisations each of which seeks a goal common to each and freely chosen by all. As a constituted dialectic, however, the group produces an action and tends to internalise that external effect as its definition. The inhabitants of the Bastille quarter did not originally exist and act as a group; it was the product of their action that presented itself to each individual as the product of a common *praxis*, and conversely, as the definition of that same common or group *praxis*. Internalising this result and definition, each member regards itself as a group-individual. But the problem that now arises

is precisely the fact that the group does not and cannot have the ontological status that it claims in its *praxis*; and it is, inversely, the fact that each and everyone produces himself and defines himself in terms of that non-existent totality. There is a kind of interior void, an impassable and indetermined distance, a malaise in each community, large and small. This malaise incites a reinforcement of integrative practices, and grows in the measure that the group is more integrated. (p. 568)

The group that destroyed the Bastille was a fusion in the historical heat of the moment; it defined itself in its action. When the moment is past, only the result of the group-*praxis* remains; each individual as individual identifies with the result, and only through the mediation of the result, a thing, can the members of the group think of themselves as the Same. The group thus rests on a dead totality, losing its character as a living totalisation. This is the foundation of the Fraternity-Terror which is, for Sartre, the archetype of the general process of group-socialisation and internalisation of norms. Because the fusion cannot be maintained naturally over a long historical time, the group must either institutionalise itself or disappear.

The institutiionalised group represents "a beginning of circular massification whose origin is the *non-substantial existence* of the community. The *being of the institution* . . . is the *non-being* of the group producing itself as the relation between its members" (p. 583). After the seizure of the Bastille, the group tends to disperse, returning to the everyday. Yet there is a new danger, the revenge of the Royalists, which may come today, tomorrow, or next week. The group must prepare to defend itself: it sends out patrols to stand watch, it begins to think about organising the defence of the quarter, it assigns responsibilities: in short, it begins to differentiate itself into sub-groups each of which is determined by its belonging to the larger group. Each of these differentiated groups is defined by a task that the group assigns. As long as each individual has internalised the demands of the group there is no danger of betrayal. Indeed, with the institution of the Oath and the Fraternity-Terror, a first defensive means has been defined by the group to prevent such a betrayal — which is always possible because once the fusing group cools down and the institution begins to emerge, the relation of each individual to the group again becomes serial, determined by Otherness. When the individual is determined by belonging and not by doing, the result is a passive determination by the Other (even though the Other here is the group of Same's), as opposed to an active self-definition. The function of the institution thus becomes the paradoxical task of preserving the being of a non-being (the group).

It is in this situation that bureaucratisation arises. With the increasing differentiation of sub-groups, the group must 'consume a part of its strength . . . in order to maintain itself in a state of relative fluidity' (p. 539).

That which constitutes the specificity of organized *praxis* is the pyramid of inertias which constitutes that organized *praxis* . . . and the fact that for any apparatus its object (its subgroups which must be united) appears as an internal external inertia which as such must be manoeuvred, whereas the same apparatus, in its relations with other organs of the group, is itself manipulated as an inertia by the apparatus above it (p. 537).

When the group, originally constituted itself in a fusion which was a means to an end, takes itself as an end-in-itself and devotes its energies to its own self-preservation, each member takes on a dual status for each other member: each is the Same, since each has internalised the same end-goal; yet each is an Other whose loyalty and efforts must be coordinated and structured. When the group becomes an end, its members become means; and as the immediate goal for which the group was formed recedes in time it becomes necessary to rule either by bureaucratic means, or continually to invent new external dangers (e.g., world imperialism, traitors in our midst, commies, etc.) — or both. In a word, the group-subject takes itself as group-object, treats itself as a thing such that its *praxis* becomes a '*praxis*-process' (p. 549). Yet, though bureaucratised, the group retains a totalising function which comes to it through the constitutive actions of individual *praxis*; hence it would be wrong to study it *only* as an object. The notion of the group as *praxis*-process points to the necessity of keeping both functions and their interaction continually present in the analysis, for even as bureaucratised the group is constituted by the constitutive dialectic of totalising individuals.

IV   The Problem of Revolution

The development of the theory to this point has been marked by an ambiguity to which I referred at the outset: the theory is a categorial or ontological theory which develops the formal avatars of the constituted and constituting dialectic to the point — at which the present reconstruction has now arrived — at which concrete history can be thought in its complexity and revealed as intelligible. None of the categorial moments that have been discussed here actually exists in isolated purity; each gets its full sense only when thought within the complex totalisation that is History. The categories are ontological, grounds of intelligibility; the concrete illustrations that Sartre offers are, like the Remarks and Additions in Hegel's *Philosophy of Right*, neither complete interpretations of specific social and historical complexes nor inherent to the theory in its pure form.[28] A look at one specifically Marxist problem in its concrete historicity will clarify the advantages and disadvantages of Sartre's approach.

The working class is defined within the sphere of the practico-inert; it is a collective of serialities interspersed with particularistic groups, which it may form or which seek to form (manipulate) it. Periodically, and under given conditions, the temperature rises and a fusion occurs. In the fusion, leaders arise, first as regulative Thirds. 'Thus, the *leader* is produced at the same time as the group itself, and he produces the group which produces him — with this distinction, that in this elementary moment of the experience, the leader is *anyone*' (p. 586). As the group begins to disintegrate back into seriality, the leader becomes the 'authority' whose function is to integrate 'the multiplicity of institutional relations and to give them the synthetic unity of a real *praxis*' (p. 587). But, due to the nominalism which indicates that this 'synthetic unity' as institutionalised is in fact no longer a group but a fixed structure which takes itself as its own end, the position of the leader shifts. Where the leader was simply the expression of the group-as-all-of-us, now we become an expression of the leader, and he or she is no longer leader but sovereign. Of course, the leader may devote him- or herself to the structuration of the group as an end which is a means to another end, and attempt to preserve the relation whereby we members of the group who agree with that final end remain related to one another and to the sovereign not as obedient subjects of the Other's will, but as our own free choice of the Same. This would be the revolutionary Party. But it is also the case that Sartre's principles 'explain' Stalin's substitution of the Party, and finally of himself, for the will of the people; Stalin, Sartre says, 'is' the constituted dialectic which must direct the constitutive dialectic of the masses in order to unify it around a common goal (p. 630).

Inasmuch as the Party (or the State, for that matter) exists within a serially structured class, its role is comparable to that of any group in relation to the series: the series is Other-directed, and the Party is one of Others competing for its attention.[29] Under these circumstances, the Party may win votes, elections, and a share of the public opinion. It may recruit new members who choose to recognise themselves in it and its goals, subordinating themselves to it in order to become no longer Others-in-sympathy-with-the-cause, but the Same as the other militants. Each militant identifies him or herself with the Party; in discussions with non-Party people (Others), each will tend to identify the Party as the Truth and goal of the class. But the problem with this theory of the Party is that it is based, paradoxically, on precisely the seriality that the Revolution aims to eliminate: if the Party wins my vote, if I follow its directions in a strike or a coup, I am still obeying the Other — whether that Other claims to be my representative or not doesn't matter. It is for this reason that Sartre finds himself admitting that the idea of the dictatorship of the proletariat 'is itself absurd' (p. 630).

To be sure, Sartre continually criticises Party dictatorships using precisely the concepts developed in the *Critique*. For example, in his brilliant Preface to the writings of Patrice Lumumba, he writes that:

> The government atomizes the colonialized people and unifies them *from the exterior* as subjects of the King. Independence will be only a word if for that *cohesion from the outside* a totalization from the interior is not substituted.[30]

The very influential Preface to Fanon's *Wretched of the Earth* is based on the argument that revolt is necessary precisely in order to substitute interior cohesion for the colonial yoke which de-humanises the colonised by treating him or her as Other. In the *Critique* itself, Sartre recognises that in any fusion the Party's directives are followed *only* if they are in fact the expression of the activity of the fusing group, and suggests that when the fusion does occur the old cadre group will find itself outside the process and will be forced to dissolve and reconstitute itself out of the movement.

Yet, the necessity that the ontological analysis reveals — that the group is not a hyperorganism, and that it must institutionalise and bureaucratise itself or disappear — forces Sartre to a paradoxical position. He asserts that 'the transformation of the class into an actualised group has never occurred anywhere, even in revolutionary periods.' (p. 644). This historical and empirical assertion is rendered intelligible by the ontological necessity that rules the formation of groups. Yet that same ontology would define revolution precisely as the *praxis* which creates a we-subject. Does this mean that revolution is ruled out, empirically and ontologically? Or that revolution is a misnomer designating a series of material reforms (nationalisations, income redistribution etc.) which are achieved in the temporary fusion and the phase of institutionalisation that follows it? And what are we to make of Sartre's comments on the role of the Party — for example, that there is 'no doubt that the entire class is present in the organized group which has constituted itself within it'? (p. 644).

V   Concretisation and Critique

In his Preface to *Les Maos en France*,[31] Sartre applies his social ontology to elaborate three themes that he sees as fundamental to French Maoism: violence, spontaneity and morality. He illustrates his theses with the example of Contrexéville, a factory where working conditions were so bad that the workers called the factory 'Buchenwald', but where, nonetheless, there had been no strikes during the twelve years of its operation.

The atomising forces acted constantly on the workers, serialising them. An ensemble is said to be serial when each of its members, even though the neighbor of all the others, remains alone and defines himself by the thought of the neighbor insofar as that neighbor thinks *like the others.* That is, each is other than himself and behaves like an other who, himself, is other than himself. The workers spoke and affirmed the serial thought as if it were their own thought, but it was in fact that of the ruling class which imposed itself from outside.

This poses the political problem for the militant who had 'established' himself at Contrexéville. What occurred in this case was that 'once an external change concerning production showed, in one specific point, the actual conditions and drew from the workers a particular, concrete and temporally specific refusal, the series gives way to the group whose behavior expresses — even though often without formulating it — the radical refusal of exploitation.' Once this *external* change had intervened, then and only then could the militant make himself heard. In fact, continues Sartre, on their own the fused workers gave up the racism, misogyny and passivity that had divided them. This would imply that the fused group doesn't need the militant. Indeed, it turns out that Sartre's illustration concerns the tasks of the militant in the serialized situation. There, he says, the militant has the double task of supporting the most 'left' tendency, however modest its actions. The militant may propose specific tasks; if these are accepted, then he/she must know how to listen to the masses, accompanying but not guiding them. Further, replying to the implicit question, why a party? Sartre suggests that its necessity is explained precisely by the inevitable return to seriality: the party is 'in a certain manner, first of all the memory of the masses. It must shorten the gap between the periods of fusion.'

Sartre's political application of his ontology poses several problems, to which allusion was made at the outset. The militant in fact finds her/himself in the position of the traditional intellectual, supporting ongoing actions once they have taken place. The theory of seriality explains the impossibility of her/his actually intervening until the fusion has begun;

and the fusion itself is said to depend on an *external* event. Moreover, not every or any external event catalyses the freedom which is present, but alienated, in the atomised seriality. Here, the suggestion would be that the militant(s) intervene through actions of violence (sequestration of managers, use of force against bullying foremen, etc.) whose symbolic effect is to unveil the exploitation and alienation, as well as the possibility of fighting back. These, of course, will not always work; they are like the external events, which may or may not activate the workers' freedom. Thus, while the virtue of Sartre's politics is its insistence on self-development, its problem is that it presents no way in which the militant can act politically to insure the rupture of seriality and the beginning of the self-developmental process. The militant, like the philosopher, either intervenes after the fact, or acts according to an abstract universal demand (e.g., exercises symbolic violence to reveal the structures of exploitation).

At one point in *On a raison de se révolter*, Sartre exposes this general problem when he asks his Maoist interlocutor what the working class in fact is during those periods when it is not acting. Victor's reply is that the class is never completely passive. He suggests that Sartre's distinction between the seriality and the group is not applicable in its purity; and that Sartre's position supposes an absolute rupture which in fact cannot exist.[32] Sartre had already seen this danger in the *Critique*. At one point, he takes up the dispute between those who hold that the proletariat can only be organised as a class through the external action of the Party, and those who argue in favour of the necessity of mass spontaneity (p. 518). He argues that the problem is a 'political' one, since both solutions have the same ontological structure. If the group is truly a group, it is based on the Sameness of all, which implies that the Party will succeed in effecting the fusion of the group only if it is the Same as the group, not external or Other to it. The fusion of a group is not the same thing, he insists, as the agreement which might exist between a worker and her boss, for example, that the laws of physics are true. Agreement on a scientific principle is an accord about an Other, and as such does not affect the existence of either person, whose relation with the Other is unchanged. When a group forms, and when the tactical or strategic unity makes itself felt, the debate that is engaged is a life-or-death matter not only for the existence of the group but also for each individual who composes it, since in this case each here is the Same. Within the group, no solution can be imposed on the Other since that would imply the death of the group as such, and consequently the victory of an individual (or faction) imposing itself on the group would be the pyrrhic success of the suicide, destroying the structure of the group. At this level of the theory, Sartre is surely consistent. But the political question becomes important in the intervention into concrete history; there, the neat theoretical structures developed in their formal isolation show their ambiguity.

While Sartre is aware of the political dangers, he is unable to avoid conclusions which contradict the New Left goals that he desires. The ontological foundation of his system prohibits *a priori* the stablisation of the group in fusion, condemning it to dispersion or to the petrification of an institution. In the concretion of history, the group, if it persists, enters into relations with other groups and series, relations which are themselves serial and which found the structures of domination whose archetype is the bourgeois state. The delicate relation thus established demands that the group-as-institutionalized take severe measures to preserve itself against the threat of inertia or dissolution. As a common member of an historical group, I must restrain myself, mold myself to the will of the institutionalised-group. Since this group is threatened from the outside world in which it nonetheless operates, I must take care that despite my subjective goals my words and actions do not get deflected by the dialectic of seriality and turn back against the group. 'The model of the institutional-group', says Sartre, 'will be the *forged tool*' (p. 585). In the same context, he speaks of the 'systematic self-domestication of man by man' (ibid.). Thus, purges are justified by the paradoxical task of maintaining the being of a non-being, the group.

Consistency with his ontology leads Sartre to conclusions which seem to violate his own existentialist premises. In *On a raison de se révolter*,[33] Sartre explains that he is a revolutionary because the thought of the group is more true than that of the series, for in the group each knows the truth, seizes it as her/his own, whereas the atomised series is a structure of separation and impotence. Pressed on this point, Sarte finally replies that he prefers such group-thought because 'That's how I am'. And, he continues: 'I think that an individual in the group, even if he is a little bit terrorized, is still better than an individual alone and thinking separation. I don't think that an individual alone can do anything.' The Sartrean individual thus becomes fully free and individual only in the group, even if membership implies a certain constraint, a 'little bit' of terror. Presumably this constraint and terror are ontologically necessitated by the continued presence of scarcity. For this reason, however, the analysis of existential subjectivity gives way, as was evident already in *Being and Nothingness*, to the precise delimitation of the structures of the objective world. Sartre presents magnificent phenomenological descriptions of that 'threatening and sumptuous opacity'[34] where, to cite a telling passage, 'With a certain distance, novels become completely similar to natural phenomena: one forgets that they have an author, one accepts them like stones or trees.' Sartre's existentialism certainly does not intend to be a kind of moralistic idealism or a return to the Kantian project. But the paradox is that, despite the introduction of the concept of the practico-inert, he overreacts to this danger: material necessity overwhelms and delimits the projects of *praxis*. Thus, we have already seen that, politically, Sartre's existentialism can only support or criticise; it is incapable of initiating.

The motive force of Sartre's transcendental social theory is his attempt to show how each formation can be understood in terms of a basic principle of which it is the concretion. This is what guarantees the dialectical intelligibility. The principle of the system is the praxical individual, who is the constitutive ground of the constituted dialectic. Sartre explicitly recognizes the danger: if the given 'is *praxis* through and through, the entire human universe disappears in an idealism of the Hegelian type' (p. 688). A materiality which is opaque and other than the praxical individual must be accounted for; but this opaque otherness must at the same time remain intelligible and explicable by the theory. Sartre's concept of the practico-inert, and the correlative notions of active passivity and passive activity are introduced for this purpose. In this manner, he thinks he can account for the weight of the world, and at the same time explain the forms of human alienation, without violating the primacy of freedom. In *On a raison de se révolter*, he criticises the Marxian perspective for failing to draw fully the conclusions from the rejection of idealism:

> Marxism presents historical development as if since father Adam the same individuals made History, whereas in reality it is different individuals born from one another. In each generation, the young appear in a society which has its ruling class, its exploited, its institutions, its conflicts; but since they are not responsable for these, they must deal with them in an other manner. Consequently, in fact, History is not at all like the Marxists see it.[35]

The implication is that Sartrean existentialism will be a

corrective to Marxism insofar as its theory of the individual will account for the formation of (class-) consciousness. It will do this both by showing the integration of the subject in the objective world, and the integration of that objective world in the formation of subjectivity. This is what Sartre understands by *praxis*.

What is striking in the *Critique*, however, is that despite the conception of the practico-inert, and the theory of *praxis* which attempts to bridge the dualistic gap, the individual never seems to have a *body*. Of course, the phenomenologist doesn't ignore its existence. In the systematic theory, the organism is shown to externalise itself in working on the environment. But the body is never a constitutive variable in the social world. Yet it would be precisely a theory of embodiment that could account for the mutual imbrication of individual and world that Sartre needs. Indeed, the unification that Sartre finally offers is haunted by the dualism pointed to in the very notion of the practico-inert. One of Sartre's definitions of *praxis* is particularly telling in this regard:

> In effect, *praxis* is a passing from the objective to the objective by means of an interiorization. The project, as a subjective move from objectivity to objectivity stretched between the objective conditions of the milieu and the objective structures of the field of possibilities, represents *in itself* the moving unity of subjectivity and objectivity. . . . The subjective thus appears as a necessary moment of the objective process. (p. 66)

Analogously, in *On a raison*, Sartre asserts that what he calls morality 'exists at the level of production itself'.[36] Such a unity of subjectivity and objectivity could just as well be the practico-inert as *praxis*. The only distinction comes with the formulation of a free project, although in this passage the project depends on the objectivities that it confronts. If the project is understood in a more 'existential' manner, as the free choice of the subject to incarnate its freedom by transcending the given, the position falls back into an idealism. Philippe Gavi confronts Sartre on this issue in *On a raison de se révolter*, insisting on the role of *pleasure* as well as that of freedom in determining people to act. Yet Sartre's disembodied individual cannot imply a notion of pleasure, and he replies to Gavi that only commonly defined projects against a class enemy, not pleasure, can be a motive.[37] Thus, *praxis* now becomes project, subjective, always equal to itself and never learning, changing or growing. This was the objection that we saw at the outset, the reason that Sartre undertook the *Critique*. In the end, it appears that he is still caught between the poles of a pure freedom and a pure objectivity. However much he insists that nothing is pure, that freedom can be alienated and scarcity and need impregnate daily our free projects, Sartre is forced in spite of himself to privilege one or the other: impure-pure subject or pure-impure object.

The Sartrean dualism is the result of his dialectical *nominalism*. The *Critique* has two major divisions: 'From Individual *Praxis* to the Practico-Inert', and 'From the Group to History.' It appeared that Sartre's categorial principle — the abstract individual and its *praxis* — would raise itself to a first level of concreteness as the human individual living in the world of the practico-inert; and that this new, concrete human would take on further depth, becoming a qualitatively different constitutive principle for the second stage of development. Historicity would thus have been built into the transcendental program; and the possibility of political application would have been accounted for. Instead, Sartre insists that

> the concrete dialectic is that which reveals itself through the common *praxis* of a group. But we also know that the fundamental condition of historical rationality is the impossibility of going beyond ... organic action as the strictly individual model; that is, the constituted dialectical Reason ... must be related to its always present but always masked foundation, the constitutive rationality [of the individual].
> (p. 643)

Although Sartre recognizes that this abstract individual has no concrete historical existence, his formulation of a theory which is *both* reconstructive and critical cannot make the kind of distinction Habermas' counterfactual truth conditions would assert. His ontological principle is taken at one time as a real, existent foundation for the theory, while at the second moment it is treated as a transcendental principle. It is always present, and can always be called into play. On the other hand, the existent world which this transcendental principle is supposed to explain is the 'impure' blending of plural *praxis* in an objective world. Theory and practice take place in the real world; yet their principle and *telos* lies in the transcendental sphere, remaining always equal to itself and manifesting its presence in those 'privileged moments' when it transcends the given conditions in an act of revolt.

The limits of the Sartrean theory appear from another point of view when we recall the earlier remark that Sartre is developing the results of Marx's *Critique of Hegel's Philosophy of the State*, which demonstrates the priority of civil society over its political form. What is often forgotten, however, is that *civil society is precisely the problem, not the solution.* Civil society is the sphere of social atomism whose principle is the particularised individual in an economic war of all against all dominated by conditions of scarcity. The Hegelian analysis, as well as the Marxian critique, show the manifold tensions, contradictions and injustices which must prevail in this sphere. Where Hegel transcends these problems by moving to a higher ontological level, the stately or political sphere, Marx calls for a revolution of civil society. The problem is to explain the source of that revolution, which for Marx is of course the proletariat as the class which is nothing and must become all. Marxian revolution is the transcendence of the conditions of civil society, whose possibility is explained sometimes strictly in terms of the conditions of civil society itself — economics — while at other times the revolution is seen as a *political* act. Marx's proletarian revolution would come about when the 'lightning of thought' strikes into the soil of the proletariat. But Marx never made more precise the mechanism by which the 'lightning' would strike — indeed his position reminds one precisely of those 'privileged moments' when the Sartrean transcendental freedom manifests itself! Lenin's distinction between trade-union and political class-consciousness confronts the problem left by Marx with the suggestion that within civil society only reformist, opportunist or spontaneist consciousness is possible, whereas the 'more' that would permit the revolutionary transformation comes from the outside, from the party. The dilemmas of Sartre's existential Marxism emerge from his uncritical acceptance of the premises of both Marx's and Lenin's posing of the political problem. The constraints that force the group to take repressive measures in order to maintain itself are inherent in civil society. Sartre attempts to practice and theorise politics by means of a space which, by its very nature, excludes the political. The world of civil society is that impure world in which free subjectivity is embedded and alienated, whereas the political practice with which Sartre identifies is motivated by the purity of the transcendentally grounding subject. For this reason, Sartre finds himself rejecting the Marxian primacy of class analysis, asserting recently that: 'It is absurd to think that one can define man uniquely according to his class. There is something more; the various alienations point directly to freedom, for only a freedom can be alienated; one cannot alienate a man who is not free.'[38] But immediately after this series of expansive commentaries on freedom as that which we all seek at all times, and as the key political variable, Sartre turns the coin when questioned about Solzhenitsyn, whose ideas of freedom, he says, are harmful because they are archaic, not adapted to the development of contemporary society! The theoretical dualism returns; Sartre can have his cake and eat it too!

Toward the end of the *Critique*, Sartre writes that 'at a certain level of abstraction, the class struggle is expressed as a *conflict of rationalities*' (p. 742). He is referring to the distinction between analytical and dialectical reason; but the implications of the statement range further. I have suggested two fundamental criticisms of the Sartrean position: its dualistic structure, and its inability to account for the political. Both of these are criticisms of the 'rationality' of the Sartrean (and, to the degree that Sartre successfully reconstructs it, the Marxian) position. Both are motivated by similar considerations. As a theory of the social atomism of civil society, Sartre's theory can at best account for social equality; it cannot explain the liberty and fraternity that must also be achieved. It must remain a moral theory, concerned with individual choice but unable to account for successful institutions of plural subjectivity. It talks about freedom, but is unable to discuss the forms and articulations of that freedom. The reason for this inability to approach the political is built into the dualistic structure of the theory. It must be stressed that the dualism is *not* the traditional empirical one of subject/object; Sartre's phenomenological acuity cannot be questioned on that score. Despite Sartre's intention of overcoming it, the dualism is built into the transcendental structure of the theory which permits a pure transcendental freedom to somehow incarnate itself in the impure, real world. This is the dualism of traditional, rationalist theory as inherited in the West since Plato. From the Forms of Plato and the Essences of Aristotle, through the Transcendental Unity of Apperception of Kant and the Spirit of Hegel, down to the Being of Heidegger and the Freedom of Sartre, a common rationality and a common problem prevail. Marx took the first, hesitating and confused, steps towards its overcoming — for example, in the aphorisms on Feuerbach — but he too fell back, to a rationalist theory where a unique principle is used to explain (away) the manifold appearances which are taken as its *principiata.*

Sartre's contribution to the formulation of a New Left

political theory shows that such a theory will ultimately depend on the formulation of a new concept of rationality, on a new philosophy. That the political weaknesses and contradictions of the Sartrean project are explicable by the type of rationality that he theorizes is significant. Despite the obvious parallels with the Hegelian theory, it is to the paradoxes of the Kantian project that Sartre's work leads. Kant's tenacious and rigorous path through the three *Critiques* had to lead to a philosophy of History where the freeing of men from their 'self-incurred immaturity' first took the form of welcoming the Enlightened Despotism of Friedrich, before running head-on into the new fact of the French Revolution, for which his theory could not account. Sartre's New Left enthusiasm opts for a long process of 'liberation from power' but he is unable to give grounds for this liberation; he is unable to formulate a theory of the political. Here, the Hegelian attempt would recommend itself, not as it has come down to us, but in the form of a reflection on the limitations of a theory of civil society. The model of individual relations in a social plurality dominated by scarcity is no more adequate than an abstract contractualism would be in accounting for the political institutions which give social life its sense. Sartre's account of the *process* by which the group forms and maintains itself is instructive. But the traditional philosophical rationality, which demands transparency in theoretical as well as personal relations, vitiates any advance by explaining away the process-character of the group. Reduced to logical permutations of Same and Other, Sartre's disembodied actors engage in a *praxis* which resolves the ambiguity of the political process into a form of the 'practico-inert' where the domination of one or the other term of this *mixtum compositum* can only be explained after the fact. In the end, it is the philosopher Sartre who dominates the existential activist; for the *praxis* and freedom which Sartre theorizes serve ultimately as the explanation, not the process to be further developed. It is precisely this style of philosophising that Sartre paradoxically typifies in his own attempt to overcome it.

Part Four
Criticising Marxism

8 From Marxism to Ontology: Maurice Merleau-Ponty

The name of Merleau-Ponty conjures forth a multitude of images, refracting against one another in ways that continually surprise. There is first of all the phenomenologist. Under his pen, phenomenology becomes less than a method and more than an attitude: the phenomenological analyses spring forth on their own from the materials, those of science, of culture, and of the everyday. The studies of expression in art and literature come to mind; but on reflection what strikes one as axial is that these studies manifest the same care and concern, the same sure hand floating with the world, as one sees in the continual working with the 'hard' sciences. And again, the same manner of cleaving to the world is present in the political choices and analyses. But then, thinking of that last and unfinished ontology in *The Visible and the Invisible*, the always-present

---

In the following text, all citations from Merleau-Ponty are indicated with a reference-sign and page number in parenthesis. All citations are from the French editions, and are rendered in my own translation. The sources cited are: *Phénoménologie de la perception* (Paris: Gallimard, 1945), indicated as *PhP*; *Humanisme et terreur* (Paris: Gallimard, 1947), indicated as *HT*; *Sens et non-sens* (Paris: Nagel, 6th ed., 1966), indicated as *SNS*; *Eloge de la philosophie et autres essais* (Paris: Gallimard, 1953, 1960), indicated as *Eloge*; *Les aventures de la dialectique* (Paris: Gallimard, 1955), indicated as *AD*; *Signes* (Paris: Gallimard, 1960), indicated as *S*; *L'oeil et l'Esprit* (Paris: Gallimard, 1964), indicated as *OE*; *Le visible et l'invisible* (Paris: Gallimard, 1964), indicated as *VI*; *Résumés de cours* (Paris: Gallimard, 1968), indicated as *Résumés*; and *La prose du monde* (Paris: Gallimard, 1969), indicated as *Prose*.

speculative moment, the sense of a mystery to be evoked which is itself the condition of a kind of philosophical lucidity, filters through the refraction of the work. Each time that we read him, new possibilities of interpretation emerge, new questions surge forth, new applications suggest themselves.

I   Why Reread Merleau-Ponty?

Rereading a thinker whose work and world exercised a formative influence on our own present and problems, we are at first surprised to find that the 'new' materials and tensions that we discover in the work are precisely those of our own present. We wonder how we could have missed them the first time around. But then we pause, and suspect that perhaps our present interrogation too will be surpassed in time. Indeed it will: a doctrine or fact, once learned, does not call out for reconsideration; but then neither does it illuminate the obscurity of choice in a changing history. That the *oeuvre* of Merleau-Ponty resonates at each new reading indicates not merely that it is a philosophy, thought in action; but, too, that it is both itself historical and a part of the history which is our today. If I chose to write or think through my own problems and doubts across the reconsideration of the *oeuvre* of Merleau-Ponty, it is therefore not because I want to offer 'the' correct reading, right interpretation, or the reconstruction of a suddenly interrupted thought which had not become clear as to its own nature or implications. Common to Marxism and to philosophy is a concern with their own self-development: each is what it is only as having become, and each is continually reinterpreting the sense of the distance it has travelled. More: each lives the paradox that the distance is only a return to the source, for the task and goal remain constant.

Two incidental aggravations which played a role in inciting this rereading ought to be mentioned, for they weigh more than I at first suspected. The first is the French forgetting of Merleau-Ponty, which is not just a refusal to recognise a debt but, in the last resort, that significant *forgetting of origins* that marks the replacement of the labor of thought by the plump search for positivity. The claim could be made[1] that the principles and problematics of what appears centre-stage in contemporary French intellectual life are rooted in Merleau-Ponty's developing interrogations. It is not the intellectual debt alone, however, that is crucial; rather, if I may use the psychoanalytic analogy, it is that, killing the father, the cannibalistic sons have not incorporated his wisdom; and that, in erecting their defence against any thought of origins, they are also denying the possibility of a history, of change, and of the new; and further, that their thought tends as a result towards the obsessive, delusional, repetitive. This is not the place for a polemic with French modernity; nor for a demonstration of its ideological structuration. What is indicative of the weakness of this modernity is, ironically, pointed to by my second *bête noire*: the assertion, by the editor responsible for the English translations of Merleau-Ponty, that *Humanism and Terror* and *The Adventures of the Dialectic* are 'two works of political polemic which, because of their dated and topical character, will probably never be published in English in their entirety'.[2] This assertion is symptomatic not so much, or not only, of a political blindness as it is of a misunderstanding of the philosopher's *oeuvre*. Datedness and topicality characterise the raw materials out of which any work emerges, scientific and literary as well as political. Moreover, a philosophy which rejects the quest for a schema of a world pictured as lying before it, and aims at taking up the task of Hegel 'who started the attempt to explore the irrational and integrate it into an expanded reason' (*SNS*, p. 109), must be specific and polemical. The philosopher who described his task as 'to restore the world as the sense of Being, Being as absolutely different from what is "represented", that is, as vertical Being which none of the "representations" exhausts but which they all attain: savage Being' (*VI*. p. 306), could only work in this concrete manner. To think otherwise is to reduce Merleau-Ponty to Heidegger — an abuse too frequent in the United States. In short, the American reading and the French forgetting have a common result: a purification of philosophy, its separation from the texture of history, and the elimination of its own historicality.

The science and sobriety with which Merleau-Ponty handles the concrete have the effect of a shock when we reread him. We remembered that assurance with which the author of *The Structure of Behavior* and the *Phenomenology of Perception* guided us through the empirical research, convincing us of the validity of one set of arguments only to point to lacunae and move onward. We remembered too in those works the play of descriptive eidetic variations, and the assertion in the Preface to the latter, that 'the true philosophy is relearning to see the world, and in this sense the telling of a story can signify the world with as much "profundity" as a philosophical treatise' (*PhP*, p. xvi). There was also the mastery of the detail of history in *Humanism and Terror*, and the political debates within *Les Temps Modernes* which, Sartre admits, was run by Merleau-

Ponty for years. What we had forgotten was the continuation of these scientific and historico-political concerns in the later works, recalling these as concerned with a never fully elaborated ontology of whose implications we were never quite certain. We had overstressed the rupture between the ontology and the early phenomenological studies; and we took too seriously the critique of Marxism, as if to say that it meant a giving up of the political project. Suddenly, it becomes clear why the concreteness was shocking: because it *is* concrete, because the philosophy must continually confront it but dares not affront it, because in the end the concrete is the precondition on which philosophy rests at the same time that it is the eternal menace which threatens philosophy's very existence. Calling forth the philosophical investigation, the concrete is at the same time its continual refutation; unable to leave it, neither can the philosopher dwell in it. Lucid, Merleau-Ponty accepts the challenge. The new ontology is defined as a 'non-philosophy', and the traditional posing of the philosophical task is reformulated.

The return of Merleau-Ponty follows after a political experience which, it seemed, satisfied the criterion he himself described in *The Phenomenology of Perception*: 'If a revolution is truly in the sense of history, it can be thought at the same time that it is experienced' (*PhP*, p. 416). From within that experience, I wrote an earlier essay[3] attempting to 'save' and even to 'use' Merleau-Ponty first of all by distinguishing the Marxism he criticised — in essence, Leninism — from the Marxism of Marx. I tried to use his analyses of the lived world, the body, perception and language to found a politics based on the reshaping of civil society and ultimately of everyday life. While this attempt was not foreign to Merleau-Ponty's own goals, experience and reflection have shown it inadequate as a philosophy or as a politics. The position I defended 'solved' the problems which revolutionary thought must address through a kind of reduction: the political was reduced to daily life, or even to embodiment, philosophy to praxis, the thickness and multivocity of history to the transparency or givenness of the real. Such a reduction robs each of its specificity at the same time that it prohibits an understanding of their relation. A theory of embodiment or the lived world can become a disguised positivism which eliminates thought in favour of the observable givens, however sinuous, ambiguous or polyvalent they appear to the describing subject. Correlatively and in the same movement, the notion of a constitutive subject for (or before) whom the world stands as ultimately understandable, potentially transparent, freely manipulable is maintained. The *diplopie* is reduced to a plump identity. Forgotten is Marx's injunction: to be eliminated, philosophy must first be realised.

Reflecting on the euphoria of that political experience poses the question: while carried along on a wave of success, where novelty led to success and success to novelty, what were we thinking to ourselves, how were we judging our own actions, in terms of what criteria were we chosing? It seems clear that the New Left was touching at the grain or tendencies and tensions of history, yet without any preordained schema guaranteeing the aim, defining the target or chosing the weapon. To cite Merleau-Ponty again, 'the revolutionary movement, like the work of the artist, is an intention which itself creates its instruments and its means of expression' (*PhP*, p. 508). Now that the stocktaking has begun and the march slowed, we strive to understand what was, and what could have been but is not yet. Strictly political, that reflection drives us directly to the philosophical: we can enunciate the infrastructural tendencies, the counterforces opposing us as well as the inroads made by our own advances; and at the same time we know very well that, at the time of our action, those forces and those inroads existed at best as undefined possibilities which only took their contours as the result of our own activity. We encounter a dual problem. Seeking to reconstruct the impasse, we find that each step of the path brought with it side-effects; and we recognise that we have encountered the indeterminacy of the Historical. At the same time, looking at our reconstructions, we find that precisely their nature as attempts at explanation negate the 'existentiality' of the real choices at the moment they were made. This dual problematic poses the question of philosophy, and rejoins Merleau-Ponty's own quest. We only encounter the philosophical problems insofar as we are situated historical beings; and, once we encounter them as philosophical, they drive us back to our situated historicality.

The point is not philosophy *or* politics but — as with the sculptor seeking to embody movement in the inert stone — keeping both feet on the ground. Merleau-Ponty knew that '[one] does not become a revolutionary through theory but through indignation' (*HT*, p. 13). He had learned with Marxism that indignation itself calls for its own theory and that even pragmatism is itself a theory. The desired theory is not simply a philosophy nor a morality. Replying to an interviewer concerning the French colonial war in Algeria, Merleau-Ponty condemned the tortures and bankruptcy of French politics; but he insisted that such a criticism is still *only* moral: from it, no politics follows (*S*, p. 408f.). Politics is to be instrumental for morality, not vice-versa. This is why *Humanism and Terror* could work along with the communists, for 'The problems of communism are our problems', (*HT*, p. 159) even though, significantly, this did not imply the subordination of the philosopher to the Party. The 1949 essay on Machiavelli explains this:

> If by humanism one means a philosophy of the essential man, who in principle finds no difficulty in his relations with others, no opacity in the social functioning, and replaces political culture by moral exhortation, then Machiavelli is not a humanist. But if by humanism one means a philosophy which confronts as a problem the relation of man with man, and the constitution between men of a situation and a history which are common to them, then one must say that Machiavelli formulated some of the conditions of any serious humanism. (*Eloge*, pp. 375—6).

The attraction to Marxism grew from its claim to be more than simply a philosophy. In his 1945 reply to Thierry Maulnier, Merleau-Ponty defends a 'Marxism without illusions, completely experimental and voluntary', while pointing out that: 'The weakness of democratic thinking is that it is less political than moral, since it poses no problem of social structure and considers the conditions for the exercise of justice to be given with humanity' ('Concerning Marxism', *SNS*, pp. 219, 180). An existential-marxism in the Sartrean mode errs in the same manner; when its moral and philosophical machinery is applied to the real, it can only approve or condemn, never propose or create. Marxism seemed to offer more, with its theory of the proletariat as the creator of history. Yet, the more the philosopher involved himself with the political realities confronting him, the less he could accept this proposal. The French colonial involvement in Vietnam led him, in 1951, to assert that: 'What is serious is that *all* of the western doctrines are too narrow to confront the problem of the valorization of Asia' (*S*, p. 302). Nearly a decade later, with France again in a colonial war, he referred to a theory which seemed to fit the facts of the situation — Serge Mallet's notion of a 'structural imperialism' — only to object: what is its validity *as a politics*? (*S*, 19—20) A theory of 'structural imperialism' could imply a politics only if it were the expression and crystallisation of an ongoing movement whose possibilities it articulates. The theory is not there to provide answers, recipes or redprints; its task is

to restore the structure of contingency, possibility and indeterminacy that is the social-historical world. Marxism seemed to
Merleau-Ponty to provide a model; and yet its practical
impotence drove him to rethink the conditions of the possibility of its very claim.

As much as he was haunted by the possibility of a politics
which would be adequate to the demands of philosophy,
Merleau-Ponty was obsessed by the necessity which, in the
everyday as much as the sciences or the political, calls forth the
reflection of the philosopher. In a certain sense, one could say
that his entire *oeuvre* is fuelled by the question: *is philosophy
indeed possible*? It could certainly be claimed that the interface
philosophy/politics was present already in *The Phenomenology
of Perception*, as the series of reflections on Marxism from the
point of view of the concrete studies engaged by the phenomenologist suggest. But the reflection of his editor and friend,
Claude Lefort, suggests something even more important: 'In a
certain way,' writes Lefort, 'Marxism taught him what he was
seeking, what his work on the body and perception had already
led him to ponder: a relation with being which attests to our
participation in being, in this case a philosophy of history which
reveals our historicity.'[4] In Merleau-Ponty's own words, 'if
consciousness were ever absolutely cut off from the true — no
thought, not even Marxism, would be able to lay a claim to
truth. . . . Marxism needs a theory of consciousness that
accounts for its mystification without denying its participation
in the true . . .' (*AD*, pp. 57—8). The attempt to do philosophy,
to make certain that one's speculations are more than just that,
demands that one go beyond the traditional subject-object
stance. The drive to do philosophy lies indeed in the everyday;
but the everyday includes more than what presents itself to the
naked eye, more than 'the visible'. In the end, and here the
studies in perception rejoin the political thrust, we are driven to
the historical. *This historical was something that we, the New
Left, were never able to think through. Stood against the wall
by our actions and their unintended results, we are summoned
to think it.*

To think our present situation is to understand it as
historical: but what in fact is such an historical understanding?
We recall that in speaking of his own contributions (in the
Letter to Wedemeyer, 5, March 1852) Marx insisted that the
bourgeois historians had long before him recognised the
existence of the class struggle and its historical effects. What is
to be avoided is the idea that events which are history can be
interpreted *as if they were the reply to some pre-given question*,

be it one of the eternal questions of philosophy or a conjuncturally defined problem which, after its resolution, we read back into the decisions which led to the new stasis. Merleau-Ponty's work on Weber convinced him that, for example, capitalism and Calvinism are not to be understood as supplying solutions of this type. Rather, such radical innovations have precisely the effect of changing the terms in which the problem itself is posed. The movement of history, he writes, 'is of the same type as that of the Word or of Thought, and finally of the explosion of the sensible world between us: there is sense all over, dimensions and figures beyond what each "consciousness" could have produced; and yet nontheless it is men who speak, think and see. We find ourselves in the field of history as we do in the field of language or of being' (*S*, p. 28). Merleau-Ponty's philosophy accepts a challenge which confronts us as well. We can reread him today not so much 'with profit' — as the phrase goes — as with the sympathetic understanding occasioned by a coincidence of problematics. We expect no answers; at best, a formulation whose rigour and honesty, and whose contradictions and tensions, draw us toward the articulation of our past-present which will open our present-future.

II   Marxism and its Politics

Merleau-Ponty's preoccupation with Marxism, as a theory and as a politics, develops through three central axes: in the period of *Humanism and Terror* he recognises that the problems of organised communism are our own (*HT*, p. 159) and is concerned with Marxism as a manner of elucidating praxis within an historical context; in the period marked by the publication of *The Adventures of the Dialectic* and its option for an 'a-communism' (*AD*, p. 248) he sees the incoherence of the Manichaeism of the Cold War, and puts into question the centrality of the proletariat and the theory of the party as its representative; finally, after Budapest, and with decolonisation showing the inadequacy of established thought, he returns to the project of Marx itself as a philosophy which is the realisation of philosophy as a 'non-philosophy' adequate to the problems of political choice in the flesh of history, recognising the need for a new ontology and with it a new conception of the political. In each of these moments we follow the sinuous dialectic between the philosophical and the political, each demanding one another as completion and sense, yet each

inevitably betraying the other. Deceived hopes, each firing anew
the quest: in the end, the object of the quest will appear to be
nothing but the question itself, sure of itself and continually
reposed.

The first return and rethinking of Marx — by which we are
tempted today as much as Merleau-Ponty was in his own
context — aimed at transforming a theory that had become an
ideology and a mask. This appears all the easier insofar as
Marxism, even in its most distorted form, has retained the
elements of a humanist goal, the creation of a society where
humans would relate to one another as persons and not as
objects. The orthodox might ridicule it as an abstraction, but
must accept Merleau-Ponty's assertion that: 'Political problems
have their source in the fact that we are all subjects and that,
nonetheless, we see and treat the other as object' (*HT*, p. 115).
Moreover, whatever we think of its practice, we must agree that
Marxism's critique of the hypocrisy of liberal society remains
valid.[5] The transformation of Marxism by returning to its
theoretical base would seem to be facilitated also insofar as
Marxism considers itself to be based on a philosophy or theory
to which it continually makes reference and even obeissance.
Hence, the uncovering of the 'true' Marxist inspiration should
have an impact on the practice of the Marxists.

One could begin the incursion into Marxism as ideology, by
observing that the 'frequently celebrated relationship between
ideology and economics remains mystical, prelogical and un-
thinkable as long as ideology remains "subjective", economy is
conceived as an objective process, and the two are not made to
communicate in the total historical existence and in the human
objects which express it' (*SNS*, pp. 232–3). The communication between the two domains could be established through an
'existential' notion of praxis; but such an attempt demands that
praxis be conceived as situated within a history, whose nature
or structuration Marxism can begin to define. 'Marxism', writes
Merleau-Ponty in the same essay, 'is not a philosophy of the
subject, but it is just as far from a philosophy of the object: it is
a philosophy of history' (*SNS*, p. 231). Here, the elucidation of
Marxism rejoins Merleau-Ponty's own study of perception. He
had already written there: 'One would be tempted to say that it
[Marxism] does not base history and the modes of thinking on
production and the modes of working, but more generally on
the mode of existence and co-existence, on interhuman relations' (*PhP*, p. 200). If we look at how Marx actually treats
history, we see that he 'wanted to provide a *Perception of
History* which at each moment would make the lines of force

and the vectors of the present appear' (*HT*, p. 105). Or, in a later formulation:

> There is history if there is a logic *in* contingency, a reason *in* unreason; if there is an historical perception which, like perception in general, leaves in the background what cannot enter the foreground, seizes the lines of force at their birth and actively leads their traces to a conclusion. ... all symbolic systems — perception, language, history — only become what they were, though in order to do so they must be taken up in a human initiative. (*Résumés*, p. 46)

The implication is that 'History is not an external god, a hidden reason whose conclusions we would only have to record' (*AD*, p. 32). Or again, human history is 'contingent and the date of the revolution is written on no wall, nor in any metaphysical heaven' (*SNS*, p. 141). History provides a bridge, or is the context from which a text emerges. But the definitions offered are still vague, calling for theoretical and practical definition.

Political practice, like the rest of our lives, is situated in an historical milieu which forces it to action and to choice. As a theory of history, Marxism attempts to trace its logic, in order thereby to open the historical to conscious human initiative. 'Essentially, Marxism is the idea that history has a sense . . . that it is going towards the power of the proletariat which is capable, as an essential factor of production, surpassing the contractions of capitalism and organizing the human appropriation of nature; and as a 'universal class', of surpassing the social and national antagonisms as well as the conflict of man with man' (*HT*, p. 139). But with this assertion of a sense of history, Marxism runs into a problem. The reconstruction of the Trials of 1937 in *Humanism and Terror* implies that Bukharin and his co-accused were led to confess precisely for 'marxian' reasons. 'To be a revolutionary', writes Merleau-Ponty, 'is to judge that which is in the name of what is not yet, taking it for more real than the real', for 'revolutionary justice takes as its standard the future' (*HT*, p. 30). What has happened is that, in political action, the *sense* of history has been transformed, Praxis has become practice, and revolution a technique; history as perceptual has become a metaphysical object, stripped of its contingency. Practice forces the issue, fixes its object in order to get a better hold on it and aim at it.

History calls for praxis, yet praxis transforms history; by negating the openness that called it forth, praxis seems to inevitably lead to its own elimination, and its reformulation as (technological) practice. Merleau-Ponty had restated Marx's | notion of praxis as

> that sense which takes form spontaneously at the junction of the actions by which man organizes his relations with nature and with others. It is not directed from the beginning by an idea of universal or total history. We recall that Marx insists on the impossibility of thinking the future. (*Eloge*, p. 59)

The exigencies of political practice put this formulation into question. Conscious action seems to demand that the acting subject know fully the nature of the objective milieu into which the actions will be inscribed. The relativisation of subject and object thus falls by the wayside; history becomes an object which can be known. Bukharin and his judges agree that at any moment there is but one and only one politics which must be chosen; Bukharin's 'crime' is to have been wrong. But, notes Merleau-Ponty:

> When one asks for a solution, one supposes that the world and human co-existence are comparable to some problem in geometry where there is certainly an unknown but not indetermination; what one seeks is a regulated relation with what is given and with the ensemble of the givens which are equally possible. But the question of our times is precisely to know whether humanity is only a problem of that type. (*HT*, p. 203)[6]

What emerges when the sense of history is transformed or translated as indicating the *real* course which history must take is only too patently illustrated by the political practice of the Communist Parties. In a 1948 discussion, Merleau-Ponty illustrates the results under the title, 'Paranoiac Politics'. He stresses the irony that 'The thought which wanted to be the most historical and the most objective, leaving aside in the last analysis all the felt and lived differences in the experience of the actors in the drama, finds itself delivered over to phantasies; it is at the height of subjectivity' (*S*, p. 316) Marked by a 'neurosis of the future' (*S*, p. 89; also *Prose*, p. 118), Party marxism becomes a 'voluntarism based on absolute knowledge'. (*AD*, p. 117).[7] For after all, if one knows the course of History, one's actions will always correspond to that sense, while those of one's opponents will fall into the realm of mere appearance, the field of error.

The Marxian theory of history which seemed so convincing

and rational finds itself transformed into a *point d'honneur*, as
Marx once said of philosophy; and this transformation seems to
be necessitated by the concrete demands of practice. The
unification of philosophy and politics seems to have failed;
politics has forced philosophy to separate itself from the real,
and as separate philosophy becomes subjective, an ideology.
Merleau-Ponty had been willing to work with, though separately
from, the Communists in 1948. Now that he has reworked the
bases of the Marxian theory, the practical question which must
be posed is whether it is the theory or the practice has led to
the deformation of communism. *The Adventures of the
Dialectic* take up this challenge, beginning with a renewed
investigation of that history whose transformation from sense
to reality was responsible the failed marriage.

If the exigencies of practice have transformed the philosophy, a renewed investigation of the specificity of the
philosophical task is necessary. This rethinking, in the incomplete *Prose of the World*, in the summaries of the courses at the
Collège de France, and in the inaugural lecture, *In Praise of
Philosophy*, takes the philosopher beyond the still vague and
unarticulated notion of history and makes possible his understanding of the deviation undergone by Marxism. 'There is no
history if the path of things is a series of episodes without
relation, or if it is a combat already won in the heaven of ideas',
he insists (*Résumés*, p. 46). Or again, in the Inaugural Address:
'History has no sense if its sense is understood as that of a river
which flows under the action of all-powerful causes towards an
ocean where it disappears. All recourse to universal history cuts
out the sense of the event, renders insignificant actual history,
and is a masque for nihilism' (*Eloge*, p. 61). And, after a
penetrating critique of Malraux's image of the *musée imaginaire*,
where the history of painting is portrayed as a linear progress
accompanied along its path by a kind of Super-Painter or Spirit,
he takes up the old problem:

> History is judge. Not History as the Power of a moment or
> a century. History as that place where, beyond the limits of
> the centuries and the countries all that we have said and done
> which is most true and most valid, given the situations in
> which we had to say it, is reunited, inscribed and accumu-
> lated. (*Prose*, 121)

History is thus reaffirmed as a logic within *contingency*; Weber's
notion of the *Wahlverwandtschaften* expresses precisely and
concretely what Merleau-Ponty is striving to understand. So too

is his intuition expressed in another area:

> The theory of the sign as linguistics elaborates it implies perhaps an historical theory of sense which goes beyond the alternative of *things* and *consciousness*. Living language is that concretion of spirit and of the thing which poses the problem. . . . The presence of the individual to the institution and of the institution to the individual is clear in the case of linguistic change . . . and Saussure may well have sketched a new philosophy of history. (*Eloge*, pp. 63, 64).

Linguistics is not language, not coincident with the expression; it is the theory of the sense and conditions of possibility of language and expression. Its status provides a clue to the question posed by the philosopher: 'History realises an exchange of all orders of activity, none of which can be given the dignity of exclusive cause; and the question is, rather, to know whether that solidarity of the problems announces their simultaneous resolution or whether there is only concordance and reciprocal implication in the interrogation' (*Résumés*, p. 44). On this question rests the problematic of philosophy and politics. It will require a reformulation of the ontological presuppositions of philosophy for the question to receive an answer.

What emerges from Merleau-Ponty's reflections at this stage is that Marxism finds itself in the tenuous and tense position of being at once a part of the very history of which it claims to express the sense. Everywhere and nowhere, it accepts the challenge of philosophy and of politics. This was of course Marx's intention, but one which was asserted rather than argued. Beyond the antinomies of a Weberian Liberalism, Merleau-Ponty sees Lukács try to render explicit the insertion and task: 'the recognition without restriction of history as the single milieu of our errors and our verifications [that will] lead us to recover an absolute in the relative' (*AD*, p. 44). But the immersion in this flux demands that we have some vantage point from which to judge.

> This immanent sense of interhuman events: where indeed can we place it? It is not, or not always, in men, in consciousness. But, outside of them, it appears that there are only blind events since we have renounced the placing an absolute knowledge behind the things. *Where* then is the historical process, and what mode of existence can we accept for historical forms such as feudalism, capitalism, the

proletariat, of which we speak as if they were persons who
know and who wish, who are hidden behind the multiplicity
of events. We don't see clearly what these prosopopoeias
represent. (*Eloge*, p. 62)

The search for a vantage-point or standpoint corresponds
exactly to the shift which was seen to transform the Marxian
theory of history when it became practice: the sense of history
is transformed into the reality of history. Lukács' theory of the
proletariat as the subject-object of history whose self-knowledge
is also the knowledge and transformation of the capitalist
totality points to the centrality of the proletariat for any
revolutionary theory, but at the same time it leads to the theory
of the Party whose 'absolute authority . . . is the purity of the
transcendental subject incorporated by force into the world'
(*AD*, p. 192). Lukács' justification of Leninism and his sub-
sequent political choices, appear to be inscribed in the
exigencies of a theory which accepts its historical insertion and
strives to become praxis.

Inserted into the tissue of history, revolution becomes what
traditional philosophy has always sought to be. For Western
Marxism, writes Merleau-Ponty, 'The revolution was that
sublime point at which the real and values, the subject and the
object, judgement and discipline, the individual and the totality,
the present and the future, instead of entering into collision
gradually entered into complicity' (*AD*, p. 12). The class-
consciousness which is essential to this process 'is a praxis, that
is, less than a subject and more than an object, a pulverized
existence, a possibility which appears in the situation of the
proletarian, at the joints of the things and its life, in a
word — Lukács takes over here Weber's term — an "objective
possibility" ' (*AD*, p. 66). What, though, is the status of this
'objective possibility'? 'The profound, philososphical, sense of
the notion of praxis is to install us in an order which is not that
of knowledge but that of communication, exchange, frequen-
tation. There is a proletarian praxis which operates such that
the class exists before it is known' (*AD*, p. 70). The brute
existence of the class must be raised to the level of consciousness; this is where the party enters. 'In philosophical terms: the
party goes beyond the revolt of the proletariat; it realizes the
revolt by destroying it as an immediate revolt; it is the negation
of that negation, or in other words it is the mediation, its action
is such that the class which refuses becomes the class which
founds and, finally, a society without classes' (*S*, p. 350). The
theory of the party is subtle, and philosophically consistent:

The party doesn't know everything, doesn't see everything; and yet its authority is absolute because, if spontaneous history has a chance to become manifest history, it can only be in it. . . . In the absence of any metaphysics of history, the dialectic of the proletariat and the party unites in itself and carries all the others: Marxist philosophy has as its final condition not what the proletarians think, nor what the party thinks that they should think, but the recognition by the proletariat of its own action in the politics that the party present to it. . . . The party is at once everything and nothing: it is nothing but the mirror in which the forces of the proletariat, dispersed throughout the world, concentrate themselves; it is everything because without it the truth 'in itself' would never become manifest, would never complete itself as truth. (*AD*, pp. 106—7)

'Everything and nothing': Merleau-Ponty had insisted that the place of philosophy was 'everywhere and nowhere'. The crucial difference is that this place is now situated, in a real history. 'The party is thus like a mystery of reason: it is that place in history where the *sense that exists* understands itself, where the concept becomes life . . .' (*AD*, p. 71). By an ironic reversal, however, the union of philosophy and history in the party does not achieve the final reconciliation. The Party is transformed into precisely that impotent philosopher with no hold on reality — save that of force. The paranoiac politics by which the party, armed with the authority of Reason, substitutes itself for a proletariat whose 'objective possibility' is now incarnate in the Party itself. Should the Party seek to avoid this ironic inversion by following or aiding the masses in the struggles which they undertake, then not only is this a violation of Leninism; more important, it is the other side of the ironic paradox: for then there is no need for the philosophy since the theory, and the unity is again broken. We recall this problem as having already been posed by he young Marx's discussion of the 'practical' and 'philosophical' parties.

III   Towards a Reformulation

That goal of Marxism which Merleau-Ponty had made his own — the unification but not the conflation of philosophy and politics — failed. In the Preface to *Signes*, he returns to the problem, looking at the dilemma facing those ex-communists attempting to understand their situation. He begins by noting

that politics is the 'modern tragedy', in the sense that everyone
had expected from it *the* solution (*S*, p. 11). Marxism's impact
had been to make history, like Hegel's morning newspaper, a
metaphysically charged experience. Even outside the party, the
tendency of many is to maintain this attitude, to expect that, in
some future, the proletariat will reappear on the stage of
history. But, even if one grants Marxism 'its pretension not to
be a philosophy, to be the expression of a single grand historical
fact', nonetheless 'since one also admits that there is not at
present a proletarian movement on a world scale, one puts
Marxism into a position of inactivity and one defines oneself as
an honorary Marxist' (*S*, p. 14). A rethinking of the fundamental philosophical options of Marxism is necessary. The question
is not 'are you or are you not a Marxist?' Rather, in this case,
error is not the opposite of truth; it is rather, says Merleau-
Ponty, a 'truth which missed its chance. (*vérité manquée*, *S*,
p. 16).

> There is an internal relation of the positive and the negative,
> and this is what Marx envisioned, even if he was wrong to
> restrain it to the dichotomy of subject/object. This internal
> relation operates in entire sections of his work, and it opens
> new dimensions to his historical analysis and makes these
> analyses such that they can cease to be conclusive in the
> sense that Marx intended without ceasing to be the sources of
> sense and reinterpretable. The theses of Marx can remain true
> in the way that Pythagorian theorem is true, no longer in the
> sense that it was for the inventor — as an identical truth and
> property of space itself — but as the property of a certain
> model of space among other possible spaces. (*S*, 16)

Marx has become a 'classic'. Those who have broken with the
Party affirm that there are other possibilities, other 'spaces',
other theatres of history with more than one dimension,
reference or source of sense. 'They have rejected a certain idea
of Being as object, and of identity and difference. They have
adopted the idea of a Being which is coherent in many foci or
many dimensions. And they say that they are not philosophers?' (*S*, p. 18). Marxism, continues Merleau-Ponty, wanted
to be the expression of the operation of history itself. 'But that
was precisely the height of philosophical arrogance' (*S*, p. 18).
It is to the reformulation of the philosophical task itself that
the critique of Marxism leads.

What emerges from the second go-around with Marxism is a
conception of history which, in its surface contours, appears to

return to the original insight. In the Preface to *Signes*, we read, for example:

> What good is it to ask oneself if history is made by men or by things, since from all evidence human initiatives do not annul the weight of things, and the 'force des choses' always operates through men? It is precisely this failure of the analysis when it wants to return everything to a single dimension which reveals the true milieu of history. There is no analysis which is final because there is a flesh of history; in it like in our body, everything carries, everything counts — both the infrastructure and the idea which we have of it, and especially the perceptual exchanges between the one and the other where the weight of things becomes also a sign, things forces, the accounting an event. (*S*, p. 28)

Here, however, the assertion is no longer formulated in terms of what Merleau-Ponty calls the 'philosophy of consciousness', or the subject/object dualism. For that philosophical stance, the problem of *constitution* through a form of interaction was the centre of concern: the proletariat was the embodied subject of history, whose traces philosophy must follow through the world which proletarian action directly and indirectly constitutes. Marxism opened up a new approach; but insofar as the history with which it was concerned was, ultimately, to be constituted by the proletariat, it could not live up to its radical promise; posed as acting in the real, the proletariat was transformed into its conscious incarnation, becoming the Party imposing itself upon the real.

The renewed formulation of the question demands a new ontology, which can deal in a world which is neither purely rational nor wholly recalcitrant to thought. The Marxism which interprets history as the product of proletarian praxis neglects the density of the historical milieu, where the effect of actions is not that which the rational actor may have intended.

To understand at once the logic of history and its detours, its sense and that which in it is resistant to sense, the Marxist had to conceptualize the sphere proper to history, the institution, which does not develop according to causal laws, like another nature, but always in dependence on what it signifies, not according to eternal ideas, but rather by bringing more or less under its laws events which, as far as it is concerned, are fortuitous, and by letting itself be changed by their suggestions. . . . This order of 'things' which teaches 'relationships between persons,' sensitive to all the heavy conditions which bind it to the order of nature, open to all that personal life can invent is, in modern language, the sphere of symbolism, and Marx's thought was to find its outlet here. (*AD*, p. 88)

This passage contains a dual hint. The 'sphere of symbolism' was already referred to in Merleau-Ponty's suggestion that we learn from the theory of the sign in linguistics. In this context, his work on the question of artistic expression could be integrated into the problematic that we are discussing here, though detailed discussion would take us too far afield. The second suggestion in the cited passage is that the 'sphere proper to history' is the *institution*. In the lectures at the Collége de France on 'The "institution" in Personal and Public History', Merleau-Ponty stresses that 'We are looking here in the notion of the institution for a remedy to the difficulties of the philosophy of consciousness' (*Résumés*, 59). This notion, which he says gives us a 'revision of Hegelianism' (id. p. 65), is explicated as follows:

We thus understood here by institution those events of an experience which give it durable dimensions, with relation to which a whole series of other experiences have a sense, form an understandable succession or a history — or, again, those events which depose in me a sense, not as a survival or residue, but as the appeal to a succession, the demand for a future. (id. p. 61)

This is Merleau-Ponty's answer in the polemic with Sartre, where he exclaims, 'The question is to know whether, as Sartre says, there exist only *men* and *things*, or whether there also exists that interworld which we call history, symbolism, truth-to-be-realized [*vérité à faire*]' (*AD*, p. 269). The philosophy of the *Cogito*, whose sophistry and violence Merleau-Ponty unravels at length in the polemic with Sartre in *The Adventures*, is incapable of dealing with this flesh which is history.

Obsessed with the thickness of the world, unwilling to leap beyond it to the comforts of philosophy, Merleau-Ponty's attention during the last years of his life was focused on the twin problems of the possibility of a philosophy-non-philosophy and the problem of nature. Of the latter, he writes:

Pure object, being in itself in which all that exists is

contained, and which nonetheless is not to be found in human experience because, from the outset, experience works [*façonne*] and transforms it: nature is for experience everywhere and nowhere, like an obsession. In seeking to elucidate this problem, one is thus not so far from history. (Résumés, p. 93)

Once again, the return of the problem of history in all its opacity! And in the same breath, nature is defined with that very phrase which continually reoccurs under the philosopher's pen: everywhere and nowhere, nature like philosophy and history is an obsession, but also an appeal. The paths to its elucidation are first of all those of phenomenology. However:

These descriptions, that phenomenology, always have something disappointing because they limit themselves to uncovering the negative in the positive and the positive in the negative. Reflexion seems to demand supplementary explanations. The description will not have its full philosophical weight until one questions the foundation of that demand itself, until the principled reasons for which the relations of the negative and the positive present themselves thus are given: this is nothing but the posing of the *Bases of a Dialectical Philosophy*. (id., pp. 72—3)

The disappointment described here is precisely the one we have been feeling as we trace Merleau-Ponty's confrontation with Marxism. Continually working within the problematic of philosophy-history-politics as posed by Marx, Merleau-Ponty seemed to be playing Marx against Marx (or the Marxists). When he went outside, it was only to phenomenological description that he had recourse, or to political facts. He knew that more was needed, that the terms of the problem could not be correctly defined if this were the only type of result which emerged. It is time that we turn to the new ontology, to the dialectical philosophy, to see whether it succeeds more adequately in enabling us to think the problems of philosophy and politics.

IV The Question Re-posed

Rereading Merleau-Ponty from the standpoint of our own political experience and political hopes, we have found nothing like a solution. The temptation for the would-be political actor is to stop the rereading, to point to the monstrous structural contradictions and human misery of the present, and to leave philosophy to the philosophers while personally turning to practical politics. It would not be hard to find ways of defending Marx despite the philosopher's criticisms; nor is it difficult to use elements of the phenomenologist's descriptive discoveries in this venture.[8] But we are struck by the doggedness with which he pursued the problem of politics and philosophy, by the combination of rigorous exposition and creative interpretation in his reading of Marx, and perhaps most of all by the insightful Preface to *Signes* which anticipated so many of our criticisms. The New Left belongs to the same revolutionary tradition as Marxism not because of a common trunk of theory or ideology, but because its spontaneous praxis, emerging from immediate indignation, carried with it the spur of theorisation, the felt presence of a sense which was striving to articulate itself across time and through human interrelations. It would be a betrayal of that experience which permitted and forced us to think for ourselves, beyond the received categories, outside the routine of the political rituals, were we to abandon Merleau-Ponty now, simply because he offers no ready-made solutions. The only honest continuation of our own project today seems to lie precisely in thinking it through to the end; and that is just another way of returning to our origins.

The 'neurosis of the future' which would demand a solution, as well as the confusion of a moral stance with a political analysis, are clear in the reproach addressed to Merleau-Ponty by Henri Lefèbvre: 'the philosophy of ambiguity justifies [the present] situation instead of denouncing it.'[9] At the time of *Humanism and Terror*, Merleau-Ponty had conceived of his own role in a framework seemingly similar to that of Lefèbvre:

> Efficacious or not, [the role of philosophy] is to clarify the ideological situation, to underline beyond the paradoxes and the contingencies of present history the true terms of the human problem, to recall to the Marxists their humanist inspiration, to recall to the democracies their fundamental hypocrisy, and to maintain intact, against all propaganda, the chances that history might once again become clear. (*HT*, p. 196)

Only a few years later, reflecting on what he had done in *Humanism and Terror*, Merleau-Ponty suggested in his Inaugural Address that 'Philosophy explains that, dialectically, an opponent, in the given conditions, becomes the equivalent of a traitor. Such a language is precisely the contrary of that of the powers; the powers cut short the premises and say more succinctly: there are only criminals in that group' (*Eloge*, p. 69). In this suggestion, the task of the philosopher is no longer that of external judge or moral consciousness; by making explicit the premises, the philosopher restores the dimensions of uncertainty, of choice, and the work of history in the making. In a philosophical text dating from the same period, this position is stated explicitly:

> Perhaps the reader will say here that we live him without an answer, and that we limit ourselves to a 'So it is' which explains nothing. ... But when it is a question of speaking [*la parole*] or of the body or of history, unless one wants to destroy what one seeks to understand . . . one can only show the paradox of the expression. (*Prose*, p. 160)

Philosophy must deliberately restrain itself, becoming 'phenomenology' in the sense originally conceived by Hegel: the science of the forms of appearance. Such a self-limitation must, however, be philosophically — ontologically — grounded, as Merleau-Ponty's political reflections have already indicated.

The phenomenological project led the philosopher to the ontological question *via* the reflection on history as the mediation and medium of social life. Subject and object were relativised, and the philosophy of consciousness or constitution (the *Sinngebung* by any intentional subject) had to be rejected. In an article of 1947, Merleau-Ponty had defined his task:

> Metaphysical consciousness has no other objects than those of everyday experience: this world, other people, human history, truth, culture. But instead of taking them all as settled, as consequences with no premises, as if they were self-evident, it rediscovers their fundamental strangeness to me and the miracle of their appearing. (*SNS*, p. 165)

More than a decade later, he restated the philosophical task in significantly modified terms:

> Philosophy has as its charge not to decompose our relation with the world into real elements, or even into ideal elements which would make of the world an ideal object, but to find the articulations in it, to awaken regulated relations of pre-possession, of recapitulation, of encroachment, which are asleep in our ontological landscape, which remain there only

in the form of traces, and which, nonetheless, continue to function in it, to institute novelty into it. (*VI*, p. 137)

In the first citation, the world is still an 'out-there' which is to be rediscovered by the subject using its analytic capacities. By the time of the second suggestion, the role of the subject is diminished and made almost dependent on the instituting activity of that 'ontological landscape', which itself is to be approached only obliquely. The second passage makes a further assertion, which carries us forward. We are neither to decompose the world into real elements, nor to constitute it out of purely ideal moments; for the stuff of the world, the Being at which ontology aims, falls into neither of these slots. Here too the assertion directed against the 'American' antiseptic reading of Merleau-Ponty finds its justification.

The turn to this 'new ontology' was presaged in Merleau-Ponty's earlier phenomenological work and made inevitable by the confrontation with Marxism and politics. The first course he offered at the Collége de France was entitled 'The Sensible World and the World of Expression' (1952—3). From the outset, the philosopher recognised that: 'Perceptive consciousness is thus indirect or even inverted in relation to an ideal of adequation which it presupposes but at which it does not look face to face' (Résumés, p. 12). The dream of truth as an adequation of thought and thing is an impossibility; the expression can never coincide with what it seeks to express. Such a collapsing of the poles would eliminate both: the coincidence of thought and thing, expression and expressed, is the dream of positivism, or of the technocrat; it makes human action, history or even consciousness impossible. The study of perception revealed a paradox whose understanding demands a rethinking of the notion of the Being which it is to perceive or express. In the *Visible and the Invisible*, this problem of representation continually recurs. 'What I want to do', writes the author in one of his working notes, 'is to restore the world as the sense of Being absolutely different from the "represented", that is, as the vertical Being which none of the "representations" exhausts but which they all "attain" — savage Being' (*VI*, p. 306). Such 'savage Being' is not to be equated with a kind of pristine nature; it is not without the effect and affect of human action, nor in its bruteness is it somehow a-logical or inaccessible. The course on 'The Problems of Passivity: Sleep, Unconscious and Memory' (1954—5) attempts to work through one aspect of the assertion, insisting that the analyses of these phenomena shows precisely the ambiguous structure at which the philosopher is grasping. Freud is invoked, for example, to demonstrate that:

> The essential of Freudianism is not to have shown that there is an entirely different reality underneath the appearances, but that the analysis of a behavior finds several layers of signification, that each of these has its truth, that the plurality of possible interpretations is the discursive expression of a mixed life where each choice always has several senses without our being able to say that one of them alone is true. (*Résumés*, p. 71)

The importance of Freud, and what the phenomenological descriptions detail, is that the most strict attention to the facts, to experience and to our praxis, discloses precisely an ambiguity, a multi-layered structure which cannot be rendered univocal without losing the experience from which one began. What is needed is a 'philosophy-non-philosophy', which would preserve the chiasm between the experience and its sense.

Formulated in this manner, Merleau-Ponty's task rejoins that the young Marx confronting the Hegelian systematisation. In the course which he was teaching at the time of his sudden death, the philosopher had chosen to confront the problem of 'Philosophy and Non-Philosophy since Hegel'. The text is symptomatic of the care and creativity which Merleau-Ponty always devoted to interpretating Marx; and his return to Marx after the seemingly (for him) conclusive refutation in *The Adventures* is itself significant. The Introduction to Hegel's *Phenomenology* confronts the relation of phenomenology/ontology; and the interesting dilemma is that at the same time that the text is to describe the advent of consciousness, this movement with its ruptures and its leaps to sense is described by a Third Party, the philosopher who has already made the journey. A double tension is thus present: that between experience and its sense; and that between this oscillating movement and the philosopher for whom there is both experience and sense, but who must avoid adding to or aiding the movement through foreign knowledge imported from without. A further tension is brought into the text through the questions that we (and Merleau-Ponty), in the wake of our own knowledge and experience of Marxism, bring with us.

In 'Philosophy and Non-Philosophy since Hegel', (1960—1) Merleau-Ponty accompanies Hegel (and Heidegger) through the path of an introduction to the tasks of philosophy and the acquisition of the philosophical armament in order to work out his own position. Beginning with immediate experience, it is suggested that what the philosopher extracts and understands is the 'inverted world', but that this philosophical experience is at the same time part of the world. In accord with the historical and phenomenological relativisation of the subject/object relation, the philosopher observes that 'The phenomenon is not object nor is it subject. Not object: it concerns me, and in presenting it I understand myself. Not subject: it still has to become for itself. It is the hidden framework of "subject" and "object" — object returning to itself, subject outside itself' (*PNP*, p. 108). Insofar as Merleau-Ponty has learned that History cannot be invoked simply as a guarantee of sense, he has to look for the sense of this experience in the experience itself. But what in fact is this experience? Merleau-Ponty had earlier insisted that '. . . if consciousness were ever absolutely cut off from the true . . . no thought, not even Marxism, would be able to lay a claim to truth' (*AD*, p. 57—8). The Hegelian text which he is following describes the quest of consciousness, first assuming that the 'object' is the Essence or Concept which theory seeks, then driven to locate the latter in the 'subject'. The task that emerges from this instability, insists Merleau-Ponty along with Hegel, is to find the standard of truth in the experience itself.

> It seems that dialectics is of course not a fact of consciousness in the sense of a spiritual motor — for then it would be *unsere Zutat* [our addition] — but it is not either an objective movement (for the same reason). It is the *Movement of the Contents*, of experience: that is, of this new ontological milieu which is the *Erscheinung* [appearance] and which doesn't exist without a relation to someone who has the experience of it. It is not a property of consciousness; it is rather consciousness which is a property of the dialectic: dialectics has consciousness (and seems impossible without consciousness through which it makes itself the production of the new object) — but an opaque consciousness, experience. (*PNP*, p. 116)

The 'new ontological milieu' is opaque; and yet it would be erroneous to think that it should be wrenched lose from its experiential axis and driven towards the univocalty and transparency of the traditional notions of truth.

> The ambiguity is not a lack of univocity. It is 'good.' There is no problem if the *Zweideutigkeit* [dual signification] is

present as such; if the absolute is that light of truth which appears in the thickness of the experience and which embraces the relativized subject and object. But if one formulates this in terms of consciousness, one has an equivocation. (*PNP*, p. 127)

The traditional rejection of ambiguity — and hence of experience as the soil on which philosophy is alone possible — is based on a philosophy of consciousness, of the subject/object dualism, of appearance and essence. 'The problem of a philosophy which *is* non-philosophy remains entire', writes Merleau-Ponty, 'as long as one thinks *Consciousness* or *Gegenstand* [object]' (*PNP*, p. 118). Rejecting the tradition, the philosopher must assure himself of his new grounds. The reference to the absolute is not accidental or insignificant, any more than is the return to Hegel, whose beginning of the attempt to integrate the 'irrational' into philosophy the philosopher had commented on fifteen years previously.

The problem that emerges is that if we are to show how experience moves towards truth, we seem at the same time forced to move away from the *lived* experience from which we began, distorting it while robbing it of its specificity. The problem is not a new one for Merleau-Ponty; he had already commented at length on Malraux's notion of a *déformation cohérente* in the phenomenon of artistic expression, and had observed a similar experience in the perceptual sphere. Here, however, the problem is taken up in the political context of Marxism.

To put the dialectic back on its feet (and one forgets that it is Hegel who said explicity that the dialectic is a world on its head) would be to destroy it. Philosophy, that is, the access to the absolute, seems to be essentially experience, that is, entry into the phenomena, taking part in their maturation, in experience. It is this because it is only in the relation of *experiri*, by existing the things, that one can be present at the advent of knowledge. (*PNP*, p. 104)

Philosophy must be experiential, but it is not conflated with the *things* of experience. Experience is a relation; neither subject nor object, it is what makes these possible, while it itself cannot be accounted for simply by their combination. The dualism tends, however, to re-emerge; we find ourselves confronted with two orders: the *idea* of experience acting from outside the experience as a control on that experience itself. This, continues

Merleau-Ponty's marginal note, is like the *idea* of the proletariat
in the form of the party becoming a control over the
proletariat. We confront a dilemma, he adds a few pages later:
'either the experience is truly taken into account, in which case
it is a wandering, sceptical one; or it is understood, transformed
into its truth, but then it is transcended. And the pretension to
get into this second order by experience is the most complete
dogmatism, for it is a dogmatism disguised as the movement of
things' (*PNP*, pp. 121—2). Such a 'dogmatism' is present in
Marx as well as in Hegel.

The young Marx seems to have recognised and confronted
the antinomic task of a philosophy which, in refusing to
transform or transcend experience, would be a non-philosophy.

> Marx critiques the pretension of philosophical *Denken*
> [thinking] to remain within itself in the other than itself, to
> contain in itself and possess its contradictory — to go beyond
> it from within or to understand it from without, without
> experience. The problem is to reconceive the philosophical
> proximity and distance, the nowhere and everywhere of
> philosophy, with the condition: not to give to conscious-
> ness — and especially to 'self-consciousness' — the power of
> carrying in itself its contradictory, of being within itself in
> what is the inverse of it. Not to construct under the name of
> *Wissen* [knowledge] a power of being everything which is
> illusory, a negativity which is so total that it digests and
> founds all and nothing. (*PNP*, p. 164)

When the young Marx posed as his task the making worldy of
philosophy and the making philosophical of the world, he
recognised at the same time that this did not mean the
collapsing of the one into the other. Philosophy, he insisted,
was both true *and* false; it was not to be corrected either by the
'philosophical party', which wished to apply it to the world, nor
by the 'practical party', which wanted to change the world
without the aid of philosophy. Philosophy and non-philosophy
from such a point of view share a non-dialectical approach, for
they implicitly suggest that the world of experience and its
philosophical understanding are separated one from the other;
and in such separation, each is false. Under the influence of
Feuerbach, the young Marx is seen to want 'a "philosophy"
which is not a philosophy of consciousness but of sensuous
man' (*PNP*, p. 159). As such, Marxism will be the 'non-
philosophy' whose task is to remain with experience in
witnessing the advent of its truth.

Merleau-Ponty had already argued in *The Adventures* that by 1850 the philosophical project of the young Marx was abandoned in favour of 'scientific socialism'. (*AD*, p. 85) Coming at Marxism from the standpoint of the possibility of a non-philosophy, his analysis is richer and more nuanced.

> It is not the passage from philosophy to science; it is the passage from 'direct' philosophy (man, nature, Feuerbach) to another conception of philosophy (man, nature attained through the experience of capitalism; that experience understood and brought to its concept uncovers the proletarian class which is the historical formation in which the understanding of capital is realized; the identification of he who thinks the functioning of capital with that historical formation itself: the latter, thus, reveals the *Corresponding Point* to absolute Knowledge, is *Erscheinende Wissen* [appearing knowledge]. *Capital* rejoins the intuition of the proletariat just as the *Logic* of Hegel rejoins the *Phenomenology*). (*PNP*, p. 147)

The discovery of the proletariat as that subject/object of history which is the solution to the 'riddle of history' (Marx) appears at first to follow within the parameters of the non-philosophy which remains faithful to the phenomenological task. Much of the analysis in the 1844 *Manuscripts* must be understood in this optic. But just as Hegel was unable to remain with experience, subordinating the *Phenomenology* to the *Logic*, so too was Marx driven by his *philosophical* presuppositions to subordinate the proletariat to the logic of *Capital*.

> Here one goes from reality (capital) to the appearance (the proletariat): the 'becoming of the truth' is substituted for the 'becoming of consciousness' just like with Hegel's *Logic*. But this is still philosophy and still Hegel — under the appearance of abandoning philosophy it is the most audacious philosophy: the philosophy which hides itself in the 'things', which is masked by an apparent positivism — philosophy precisely in the sense that it doesn't want to be philosophy. And, inversely, the explicit philosophy of 1844 is not far from the concrete. (*PNP*, p. 160)

The move here is that insofar as the proletariat is the truth of the experience of capitalism, while at the same time remaining itself experiential and praxical, it itself needs to be brought to its truth, which is the science of *Capital*. The reality of capitalism is itself an 'inverted world', insists Marx repeatedly; it thus stands to the concrete proletariat as philosophy does to experience. From here it is but a short step to the assertion that *Capital* is nothing but the experience of the proletariat brought to its truth or concept; and precisely insofar as the relation philosophy/experience is implicitly maintained, Merleau-Ponty is correct in indicating that we have here a disguised philosophy hidden in the movement of the things themselves. At the same time, we have the transformation of the experience of the proletariat into its logic or truth. This latter 'mystery of reason', as Merleau-Ponty had referred to it in *The Adventures*, forces us back into the dilemma of philosophy-non-philosophy: i.e., that the idea of experience dominates over the experience itself, making way for a dogmatism which justifies itself as being the movement of the concrete itself, the expression of the truth of History.

In this consideration of Marx and Hegel, the contribution of the new ontology begins to make itself felt. Both were caught in a philosophy of consciousness, with its corrollary, a philosophy of the object. The tension could not be maintained, with the result that the absolute was imported to bridge the gap: for Hegel, from the side of the Reason; for Marx, from the side of the things.[10] As opposed to this, Merleau-Ponty had argued in his course, 'Dialectical Philosophy', (1955—6):

> There is thus a dialectical absolute, which is there only in order to hold the multiple in its place and in its relief, to oppose the absolutization of these relations. It is 'fluidified' in them, it is immanent to experience. This is by definition an unstable position . . . (*Résumés*, p. 82)

If the instability cannot be maintained, the possibility of philosophy itself as the concern with the advent of knowledge in experience is put into question. This question is dealt with in the course of 1958—9 through an investigation of Hegel's legacy as seen through Husserl and Heidegger. Concerning the latter, Merleau-Ponty writes that:

> The term Being is not, like other terms, a sign to which one could find a corresponding 'representation' or an object: its sense is not distinct from its operation; by it we have Being which speaks in us rather than we speaking of Being. (id., p. 155)

Heidegger fails because he seeks a direct expression of Being,

even while knowing such an expression to be impossible.
Merleau-Ponty's option, to approach the problem of Being
through the beings of Nature, finds a congenial resonance in
Marx. The philosophy elaborated in 1844, he says, seeks

> a single Being where negativity is at work. Thus: nature will
> not be defined as a pure object, exteriority, but as 'sensible',
> sensual, nature as we see it. Natural beings have a preordered
> internal relation to one another. Man will not be defined
> either as pure subject or as a fragment of nature, but by a
> sort of coupling of subject/object with two faces: relation to
> an object, or active object and thus as essentially relation to
> other men, generic being (*Gattungswesen*], society — this
> relation being transformation and result of the natural
> relation of a living being to external beings. History being in
> this sense the flesh itself of man. (*PNP*, p. 168)

Both the unstable dialectical absolute and the Being whose
sense is its operation are thus returned, along with Nature, to
the flesh of history. 'The task of philosophy would be . . . to
elaborate such a concept of Being that permits the contradic-
tions — neither accepted no|"surpassed" — to find their place in
it' (*Résumés*, p. 128). Such a philosophy would depend on a
different ontology than the one dominated by the simple
perceptual metaphor of a subject seeing an object; and it would
demand a different conception of truth than that of adequation
or expression. History would not be a future conceived spatially
and linearly — be it as judge, openness or determined; or be it
even as that *vérité à faire* which Merleau-Ponty (along with the
Frankfurt School) had accepted. History would be our present:
a task always to be begun anew, whose accomplishment would
be our end.

With this, we have returned to the question from which we
began; and to the accusation of a quietism. It could be claimed
that Merleau-Ponty has returned us to Marx's own starting
point; and that he has explained the ontological presuppositions
that led Marx astray. More than that, when Marx speaks in 1844
about the 'positive' in Hegel he expects to find there a solution
to the 'riddle of history' by means of the negation of the
negation. 'Marx', writes Merleau-Ponty, is a 'positivist for a
far-off future, beyond communism' (*PNP*, p. 168). Alienated
objectivation is to be replaced by its non-alienated form, argues
Marx. But this is precisely the vision of the positivist, for
whom — exactly like the hated enemy, Hegel — the concrete
world delivers up its essence immediately to a disincarnate

consciousness who is a pure receiver. 'Positivism, in a sense — ironically — produces the same result as the absolute negation or the negative absolute of Hegel: i.e., the hidden sense of history, combat of the gods. Stalinism and Hegelianism. One could even say that Hegel maintains more the sense of negativity, of tension' (*PNP*, p. 173). Merleau-Ponty's claim is that the 'sense of negativity' which would find its expression in the new ontology cannot provide grounds for the elimination either of philosophy or of the sensuous and opaque structure which is historical experience. As such, his reply to the accusation would be twofold, with Marx and against Marxism. In *The Adventures*, he had written:

> . . . it is correct to say that there is not much sense in beginning Bolshevism anew at the very moment when its revolutionary failure is evident. But there is not much sense either in beginning Marx anew if his philosophy is involved [*en cause*] in that failure; no sense in acting as if that philosophy emerged intact from the affair, as if it were in fact the end of the interrogation and self-critique of humanity. (*AD*, p. 124)

So much for Marxism! As to Marx himself, Merleau-Ponty would return to that original problematic, replying to the accuser as Marx had replied: philosophy cannot be eliminated without being realised. This does not of course exclude politics; but it avoids the conflation of theory and experience which wreaked havoc with the Marxian project.

V   And Now?

We turned to Merleau-Ponty with a political question; and after finding that same question running throughout his work, we were denied an answer, receiving only the promise of and demand for a 'new ontology'. It is not simply that death denied him and us that answer. The thrust of Merleau-Ponty's work was interrogation, the discovery of the impossibility of thinking within the inherited framework, and the attempt to formulate anew. At the beginning of the Preface to *Signes*, he had offered an ironic comparison:

> At first glance, what a difference, what a disparity, between the philosophical essays and the circumstantial remarks, nearly all of them political, which compose this volume. In

philosophy, the path can be difficult, but one is certain that each step makes others possible. In politics, one has the oppressive impression of a breach which must always be begun again. (*Signes*, p. 7)

The point is that when they are thought through, philosophy and politics in fact share a common fate, accept a common task, and run against common obstacles. Only when each is conceived in its traditional or liberal guise do they appear distinct. The unstable absolute of dialectical thought, and the Being never to be exhausted by any representation, define the parameters of politics as well as philosophy. As the end of history would be the end of humanity, so the end of politics, its realisation, would be the disappearance of society.[11] There is no single positive politics to be followed at any given moment, any more than the expression exhausts the expressed, the perception the perceived, or the signifier the signified. As each artist begins anew the task of making visible the world, and each philosopher begins anew the interrogation of Being, so each political action is the renewal of humanity's questioning its own sociality and society.

Rejecting Marxism, Merleau-Ponty did not reject the project of Marx. That Marx's project can not be taken over intact, and that his work has become a 'classic', does not mean that we have nothing to learn from him — as Merleau-Ponty's repeated confrontations with Marx themselves indicate. When we reflect on Marx's politics precisely from the standpoint of the project, we learn to elaborate our own; to understand our own choices, their implications and echoes. An illustration of the attitude suggested is clear in one of Merleau-Ponty's reflections on literary expression:

This is what Marx understood perfectly when he espoused Balzac. ... Marx wanted to say that a certain manner of *making visible* the world of money and the conflicts of modern society was more important than Balzac's ideas, even his political ones, and that once that vision was acquired it would bring with it its consequences, with or without the consent of Balzac. (*S*, p. 96; also *Prose*, pp. 125—6)

What Balzac's novels present is precisely the weight and thickness of the world as the individual strives to understand him/herself in action and through action. In this, Balzac writes the world the way Marx tried to think it. Though we cannot think with Marx, we cannot think without him either. From him we learn a certain philosophical task and, when we read his historical/political writings, a manner of understanding the specificity of the political action. We learn that politics is the realm of choice and chance, in which there is no pure action whose consequences the philosopher could calculate in advance. The thrust of the polemic against Sartre in *The Adventures* is to demonstrate that his schematic Marxism warmed over on the categories of *Being and Nothingness* misses precisely this element in Marxism. For example: 'In a word, for the Marxists, consciousness can be mystified. For Sartre, it is bad faith. For the Marxist, there are fools (*sots*); for Sartre there are only scoundrels (*canaille*)' (*AD*, p. 213). From Marx we learn the weight of history; and we learn too an appreciation of the creativity of human initiative.

What emerges for a political reflection is in the first place the situating of that reflection itself. We are not outside of the action in progress; politics has no technology which it applies to the given situation to achieve a desired solution. We cannot undertake a political reflection as if we were building a bridge or repairing a machine. The historical flesh into which the political project seeks to engrave itself is not transparent, a world of univocal significations whose sense could be determined, nor is it dead objectivity awaiting the inscription by praxis. A politics based on ethical imperative becomes precisely that pure violence which Hegel denounced in the French Terror, and Merleau-Ponty in Sartre.

> If [as opposed to Sartre] one agrees that no action assumes as its own all that takes place . . . and that all action, even a war, is always symbolic and counts as much on the effect that it will have as a signifying gesture and the trace of an intention as it does on the immediate results; if, in other words, one gives up 'pure action' which is a myth (a myth of the spectator consciousness), it is perhaps then that one has the most chance of changing the world. (*AD*, p. 270)

What is to be opposed is the abusive totalisation of the world, rendering all political or all philosophical. 'If all action is in fact symbolic, then books in their manner are actions and they are worth writing according to the rules of the trade, without giving up any part of the obligation to unmask' (id.). With the recognition that the world is not all of a piece, that there are spheres each of which has its own demands and techniques, and that these interact at the level of the flesh of history, comes the possibility of coherent political action, of changing the world.

This change is the act of *institution* of a common world and in a common world. The recognition of the nature of the task is a first stage, not towards developing the *techniques* of revolution, but for understanding what it is that we actually do.

In the introductory section to *The Eye and the Mind*, in which the philosopher exemplifies his new ontology across the quest of the painter, there is a deceptively simple passage which speaks to the heart of our own dilemma:

> But art, and especially painting, draw from that sheet of brute sense of which activism wants to know nothing. They are even alone to do it in all innocence. One seeks counsel or advice from the author or the philosopher; one does not permit them to hold the world in suspense; one wants them to take a position, they cannot decline the responsibilities of speaking man. . . . No one attacks Cézanne for having lived in hiding at L'Estaque during the war of 1870; and everyone cites with respect his 'life is frightful', when the least student, since Nietzsche, would roundly repudiate philosophy if it was said that philosophy did not teach us to be great beings. (*OE*, 13—15)

We all want to be 'great beings', to have 'counsel or advice' to give and 'responsibilities' weigh heavy on us. We all want to be 'Little Lenins'. Perhaps we are wrong. Certainly the thrust of Merleau-Ponty's critique of the traditional philosophical stance suggests that we no longer dare arrogate to ourselves the standpoint of the subject above or outside or even determine history. And the philosopher's critique of Marxism's pretension to be the incarnate voice of a still unconstituted proletariat takes from us that option of thinking of our words and deeds as being somehow the expression of that brute force of history which will make the revolution. We fall back on our own. And that was where we began.

9 Bureaucratic Society and Traditional Rationality: Claude Lefort

The work of Claude Lefort highlights one of the paradoxes of the Marxian tradition. Despite its claim to be the theory *of* the revolutionary proletariat, developing dialectically with the advances of the working class, the fact of the matter is that a specifically Marxian approach to sociology and political theory has not yet been developed. This might be claimed to result from the 'traditional' structure inherent in these disciplines, whose aim is prediction and manipulation of human objects. It is more likely, however, that the reasons behind the neglect of the political, and the specific approach to the sociological taken by the early Frankfurt School are typical.[1] The assumption is that classical Marxism provides a theory of the inherently contradictory and exploitative nature of the societal infrastructure, leaving the contemporary theorist with the task of elaborating the more or less independent tensions in the superstructure.

The relative weight accorded to these depends on the particular theory; in all events, the superstructure, or forms of consciousness, are at best seen from the point of view that looks for a trigger, for the potential catalyst that will ignite the already existing latent contradictions. This is certainly not the manner in which Marx himself proceeded, in his social investigations or political practice. Yet, with the possible exception of Rosa Luxemburg, the poles of theoretical reflection, empirical social analysis and political practice which Marx wanted to unite remain separated from one another. The theorist reconstructs what he/she takes to be the Marxian breakthrough; the social analyst works with an often unstated model of this breakthrough, adapting the empirical materials to it or working out new permutations of the historical development; while the political actor makes choices and tries to understand and justify their logic in terms of the theory and the sociological corrollaries. Lefort's work suggests that it is this separation of what was united by Marx that accounts for the underdevelopment of the practical side of Marxism; and that, correlatively, there are not just accidental grounds, but grounds in Marx's theory itself, that account for this underdevelopment and the various deformations of Marxism.

From another point of view, one could suggest that Lefort is carrying out the philosophical programme of Merleau-Ponty, his high-school teacher and close friend, whose posthumous works Lefort edited. Or, more accurately, one should point to the mutual fructification of their interchange. At the time that he broke with the IVth International to join in the founding of the group 'Socialisme ou Barbarie',[2] Lefort also joined Merleau-Ponty at *Les Temps Modernes*, taking part in the editorial discussions and writing for the journal. His collaboration ended — as did that of Merleau-Ponty[3] — with Sartre's move toward the Communist Party in 'The Communists and the Peace'. Lefort's critique of Sartre, and his reply to Sartre's rebuttal, are masterful applications of that unity of theory, social analysis and political judgement which one finds in Marx at his best. As generally in his political writings, Lefort's answer moves beyond the *programme* that Merleau-Ponty was elaborating, toward its realisation. Merleau-Ponty's penetrating critique of Sartre in *The Adventures of the Dialectic* remains at the level of the theoretical (opening, in a sense, to the theory of the political), whereas Lefort brings the social as the axis around which theoretical and political elaboration occur. The movement of Lefort's thought begins with Merleau-Ponty's critique of the rationalist illusion that theory can grant absolute knowledge of a social totality which is the 'really-real'; but it moves from this starting-point to the social and historical experience by which a society reproduces itself and its members, thus rejoining the work of Marx's own investigations.

Lefort's development is complicated by his insistence on working with Marx and against the consequences of Marxism. From the break with the IVth International through his second split with 'Socialisme ou Barbarie' (1958) and the foundation of the group ILO (Informations et Liaisons Ouvrières, later ICO, Informations et Correspondances Ouvrières), the struggle against the form of *bureaucratic* domination was foremost in Lefort's political concerns. Beyond the critique of the Soviet Union and the orthodox Communist (and Trotskyist) organisational forms, Lefort was attempting to elaborate the conditions of the possibility of the self-organisation of the revolutionary struggle. While he agreed with the critique of Marx that Castoriadis was developing in *Socialisme ou Barbarie*, Lefort felt that it did not go far enough. Following an argument from Merleau-Ponty, Lefort insists:

> I wanted to show that the concept of Leadership [*Direction*] was tied to that of Revolution in the sense that we inherited it from Marx. The root of the illusion was the belief in a point of radical rupture between the past and the future, in an absolute moment (even if it is stretched out temporally) in which the sense of history is given.[4]

As he worked with the Marxian notions of alienation and ideology, examining the phenomenon of History and the conditions under which a society reproduces and interrogates its self-identity, Lefort articulated a reinterpretation of Marx that permits an explanation of the devolution of the Marxian project. With Marx, against Marx, he elaborates a theory of the thought, sociality and politics of revolution in its historical specificity. Interestingly, the central theoretical articles in which Lefort lays out this approach were not published in *Socialisme ou Barbarie*. There, at first under his pseudonym, S. Montal, he published practical texts, on organisation, on specific conjunctural events, on the tasks of the militant. Since he felt himself still bound to Marxism in some form, it takes a careful reading to see the originality of his approach as compared with such variants as the Dutch Council Communists. Nonetheless, the brilliant analysis of the 20th Congress's revelations about Stalinism, the critique of the 'progressive intellectuals', and the lucid analysis of the 'proletarian experience' show the direction in which he was moving. The political critique of bureaucracy in the Soviet Union, as well as in the Marxist Parties and Sects, opened toward a general interrogation of the interpenetration of the social and the political.

Lefort's is ultimately a theory which is a critique of the pretensions of all theory; an analysis of the social laying bare the structuring principles of its *ir*reality and dependence; and a politics destroying the possibility of political solutions. This neither makes it a scepticism nor sets it above the fray. In his own words:

> In short, it is the belief in a solution, in a general formula for the organisation of society which I had to denounce as illusory by showing that the power of the bureaucracy had built and builds itself on that illusion, and by showing that

breaking with it (or attempting to break, for this is a break which must continually be begun anew) is the fundamental condition of a struggle on all terrains against the actual or potential forms of domination.

It is a struggle against the strata which monopolise the decisions which affect the fate of the collectivity in each sector of activity; a struggle against the monopolisation of the means of production and of knowledge; a struggle which prevents the petrification of the social due to the effect of a coercitive power which is necessarily driven to grow, to close in on itself, to imagine itself as the origin of the institution of the social; a struggle, therefore, which does not have to determine its nature in terms of the alternative reform or revolution, global or partial objectives, but which has its own internal justification by virtue of the fact that its effects are felt at a distance from the place where it develops, that its specific efficacity is at the same time a symbolic one, that is, that it threatens the established model of social relations which heretofore was taken as natural.[5]

Theory that pretends to give knowledge of the real, like a sociology describing preformed facts and a politics that would resolve all social contradictions, falls into the rationalist dualism which must either give all power to the 'facts', or to a transcendental principle floating above the real. In both cases, thought or praxis is alienated, separated and particularised; in both cases, the result can only be ideological, taking the part for the whole, imposing univocity on the multivalent. It is here that the rejection of Marxism, based on the work of Marx's own analyses, becomes most controversial. Indeed, as Castoriadis has asserted, Lefort appears to be forced to give up the idea of revolution itself! Lefort denies this. The difference of the two positions is clear in their respective analyses of May 1968, where as opposed to the practical steps that Castoriadis proposes, Lefort's essay sees in May the realisation of the beginning of a revolution of a new type whose advent his critical confrontation with Marxism demanded. Lefort had insisted that what must be abandoned is the traditional, philosophically rooted, notion of revolution as the completion of a rational system — Marx's making philosophical of the world and making worldly of philosophy — for it is this that leads to totalitarianism. Given up is the idea of the Good Society where all contradictions are resolved, the world made transparent to itself, and human praxis stripped of its contingency and ambiguity. The Good Society is not a state to be realised, an end to (pre-)history, or Engels' famous replacement of the government over people by the administration of things. Lefort shows that it is precisely the *myth* of revolution, anchored in that traditional philosophy that expresses the world and world-view that the revolutionaries combat, that is responsible for the degeneration of revolution. If one can speak of a 'convergence' between East and West, its roots are not in shared industrial techniques, but rather in a shared *logos*, whose source is traditional philosophy.

Lefort begins from the phenomenology of Merleau-Ponty, attempting to lay bare the structure of the *experience* of theory, sociality and politics. The very style of the analyses recalls the manner of presentation adopted by Merleau-Ponty: rejecting the transcendental, non-situated or constitutive subject, moving from one argument, showing its seeming necessity, only to drive it to the limit where it inverts and opens a new path. This *experience*, the *work* of interpretation, *is* in fact the object being analysed. Truth is not adequation of thought and thing, but the process which includes the situated thinker/actor. Through an analysis of the various historical representations of Machiavellism, and a confrontation of the lacunae of the traditional interpretations which pretend to establish *the* meaning of the work, Lefort prevents the reader of his monumental *Machiavelli* from imagining that the work of Machiavelli's thought could be reduced to a univocal message. He then follows the path of the work, confronting its ambiguities, lapsuses and contradictions. Sociological and historical materials are introduced, not as a criterion of falsification but to illuminate the *sense* of Machiavelli's chosen deformations. Not a word is wasted; the reader is engrossed. The 776 pages of this volume could no more be condensed than the equally admirable application of Lefort's interpretative technique to La Boétie's *Discours de la servitude volontaire*: a sinous thought, doubling back on itself, opening and closing, restoring finally the *in*determination of the text whose movement or work is its sense. In Lefort's own terms:

I therefore said that the question of interpretation already implies the question of the political. Through the discovery of the illusion of a disembodied thought taking an overview [*pensée de survol*] which gives the interpreter his power, I am led to understand what Machiavelli said from the point of view of the Prince who, blinded by his position of power, hides from himself the fact that this position is engendered in the division of the social, that the Prince himself is *caught* in that division.[6]

What makes a work live and become an object for the thought of successive generations is not its message but the interrogation which it is and to which it gives rise. The author does not impose a view but guides the reader's questioning. The situation of the Prince, or La Boétie's apparently naïve questioning of our submission to the Name, and thus the power, of the One, interrogate the *experience* of the political. Similarly, what makes Marx a source of continual discovery is not the results which emerge but rather the work of interrogation which bares the tensions and contradictions of the experience of capitalism, making Marx's work precisely a theory *of* the proletariat.

The danger for theory is structurally identical to the risk that drives politics to become a form of domination rather than the sphere where a community debates and articulates the form of its communality. In politics, it is the danger of the *One*, the Prince or the Party who becomes the unification and incarnation of the Good Society, separate from it and dominant *over* it — and thus is driven to totalitarianism, or faced with revolt from the society whose unity it no longer expresses. In theory, the danger is also the *One*, the Truth or Being which is taken as the 'really-real', that determines the nature of the appearances but which is either lost in the appearances or forces neglect of them due to the position of overview that it accords to itself. This does not mean that a phenomenologically-based metaphysics becomes either the last rampart against invading totalitarianism, or that a metaphysics would be the theory *for* a revolution which would, at last, be adequate to its human goals. Lefort's Marxian heritage served him in good stead; the logical structure opened by phenomenology must be articulated in terms of a *social* theory. The elaboration of Lefort's social theory was begun within, yet already pointed beyond, the Marxian framework. Marx moved from the critique of the political to a theory of the social, but remained then at the level of civil society. Lefort does not accept this reduction, for it claims to have found the positive, 'really-real' base on which all else is seated, and thus becomes a traditional theory. Lefort's phenomenological stance demands the interrogation of the *experience* of the social. It is to the growth of this interrogation that we must first turn, in order to see how Lefort's contribution to that active inheritance from Marxism fits into the framework of a New Left politics for which we are reaching.

I   Developing Theory and Developing Society

(a) Politics and the Social

In his polemical reply to the 'ultra-bolshevist' panegyric, 'The
Communists and the Peace', which marked Sartre's political
conversion (as he himself describes it in his essay on Merleau-
Ponty), Lefort attacks Sartre's atomistic and volontaristic
conception of the proletariat. Following the stress of his earlier
essays on the notion of the proletariat as its accumulating
experience,[7] and presenting a subtle interpretation of Marx's
analysis of the modern industrial process, Lefort points out that
Sartre begins from the *idea* of the unity of the class, not the
everyday experience of the class itself; and that Sartre ends up
with the class as a pure act, without material conditions, by
which the individual transcends him/herself to a social
universality and therewith to freedom. Lefort stresses that this
omits the *social*:[8]

> in its premises, because it mentions only the individuals; in its
> conclusions, because it ends with a collectivity united by the
> same will, identifying itself in action, perfectly present to
> itself and clear to itself. But this is only apparently what is
> designated by a collectivity; in reality, it is nothing but an
> individual, or better, a consciousness.[9]

Two central themes of Lefort's theoretical work already emerge
here: the notion that the self-transparence of the social is
impossible — such self-transparence being the old rationalist
dream of a perfect, god's-eye view, or the new dream of the
bureaucracy; and the attempt to pinpoint the *specificity of the
social*, its relation to the individuals who institute it, and who
are instituted by it. The political translation of a misunderstanding of this specificity is found not only in Sartre's naïve
acceptance of the Party as incarnating the class from the
standpoint of History; it is typical of what Lefort castigates, in
a brilliant article, as 'The method of the progressive intellectuals'. This position is rooted in philosophical dualism. From
such a stance, the particular (individual, as well as the brute
particular facts) and the Historical are rendered separate; the
Historical, which is said to be the truth of the particular, the
universality and transcendence of its particularity, dominates
the particular individual, whose action and errors appear as only
incidents in the linear course of History. One then reasons
about the choices posed by concrete historical situations.[10] The
upshot is that the *experience* of the class is neglected and one

cannot understand the possibility of autonomous activity. Instead, pure reason, or its inverse correlate, pure will, govern the historical process. Thus, summarising his argument in the counter-polemic to Sartre's 'Reply to Lefort', Lefort writes:

> I accused you of confusing the party and the class, and I saw at the source of that error your incapacity to define the class as an economic, social and historical reality. I tied that incapacity to your narrow rationalism which locked you into the oppositions of activity and passivity, subjective and objective, unity and division; I thought that that rationalism prohibited you from understanding the idea of praxis, which you understood in fact as the pure act of a pure organism, and which, in my opinion, supposes an interweaving of all the economic, social and political determinations.[11]

The suggestion here that a specific rationality and the nature of the social mutually implicate one another is basic to the first thrust of Lefort's theoretical work, the interrogation of ethnographic materials with an eye toward specifying the domain of society and history.

(b) The Origin of the Social
In his 1951 article, 'L'échange et la lutte des hommes',[12] Lefort took the occasion offered by Lévi-Strauss' Introduction to the republication of Marcel Mauss' works in order to clarify his notion of reason and of the social. Mauss, he writes,

> proves to be one of the most representative authors of our epoch which is attached to the project of defining a new rationalism in the sense of Hegel, Marx and Husserl. His constant preoccupation is not to explain a social phenomenon in terms of another which is judged to be its cause, but to tie together all the economic, juridical, religious and artistic traits of a given society, and to understand how they work together in the same sense. (op. cit., p. 1400)

Mauss' 'Essai sur le don' studies nothing less than the foundations of society itself. Exchange is seen to be a 'total social fact'; its sense is not only economic, but juridical, moral, religious and aesthetic. Exchange relations exist before the 'economic' forms of reciprocity which we know as barter. The *potlatch* is but one illustration of an exchange relation that cannot be explained in terms of economics alone; there are a manifold of others studied by anthropologists, which Mauss brings together in his essay. To explain these social forms, one must go beneath the empirical. 'Overall,' writes Lefort, 'the greatest error is to want to treat exchange as a fact' (id., p. 1406). Yet Lévi-Strauss' Introduction to Mauss sees his importance precisely in these terms: in his early efforts at mathematization, and in his reduction of social phenomena to their symbolic nature. In Lévi-Strauss' reading, Mauss' importance lies in seeing that it is the fact of exchange itself, not the operations which are its manifestation, that is the crucial phenomenon. The task would be to analyse exchange itself, in order then to be able to understand its operational variations in terms of its own structure. This, however, verges either on a mechanical causal explanation, or the appeal to a kind of Kantian transcendental consciousness which is to be the seat of the categories in terms of which alone the world of experience is possible. Lefort disagrees:

> The unconscious, Lévi-Strauss tells us, would be the mediating term between me and the other person, because it gives us 'forms of activity which are at once *ours* and those of the *other*, conditions of all the mental lives of all men and of all times'. But this is to forget that from the perspective of such a collective consciousness, the notion of the other person — as, in fact, that of myself — have no longer any sense. (id., p. 1408)

Lévi-Strauss' position returns again to a rationalism which dissolves the specificity of the particular in the universal. Hence:

> What must be criticized in Lévi-Strauss is that he grasps in society '*rules*' rather than '*behaviors*,' to use Mauss' terms; that he gives himself artificially a total rationality in terms of which groups and men are reduced to an abstract function instead of basing that function in the concrete relations that people establish among themselves. (id., p. 1409)

Crucial to the experience is not the symbolic but the signifying; the immanent intention in action and not a logical order which would underlie and found the concrete appearance, must be analysed.

The potlatch offers the most paradoxical form of exchange relation: in it the individual manifests reciprocity with others and with nature through the *destruction* of the gift offering. For Lefort, 'not only is this an act, but the act *par excellence*,

through which man conquers his subjectivity' (id., p. 1413).
Mauss proposed as a first explanation of the reciprocity
involved in the potlatch the idea that destruction of the goods
was conceived as a kind of exchange with the gods. The
problem with this is that we know that the potlatch phenomenon also serves as a form of competition: whoever destroys the
most goods becomes chief, receives recognition, or honours.
Mauss makes a second suggestion: in destroying the goods, the
giver is in effect putting the other under an obligation which
cannot be repaid, thereby establishing a relation of domination.
The problem is that if this were the case, it would destroy the
reciprocity on which the gift relation in general is based. One
must go further: the destruction of the goods implies that the
giver is independent of the goods, independent of external
things and of nature. The domination that is established thus
appears to be based solely and simply on the persons themselves, not on external signs of power; in Hegelian terms, the
confrontation with the other is effected through the mediation
of the confrontation with nature. The goal is thus not simply
the submission of the other, but wrenching free from nature
itself. In this manner, the establishment of the independent
personality is also the establishment of a specific *sociality as
distinct from nature*. Lefort writes:

> We thus see that our analysis leads us to a more profound
> reality than that of individual relations: social reality itself.
> Exchange by gifts appears at first to offer the double
> character of opposition between men and opposition of men
> to nature which we discovered in the potlatch. In a first
> sense, it is the act by which man reveals himself *for* man and
> *by* man. To give is just as much to put the other person in
> your dependence as to put yourself in his dependence in
> accepting the idea that he will return the gift. But that
> operation, that initiative in giving presupposes a primordial
> experience in which implicitly each knows himself to be tied
> to the other; the idea that the gift must be returned
> presupposes that the other person is an other than myself
> who *must* act like me; and his act in return must confirm to
> me the truth of my own act, that is, my subjectivity. The gift
> is thus at once the establishment of the difference and the
> discovery of sameness. (id., pp. 1414–15)

The opposition and difference without which the gift relation
could not exist only becomes real when the other returns the
gift, hence in a sense suppressing the opposition. The 'real' is

not seen from without, by an observer; it is instituted in and by the social relation. 'One does not give in order to receive', writes Lefort in italics, 'one gives in order that the other give' (id., p. 1415). In this manner:

> Behind the struggle of men for mutual 'recognition' there appears the movement of a collectivity which attempts to behave like a collective subject. But far from abolishing the plurality of subjects, this 'we' only exists insofar as each affirm his own subjectivity by the gift. The behavior of the empirical subjects cannot be deduced from a transcendental consciousness; such a consciousness, on the contrary, constitutes itself in experience. (id.)

The obligation to return the gift is not simply an obligation between two private persons; it is a 'social' obligation which, if broken, would threaten the society itself, the human reality which has ripped itself free from nature and constituted itself as a society. The social is more than the sum of individual actions, and less than the self-transparence of a pure subject.

At the conclusion of the essay on the exchange relation, Lefort indicates the direction for further reflection:

> These remarks, which see themselves in the prolongation of the analysis of Mauss, should have the advantage of permitting a *confrontation of the social and the historical*. It is striking that the exchange by gifts in its generalized form, and the institution of the potlatch, predominate and maintain themselves in societies that are incapable of developing a history. (id., p. 1416, my stress)

The social relations instituted by the potlatch regulate the rivalry between men and others as well as their relations with nature. The society which they institute still has competition among its members. But the competition remains at a level of immediacy, never threatening the social relations that have been instituted. The question that arises is that of the mediations which are the conditions of the possibility of a history, of an accumulation of experience going beyond immediate relations. More generally, what is history itself?

(c) Societies without History and the Origin of History

Lefort's 'Sociétés sans histoire et Historicité' presents the specificity of the social which we have just sketched through an analysis of what he calls a problem for 'all rationalist theories of human history'.[13] Be it the idealism of a Hegel or Husserl, or the materialism of a Marx, the problem of the *origin* of historical society remains opaque. Once a given historical course is engaged, the rationalist does fine. But we know that there are societies which never enter into the path of history, or at least don't do so of their own will and logic. The question is analogous to the one just posed: by what human *decision*, through what bestowal of sense, does history emerge as structuring the interrelations of humans among themselves? Not that we need postulate a 'first town meeting', or some such; it is not important, and not demonstrable, that such an event existed or could have existed. Important is that individual behaviour finds itself determined by a collectively assumed decision which wrenches it from its naturalness and structures its behaviour.

Non-historical societies are not free from conflictual behaviour: jokes hide hostility, counter-magic is used against the spells of the other, paternal love for the son conflicts with duty to the nephew in matrilineal societies. Yet the society continues, reproduces itself daily. Lefort suggests that

> social reality is never totally given in its present; the synchronic order always encloses a discordance between its elements; and the harmonious configuration itself doesn't reveal an essence but presents itself rather as a *solution which has come into being* [*solution advenue*], as an ensemble of concordant replies given to past situations even though the sense of these situations escapes the present people (an encounter with another people, discovery of a new mode of production), and hence one doesn't know in what sense this is a reply. (id., p. 98)

In other words, *the lack of a past is not nothing*; 'its absence calls it to our attention, suggests a style of becoming which can at least be described' (id., p. 99). The attempt to deal with the question of social origins, the institution of institutions, has more than an academic or antiquarian payoff.

The particular mode of becoming of non-historical societies suggests the need to reconceptualise the notion of history.

What is specific to an *historical* society appears to us to be that it envelops the event, and has the power to convert it into a moment of an experience, such that it appears as an element in a debate which men pursue among themselves. Thus in it the transformation is not essentially the passing from a state to another, but the progress of an intention which anticipates the future by tying it to the past. (id., p. 102)

History is 'a style of collective behavior', giving sense to the world and defining social relations (id.). For this reason, historical *memory* becomes crucial:

> If a society preoccupies itself with interpreting its past and with situating itself with relation to that past, if it explicitly formulates the principles of its organization, if it relates its factual activity and everything *new that happens* to it [*lui advient*] to its consciousness of its role and its values — this supposes a particular type of becoming. (id., p. 103)

The question then becomes, how can we explain the manner in which non-historical societies *live* a collective past? What is the sense and structure of the *decision* of societies without history? And how can we understand the *representation* of the past or future through which a society becomes conscious of its own identity? (The latter question poses the problem of ideology in its socio-historical specificity, and the question of the Power in society, around which Lefort's recent work has turned, and to which we will return.)

Lefort uses Bateson's analysis of Bali as a 'schismogenetic' society, showing how the conflict-ridden Balinese society has established a variety of mechanisms to preserve itself from upheaval. Crucial in this account is that the Bali society depends on a rigid set of orientations in time, space and status. Outside these coordinates, the individual is lost, quite literally becomes neurotic. This is not to be explained, as Bateson suggests, by psychoanalytical concepts.[14] In such a society there are no neutral situations; all behaviour is governed by the social relations that cement together the society and constitute the individual as what he/she is. The past and future too must be brought into the structure of the presence of the present, for otherwise the experience of indetermination would destroy the capacity of the socialised individual to function. Non-historical social relations thus serve as a way of avoiding the outbreak of social conflict, legitimating the forms of domination that give the society its particular character.

What then are the conditions which permit the passage from non-history to history? Lefort's suggestion is that the non-historical societies are structured as if the only goal for the individual is to relate to others, and to constitute themselves with these others as a 'we', separate from nature and continually reproducing itself through the network of immediate relations to others. All activity is multi-valued, with economic, moral, religious and aesthetic values coming together such that none is taken in its own domain, but simply as an expression, open to many interpretations, but never neutral or valueless.

> On the other hand, it is when activity becomes *labor* that it fixes its signification, that it acquires objectivity in showing the adequation of an intention and an object, that it turns men from their debate among themselves to draw them into a finality which was not given with their simple co-existence. (id. p. 113)

There is nothing necessary in this development, nothing pre-inscribed in the non-historical society, that prefigures the transformation to a new social form based on a new temporality. There is no reason why the previous experience of social division should have its legitimacy and its sense suddenly changed. Nor is the process one of natural, gradual evolution. Where in the stagnant society production was subordinated to the confrontation and integration of people into the collectivity, 'it is by a revolution in historicity that men transform production into productivity, disengage themselves from that investment in the other person which was their primitive situation, and inaugurate a history' (id.). The paradox, in other words, is not what it appeared to the rationalist — that there exist non-historical societies — but rather what appears is an '*adventure*' in human relations which surges forth without necessity, yet of course not without anterior conditions. To look to causal explanation would be to lose the specificity of the social which was just presented: the object explained would no longer be the one which concerns us.[15]

For Lefort History and society are the institutions (in the transitive sense) which emerge from human co-existence, but which are not necessitated by any material or moral preconditions. In a later, unpublished, reflection on this stage of his work, Lefort suggests that a further question must be posed:

> What ethnologist, I ask, has questioned the conditions which give him access to an experience of the world incommensurable with his? Who examines the fact, nonetheless unavoidable: that it is in this time, in this space where we are anchored, that there is the possibility, perhaps one should say necessity, of knowing the meaning of other human societies,

whereas within the frontiers of these latter, at least for savage societies, there is not a *view* on the foreign world.[16]

This is not the well-beaten problem of cultural relativism. Lefort is re-emphasising the argument about the place of memory and representation in an historical society. This conclusion is reinforced in an article written during this period, 'Capitalisme et religion au XVIe sièclè,[17] where the economic determinist views of Robertson are constrasted with the more open interpretation of Tawney. In question is Weber's Protestant ethic thesis; but more importantly, the question of 'revolution' emerges as central:

> A revolution supposes ... a vision of the past and an apprehension of the future as the negation of the past, a heterogeneity of time or of temporality; or further, an *act* whereby men join together in opposing, as *we*, other men whom they dispossess of their sense. (id., p. 1897)

While one can point to 'capitalist' behaviour and institutions as early as the thirteenth century, and while at least the Jesuits attempted to adapt Catholicism to the new conditions, Lefort's point is, on the one hand, that neither the economy nor ideology alone can be said to univocally determine anything; and on the other hand, and more importantly, that the Reformation has a revolutionary signification precisely insofar as, in introducing a new attitude to the world, it marks a rupture with the established mode of representation. A 'capitalist' in the world of universal Catholicism could not affirm capitalism as such; only through the opening of a new signification could the capitalist come to know himself as a self-conscious subject. In other words, once again, the *institution* of a form of *sociality* shows itself as central to Lefort's *political* concerns. This position emerges more sharply in his next major theoretical advance, 'L'aliénation comme concept sociologique', in which the particularity of *historical* society is played out. In the attempt to avoid the essentialist vision of alienation as *une condition humaine*, Lefort is led toward the themes which dominate his work today.

(d) Alienation, Ideology and the Real: the Structure of Capitalism

Lefort's turn to the concept of alienation was outwardly conditioned by the times. Marxism was becoming respectable, among professors and Catholics, and in a peculiar fashion. Landshut and Mayer, in the Introduction to their edition of the *1844 Manuscripts*, had already suggested, for example, that Marx's 'All history is the history of class struggle' could just as well read: 'All history is the history of alienation.' In this manner, Marx becomes simply a consistent Hegelian, taking the dialectic a step further. Lefort's counter is remarkably penetrating, using anthropological materials to make his point. He summarizes Evans-Pritchard's description of Nuer society — a society which, at first glance, appears nothing but reified, alienated, mystified by one commodity which, though important, is not its life source: cattle. All social relations are expressed in bovine terms: lineage, marriage, exchange, aesthetics and religion. Indeed, the language of the Nuers seems to have a manifold of nuances when it comes to cows, while it is impoverished elsewhere. Nuer life is not solely dominated by cattle; but its world of representation is, down to its metaphors and proper names. A truly fetishistic society, *it seems.* Even the use of cattle is not as 'economically rational' as it might be, for it is the *image* of the cow, its fetish, that is crucial, rather than the full exploitation of one's bovine resources. Wars, quarrels, personal relations are all hidden behind bovine mystifications. Finally, completing the analogy, the Nuer dream content seems to indicate a latent hostility to the cow, as do its myths and rites. For the 'Marxist' professor, an incipient revolt must be brewing in Nuer society! The problem, however, is that this is a view from outside; from within, the society functions harmoniously — as one would expect from Lefort's analysis of Mauss or the problem of non-historical societies. What sense, then, does it make to talk about alienation and its correlates in this context?

On its most general level, Marx's notion of alienation is derived from the difference between an historically specific reality and irreality: the socialised nature of productive labour is a reality in capitalism; but the commodity form in which it appears is an irreality, an appearance which hides and deforms the reality. Alienation is this unity in difference. It is not the case that there exists a 'natural' form of labour which is deformed or exploited under capitalism and which thus grounds alienation. In insisting on the specificity of the capitalist form, Marx shows that the socialisation of labour is not natural, but is an *achievement* of capitalism; the same is true for the equality among human labours (the notion of abstract, socially necessary labour) which did not exist before capitalism. To have recourse to a critique rooted in 'natural' human qualities returns alienation to the domain of traditional philosophy. What Marx did is, to the contrary, to insist on social and historical specificity. Moreover,

Marx always points out that the alienated fetishised forms are *nonetheless* real, actual conditions. When he criticises a situation where the movement of things dominates people's activity and self-understanding, Marx always notes that it is not things but people acting through the things who create these conditions of domination. Domination, however, has existed in manifold forms and societies; in all but capitalism it has not had the double structure of alienation in Marx's schema: negativity with positive implications. What is it that specifically permits capitalist social relations, and only them, to be the antechamber to the realised socialist society?

The attempt to specify the notion of alienation also clarifies an ambiguity in Marx's own analysis: is capitalism simply the process defined by the formula 'M - C - M'? What is its specific mode of sociality? Marx's discussion of the phases of development which emerge genetically from manufacture to what he calls 'Machinery and Modern Industry' suggests that where the manufacturing phase subordinated the worker to a total process, this worker still remained an individual, with particular and personal skills, working in specific branches, etc. In the further development, however, the personal skills (and limits) are surpassed; the individual becomes simply a cog, part of the 'collective worker' whose work is ever more decomposed into its component parts. The result is that any possible view of the totality or sense of the work process is lost, one's job becomes a bit-part in a mystery play, *and* the interdependence of each on the others is increased. Modern industry thus presents a Janus face:

> It appears, in effect, that the specific movement of industry by which the unity of all the productive acts is established — a universal society — is at the same time the movement by which separate spheres of activity are constituted...[18]

The social and socialised character of production is patent in the activity of work itself; and at the same time, the division of labour into separate spheres, its constant decomposition into partial processes, separates the individual within the productive unity. Whereas in true manufacture the labour which gave value to the product was that of individual craftspeople, in modern industry that which gives value is precisely 'average socially necessary labour', as Marx puts it. For manufacture, and the social forms which preceded it, this measure was the theorist's reconstruction; in modern industry *it is the structure of the*

experience of reality itself: the unity of labour is effectively
given in the multiple tasks which compose the totality; but each
task is in only a fragmentary relation to that unity. The
technological form of a given productive task gives that
production a (historically specific) universality; while the
division of capital and labour, mental and manual, makes each
activity particular. In this sense, the actual process of assembly-
line production, for example, incorporates a contradiction: each
gesture is at once radically particular (turning this bolt, welding
this joint) and effectively universal (as part of the total social
process). But the terminology borrowed from philosophy
should not mislead.

> The contradiction is not that between universalization and
> particularization, but rather consists in this, that the experi-
> ence of the particular criticizes itself because it presents itself
> as privation of the universal, because the experience of the
> universal degenerates into the particular. (id., p. 51)

It is not that my work is somehow robbed of its essence,
deformed and distorted. Nor is this the *condition humaine*,
caught between heaven and earth, good and evil.

> From this perspective, one cannot speak of a society
> alienated in technology, in money or whatever; or of an
> alienated man, as if it were possible for the being of the
> society or the man to become Other. Alienation is not a
> state; it is the process in which activity is cut up into a
> manifold of independent spheres at the same time that each
> of these divided activities is subordinated to a single
> productive schema. (id., p. 52)

The individual is destined at once to have a profession, a
concrete form of activity in which he/she objectifies and
socialises him/herself; and at the same time, such stable activity
loses its sense and becomes particular, a fragment within a social
process continually changing but always riven by the contradiction between the socialisation which renders it universal and
the particularisation of the activities of the individuals.

The implications of this specification of alienation *within the
structure of capitalism itself* are both a development and a
critique of Marxism. The notion of ideology can now be
grounded sociologically. Ideology is defined by Marx as an
inversion of the real, an inversion which is not the fault of
consciousness but built into the social structure itself. In

theoretical terms, ideology is the transformation of the particular into the universal, taking the part for the whole. The necessity of this transformation can be seen in the above description: the fragmentation and atomisation of the worker and the act of production in modern industry which has as its defining characteristic the socialization (i.e., universalisation) of society. Each particular domain, from the menial to the mental, from production to juridical or artistic activity *is* effectively particular, and yet within the socialised totality, historically universal. Each particular facet of the division of labour tends, therefore, to attempt to realise the universal in its activity, to generalise from what it does to what the social totality as a whole *is*. The result, of course, is self-deception and the impossibility of having a totality view on the society, because each sphere, as particular, is closed in on itself, not in communication from within to without; and yet each does effectively, structurally, communicate in spite of itself. Ideology is thus not just a form of consciousness *within* a given social formation; *ideology is the structure of capitalism itself*. It is therefore incorrect and misleading to speak of ideology when one is talking, say, about religion, or of the function of philosophy or culture in a pre-capitalist social formation. These pre-capitalist forms are based on reference to an *external* or *transcendent* universal, whereas in capitalism's socialised society, the universal is immanent in the activity of the particulars.

At the same time, however, that it makes more precise what Marx was driving at with his notion of alienation, this analysis carries a further implication to which Lefort's work in the 1960s increasingly turned, culminating in his *Machiavel: le travail de l'oeuvre*. The problem of alienation, and of ideology, poses the problem of reality and of truth. That which is most real, immediate, appears in fact to be that which is least real. The occultation of reality is built into the structure of capitalist social relations. Marx thought that his analysis uncovered the really real, the basis of capitalist reality itself; but in fact, because of the logic of the very structure which it uncovers, Marxism must be seen itself as a part of that structure: thought in alienation thinking alienation; ideology thinking the structure of ideology. The demand for totality, built into but denied by the social structure, becomes the demand for a kind of truth or rationality which is systematically and structurally unattainable. The result is not an irrationalism or existentialism; rather, it calls forth a redefinition of the task of theory. Theory, carried within the social structure and governed by its operation, becomes the society's own self-interrogation; philosophy is no longer the unveiling of a truth which was always there but somehow occulted; it is the continual process of interrogation, destined to ambiguity, prohibited from absolutising its results. In this way, the kinship between the 'philosophy of ambiguity' of Merleau-Ponty and the political development of Lefort, re-emerges. Lefort concludes his essay on alienation:

> If the idea of alienation in the last analysis calls forth that of truth, it is on the condition that we find its properly sociological content. (id., p. 54)

This will be the grounds for a double operation: critique of the presuppositions of social and political analysis and action, and at the same time a return to and re-evaluation of philosophy. Traditional Marxism and its definition of theory, praxis, and of revolution are thus called into question.

II   The Political and the Philosophical

(a) The Proletariat and the Problem of the Real and the True
In 'La politique et la pensée de la politique', a remarkable homage to Merleau-Ponty written shortly after the latter's death, Lefort tries to understand the inability of the Left to deal with the Algerian Revolution and its implications in France. During the Revolution, the French Left united in its support of the FLN; with the victory, the FLN itself showed its divisions, and the Left saw its transferred enthusiasm shattered on the realistic decisions imposed on the Front. In France, the war's end did not bring an upsurge in political action and consciousness, but a depression and decompression. What bothered Lefort in the attitude of the Left was that

> politics increasingly bases itself on a moral perception of the world in terms of which one must chose at each instant between two principles which exclude one another; and since these principles express themselves in men and structures, one must give one's unreserved adhesion to the party of revolution whose very existence is its justification.[19]

This is different from traditional Marxism which is based on a rational image of society as joining revolutionary consciousness and structural necessity in a capitalism whose decline points already to the socialist future, and whose gravedigger is

produced from within. The new 'revolutionary' morality replaces Marxism's rational interpretation of history. Typical of
this position is, of course, Sartre. The counter-position is that of
Merleau-Ponty.

For Meleau-Ponty, the question of revolution and that of
reality and truth were inseparable.

> In a sense, Marxism taught him what he was looking for,
> what his work on the body and perception had already
> opened to reflection: a relation with being which testifies to
> our participation in being, specifically, a philosophy of
> history which uncovers our historicity. The proletariat is
> precisely that singular being where we find the genesis of
> history, where the past lives on in its sense, where the truth
> of what is not yet announces itself. (id., p. 58)

Lefort's detailed analysis of Merleau-Ponty's attitude toward
Marxism, in *Sense and Nonsense*, then in *Humanism and Terror*,
shows how the 'singular being' of the proletariat becomes the
central axis on which Marxism turns. Attempting to remain
within the opening that he found in Marxism, Merleau-Ponty
confronted it with its empirical correlates, bringing together the
theoretical proletariat and its actual incarnation. The opening of
Marxism is its rejoining in one subject of the empirical and the
true, praxis and theory. Yet this unique opening, the passionate
analysis of which makes *Humanism and Terror* appear at times
like a defence of Stalin's purges, is precisely the grounds for the
degeneration which Merleau-Ponty would trace in *The Adventures of the Dialectic* a few years later. If the proletariat is taken
as the Truth which coincides with the Real, and if its project is
defined outside its control, then the empirical proletariat and its
activities no longer enter into the dialectical interaction.
Correlatively, if today's empirical proletariat is looked at in
itself, the truth claim essential to the revolutionary project can
no longer be maintained. If one sticks to the premise, the result
is the theory of the Party-as-Truth, as Moral Absolute, or as
Revolutionary Will, as appears in Lukács, Trotsky and Sartre.

The result of Merleau-Ponty's series of confrontations with
Marxism is a reformulation of the dialectic of being and truth,
history and historicity. Marx's error is that he attempted to find
a *place* in history which would be the incarnation of his theory.
He thinks of history in terms of totality, in terms of the
principle of the *constitution* of that totality. This, however, is
to fall back into *representational* thought, and thus to deny
truth and historicity:

Society cannot become an object of representation, or a
matter which we would have to transform, because we are
rooted in it; we discover in the particular form of our
'sociality' the sense of our projects and our tasks. (id., p. 67)

The task of political theory is not to explain and express our
attachment to a society and a history which determine us. On
the contrary: what must be restored is the fundamental
*in*determination of our historical situation. The path to this
restoration is the process of *interrogation* of the real.[20] This
implies politically the rejection of the goal 'of instituting a
regime freed from the exploitation of man by man, which
translates into the program of a party which would demand
Power' (id., p. 68). The class struggle still exists; modern
capitalism makes resistance all the more necessary. Still,

The idea of a thought committed to indetermination and of a
politics committed to contestation, is not foreign to the spirit
of Marxism . . . In the image that Marx has of the proletariat,
we can recognize the symbol of a rupture of the social unity,
and of a questioning, in the movement of history itself, of
the relation of man to being. (id., p. 69)

This aspect of Marx's theory of the proletariat and its praxis has
been covered over, not simply by the epigone or by the
changing structure of capitalism. Lefort's 1964—5 Sorbonne
lecture series, 'Réalité sociale et histoire', shows why.

Marx's claim is that the critique of theory in specific social
conditions is the critique of reality itself. This can be
understood on the basis of the above analysis of capitalist social
relations as a process of alienation, necessarily giving rise to the
forms of consciousness known as fetishism and ideology. The
socialisation of society accompanied by the continual and
increasing division of labour means that from within the society
knowledge of the social totality — the self-knowledge or trans-
parance of the social — is not possible. As the impossible
attempt to know society from within, bourgeois theory
manifests bourgeois reality in its contradictoriness. It is ideological in the sense defined above. But Marx would appear to fall
under the same strictures — unless he can claim that his theory
is *itself* the praxis of a class of society, a social reality, which is
not subject to the distortions of the alienation process. This is
why Marx is driven to find anchorage in a *place* that is both
within society, a participant undergoing its processes, and which
yet escapes the fate of society. This praxis, this place, is of

course the proletariat. Lefort explains why Marx can make this claim, looking at the commodity nature of the proletariat, its actual functions in the work process, and its political role. As the commodity labour-power, the proletarian is a formally free contractual partner; which means that in selling his/her labour-power, the proletarian lives the contradiction of being a commodity and being a proprietor. Moreover, the particular commodity labour-power has no fixed value; its value is determined through the process of the class struggle itself. The proletarian enters the labour process at first as a private individual; but the hours at work are lived as part of a collective, to be followed by a return to the private concerns. This movement from individual to collective and back to individual again takes place not in the sphere of circulation but in a specific kind of production: in modern industry (as opposed to the still artisanal manufacturing process), where the veils are lifted and the worker experiences the material social reproduction. Modern industrial production functions in terms of a double demand: that the worker do what he/she is told; and yet that the worker participate, want to produce, confront the unexpected quickly and creatively. The proletarian thus experiences rationalisation; but, not tied to one branch or job, and especially not tied to the commands of profit, the proletarian experiences too the perversions of that rationalisation. When the proletarian emerges to a political role, it is not simply a defensive one, but tends toward a struggle for social control. In this expression of its goals, the proletariat does not need to conceal its intentions, whereas the bourgeoisie must continually hide from itself and its supporters the structure of domination which its rule perpetuates.

These structural conditions imply the possibility of true social knowledge for the proletariat. An infinite dialectic is established in which the proletariat, still a part of bourgeois society, continually engages in its own self-critique. Is this a circular argument? Marx presents a description of the proletarian situation, and then claims that the description grounds the truth of the description, its revolutionary implications. Theory is subordinated to praxis — but still from the point of view of theory. One might say that this is precisely the dialectic of theory and praxis which refuses to make the one depend on the other; and the continual self-critique would prove the virtue of this approach. But once the validity of the option for the proletariat is *assumed*, the dilemma of falsification emerges, for the infinite dialectical self-critique supposes an end which can never be reached. One can point to tendencies which seem to confirm the analysis; and to others that deny it. These latter are the problem. Can we reduce them to mere accidents, appearances of the Essential Reality that is History? That would be the 'method of the progressive intellectuals'. The development of a workers' aristocracy or the increasing interference of the state, to name but two frequently mentioned problems, can be accounted for by the theory. They are not merely accidental or conjunctural appearances. Their existence, however, does not necessarily invalidate the theory: other tendencies confirming it can be cited. Lefort suggests that to get around this indefiniteness which continues to affirm the truth of the Theory by adding new corrollaries, we need to ask about the theory's premise:

> Can thought ever postulate that there is an empirical place where history and society uncover themselves in their totality where all equivocation is dissipated, where the institutions, collective behaviors and symbols become transparent, where all the significations of the event are recuperated in the same truth?[21]

The question goes to the heart of Marxism. One could reply that Marx doesn't treat the proletariat as already universal, fully conscious, free from contradictions; and that he doesn't suppose that society can be fully known but, on the contrary, stresses its contradictory character. Not only this — Marx insists that history need not conduct us to socialism: barbarism is also a possibility. Here, however, the problem re-emerges:

> How can there be a correct relation with history, an exchange between social theory and social praxis, open investigation and true interrogation, if we have only the choice between the continual affirmation of an absolute sense and the negation of this sense which becomes the negation of all sense? (id., p. 69)

If the task of History is the achievement of socialism; if particular historical events and social configurations are to be interpreted in function of the movement toward this goal; and if these phenomena which stand in the way of this movement are either integrated into the process or ignored in the press towards action; if, in other words, the contradictory reality is taken up only in what it shows as positive, then the dialectic is eliminated, experience cannot do more than modify a presupposed truth, and theory becomes empiricism — the 'method of

| the progressive intellectuals'.

> The result is thus paradoxical. Pretending to discover within
> history, at the level of the phenomena, an absolute founda-
> tion, the theorist rejoins the position of the philosopher who
> flies above history and subsumes empirical reality under the
> idea of a transcendental becoming of truth. But this paradox
> should not surprise us, for if the two procedures coincide,
> this is because in both cases thought postulates an adequation
> of sense and being (of the being of society and the being of
> history). (id., p. 70)

One thus falls back into the myth of possessing the entirety of
the phenomenon — precisely what the analysis of the alienated
structures of capitalist society warned against. The theory
becomes ideological.

Marxism opens the question of the reality and truth of the
social; and yet it closes it off hastily. Its error is to equate the
signifier and the signified, to become a representational and
rationalist thought in the classical sense. Lefort shows in his
lectures that Marx doesn't always fall into this error. The
analysis of the Asiatic society, for example, or the discussion of
the peasantry in the *18th Brumaire* show the role of the
symbolic in social constitution. Rather than follow Lefort
through these analyses, it will be more useful to turn to the
article, 'Réflexions sociologiques sur Machiavel et Marx: La
politique et le réel', where Lefort develops his interwoven
political and theoretical argument through a critique of Gramsci's attempt to reconcile Marx and Machiavelli.

(b) Political Realism as Interrogation
Gramsci suggests that beyond their obvious differences, Marx
and Machiavelli share in a common *political realism* which
opens up a new *experience* of the world, a new conception of
society and truth.

> What constitutes the common originality of their work is that
> both begin from the certainty that the real is what it is, and
> that in a certain manner there is nothing to be changed in it;
> and yet both induce from this a practical task[22]

Marx's 11th Feuerbach Thesis is not at all the rhetoric of
engagement, moral choice or spontaneous activism. It is the
assertion that the real is through and through praxis; and that
precisely the praxical contradictions of the present point

beyond it. Similarly with Machiavelli, we find an anticipation of the philosophy of praxis:

> Knowledge of the past teaches what men are; the reading of empirical history is a reading of human nature. Realism consists in acting such that, the present situation being brought back into the terms of a past one, we can either apply the adequate remedies previously conceived, or imagine other ones, since we are aware of the errors that have been committed. In all events, our power of intervention is based on the consistency of human passions and of the struggle which opposes everywhere a privileged class and the people, which is the origin of all the difficulties and all the solutions. (id., pp. 117—18)

Though they were apparently writing for different classes — Marx for a revolutionary proletariat, Machiavelli for the Prince — a moment's reflection shows that in both cases the relation of the work to its public was similar, notes Gramsci. True, the *Prince* was in appearance for the ruler; but the ruler has to justify domination — which means, in fact, hide it. Machiavelli's recipes may be correct; but the Prince could never publish them! The implication is that Machiavelli was writing for someone else: the rising, yet still timid, bourgeoisie.

Machiavelli is said to be a political realist insofar as he recognises the historical task which the new bourgeoisie, blinded by tradition, has not yet understood.

> If he draws our attention to the nature of power, reveals that it is a human creation arising from the permanent conditions of social struggle, it is because he is speaking to those who are blinded by the Power, who haven't yet understood that it is within their grasp if only they are the stronger. And he shows the price of its conquest. (id., p. 120)

The Prince thus appears to have the same demystifying function as the 'philosophy of praxis', as Gramsci calls Marxism. There arises the idea of an historical task, which the Prince recognises and must render accessible to the consciousness of the people. In this sense, the Machiavellian Prince easily becomes the 'Modern Prince', the Leninist Party. The Prince/Party has the task of understanding the historically necessary, seeing in it the actuality of the people's will whatever the present mystified form of that will may be. The Prince/Party is the mediator. 'In such an interpretation, Marxism permits us to rediscover the sense of Machiavellism; but Machiavellism rejoins, defines in its place, the Marxist intention' (id., p. 123). Overthrowing the traditional authorities and mystifications permits the establishment of a new authority, the *task* to which all else is subordinated.

The political implications of this realism are the separation of the class struggle from the daily life of the class. The sphere of politics is circumscribed and separated.

> Precisely because of the opacity that it maintains with regard to the masses, it calls for the elaboration of a particular strategy whose objective is to obtain and to maintain their *consensus*, to convince them of the legitimacy of their leaders and the utility of their own sacrifices. (id., p. 124)

Moreover, this position lends assurance to the leaders, gives them the certainty that they are the agents of History, that they are correct in subordinating all to the achievement of their task. The writings of the political realist are taken only in their functional usage, to be judged by the success or failure of their appeal. And since the appeal is to the universal, the particular cannot disprove but only confirm the position of the realist, or remain silent. When this is applied to Marxism there arises a specific problem. While the bourgeoisie exists as an economic class, but needs political representatives insofar as the basis of its economic unity is competition, the proletariat cannot operate through representatives. It is itself only when it struggles, not as represented in a separate political sphere. This means that if the Prince/Party is the truth and universal, then it cannot be criticised, for the foundation in being of this truth is denied, and *a truth which cannot relate to or account for its origins is nothing but ideology*.

Pursuing the notions of indetermination and interrogation, Lefort suggests that it is precisely this realism which must be put into question; and that a careful look at Machiavelli's originality confirms this approach.

> That originality does not consist in certain propositions which would support an essential thesis. It consists in an approach which makes the writer pass from a position to another, which permits him to outline successively this or that thesis and to destroy them as theses; to conserve in this movement certain indications [*repères*], to multiply them, and thanks to them, to circumscribe an order of phenomena

whose unity had never been perceived before this. (id., pp. 126—7)

This movement from thesis to thesis, this multi-level unity in difference, is of course similar to Merleau-Ponty's philosophical interrogation. Lefort is not forcing a thesis on Machiavelli. It is the nature of the *reality* in question to only expose itself in this manner: it is an historical reality, not in the sense of a series of circumscribed events in objective space and time, nor as a progress of humanity to knowledge of itself:

> In the infinite of the life of peoples history is the repetition of the project which constitutes society: the assembling of men who situate themselves as depending on the same public thing, acquire a collective identity, inscribe their respective positions in a common natural space, their institutions in a common cultural space, and determine themselves as a private community vis-à-vis foreign people, find a certain equilibrium in their relation of forces (even if they constantly put it into question), and are led by the will of the Master, that of the most powerful or that of the majority among them, to find the means for their security and their development. (id., p. 129)

This is no contradiction, no dissolution of change, as the earlier considerations on the nature of society and history indicate. Historical reality is a repetition; but the repetition itself is historical, taking place in specific milieus, specific structures and institutions which offer a finite number of choices. Machiavelli's richly illustrated and multi-signfying writings on Rome, for example, show clearly the social divisions out of which equilibrium emerged; show this as threatened by ignorance, rapacity and fear; and insist that the equilibrium is only maintained by the singular combination of the Republic and its imperial ventures. This is but one variant: Machiavelli leads us through arguments from different positions — the people is good, but can be misled; the Republic chooses the best masters, but as theatre of civil strife it can be dominated by one stratum; and so on. There is no one good regime, no positive politics; there is the real-historical, indeterminate and constantly changing.

Lefort's suggestion is that the 'realism', of Machiavelli consists precisely in the denial of any system of fixed representations. This is the 'realism' of the phenomenologist. The same is true, he argues, of Marx.[23]

If Machiavelli's thought has come down to us, it is because it forces us to embrace simultaneously these diverse perspectives. We make his realism our own when we observe that the conquest of the real is accomplished in the critique of each image at which we would be tempted to stop. (id., p. 132)

What emerges from Lefort's analysis of Machiavelli is the project of defining an interrogation of the *logic of the political*.[24] 'Doesn't realism consist precisely in defining the *terms* of a situation, in ordering them in the form of a question?' (id., p. 131). The question is more fundamental than the explicit problem of classical political philosophy — that of the good life in the city. It is the *political* question which grounds the *social*. And it poses the question of rationality, truth, and the nature and goals of theory. That emergence of the social to itself which preoccupied Lefort in his earlier writings emerges as fundamental to a redefinition of the political.

(c) The Logic of the Political

Lefort's logic of the political is not the traditional onto-logic: it is historical and social in the sense that these terms have been redefined. The political as such is constituted along with and inseparately from the social as such, and it institutes a specific mode of experiencing the historical. We saw in the discussion of the gift relation that the social is a wrenching free of interpersonal and communitarian relations from their natural insertion, defining at once the individual and the community. With this *institution* of the social, the political surges forth necessarily. It may, however, be lived in a mode of non-recognition, through a concerted effort to avoid the decisions and divisions that it consecrates. The 'society without history' appears as a society without the political. Indeed, as Pierre Clastre's ethnographical analyses show brilliantly, though we can look back and see division within primitive societies, there is a tendency in them toward an organisational principle based on the denial of that division: denial either that it is a difference that makes a difference (i.e., justification from a transcendent, external source), or denial of a separation of the spheres of life (the economic, political, religious, etc., remaining immediately interwoven). The political cannot be separated from the social. But it does not, for that reason, exist in the same manner, on the same level, as determined by, or as determining, the social. It is not as if one could say that these phenomena are political, those are cultural, those others economic, and so on. The political is co-institutional with the social. It is a society's self-reflection, the image that it gives itself of itself in the attempt to conjure away and defuse the problem of social division. The political is representational, symbolic; but as such it cannot exist separate from or independent of the social that it represents or brings to self-awareness — any more than the latter can do without it. Were it to be separated, it would lose its grounds, its origins, and become ideological. Lefort suggests that

It is from that general division, where the power takes form, that it is necessary to begin in deciphering the political and knowing how a power is effectively circumscribed, how it is represented, how it represents itself to others — how the collective representation invests it in the social body and what simultaneously happens to the determination of nature and the gods; how it separates itself, is perceived as *Other*, at a distance and 'above' society; how the position of the separated power is modified and, to examine all the consequences which come into being in the forms of representation and the effectiveness of socialization.[25]

This is the general task which the political in any society — even when it is not articulated self-consciously as the political *different* from other forms of experience — must fulfil. A logic of the political can thus be established. It will be the logic of a unity in difference whose differentiations are not *aufgehoben* but remain open to the contingencies of historical creation. The system is unstable, riven by conflict; change is always possible, never necessary.

The sense of Lefort's approach can be seen when we think of the advent of democracy in Greece. We don't know why it occurred, can't explain its necessity in socio-historical laws. Yet with democracy came new forms of sociality: the space and time of life within the city took on a different sense, the relation to nature and other humans was modified, and discourse took on a new meaning and indicated a new relation among the speaking subjects, becoming the interrogation that is philosophy. Simultaneously, the political and the image of power, changed: politics and power moved into the centre of the city, not as a form of domination, but rather as the interrogation by society of its own nature and goals. Lefort sees this as a society attempting to carry within itself the law of its own origin, its own institution, breaking with the transcendent justification heretofore typical. Groups and their articulations are to be in constant communication; their interrelations are to be openly readable in the social space. In a word, the society seeks its self-transparence. This, however, is specific to democracy, which is:

> An attempt which culminates or roots itself in the idea of a power which is *de jure* inoccupiable, inappropriable, at an equal distance from all those who are bound to it; no one's power, *neutral*, and as such, *instituting* the social; at once the instigator and guarantor of the Law under which each finds his name, his place, and his limit. (id., p. 2)

Politics does not become a separate sphere of discourse; it is interwoven throughout the society and the socialisation of the citizens. Not that politics is the whole which gives sense to the parts that would be metaphysics, yielding to representational thought and occluding the question of origins. Rather —

> It is that the interrogation of the political is born in a society where, by the effect of an identical historical rupture, both power and knowledge are put into question. Power is questioned in the relation it maintains with the social division in all its forms; and at the same time the knowledge carried in the multiplicity of social discourses — and beyond them, the knowledge of the benchmarks [*repères*] of the real and of the law — is opened to question. (id., p. 2—3)

The linkage of the political and knowledge occurs through the medium of the discourse which carries both, in which they represent themselves and are instituted in and institute the process of socialisation. Here, as we shall see, Lefort's analysis of the political and that of knowledge show their similar structure. The logic of the political is not only referred to the social, but to the discourse of knowledge; the questions of reality and truth that so much governs Lefort's work are linked in the political.[26]

Lefort spells out his logic of the political in a long article, 'Sur la démocratie: le politique et l'institution de social', written with Marcel Gauchet, and in his book, *Machiavel: le travail de l'oeuvre*.[27] We can give the flavour of the approach by taking as an example the dilemma of the Prince — democratic, tyrannical, self-proclaimed socialist, or whatever variant thereof. The Prince is to incarnate the unity of society; as such, he is the symbol of the Law. As incarnation, however, the Prince has no proper function; the political has no independent existence.

Then, however, the society itself has no delimitation; it cannot properly be called a society, since without reference to an Other or Outside different than the collective and incarnating its self-representation socialisation cannot take place, group consciousness and historical memory are not possible. The Law must be greater than and different from the individuals in order that these latter be able to find themselves in it. As a result, the Prince must assert the separation of the political and the independence of the Law. This, however, poses legitimation problems. Either the Prince must attempt to rejoin society — but this defeats his purpose since he is then no longer the Law, but dependent on society — or he must impose the Law upon the citizens. That, however, would risk revolt. The dilemma of the Prince is that he is at once the incarnation of the social yet distant and distinct from it. The dilemma is not only that of the Prince's subjective position; it is society's problem, for it rips itself free and constitutes itself only in the move to its political self-representation. Navigating between these two poles, a variety of mediations can be established — corporations, legislators, courts, local governments, etc., etc.; yet ultimately the dilemma remains to be confronted at every step. The courts are to be the Law, yet must be open to the new; legislators are to be representatives and yet to find the Law for all; pressure groups and political parties have to act from within society in their specific positions, yet in the name of the entire society. What emerges here in this dual claim to be within and yet without, particular and universal, is of course the danger of *ideology* if the *experience* is reduced to one or the other pole. At the same time, the domain of political discourse is opened to precisely those questions of interrogatory philosophy: reality and truth.

The interdependence and interrelation of the phenomena of ideology and the political go beneath that of structural analogy: both are implicated in the self-assertion and self-maintenance of the social and its discursive character which is lost when the *political* experiences collapsed. Commenting on his use of the term 'political', which may appear either too vague or too broad, Lefort writes:

If we nonetheless call political the 'form' in which the symbolic dimension of the social uncovers itself, this is not to privilege the relations of power among all other relations, but to make it clear that the power is not 'something' empirically determined but is indissociable from its representation, and that the test that we have of it is simultaneously a test of knowledge and of the mode of articulation of the social discourse, and is constitutive of the social identity.[28]

Perhaps the most striking illustration of this thesis is, in our context, Marx's discussion of Asiatic Despotism — whose very name indicates that this 'mode of production' is articulated in terms of something other than the productive base itself. What struck Marx in the Asiatic society is its permanence throughout all types of change, preserved by the absolute separation of the political Power from the rural community. The absolute separation of this Power, neither founded by nor accessible to the social, gives it its transcendent legitimation, diffusing the potential arising from the division inherent in the society. The efficacity of this Power is what Lefort calls *l'imaginaire* — the Freudian term which, in the work of Jacques Lacan, conceptualises the representational dimension of psychic functioning, the image of itself which the human needs in order to function as a social being. This self-image is articulated by Lacan in terms of the Ocdipal drama where the Father represents the Law, indicating to the male child what is socially forbidden, and therewith teaching the child his place in the society. Analogously, the social *imaginaire* would represent the Law of society's structuring, telling it what is and is not legitimate, what can and cannot be changed, and ultimately defining and limiting its self-identity. The *imaginaire*, symbolically articulated, structures the scientific, religious and aesthetic discourse through which a society comes to know itself. Its function is to neutralise the conflictual *origins* of the social, to create the illusion of permanence and necessity which characterised the 'society without history'. This task must ever begin anew, and engender the logic of the political; to imagine that the political or ideological could succeed in conjuring the menace is to believe in a society without origins, a thought without its situatedness, a self-transparence of the real . . . a positivism!

(d) Politics and Ideology

The interdependence of the political and the ideological is articulated through the discourse on, and knowledge of, the social. To be, the political must articulate itself, enunciate the Law. In so doing, however, the logic of its own situation leads it to neglect its origins in the social. Crucial, at this point, is that the division of the social only takes on *reality* in the articulation in this discourse. Here, the error of Marx manifests itself, conflating the discourse *on* the real (or social) with the discourse emerging from the real itself. This is the dilemma of the theory *of* and theory *for* practice. Even though he gives the mode of production the broadest possible interpretation, encompassing not only material production but social reproduction including the spheres of language, consciousness and community, Marx deploys this social self-production in the naturalist space of a linearly progressing Humanity. As to the question of origins, he turns back to empirical data, ultimately to the division of 'labour' in the sexual act. 'Here', writes Lefort, 'Marx's positivism is unequivocally unveiled'.[29] Better: Marx's naturalism. In effect, the suggestion is that from some fact — without entering into the question of how that 'fact' is instituted such that it comes to signify for us — there emerges a sense or meaning. There is no bridge between a supposed natural or primitive state and the sphere of meaning or sense which is attached to it. It is precisely this bridge which Lefort's logic of the political as the institution of the social intends to lay bare. Not that he pretends to give an explanation of how and why it occurred; the point is that already here, in a limit condition, we have an illustration of the interaction of the symbolic and the real, the political and the social. This is but one of an infinite manifold of cases; it points our way toward the continual interrogation of the articulation of the real which, we saw, constituted a 'realist politics'.

Lefort's discussion of contemporary ideologies follows this path. He suggests that we have to follow the move of Marx's own *discovery* of ideology, not that of contemporary 'critiques' of it. The latter criticise a specific discourse as 'ideological' because it veils the real. This supposes, however, that the critic knows what the 'real' in fact is. That is precisely what Lefort's work puts into question. Marx himself took a different path from his followers:

> From the 'Critique of Hegel's Philosophy of the State' to *Capital*, one principle of interpretation is maintained, which invites us to discover in the social structure the process of representation, first of all circumscribed in the limits of the philosophical, religious or political discourse. And it does not seem exaggerated to say that if Marx became disinterested in Hegel, it was because the identification of the real and the rational which he had criticized showed itself to him in the capitalist system as such, in the structuring of the form [*mise en forme*] of the relations of production where the logic of operations exhibits itself thanks to the obliteration of the conditions of their appearance. But such is the virtue of the deplacement effectuated in *Capital* that ideology shows itself

there not only rooted in but pre-formed by the mode of production; that capitalism shows itself to be, in a sense, the original ideological discourse — a discourse, it will be recalled, that the author designates explicitly as such several times by making the protagonists speak.[30]

We have already discussed Lefort's argument that ideology and alienation are the very structure of capitalism. Here we need to look briefly at his analysis of bourgeois ideology, totalitarian ideology and what he calls the contemporary 'invisible ideology'. It must be stressed that these ideologies are not the conscious representations of individual actors; they are the structures of the social reality itself expressed in the *imaginaire* of the given social and historical situation.

Ideology is articulated in the attempt to re-create the society without history. The neglect of origins, the denial of the division, and the pretence of rendering the social space self-transparent are its characteristics. Bourgeois ideology is specified by its continual reference to Ideals (Humanity, Justice, Democracy, Progress, etc.), its belief in Rules guiding action, and the multiplicity of accepted discourse. Common to these is that the distinction between the Ideal and the Real, the Rule and its Application, the Power and the Social, appears fully. It is admitted that the Ideals are not (yet) realised; the Rule is assumed, yet believed only when its effects manifest themselves; and the multiplicity of discourses bears witness to the ongoing attempt to bring together the poles. A 'logic' similar to that of the political manifests itself: in articulating itself, the social pretends to self-transparency, yet its articulation separates itself from it; and as separate it is open to question, challenge, revision; and a new articulation or discourse emerges. Bourgeois ideology is vulnerable for this reason; yet from within its own logic, any challenge simply becomes grist for its mill, is caught up in its structure and the belief in progress, in the advance of Enlightenment and History.

The traditional Marxist critique of bourgeois ideology is certainly correct in pointing to its mystifying nature; but what the Marxist cannot explain is why the overthrow of bourgeois ideology took the form of totalitarianism. Lefort's 'meta-sociological' suggestion is that the bourgeois logic of indefinite repetition is 'haunted by tautology'.[31] Totalitarianism tries to achieve in reality the 'reconciliation' of the poles which bourgeois ideology holds apart. The separation typical of bourgeois ideology is to be eliminated in a new sociality with no barriers between the spheres of life. Totalitarian ideology attempts to incarnate a mastery of the social reality within the society itself; it is a politics which denies its separateness from civil society. It does not speak of the real, but attempts to incarnate itself in it, particularly through the vehicle of the mass party. Typical of the totalitarian ideology is a 'new social agent', the militant, who in his/her particularly pretends to incarnate the universal.[32] The militant is both in the social and of it; and yet the militant is also said to know its reality and its immanent goals. The question of subjectivity is covered over, as is the problem of interpersonal relations. A new functionality becomes operational; precisely the artificial nature of the party becomes a virtue, representing a smooth logic of operations claiming to function in terms of the image of the totality. The functionalism of totalitarianism closes the society in on itself; there is no external source of identity, legitimation or socialis- ation. That this is a change in the nature of the social itself explains how totalitarianism differs from previous despotisms which were marked by the separation of the Prince. It also explains its instability, and the concomitant function of the Terror, which is not accidental. The goal of the totalitarian is to abolish the difference between the political and the social, the ideal and the real, signifier and signified. At the same time, it must *show* what it has done, identify itself as absolute Power. Where the bourgeois ideology spoke of the social, yet did not claim to be fully incarnate in it, the totalitarian has no distance; hence if the organisation goes awry, the plan fails or the bureaucrat misuses power, the whole edifice is put into question. Terror is necessary not only for this reason; more essential is that it renders each individual contingent and particular, alike in that the Terror may strike anyone — with the result that the desired fusion and elimination of the division within the social is effected. The edifice is fragile, yet viable. It need not fall on its own.[33] Its grotesque forms — in Nazi Germany or in Russia, for example — suggest that perhaps another means for conjuring the division which marked bour- geois ideology is possible, that our modern Western societies may be taking another path.

The happy-go-lucky Western complement to totalitarian practice is what Lefort refers to as 'the invisible ideology'. Reacting to both bourgeois and totalitarian ideologies, the attempt, again, is to close over the distance between the representation and the real which threatened bourgeois ideo- logy, while at the same time renoucing the completion of the representation within the real through its totalisation, as is the case with totalitarianism. Typical of the invisible ideology is the role of the group, which is both an expression of, and the goal of, social communication. What is communicated is not important: important is bringing all together in a homogeneous here and now such that the impression of a mastery over the social is felt by each. Personal presence is stressed, even though the person and the message are dissolved in the ritual of communication itself. Nothing is taboo: 'in no epoch has one talked so much . . .' (id., p. 45). There are no Masters, no Rules or Ideals, and no image of the Historical Totality; there is just the information which is lived as being the social itself which we all share. The result is to cloak the social division. Not that one can't talk of class, social contradictions and the like; this too enters into the mill and becomes part of the socialisation process. All is communicable, sayable, intelligibile; nothing is sacred, but everything is equal, equally real. Science too changes: no longer acting on the real or a theory of it, science is the real itself. Organisation is not acting on the real but obeying its dictates. There are no longer bosses and employees, workers and machines; all are part of a functioning whole, organised by a rationality independent of desire and human choice. Science spreads further insofar as all is to be equally intelligible; Nature, Psyche, and Society are united through the artificialism of method, be it formalism, operationalism or systems theory. A further facet of this machinery is the modern ('structuralist' in the broadest sense) attempt to eliminate the subject in favour of the text. Pedagogy plays its role too, with its measurement techniques and ultimately the notion of self-evaluation which eliminates the role of the Master such that knowledge is not related to the Truth or the Law but only back onto the supposed real itself. This real is transmitted through information, which all must possess on every conceivable subject in order to join the others in the group. Yet this knowledge is not a closed system; everything can and must be said, for there is to be perpetual novelty in a present which never becomes a lived past nor opens onto a future.

The description could go on, through the ideology of consumption, the transformation of nature into environment, the role of psychology, changing fashions, and still onward. What is at issue is (a) the attempt to destroy or deny the historical dimension of society through the 'novelty' of a perpetual present; (b) closing off the question of the origins of the social by instantaneously and continually re-creating the group personality; (c) denying the division which institutes the social and creating the illusion that through the plethora of information and communication the social itself is speaking; (d) homogenising the real such that it no longer poses a threat through its divisions and difference; and (e) socialising the individual in such a manner as to limit the possible expressions of desire to a sphere defined in advance as the real.

The 'logic of the political' which governs Lefort's analysis of ideology is articulated in a terminology at once more rigorous and more difficult than that presented here. The basic principles of the analysis emerge as early as the essays discussed in Section I of this chapter, which attains greater clarity from this retrospection. Reconsidering his work, Lefort talks about 'a new approach to what I have called the institution of the social':

> the discovery that the *form* is tied to a structuring of the form [*mise en forme*], and the latter to a structuring of the sense [*mise en sens*] — a term which I borrow from Piera Aulagnier[34] and that both (the same movement divided in two) presuppose a putting into question [*mise en jeu*] of the social identity in a general division such that all particular divisions are inscribed in the same register of the Law and the Real (a register which shows itself to be the same where what is forbidden and the nonsensical coincide: that which cannot be).[35]

The double register of the Law and the Real which is the social as instituted cannot be brought together any more than it can be ignored. It defines the fundamental and constituent in determination of the social to a subject or discourse from within it. This is not to be descried, but its implications must be understood. It poses the question of theory as *interpretation*.

III Philosophy Again

At this point, one could begin anew the analysis of Lefort's recent work in the light of its *theoretical* structures and implications; or one might ask what has become of the *political* goals which accompanied Lefort along his way. In the first case, the theory of the *oeuvre* would have to be analysed through his monumental *Machiavel*. In addition, one would have to reconsider the work of the late Merleau-Ponty, and this particularly in the light of Lefort's rereading of Freud in the 1960s, and the influence of the Lacanian interpretation.[36] In the present context, that is impossible. A reflection on Lefort's politics will, however, serve in its stead.

Concluding a long review of Lefort's *Machiavel,* Marcel Gauchet writes that 'he restores for us the possibility of thinking about society in a manner which is *philosophy* and knows that it can *only* be philosophy.'[37] From the time that he broke with the IVth International, Lefort had rejected the theory of the party as leader of the proletarian revolution in any way, shape or form. He split twice with 'Socialisme ou Barbarie' on this issue, and has analysed it extensively, most recently in *La Brèche.* It will be recalled that Lefort's insistence that the proletariat alone can make its own revolution through its own experience earned him epithets from Sartre for being a 'pure consciousness' above the fray. While he has abandoned the theory of the proletariat in its classical form, Lefort's attitude towards social change has remained constant. A theory of the social which knows that it can *only* be philosophy is all that the intellectual — or anyone else, for that matter — can claim. To think that you're doing more is not only self-deluding but dangerous. At best, such a theory which ignores its own limits can be an honestly bourgeois ideological stance; at worse, ignoring its own origins and claiming knowledge of the totality, it falls over to the totalitarian side. But this limitation of theory does not imply an 'existentialism' of some vague sort: that would be to enter 'the invisible ideology'.

In his essay on Merleau-Ponty, 'La politique et la pensée de la politique', Lefort had stressed that the result of a Merleau-Pontean reflection would be to support the proletarian goals insofar as 'we can recognize the symbol of a rupture of the social unity, and of a questioning, in the movement of history itself, of the relation of man to being'.[38] That rupture is not only due to the proletariat. Within the context of totalitarian and/or invisible ideologies, the rupture is open and inevitable, though inarticulate and unaware of its own nature. The task, however, is not to play the Modern Prince. One participates from one's own place: one analyses, writes, talks. No more can be done. This is not the pure spirit watching the contradictory particulars fight it out, though it certainly isn't Lenin in the library reading Hegel. It is the place of lucidity guided by theory; the place of theory and the place which the individual cannot but occupy within a social written in the double register. To want to be the leader, or to think of oneself as the militant, is to be open to contradiction in one's own attitudes and from the social reality itself.

This does not mean that there will not be social change, that all horizons are blocked, and that the exploitation and domination of the present will continue. We saw that Lefort's position is not a quietism, and that he expects struggle to continue in all domains. But social change will not follow a linear logic any more than it follows mechanical laws. It surges forth. We can recognise that not everything that calls itself 'revolutionary' is in fact revolutionary — be it the orthodox communist parties or those ideologues of the modern whose effacement of the individual, ideology of desire or practice of spontaneity is structured by the modern *imaginaire* which Lefort traces as the 'invisible ideology'. Lefort's contribution appears to be limited to nay-saying, to an always awake attentiveness to the dangers of bureaucratisation and renewed forms of domination. But there is more than just that. In the domain of theory — as philosophy, but also as an approach to a radical sociology and political theory — Lefort's work elaborates the insights which, from its own point of view and through its praxis, the New Left has gropingly acquired. He does not provide us with a Grand Theory, hardly even a Methodology. Rather, through Lefort's attempt to renew that unity of the theoretical, the social and the political which Marx had begun to elaborate, we as practical persons and we as theorists are put back in touch with the origins of our experience. This is all that a theory can do; and that is Lefort's point.

10 Ontology and the Political Project: Cornelius Castoriadis

> Marx says that revolutions are the locomotive of world history. But perhaps things are very different. Perhaps revolutions are travelling humanity's grabbing the emergency brake. W. Benjamin

For those of us who emerged from the political upheavals of the 'New Left', it has become at once more difficult and easier to be a Marxist. The difficulties are evident: numerical decline of the industrial proletariat as well as its depoliticisation and domination by labour bureaucrats; impossibility of deluding oneself about the heirs of 1917 and the kind of society they have instituted; the seeming displacement of the axis of contradiction to the Third World, leaving only a vague cultural malaise easily co-opted and ephemeral. The paradox is that precisely these difficulties (and their manifold extensions) make Marxism even more attractive. Blocked in our political practice, Marxism presents us with a theory of the 'essential' course and agency of history. Marxism is a theory tied to praxis. It defines the nature of revolution, condemning all reformism. That the praxis with which Marxism is bound up is that of the proletariat, and that this proletariat is not the empirically present one (which is only *an sich*, potentially, the revolutionary subject), leaves the intellectual both a theoretical and a practical task: the empirical appearances must be mediated to the essential structures; and these theoretical mediations must be propagated in order that the proletariat find itself in its praxis.

The Marxism to which the difficulties push us is a *theory* which needs a practical mediation: an organisational form. The concept of 'theoretical practice', along with more or less immediate journalistic work, cannot fill this gap. Hence, we are again confronted with a succession of debates, from Marx/ Bakunin/Proudhon to Lenin/Luxemburg/Trotsky, passing through Gramsci's organic intellectuals and the Council Communists. For some, crystallisation in a party (or 'pre-party party') is the essential task; for others, local activities on different levels are to be pursued, until the temperature of fusion is reached. For all, implicitly or explicitly, the theory serves as a rallying point. However interpreted, the theory is the source of meaning, the glue holding together our fragmented activities and lives. Even when we question it in this or that aspect, we assume that there must be 'the theory'.

In the face of this problematic, the development of the group 'Socialisme ou Barbarie' and its *spiritus rector*, Cornelius Castoriadis, thrust up a critical mirror which may enable us to better understand — and change! — our situation. Castoriadis' writings are now being published in a widely diffused paperback format. Written under pseudonyms (Pierre Chaulieu, Paul Cardan, Jean-Marc Coudray, among others), or distributed only within the group 'Socialisme ou Barbarie', they provide the record of a rigorous and consistent self-critical Marxist attempting to come to grips with the problem of revolution in contemporary capitalism. In following Castoriadis' evolution, it must not be forgotten that until the dissolution of the group, his work was part of a collective project.

A member of the Greek Communist Youth Party under the Metaxis dictatorship, Castoriadis recognised during the Occupation that Stalinist politics was radically opposed to the project of proletarian self-liberation. Joining the IVth International was the logical step, which meant spending the Resistance years dodging not only the fascists but Stalin's thugs as well. Moving to France after the war (to study philosophy), Castoriadis quickly found himself in opposition to the dominant tendency of the IVth International, not simply on conjunctural questions, but concerning basic issues like the nature of the Russian regime, the structure of capitalism and the problematic of the crisis theory, and the role and function of the Party. With Claude Lefort (pseudonym: C. Montal), he took the lead of an oppositional tendency within the IVth International. The final rupture came in 1948, and led to the founding of the political group and journal, *Socialisme ou Barbarie*.[1]

As 'Socialisme ou Barbarie' strove to relate theoretically and practically to the political and social changes of contemporary capitalism, its approach was coloured by an increasingly critical attitude towards the ambiguities in Marx's work itself. The basis of the critique was the insistence on taking Marx seriously — Marx as revolutionary, not Marx as thinker or theorist of politics. In the last five issues of the journal (numbers 36—40, April-June 1964 to June-August 1965), Castoriadis published a lengthy article, 'Marxism and Revolutionary Theory', in which he argues for the basic incompatibility of the two, opting for the latter. Shortly thereafter, a letter was sent to the journal's subscribers, announcing the cessation of publication. The correctness of the journal's analyses was stressed, as was its growing audience. Yet, the letter continued, this was not accompanied by political action; the audience remained consumers of theory, and the theory itself (for important reasons, discussed below) did not indicate any political archimedean point. 'Marxism and Revolutionary Theory' had concluded with the promise of a further article, under the title 'On the Status of a Revolutionary Theory'. In the letter, Castoriadis indicates that the theoretical retooling for which he was calling could not be accomplished along with the attempt to maintain the journal as part of a political project. Hence, both the journal and the group were dissolved.

The analyses which appeared in *Socialisme ou Barbarie* appeared to many to have come to their first fruition in May 1968. Personally, despite their different ages and backgrounds, its ex-members found themselves completely at home in that movement which, as Castoriadis wrote, was not the demand for but the affirmation of revolution.[2] Along with Edgar Morin and Claude Lefort, Castoriadis published (under the pseudonym, Marc Coudray) a volume of essays in early June 1968, attempting to contribute some analysis to the events in process. Yet the group did not reunite. After May, Castoriadis left his job as a professional economist (acquiring French citizenship, which permitted him to publish under his own name), and devoted himself mainly to theoretical tasks. He began the publication of his writings, became a practicing psychoanalyst, and completed the promised essay on the status of revolutionary theory, which was published as *l'institution imaginaire de la société* and which, as we shall see, goes far beyond what had been originally promised, laying the groundwork of a systematic ontology.[3] He began teaching a course on political economy at Nanterre, and with Claude Lefort and Marcel Gauchet was a member of the editorial board of the journal *Textures*. After a recent split (1977), a new journal, *Libre*, began publication.

I   The Political Critique of the Economic and the Economic Critique of the Political

In discussing the evolution of 'Socialisme ou Barbarie', Castoriadis once remarked that they had 'pulled the right string' — that of bureaucratisation — and had simply and ruthlessly kept pulling. Emerging from Trotskyism, this starting point is not surprising. A demystification of the results of 1917 was an essential political task. The tools chosen by Castoriadis were those of orthodox Marxism. Yet the implicit logic of his political approach contained in germinal form an essential element of his later critique of Marxism, which bears mention here. The working class will continue to revolt against its immediate conditions, showing its willingness to struggle now for a better life. Yet so long as that better life is imagined in Russian tonalities, the political translation of this immediate struggle can only be the Communist Party. What is important here is not simply that this strengthens the manipulatory capacity of the Communist Party. Implicit is the suggestion that it is the stunting of the creative imagination of individuals, due to the existence of a socially legitimated collective representation — an *imaginaire social*, as Castoriadis refers to it later — which must be analysed. The imaginary social representations are, in effect, a material force in their own right. To come to such an 'idealist' conclusion, Castoriadis took a strictly 'materialist' path.

The position of Trotsky stood and stands as a pole of atraction for those who refuse to recognise in Russia the translation into reality of their struggles and hopes. Yet a moment's (Marxist) reflection points to the inadequacy of Trotsky's notion of Russia as a 'degenerated workers' state'. If, in spite of everything, Russia is still essentially a 'workers' state', then the implication is that the elimination of private ownership and the replacement of the anarchy of capitalist production by the Plan are the essence of socialism. The 'degeneration' would concern only the form, not the essence, of the Russian social formation. But this confuses the juridical forms of property with the actual relations of production themselves. For Marx, it is precisely these relations of production which determine the forms of distribution and their (deformed) superstructural reflection. The vacillations in Trotsky's own analyses — for example on the question of 'Thermidor', or on the tactics to be followed by the Opposition — stem from the identification of form and essence.

Castoriadis' article, 'The Relations of Production in Russia'

(1949),[5] takes up the empirical problem with which Trotsky had not dealt, developing positions he had raised internally in the IVth as early as 1942. From this virtuoso Marxian analysis, which remains only too actual today, and not only as an illustration of what consistent Marxism can propose to empirical study, Castoriadis draws political conclusions as well. By 1934, Trotsky had been led to recognise that the working class was effectively excluded from control in the state, and that a new revolutionary party was necessary. Castoriadis' critique of the priority given to the juridical representation leads to an examination of the social relations that underlie it. His conclusion is that: 'The dictatorship of the proletariat cannot be simply the political dictatorship; it must be above all the economic dictatorship of the proletariat, for otherwise it will only be a mask for the dictatorship of the bureaucracy.'[6] This conclusion is perhaps nothing astonishingly new today. More important is the manner in which it is established: precisely by following the young Marx's own example of the demystification of the juridical, and the examination of the relations of the socio-economic to it.

A further consequence of the analysis of 'The Relations of Production in Russia', is the demonstration of the central, and independent, role played by the bureaucracy. The critique of the Trotskyist position could have led to the theory of 'state capitalism'.[7] Such a position suggests that the State (or Party) plays the same historical role in developing the forces of production that the capitalist class played in the West. The implication is that what exists in Russia is still a form — the most advanced, and therefore presumably the most contradictory form — of capitalism. It follows that the laws formulated in *Capital* are still valid in Russia, and a proletarian revolution can be expected. What Castoriadis' analysis of actual conditions in Russian industry (and agriculture, to which a separate article was devoted) showed, however, is that the role of the state is precisely to set these laws out of play. A *political* intervention occurs, making it impossible to claim that the state is a collective capitalist in the traditional sense, and demanding the recognition that Russia presents an *historically new social formation with a new form of domination: the bureaucracy.*[8]

The recognition of the *political* role played by the state implies a specific reading of the Marxian notion of political economy, and carries implications for the idea of revolution itself. Marxism is not understood as a (technical) economic theory, nor as a closed system in the classical rationalist sense. Marxism is a theory of social relations. The critique of Russia with its demystification of the juridical mask and the uncovering of the human relations that permit the continuance of the bureaucratic form which structures these relations can be extended to a critique of capitalist society as well. Bureaucracy is not simply a political category. With the appreciation of the bureaucratic 'string' comes, necessarily, a re-evaluation of the *content* of socialism. This further break with Trotskyist essentialist formalism was confirmed and furthered by the events in East Germany, Poland and Hungary. The idea of self-management that had been central since 1948/49 is transformed and developed into a concrete and elaborated demand for the restructuring of daily life in the 1955 essay, 'On the content of Socialism', whose second and third parts were published in 1957—8.[9]

The *political* critique of bureaucratic society demanded a re-examination of the *economic* base of Marxian theory. The political critique had been based on precisely that economic theory. The tensions and antinomies it laid bare in the area of the political rebound, putting itself into question. The theoretical lesson is: there is no privileged position from which to observe the goings-on in the world, no detached observer and no mythical proletarian subject-object of history.[10] Neither economics nor politics has a God's-eye-view of a once-and-for-all world structure. Just like the original economic thrust into the political, the political rebound into the economic turns out to destroy its own foundations. In one of the young Marx's favorite hegelianisms, 'Its victory is at the same time its own loss.'

The economic critique of the political points to the central role of the *relations* of production. What then determines the relations of production? Of course, the relation of capital to labour, of command over the means of production which, in the totality, assures the command over a single commodity, labour-power. In Marx's economic theory, once capitalism as a system of production and of social reproduction achieves dominance, capital tends to accumulate at the expense of labour, new and more 'scientific' modes of exploitation are devised; and there ensues, depending on your reading, either an absolute or relative pauperisation of the working class. Of course, Marx points to countervailing forces — most importantly, the class struggle as manifested in the growth of union power. Others have analysed the importance of the relative privilege of the working class in the advanced countries due to imperial or colonial domination. Nonetheless, the point remains that Marx thought of his system as indicating economic *laws* (or, at least, 'scientifically' established tendencies). In doing so, Marx had to assume a level of wages, determined by 'historical and moral factors'. Yet in fact nothing in his own theory permits this level to be established; nothing explains why the union movement cannot succeed, for example, in decreasing — rather than increasing, as the theory supposes — the rate of exploitation. Thus, the political stress on the creative activity embodied in the social relations of production is destroyed in its economic translation into a 'law' of increasing exploitation and pauperisation. For the law to hold, the proletariat must be an object, conceived in its reified form in alienated production. That, however, implies a dilemma: *either* the proletariat is dead, objective material doomed to continued exploitation and impoverishment at all levels of life, in which case it is difficult to see the positive content, or even possibility, of socialist revolution and its difference from the desperate revolts of the downtrodden which have coloured history; *or* it is a creative human force seeking self-assertion and struggling continually for its freedom in different socio-historical conditions, in which case the law of value and its scientific certainty of capitalist collapse falls, and with it falls the edifice of *Capital.*[11]

A further aspect of the problem, made evident in the analysis of the relations of production in Russia, is effective also under the contemporary form of bureaucratic capitalism. Were the law of value to be maintained, not simply as concerns wages but across the board, that would suppose the existence of competition and a free market situation. The competitive free market is that which, to give but two instances, permits the determination of the value of a commodity (in Vol. 1) as measured by the amount of *socially necessary* labour time it contains; and (in Vol. 3) it explains the difference of value and market-price as determined by the *equalisation* of the rates of profit. Yet precisely what occurs under the bureaucratic domination is the interference of the political factor — political in the technical sense, i.e., concerned with total system maintenance — within the play of supposedly free forces. The implication, then, is a *limitation on the domain of validity of economics as science.* For the Marxist used to looking to the material base of political activity, there ensues a fundamental *indetermination* of the process of revolution.

The political critique of the economic, like the economic critique of the political, sends us back to square one — save that we have passed 'Go' and collected a metaphorical two hundred dollars. We now know that neither has a 'monopoly'; both have deeper roots, a human content. Indeed, even to talk about a 'content' to socialism is somewhat misleading insofar as it implies something fixed, out-there, which can be possessed. In fact, writes Castoriadis, 'the absurdity of all inherited political thought consists precisely in wanting to resolve men's problems for them, whereas the only political problem in fact is this: how can people become capable of resolving their problems for themselves?'[12] The 'content' of socialism can only be the *process* of self-management, which Castoriadis later reformulates as the auto-institution of society. Indeed, as his political reflection was driven towards an increasingly virulent critique of Marxism as being finally a hindrance to revolutionary activity, Castoriadis went beyond the conception of self-management as an economic notion: revolutionary self-management must be total if it is to cope with the problems created by the socially inculcated tendency towards privatisation, isolation and consumptive mystification typical of the bureaucratic project. A revolutionised society would be one in which the relation of the individual to the institutional is at all levels involved in a continual process of self-criticism. The problematic of the *institution*, as instituted and instituting, becomes central once the antinomies of the economic and the political are worked through by a consistent Marxism.

II Organisation: the False but Necessary Debate

Certain of the orthodoxy of their Marxism, and the implication that the self-management form was the only one adequate to a revolutionary society, the group 'Socialisme ou Barbarie' was confronted with the question of their own identity. Many members were strongly *ouvriérist* in their attitude, and had been convinced by the experience of the IVth International that it was not simply a 'good' party replacing the Communist Party that was needed. They were attempting a return to the Marxist theory of the revolutionary class, and were striving in their journal to combine a language and approach accessible to the class with a hefty theoretical rigour. They had to find a vehicle for relating to the class without at the same time claiming to bring them, or impose on them, a theoretical consciousness from without. To this classical Marxian dilemma was added the problem, which they had already recognised within the IVth International, that the organisation itself risked becoming a bureaucracy instead of itself incarnating a microcosm of the future self-managed society. The splits of Lefort, and his constant criticisms, were an important counter-balance, though they added no positive solution. Moreover, the combination of the economic critique of the political and the political critique of the economic led to a stress on the less traditional, innovative aspects of the class struggle — and ultimately, over the years, to the elimination of its postulated centrality as the mythical and mystified image of revolution was rejected.

'Socialisme ou Barbarie' functioned according to principles perfectly consistent with the Marxian theory they adopted. Members paid a steeply proportional percentage of their income as dues, and accepted the tasks which the majority of the organisation assigned to itself. There were general assemblies on a regular basis, and special groups with specific tasks, responsible to and revocable by the group as a whole. There was a constant attempt at the development of the self-education of each of the members, both in terms of theoretical analysis and awareness of ongoing struggles and the forms in which they were being fought. The journal which they published was the organ in which both forms of this self-education were expressed. The stress on the self-education of the proletariat which must take its own fate into its hands meant that the group did not attempt to 'parachute' outsiders into ongoing struggles. They organised where they worked; published their views, in the journal, in leaflets, and later, after 1959, in the small newspaper *Pouvoir Ouvrier*; they held public meetings, and attempted to recruit new members who shared their views. Some members were active in an industrial milieu, some in white-collar areas, and later there were some student members; and there were international contacts (one of which, 'Solidarity', still exists in England). In short, from this point of view, there was nothing unusual about the group.

The 'bureaucratic string' created a series of tensions around the question of organisation. In the first place, there was the question 'What is important?' If one opts for the traditional view, that the proletariat alone can seize power, and to do so must conquer and destroy the bourgeois state, then one's attention is centred on the workplace and its attendant struggles, and on their political unification at a national level. But if one sees bureaucratisation as a *social* phenomenon, one begins to concentrate on the everyday. One's task becomes to convince people that their concerns are in fact socially important and worth struggling over. One sees that one manner in which capitalism remains in control is by convincing people that only the concerns of the experts really matter. This turn to the everyday implies a jolt for the traditional conception. But, it also implies that, in a sense, the organisation does assume a directive role. One goal of some members of the group was that there be a newspaper, or part of the journal, which would be given over to the readers. The problem is first of all, they don't think that what they have to say is 'important', and secondly that if they do begin massively to contribute, one does ultimately have to make a choice. Similarly in the selection of sheerly factual material that appears in the journal, one does again choose, and in terms of very specific criteria. Would it not be a disservice in the end to simply make the choice without explaining why? For Castoriadis, the simple fact of adhering to the organisation meant that one agreed with the general lines of its analysis; hence, any dissimulation of that analysis would be both dishonest and a disservice.

The 'bureaucratic string' poses an even more central question for the organisation: that of its own existence. The problem is not that organisations tend necessarily to bureaucratise themselves, separating themselves from the ongoing struggles and concerns. From a Marxist perspective, such bureaucratisation must be explained historically, materially. Bureaucracy is a constant risk for the organisation, which must try to counter it. Further, insists Castoriadis, 'Am I to govern my whole life on the supposition that I might one day return to infancy?'[13] Those who oppose any organisation, as Castoriadis sees Lefort's position, for example, are in contradiction with the implications of their own analyses, for they then separate theory from practice. The existential problem for the organisation is more acute once one recognises the results of the analysis of the 'Relations of Production in Russia', i.e., that there is no privileged position from which to survey the ongoing struggles. This would be Lefort's reply, for implicitly, the organisation's own existence postulates that it itself has precisely that heavenly perspective! Were it not to make that assumption, implicitly or explicitly, it would be only another particular group pushing its own particular phantasies. That it intervene in the ongoing struggles in the name of a theory, and with the goal of aiding a practice, presupposes that it has an access to knowledge not available to the participants. From this implicit assumption flows the danger of bureaucratisation. The group takes itself as the General Staff of the Revolution; its activities become rigid and formal; it passes resolutions and debates as if the eyes of History were constantly upon it.[14]

What is important in the organisational debates and schisms within the group is that, despite the growing critique of traditional Marxism and the greater depth and extension of the notion of revolution that followed, there was (at least until 1958, and culminating in the split of 1961—3 when Lyotard, Souryi and Maille's continuing Marxian orthodoxy led them to radical opposition to Castoriadis' new elaboration) a shared and usually implicit *ouviérism* animating their perceptions. Once this perspective is presupposed, the unbridgeable dualism of organisation/organised, with the attendant problems of manipulation and bureaucratic domination, is inevitable. No matter how resolutely one insists that the revolution will be made by the working class itself, one separates oneself from that class; and with the separation must come if not the distinction between trade union and party activity then at least that between sheerly defensive economic activity and revolutionary political activity. A distinction between the immediate activity and the historical sense of that activity is introduced, thereby implicitly defining 'what is important'. Even if a 'Luxemburgian' perspective were adopted, this would be at best simply a pedagogical innovation: as opposed to the learning brought to it from the outside, one suggests that the class, like the young child, will learn better and more meaningfully by choosing its own pace and objects, by making its own mistakes and then correcting them. The revolutionary organisation seems to presuppose that there exists a concrete and real goal which can be defined and known by that organisation; and whether it is the main actor, crucial mediation, or simply a tolerant pedagogue, as well as the details of how it will play the role it allocates to itself, are issues about which one can debate, around which schisms can occur — and through which, if the debate is carried through consistently, one is ultimately driven to put into question the premises of the question itself!

If one attempts to deal with the organisational question by a return to the texts of Marx and the tradition, it becomes rapidly apparent that it is no accident that the weakest and least developed aspect of the Marxist theory is precisely the nature of class. Castoriadis sums up its implications in a provocative passage:

> One sees here the profound duplicity of all the Marxists: that revolutionary class, to which superhuman tasks are attributed, is at the same time profoundly *irresponsible*: one cannot impute to its action what happens to it, nor even what it does; it is *innocent* in the two senses of the term. The proletariat is the constitutional monarch of History. Responsibility belongs to its ministers: to the old leaderships which erred or betrayed — and to us, who once again, against all

opposition, are going to construct the new leadership. . .[15]

In Marx, the proletariat is defined and created by its relation to the means of production; and its revolutionary activity, which transforms it from a class in itself to a class for itself, is the result of its social-economic insertion in the process of production. This implies that the class is defined by its *being* and not by its *praxis*, as a production which, somehow, must become a producer. On the other hand, ironically, in Marx's own presentation the bourgeoisie is by definition creative, praxical, changing the world. In accounting for the origins of capitalism, Marx vacillates, but ultimately shows that there were no necessary material reasons why it had to spring forth; it was not the product of a mode of production or a technology but rather, seizing upon the accidents which Marx designates in *Capital* as 'Primitive Accumulation', the bourgeoisie created its own world, in which technological change, ever-expanding reproduction and rationalisation became the dominant modalities of social life. The proletariat, on the other hand, is generally described by Marx as defined by the economic-technological conditions in which it reproduces itself and society. Hence, one finds statements like the famous assertion that what counts is not what this or that proletarian does or thinks, but what the class *is* and *must* do. And, when the class doesn't appear to be following the lines laid before it by history, instead of defining it by its *being*, the class is made into an *essence*, whose temporary manifestations are only accidents or moments of pause on the way to its self-realisation as laid out by the rationality of Historical Materialism.

In their practice, Marxists obviously have to go beyond this metaphysical definition of the proletariat; and yet, insofar as it defines the parameters of the organisational debate, the Marxian theory of the proletariat falsifies that debate. Immense amounts of empirical work can be, and have been done in the attempt to circumscribe empirically the working class; one can examine the effects of technological change on it, correlate its activities and attitudes with social changes, with rising and falling prices, political crises, shifts in social mores, and much more. In all of this, the presupposition is that there is something, some thing, which is the class, which the research aims at pinpointing ever more sharply. But what *is* the class? Castoriadis argues that the class is its praxis; and that the praxis of the class is what defines the social conditions in which it finds itself.[16] Of course, that praxis is not a free creation apart from the social conditions in which it finds itself. But those conditions themselves are continually changing, always affected by the praxis of the class, apart from which they are meaningless. And there is the further structurally-conditioned circumstance, that in capitalism the proletariat is not simply an appendage to the productive machine, but rather its motor without whose active contribution the machine slows, turns with difficulty, or halts. While in their practice Marxists have often tried to take account of the praxis of the proletariat, their theory proves a hindrance. It is always in terms of the class-as-essence that 'what is important' is defined. Struggles which don't fit into the schema are either ignored or, if they attract numbers so great as to force themselves to attention, they are opportunistically integrated into the schema. The explanation of the 1917 Russian Revolution by the theory of the 'weakest link' is probably the best-known example of this rationalistic fudging.

The essentialist view of the proletariat brings with it a blindness not only to non-conforming struggles, but even more, insofar as it entails a philosophy of history which defines the possibilities of revolutionary practice, there is also present in it a specific set of blinkers in terms of which the results of proletarian praxis are measured and evaluated. Reading *Capital* from the point of view of proletarian praxis instead of opting for its implicit philosophy of history, the *capital-immanent* results of proletarian struggle become apparent. The simplest example is the discussion of the transition from absolute to relative surplus-value production, as well as Marx's further hints about how machinery is introduced to control the proletarian struggle. Extended, this suggestion would mean that the capitalism which we know today is precisely the result of the class struggle; and even more, that it is probable that capitalism could not have survived without that struggle! Technological development, the internal expansion of the market creating the consumer society, and the ideology which accompany these are necessary to capitalism's continuation. If this is the case, might it not also follow that, for the proletariat, 'its victory is at the same time its loss'? Or at least its radical transformation, such that the struggle today will be located outside of the parameters of the traditional view? Does it make sense any longer to operate with the essentialist view of the proletariat and the historical metaphysics that are inextricably intertwined with it? Would it not be more faithful to the *praxis* of revolution to recognise the new situation which the class struggle has in fact *achieved*?

Spurred on by the continued existence of struggles against capitalist domination, within, around and outside of production, Castoriadis' interrogation had to put into question the foundations of Marxism itself. He could not 'solve' the organisational problem, simply because the question itself was posed in terms of a situation which no longer existed. That did not imply that the problem was abandoned. Continual reflection upon the exigencies to which it pointed was crucial to the critique of Marxism. Negatively, the classical formulation of the theory of the Party in those famous and curious passages of Lenin's *One Step Forward, Two Steps Backward* — with its glorification of factory discipline, the division of labour, subordination to the leaders and the like — and its corollary of a technologically reduced politics paradoxically based on the political will of the Party which is at the same time said to be subordinated to objective laws, had the advantage of focusing on the central issues. Positively, the always-present demand for organisation and action were coupled with the insistence on casting off the blinkers to recognise the new and interrogate its political sense. Writing in June 1968, Castoriadis still insisted on the need for organisation, pointing out that it was not for a night but for a life of love that we were struggling. The organisation of which he conceives would not make the claim to be the direction of the ongoing struggles; its task would be theoretical, thematic, and praxical in the sphere in which its members were involved. The necessity of an organisation springs from the practical needs of its members: there are many who would share the kind of analysis he is suggesting, thinks Castoriadis; they must come together, to talk, learn and act. What such an organisation would do can only be defined in the concrete situation in which it exists. This is not a 'solution', admits Castoriadis. Indeed until the theoretical reconstruction for which he called at the time of the dissolution of 'Socialisme on Barbarie' is realised, the question itself will remain to be posed anew.

III Marxism: the Problem of Metaphysics

Using Marx to critique Marx poses finally the question: what in fact is Marxism? If we make the strongest case possible for Marxism — which neither the Marxists nor Castoriadis always do — the first answer is that while it is articulated as a theory, Marxism claims to be more than the traditional conception of theory would permit — not knowledge for power, or even theory for practice. Marx wanted to break with the contemplative dualism which placed theory off to one side, while the world about which it was to give knowledge stood separate from it. Marx's theory was to be a theory *of*: history, revolution, and the praxis of the proletariat. It was a theory of history because its own conditions of possibility were historical: prior to the socialisation of society and creation of a real totality by capitalism, no theory of this type was possible. Insofar as the capitalism which had given rise to this new type of totality-comprehension was itself based on constant innovation and change, the theory had to be mobile, open to the changing course of social relations and, most importantly, revolutionary. The revolutionary nature of the theory springs from its being the theory of the proletariat: that class which is nothing, to which no specific wrong but general dehumanisation is done, is created by and constantly reproduces capitalism; it is the concrete negation of capitalism, and the theory which expresses its actual position and struggles is thus at once historical and revolutionary. The theory is a part of the revolutionary praxis of the proletariat which is historically rooted and which must, with the aid of the theory, come to an awareness of the task history has legated to it: the overthrow of the social conditions of which it is the negative product.

The specific character of Marxism *as a theory* means that it must analyse and describe social relations of which it is itself a part; and at the same time it must be involved in and aiming at changing those very conditions. To be able to make this claim, a view of history is presupposed: most generally, history as the history of class struggle. On this basis, Marxism escapes the reproach of avoiding the dilemma of a separate theory which, paradoxically, becomes an empty pragmatism. At the same time, this view of history designates to Marxism its concrete insertion, permitting it to decipher the ideological nature of concurrent theories, and to learn from the ongoing struggles of the proletariat. The process of Marxism's continual transformation through self-critique and learning from proletarian praxis is built into the theory, permitting it to come to grips with the social-political situation which constantly changes as a result of its own intervention. The basis of this learning process is that the theory's historical insertion tells it 'what is important'. It can do this because, at the same time that it is historical, it is also based on a specific science which recognises the definitional role of praxis in the formation of the social world.

If today's Marxism, and the results of Marxian practice, do not live up to Marx's project it is incumbent on us to ask how such a devolution was possible. A first attempt to salvage Marx's theory is that proposed by Lukács: Marxism is true *as a*

method, and even if all of the concrete empirical results of
Marx's own researches were proven wrong, this method could
still be applied anew to give results which would be revolutionary. While the suggestion is tempting, the historical insertion
which Marxism claims for itself speaks against it. The method is
only possible in specific social conditions; and Lukács himself
admits (in the article, 'The Changed Function of Historical
Materialism' in *History and Class Consciousness*) that it is not
universally applicable. A method is only valid for specified
contents; and if these are not present, the method cannot do
what is claimed for it. Yet the argument might continue that
only through the application of the method itself can we know
what the conditions in fact are; and that insofar as we still live
in a society which is *essentially* capitalist, we should not be
deceived by the appearances. If we lay aside the criticism of
such 'essentialist' arguments, the devolution of Marxism as
theory and as practice would then be explained by the
erroneous application of the method to the appearances instead
of using it to find the essences. In this case, however, a double
problem emerges. First of all, the distinction of essence-
appearance is one taken over from the traditional contemplative
philosophy; and the notion of essence is, by definition,
a-historical. Second, the historical nature of the Marxian theory
suggested that the praxis of the proletariat, of which Marxism is
to be the historical theory, has precisely the effect of changing
the world. In its desire to be a *historical science*, Marxism works
with a combination of the Aristotlean notions of efficient and
final cause; but as the theory of the revolutionary proletariat, it
is a theory of struggle and change whose results may well be the
elimination of the conditions in which the theory was valid. In
this sense, Marxism *is* responsible for its destiny.

What of Marx's own concrete analyses? It might be suggested
that we have to criticise certain aspects of his theory, while
keeping others. We could develop a version of the 'two-Marxes'
theory. We might try to explain away the undeniably scientistic
aspects of Marx's work, perhaps as due to the problem that any
discoverer of a 'new continent', as Althusser would have it, is
forced to describe the voyage in the language left over from the
tradition. In this case, however, we have no longer the theory of
Marx, but our own theory, expressed through our borrowings
and our syncretism. Marx did, after all, make the claim that his
theory was capable of explaining the course of history,
including the conditions of its own possibility. To suggest that
Marx can be used otherwise is not to treat him as a Marxist but
as merely another philosopher. In effect, we can also learn from

Plato, Aristotle and countless others. Marx wanted his theory to be different from theirs. If we deny that claim, then what sense does it make to pretend to be inheriting his legacy, to act in his name? It is confusing and scholastic to make the attempt to preserve a 'true' Marx untouched by time and history. And it is ultimately ideological to suggest that we are the heirs of *this* Marx, Marx the philosopher.

Marx spoke of his theory as the theory *of* proletarian praxis; and in its best elements, this is precisely what it was. The discussion of the revolt of the Silesian weavers (1844), which draws the implications from a collectively undertaken praxis, is an early example; another is the description of the meetings of revolutionary workers in the Paris of 1844; and hundreds of others could be added from Marx's properly historical descriptive analyses. Further, E. P. Thompson has shown in *The Making of The English Working Class*, that many of the constitutive ideas which Marx wove together into *Capital* were on the tongues and in the minds of the English workers well before Marx crossed the Channel. And yet, we know that at the beginning Marx's ideas did not penetrate the movement, which was more influenced by a Proudhon, a Lassalle, or even a Bakunin. When Marxism finally made its organised appearance, it had become something else — despite Marx's own misgivings — a catechism masquerading under the veil of science. Castoriadis is not concerned to salvage a 'good' Marx. Whatever the validity of the various attempts at Marxist reconstruction, these are *theoretical* efforts. The crucial point is that if we are faithful to Marx's own goals, to a theory and practice of revolution, then we must admit the fate of Marxism, taking into account its absorption into bureaucratic practice. Analysis of Marxism from this point of view tells us something about our present society.

> Marxism can from now on serve effectively only as an ideology, in the strong sense of the term: an invocation of fictive entities, pseudo-rational constructions and abstract principles which, concretely, justify and hide a social-historical practice whose true signification lies elsewhere. That this practice is that of a bureaucracy which imposes its exploitation and totalitarian domination over a third of the world's population — one must really be a marxist to ignore it, to consider it as anecdotal, or to rationalize it as accidental.[17]

Castoriadis finds that Marx-as-ideologue is the purveyor of

capitalist ideology: the primacy of production, inevitability of capitalist technological forms, justification of unequal wages, scientism, rationalism, blindness to the question of bureaucracy, and the adoration of capitalist modes of organisation and efficiency. How could Marxism become, in his words, 'the flesh of the world we combat'?[1][8]

The historical specificity of Marxism as a theory of capitalist society gives a foothold for its further interrogation. It is only in capitalist society that the economic sphere achieves its full independence and reveals its essential social function. The implication is that in precapitalist societies, this essence revealed itself only indirectly, through manifold appearances, but that it was nonetheless dominant there too. Yet, for Marx himself, the specificity of capitalism is that it is not simply production of commodities, but that it is the continually expanded drive for the augmentation of social reproduction (M-C-M', in Marx's formula). Under capitalist social relations, the economy dominates all the other spheres of society; and the model of its organisation — rationalisation in all spheres — spreads its corrosive influence over custom and tradition, creating among other appearances a proletariat which is the nothing that can become all, whose praxis as understood by Marxism is the condition of the possibility of an all-encompassing theory of history. In spite of the difference between the capitalist function of economics and that of precapitalist societies, Marx's suggestion is that we can understand history and historical transformations in terms of the development of the economic base. Though it is of course true that you can't eat religion, the law or even democracy and philosophy, the question must be posed: what does this systematisation say about Marx's notion of 'human nature'? And, what kind of theory could make this claim?

A theory of human history must be able to account for the social change which overturns a prevailing mode of social relations. For Marx, the motor of history is of course class struggle. Marx offers two explanations of the origins of class society. The first is functional-rational, suggesting that history be read in terms of adaptations to the productive base. To the windmill corresponds feudal society, to the steam engine corresponds capitalism — and perhaps, socialism would be, in Lenin's aphorism, 'soviets plus electrification'! Yet, ethnography gives us literally hundreds of examples of societies whose productive and technological bases are identical, yet whose social structures are radically different. And what of the multiplicity of social formations which, today, East and West, exist on the same technological basis? The second suggestion offered by Marx might be introduced as a reply. In a given society there arises a surplus which permits certain social strata to live from the work of others. They then arrange conditions to preserve their life-style. This is an unsatisfactory explanation, however, not only because the ethnologists have shown that there exist many societies which indeed have a surplus without an exploiting class, but also because it leaves unexplained why there would occur a shift in social attitudes permitting this division of the society. The existence of a surplus explains the origins of class society only if the nineteenth-century model of *homo oeconomicus* or *homo dominator* is read back into the analysis. Precisely the difference between capitalism as expanded reproduction for profit and pre-capitalist economic formations should warn us against this imposition.[19]

It could be objected that in his theory of ideology Marx does not really define human being in terms of an overly simplified and capital-centric perspective insofar as from this primary factor he develops a more complex and articulated perspective in which production is only one determinant, alongside of social interaction, language and species possibility. While there are non-reductionist elements in Marx's discovery of the ideological structure of capitalist society, the general tendency of his theorising is in fact quite aptly summed up by the infrastructure/superstructure approach. Clearly, however, the dependence of the superstructural forms on their infrastructural base makes sense only if the two structures communicate in some manner or another. Expressed as an action of the forces of production on the relations of production, the assertion is at least logically consistent, since the *relata* are both forms of production. But in this formulation, the dominance of production over all other modes of social activity is assumed. This is ultimately an ontological assertion, which will be criticised below. What emerges at this point is a Marxian *functionalism*: once the system is defined as oriented to its economic reproduction, all of its elements have an economic signification, and hence the dominance of the economic is assured. But the premise is not self-evident; it is a presupposition, whereas the point was to demonstrate its validity. There does not seem to be any *a priori* reason to assume that philosophy and democracy, let alone dionysian cults or matrilineal kinship systems, have solely or even primarily economic signification.

It could be objected that Marx does not abusively reduce *everything* to economics and that, indeed, the notion of the economic is not intended to refer solely to production but also to the *relations* of production and the forms of social intercourse in a given society. This defence would also assert that Marx considers the relations of production themselves to be one of the primary forces of production. But that is just the point: there are times when *Marx* at his best appears to think just like the *capitalist* at his worst, i.e., treating the whole world as simply part of a system of production for profit. To reply that 'this is how capitalism is', and that Marx is, after all, presenting a description of capitalism in its contradictory nature only moves the problem back one step. For in that case, how would he defend the thesis of the inherently revolutionary and negating character of the proletariat: the proletariat itself would be more capitalic than the capitalists! Castoriadis' critique of the theory of the proletariat as the unique revolutionary subject has already been examined. To that analysis we have now to add some further critiques of the presuppositions of Marx's theory *qua* theory. It will then appear that Marx's position is brutally consistent in its formal logical development and yet, at the same time, unable to achieve its professed goal. The reasons for its failing drive Castoriadis beyond his immanent critique in terms of Marxism to the elaboration of a philosophical theory which entails the rethinking of the revolutionary project itself, in all of its dimensions.

Escaping from the accusation of reductionism, but nonetheless on the defensive, Marxism finds its more nuanced defence through the application of categories from that sphere which Hegel calls Essence. While this is not the place to demonstrate the details of the structural parallels between the second Book of the *Logic* and Marx's theory, it should suffice to recall that, for Marx, capitalism is the explicit self-presentation of the economic essence on which all societies rest, but which they reveal only through more or less oblique, metaphorical, or mediated appearances. In this sense, it could be suggested that Marx's premises are not simply Hegelian but, in the end, Aristotelean: there is a potentiality, and what the theory describes are the paths to its necessary actualisation. Or, to express it in terms of another tradition which, paradoxically perhaps, is not logically foreign to the Marxian: we have the description of the Golgatha Way which the human species must traverse before arriving at the final Salvation.[20] From Hegel to Aristotle to that Speculative Christian mystery: the point that shocks is the *Rationalism* of Marx's own system. 'It is completely indifferent', insists Castoriadis, 'whether we say that nature is a movement of the *logos*, or that the *logos* arises at a given stage of the evolution of nature, for from the outset both entities are posited as being of the same — i.e., of a rational — nature.'[21] For the dialectic of the negation of the negation to work, there must be a *system* which provides for a homogeneity of the objects which relate to one another. This homogeneity could be supplied, we saw, by an assumption about *homo oeconomicus*. Or, in a more theoretical formulation, the assertion would be that Marxism as critical theory has the task of extracting the *rational* kernel, the reality beneath the mystification, the essence hidden by the appearance. The important point is that here *rational equals real equals essential.* Think of the oft-quoted aphorisms, such as that the rational has always existed but not always in a rational form, or the continually recurring womb metaphors, and the accompanying assertion that theory is there to lessen the birth-pangs of the new society. The assumption is that history and its milieu are ultimately rational, ultimately progressing towards a goal which is already 'essentially' prefigured in the present. A *telos* is presupposed — one which seems different from the Hegelian because it is posed in historical garb, but whose rational essence is ultimately the same: fully realised humanity, generic being.

From this stance there emerge two political positions with identical premises worth analysing. The suggestion is that the present is ripe with a futurity or potentiality which renders it unstable and opens it to the possibility of change. From the standpoint of the *telos* of a realised humanity rid of conflict, the present is found wanting. This permits the Marxian functionalist analysis of superstructures which can provide often insightful analyses, for example into the contradictory role of the present educational structures, the family or male dominance in society. At the same time that the system-preservative aspect of these institutions is demonstrated it is shown that their function is not perfectly fulfilled; and that their inadequacy creates the space for political practice. But then this practice is defined with reference to, or in dependence on, the search for functional sociological adequation. Such functional adequacy, however, can be perceived only from outside the system, from the God's-eye view of the philosopher or party bureaucrat. In a word: *politics becomes sociology*, a field for experts who control and direct, who fill in the gaps, who strive for harmony and unification, who direct from without. When politics becomes sociology, the bureaucracy is implicitly seated in power: the social present is defined as wanting, and the point of view from which that lack is deciphered is that of the potential new power, the agent of reconciliation. Sociology as politics with its assumption that the contradictions or dilemmas to which the politician must address her attention are those of an appearance (or superstructure) inadequate to its essence (or infrastructure), leads directly to Leninism and its consequent development in the Russian form of bureaucratic society. If there is a rationality to the world, and if history has ultimately a progressive direction, then those who can apply the theory to understand the 'really real' beneath the appearances need to guide and direct those still lost in the shadow world. In this sense, it is true that what counts is not what individuals may think but what the class is; the law-like activity of the infrastructure tells the naked truth of the future. Theory becomes science, and the Party with its specialists easily becomes the stand-in for the class. Substitutionism is justified; socialism becomes the Plan. And, concludes Castoriadis, 'humans no more make their history than the planets 'make' their revolutions; they are 'made' by it. . .'[22] Politics becomes technology; praxis becomes rational-bureaucratic.

The root error here is that the totality (or systematic) standpoint, which is essential to Marx's contribution, is taken as realised (or at least in principle realisable) in reality. Once that assumption is made, the question becomes that of the practical means of incarnating its reality. As the example of Lukács shows, one makes the move *from a category to a reality*: the Party. Totality becomes totalitarian! The theoretical problem is that the realised totality would be a contradiction in terms. Were it to exist, we couldn't know it, for we could not stand outside it and have it as an object of knowledge; if it in fact existed, we would be the totality, and it would dissolve itself into our monadic individuality. Further, if the totality exists, no praxis is possible; pure rationality is nothing but pure contemplation, absolute obedience, positivism. 'The idea of a complete and definitive theory', insists Castoriadis, 'is nothing but a phantasm of the bureaucracy', serving the better to manipulate the masses.[23] And yet it is precisely this sort of theory which Marx needs if he is to claim a *necessity* for the revolutionary process; and if he is to claim that his theory is a 'scientific socialism'. The move from philosophy to science in Marx is thus based on a traditional assumption about what theory must in fact be, despite Marx's attempt to open a new style of theorising.

The reason that Marx falls back into this paradigm of contemplative theory is that he has not succeeded in radically historicising his own historical theory. His claim is that proletarian revolutionary theory is the product of history; but he does not consider the possibility of history's rendering the theory itself antiquated. What emerges from reflection on this position is Marx's *linear* conception of history. Marx's essentialism and rationalism already implied this view. History is taken as just the working out — through innumerable trials and tribulations — of what already was given with the birth of humanity. Indeed, when Marx asks himself what is the specifically human, he comes up with the famous distinction between the architect and the bee: the bee creates instinctively, whereas the architect works from a mentally created plan. Convinced at first glance, one would have to ask: whence comes the architect's plan? Was Manhattan there, potentially, essentially, with the birth of humanity; and was Greece present, somehow, alongside it, perhaps a more pale or incomplete image? Why this plan and not another? Why this invention, at this time and place? If we say that, of course, the content which the plan takes on in its specificity depends on the material circumstances in which it is formulated, then we have returned to the sociological functionalism and are looking from above and outside at a 'really real' material world; and at the same time, we have precluded the possibility of revolution. Either the revolution, or the architect's plan, are there from the outset, working through the Golgotha of their realisation; or they are simply reactions to given social conditions. In the former case, history is just an illusion, a chimera with no real meaning; while in the latter case, history is reduced to natural history — which is conceived of as either essentially rational (in which case we return to the first situation), or as accidental, in which case we have no reason for supposing that revolution is inevitable, as the Marxist teleology must.

The long and the short of it is simply this: Marxism is a metaphysics, whose structure, premises, and even elaboration are simply an adaptation of the givens of an historical moment to the demands of traditional theorising. Marxism claims to be a revolutionary truth insofar as it is the bearer of the solution to the riddle of history. Its justification of this assertion is, however, its own theory of history, which is itself based upon the primacy of the proletariat, whose praxis is to be expressed by Marxism. What appeared to be a radically new type of theory emerges a tautology: Marxism is true because it is the theory of the proletariat; the proletariat is the truth of history because Marxism has shown this to be the case; hence Marxism is true. Twist and turn as one will, Marxism turns out to be based precisely on premises which make the realisation of its self-defined goal impossible. A new conception of theory is necessary.

IV Ontology: The Status of Theory and the Political Project

The tensions to which the critique of Marxism led became apparent in the 1964 programmatic article, 'Recommencer la révolution', which tried to define the parameters within which a political practice of the group was still possible. After an elaboration of their differences with classical Marxism, the article stressed the everyday struggle waged by the working class against the hierarchic, bureaucratic organisation of labour. Castoriadis had already insisted that 'labour-power' differs from the other inputs into production precisely because of this struggle: the capitalist knows how many calories of heat will be produced by a ton of coal, but not how much labour is actually purchased by the wages paid. The implications of this struggle go beyond the economic, expressing the antagonism between command and execution which structures capitalist social relations. Through the application of a variety of industrial psychological techniques, and by virtue of the formal and informal structure of work, the worker must be included in the productive mechanism, and at the same time excluded from the central decisions. This combination of activity/passivity spreads beyond the workplace to all the institutions of society, from the consumer to the student, patriarch to patriot. While it is easy to describe, the analysis of the mechanisms of its spreading and the grounds of its dominance demand theoretical elaboration. Analogously, discussion of Russia, drawing the logical conclusions from the primacy of industrial class struggle, leads beyond itself. The structure of work in bureaucratic society does not rest on the primacy of industrial labour; the 'new strata' created by bureaucratic imperatives become crucial, not simply negatively but also for their positive role in advancing the demand for self-management. 'Capitalism will not by its own functioning produce in any predictible future a class of workers who will already be, in themselves, a concrete universal', insists Castoriadis.[24] At the same time, however, he points out that 'one cannot reduce alienation by 3% per year'.[25] Politics and collective creativity become the primary means by which the revolution is to be made; and no infrastructural guarantee of success remains to guide or insure this politics.

Castoriadis' assertion that the point 'is not to deduce the

revolution but to make it'[26] does not suffice to elaborate a politics; nor does the insistence that it is the distinction between command and execution that divides bureaucratic society. Castoriadis' three-part article, 'Sur le contenu du socialisme' (1955—8), attempts to spell out the implications of his position beyond the vague notion of industrial workers' councils.[27] A second three-part article, 'Le mouvement révolutionnaire sous le capitalisme moderne' (1960—1), takes the elaboration a step further, eliminating (in Castoriadis' eyes, though the schism that culminated in 1963 was based on his opponents' maintenance of) the traditional theory of the proletariat. But if he was to avoid the reproach of 'existentialism' or volontarism, Castoriadis' critique of Marxism had to be supplemented by positive results, a new theory which would help those who continue to struggle against the bureaucratic logic of capitalist domination to understand the implications of their own choices. This task was taken up in the five-part article, 'Marxisme et théorie révolutionnaire' (1964—5), and completed in *L'institution imaginaire de la société*, whose first part is that series.

The field of revolutionary activity, and of its theory, is history. Marx tended to reduce the creative ambiguity of choice in history, conceptualising it in a linear-progressive fashion and subjecting it to a philosophical rationalism. The past was seen as absorbed into the present, itself pregnant with a future which would, ultimately, eliminate irrationality and scarcity — and, finally, (pre)History itself. But this end of History is a myth. If we analyse the historical actor, we see 'that the living being is more than the simple mechanism because it can give new responses to new situations. But historical being is more than the mere living thing because it can give new responses to the *"same"* situations, or create new situations.'[28] The idea of the *creative* ability of human praxis, producing a radical alterity and thus historical change, is fundamental to the new ontology that Castoriadis sees as necessary. The new responses and new situations are not simply the working through of what is already there; nor are they the product of a (materialist) Cunning of Reason. The projects which animate human praxis, and the rationality we attribute to it, are themselves historical products. It is not possible to suggest that a material situation or a new technology *of themselves* call for social praxis; nor that an essential rationality was always present implicitly as guide. 'After the fact', writes Castoriadis, 'we can always say of any phenomenon that it was ideally possible. That is an empty tautology, which teaches nothing to no one'.[29] Rather:

Activity [*le faire*] implies that the real is not thoroughly
rational; it also implies that it is not either a chaos, that it
contains . . . lines of force . . . which delimit the possible, the
attainable, indicate the probable, permit the action to find
support in the given.[30]

If this ambiguity which is constitutive of praxis is to be grasped,
the phantasm of true theory, of total knowledge and disembodied thought must be given up. Neither engendered by
material conditions alone (and therefore, a-historical), nor the
result of a pure knowledge applied to brute matter (also a denial
of history, formulated as technology), the activity of everyday
life itself is praxis. The educator, artist or even doctor does not
'know' the final result he/she seeks; nor does he/she simply
follow material lines of force, as if there could be somehow read
directly from the given, as if the given were immediately and
univocally signifying, as in the dream world of the positivist.
There is an indeterminateness in every praxis: the project is
changed as it encounters the materiality of the world; and the
visage of the world is altered once my project contacts it.

The problem is to account for creativity, for the creation that
is history. Castoriadis' approach is ontological rather than just
phenomenological. In order to motivate his approach, he first
uses a phenomenological approach similar to that of Merleau-
Ponty and Lefort. Praxis is not simply individual. As embodied,
the individual is always-already-social; the pure thinker and
knower, just as the pure actor or action is a fiction based on
abstraction.[31] Embodiment is impurity; and it is also the
condition of the possibility of thought or praxis. I can never
have exhaustive knowledge of myself; in psycholanalytic terms,
the I can never replace the It. The unconscious, the multivalency of representation, desire — these cannot be eliminated,
and are crucial to the creativity of the social-historical process
itself. Where the rationalist strives for their elimination, the
concrete question is that of our relation to them. I can relate to
them, act on and through them, only because they *are* Other,
always-already-present and continually changing. They are the
horizon that gives sense to thought and action, the condition of
the possibility of creation. Their constantly changing nature
poses a problem for the contemplative rationalist theory for
which Being and beings are defined and known by the fixed
determinations which, ultimately, they are. This calls for a
reformulation of the traditional notions of theory and of Being,
of political theory and political practice.

Embodiment implies sociality not simply because it gives us a physical co-presence, but rather insofar as it entails a historical partaking in an intersubjective world of symbolically mediated discourse. My body opens me to the discourse of the Other just as it does to that of the unconscious. Again, the temptation of the philosophical narcissism of the rationalist must be avoided. 'Autonomy is . . . not the elucidation without residue and the total elimination of the discourse of the Other who is not known. It is the institution of an other relation between the discourse of the Other and that of the subject.'[32] Elimination of the social Other would imply the end of history, just as elimination of the body implies the end of praxis. The social Other and the body are constitutive of the historical present and project. In this sense, I have always-already a theory, plan or project which is *mine*; I do not act as the result of my finding some objective 'gaps' or contradictions out there, in the structure of a brute given reality. The real is not immediately signifying — the steam engine does not immediately imply capitalism; humans do not act solely from physical need. The world which I and we confront is *instituted*; and as an institution it is also active, instituting forms of individual and collective praxis. The social institution is not transparent or purely rational; nor is it the wholly opaque product of accidental interactions. 'The social', writes Castoriadis, 'is that which is everyone and that which is no one, that which is never absent and nearly never present as such, a non-being more real than any being, that in which we are wholly immersed but which we can never apprehend "in person".'[33] In this formulation, the terms of the political project are radically altered; and at the same time, the basis for the necessary reconsideration and reconstruction of the tradition of philosophical discourse is laid.

Politically, the theme of alienated praxis takes on a more specific meaning. The problem is not simply that I am dominated or determined by an Other; for precisely that Otherness is the condition of the possibility of praxis or creation. Were alienation defined as simply dominance by the Other, then, for example, speech would be alienated by definition. Rather, what constitutes alienation is that the Other to whom I relate *disappears*, slides into an anonymous collectivity (the law, the market, the plan, etc.). Of course alienation is more than a subjective phenomenon: it is backed up by the force of those who stand to benefit from it. But as opposed to exploitation, alienation is concerned fundamentally with the relation of society to its own institutions. Revolutionary politics, concludes Castoriadis, 'is henceforth a struggle for

the transformation of the *relation* of society to its institutions.'[34] When the 'string' of bureaucratic society is played
through, its contemporary specificity shows itself in that 'the
phantasm of the organization as a well-oiled machine cedes its
place to the phantasm of the organization as a self-reforming
and self-expanding machine.'[35] The kinds of struggle which one
finds occurring today, in all spheres of society, from the family
to the military, from the ecological to the ethnic, including
many of those at the workplace, find their unification in a
revolt against the manner in which bureaucratic society perpetuates itself through this phantasm. As such, they can be seen as
attempts to reinstitute a praxical relation to the social institution.

Through a series of historical examples, Castoriadis attempts
to demonstrate that no 'rationalist' or 'materialist' explanation
can be offered for fundamental social-historical transformations
such as the invention of democracy and philosophy in Greece,
of monotheism by a small Semitic people, of political thought
in fifteenth-century Florence, etc. These inventions are historical leaps. History is *discontinuous* — the introduction of *alterity*, the space of *creation* which constitutes temporality.
History in this sense manifests the effects of what Castoriadis
calls the '*imaginaire radical*':

> it operates in the implicit, is not specifically aimed at by
> anyone, fulfils itself through the pursuit of an indeterminate
> number of particular goals ... which show themselves in
> their effects to have been overdetermined by that central
> signification which was in the process of instituting itself.
> That central signification can thus be seized after the fact, as
> the non-real condition of the real coexistence of the social
> phenomena: a non-real but eminantly effective [*wirklich*]
> because effectuating [*wirkend*] condition.[36]

As it is formulated here, the *imaginaire radical* appears as a kind
of traditional transcendental 'condition of the possibility' of the
existence of the historical. This is not at all what is intended.
Were it some kind of super-individual subject constituting the
individual and its historical world, then Castoriadis would have
fallen back to a kind of Hegelianism (or worse, since at least
Hegel shows how his principle constitutes itself through the
labour of the concept). The new ontology formulated in
L'institution imaginaire de la société fulfils the promise made
ten years earlier, articulating itself through Castoriadis' work in
the history and philosophy of science and mathematics (boldly

and provocatively summarised in *Le monde morcelé* and in *Science moderne et interrogation philosophique*) as well as the sustained reflections on the theory and practice of psychoanalysis. In making clear the manner in which Castoriadis explains the possibility of the new, and thus of the historical, without falling into the reductive pattern of transcendental philosophy, we will see at the same time how a renewed ontological reflection becomes the key to a theory of revolution which avoids the dilemmas of Marxian theory and practice whose results have thus far been criticised.

History is *alterity*, the radically new which did not exist in any form prior to its advent. Yet, for there to be a society at all, and therefore, in order that there be a history, a world of common significations must be instituted: all members of the society must be able to identify this thing as a cow, this other one as a law, and this third as male or female. The cow may also be a god, the law a heritage from ancestral struggles, the male or female an uncle or mother — but whatever they be, all members of the society must recognise them in their discourse. The first social institution is that of a shared universe of discourse, obeying the rules of what Castoriadis calls an 'identitary-ensemblist logic'. That is, a thing must be identified as *this* thing; and at the same time, these things which are identified must be collectionable into an ensemble *different* from those things. *What* this thing signifies, and those things are, differs in different social formations according to the *imaginaire* of each of them. Correlative to this *central imaginaire* of a given social formation is the institution of a 'logic' and a 'technology' — what Castoriadis calls the *Legein* and the *Teukhein* — which are the means through which this central institution manifests itself. The result is the social universe which, for any given society, is the 'real' universe in which it functions. The forms in which the world, individuals and technology are instituted can vary indefinitely; the only constant is that there must be a commonality established which permits society to exist and to have an identity. The natural givens (climate, geography, etc.) obviously play a role in these institutions, and must be taken into account. However, the role of nature is minimal; it does not decree *how* any social-historical institution takes account of it, only *that* it must be considered. Using a concept from Freud, Castoriadis suggests that nature serves as the *anaclitic* foundation for the institution.[37] As anaclitic, nature cannot explain the advent of its institution. The institution, however, can explain nature (as 'this' nature); it can explain the individual, the social, the technological, and all the rest of what Castoriadis calls secondary institutions and secondary forms of the *imaginaire social*. But what it cannot explain is its own advent; for to do so, it would have had to be present before its own institution, which is impossible.

The first institution, which wrenches humanity from nature and makes it at once historical and social, is the *institution of the institution*. This is only apparently paradoxical or tautological. A more concrete example makes the point clear: 'the first law is that there is law' suggests that before a legal structure is established, the society must institute the signification 'law' as having a common meaning and necessity. Only when 'law' is instituted can the society look at its material social conditions as presenting the need for legal codification or alteration. This institution changes the world. The relations which previously existed form the anaclitic basis for the institution of the legal system; but with the institution of 'law' they are effectively altered, new aspects are opened up and new possibilities emerge from them. No Theseus institutes the law; no material conditions send Moses to the mount. The institution may be attached by posterity to the name of an individual; but posterity is living in the wake of the institution, in the significations it instituted and its material results. The institution is an anonymous collective product:

> It is doubtful that one can directly grasp this fundamental phantasm; at best it can be reconstructed from its manifestations because, in effect, it appears as the foundation of the possibility and unity of everything that makes up the singularity everything which, in the life of the subject, goes beyond its reality and its history. It is the ultimate condition permitting the *surging forth* [*survenir*] of a reality and a history for the subject.[38]

Once it is instituted, the institution in its turn institutes a manifold of reorganisations, redeterminations, reformations of the already present social significations in society. Thus, the institution of capitalism with the dominance of the economic motive was able to build on and reorganise a variety of already-present tendencies and structures in order to affirm itself. These already existent forms — banks, centralised government with its financial needs and standing army, the influx of Spanish gold, technological advances, etc. — did not cause the institution of capitalism; but once it was instituted, their nature became capitalist and their contribution was put to work, and new forms brought into being. This notion is already present in assertions by Marx, when he talks about the fact that a machine is a machine, and only becomes capital in certain social conditions. But, for Marx these social conditions are seen as 'real' material existences; and the best that is offered is the 'dialectic' of quantity and quality as an explanation of their sudden change in signification.

To exist and reproduce itself any society needs two fundamental institutions, reciprocally dependent on one another, whose designation as the *Legein* and *Teukhein* points to their ontological signification and difference from their more common derivatives, language or logic and technology. The *Legein*, translated as 'distinguish-choose-pose-assemble-count-speak', is that institution by which the 'thing' is constituted as self-identical and distinct from other things. The *Legein* does not tell us *what* the thing is, only *that* it is: that it is a this, self-identical and different from other things. Nature obviously lends itself anaclitically to this operation, which is the imposition of a code, but the institution of the *Legein* is not simply or naïvely the result of the observation of empirical constancy in nature. The *Legein* institutes not only the self-identity of the thing and of *the sign itself*, but also the *relation* sign/thing. While it thus gives the possibility of language as a code which organises and fixes signification such that social discourse is possible, the institution of this *relation* carries with it ontological consequences whose elaboration can be demonstrated to give the fundamental operators in terms of which the tradition of Western metaphysics is both possible and necessarily limited.[39] Castoriadis stresses the originality of the institution of the *Legein* with a telling example: 'One cannot reflect too much on this simple fact: the word dog and the dog belong together — and in a manner totally different than the paws and the head of the dog belong together.'[40] The institution not only institutes a whole gamut of relations, but simultaneously institutes itself as the condition of the possibility of these relations. This is inherent in the nature of the institution as originary; and its consequence is that the code of significations which it established consists in an indefinite series of relations to others, while at the same time (as against a structuralist reading of this consequence) the *relation* of signification can never be exhausted. The institution thus institutes a stability which is necessary; but at the same time it never stops instituting, remains active, and retains the possibility of restoring the alterity which it is.

Dependent on, but in another sense constitutive for, the *Legein* is the *Teukhein*, which Castoriadis translates as 'assemble-adjust-fabricate-construct'. The activity of the *Teukhein* obviously depends, in the first instance, on the *Legein*'s having instituted the code, the identity of the thing and the sign, as well as the signitive relation. But the *Teukhein* is not simply a further elaboration of the logic of the *Legein*; as the dimension of social activity, the *Teukhein* is itself an originary social institution. To the functioning of the identitary-ensemblist logic is thus added the notion of a goal or end of the action undertaken; but this goal is itself necessarily structured by the instituted logic of the *Legein*. If we take the example of the law, the assertion would be that there must first of all be instuted the code and the signitive relations that make an event have the signification 'legal' or 'illegal'; but beyond this, or rather, co-originary with the institution of the legal logic there must also be instituted a legal activity, for the legal logic only makes sense when it is actionable. A code of relations governing the growth of weeds in my garden might be highly consistent and subtly developed; but without being actionable it would be senseless. More generally, if a society is to reproduce itself as society, it must not only institute the *Legein* but also the *Teukhein*: 'constituting . . . starting from . . . in a manner appropriate to . . . and with the aim of . . .' What is constituted, from what one begins, in what manner one acts, and for what aim: all of these aspects of the *Teukhein* vary indefinitely with the specific social institution of the central *imaginaire* of a society. The *Teukhein* must be instituted; we need technology in order to invent it. Hominoids may use a branch or stone in a way that we, reading backwards, see as indicating a rudimentary technology; but in fact it is only with the *Teukhein*, when the branch or stone is distinguished-separated-sought-after, in order to make . . . in a manner appropriate to . . . and with the aim of . . ., that technology is in fact socially instituted within the horizon of a finality of some sort.[41] It is important to stress that the *Teukhein* of a society is thus not just its tools and techniques, but also the human productive relations that it establishes, be they determined by the logic of bureaucratic domination or some other form, say Mumford's 'mega-machine'.

The aim of Castoriadis' theory thus far has been to account for the possibility of historical creation — indeed, for history itself as the invention of the new — by showing how society is instituted in a manner that makes its *stability* and *self-identity* possible. He has to show how *instituted* society comes to ignore its own nature as *instituting*, and thus is structured by alienation. The suggestion could be articulated if we think of human History as following a scheme whereby in a first stage society's instituting character is denied by referring to some external source of its institution (Ancestors, Spirits, Gods, etc.); in a second stage, we could suggest that the instituting character is attributed to nature and/or rationality (the development of the capitalist *imaginaire*, culminating in the bureaucratic mentality); and finally, the thrid stage would be the explicit overcoming of alienation (but not of History) insofar as the instituting character of society would be explicitly recognised and self-consciously thematised. There is no necessity in this development. Before this perspective can be developed further, Castoriadis has to take up and thematise through his ontology the traditional problem of the individual actor. What has been said thus far has concerned the social-historical; and from this perspective, the individual would be instituted in the same manner as the cow or the tool. From such a perspective only a determinism — in an 'idealistic' form — could result. While the individual is indeed socially instituted, it entails a significant 'more'.

The brilliant reinterpretation of the Freudian theory that Castoriadis offers to account for the individual's sociality also serves to elucidate the analysis of the social-historical that has just been sketched. The unconscious presents itself *as*, not through, a flux of representations. The representations are over-determined, interwoven, continually fleeing determination: the dream whose manifest content appears in a (more or less) identitary-ensemblist form shows itself as a multi-layered set of signitive relations. The stubbornness of the unconscious, which knows neither time nor contradiction, which condenses and distorts, uses jokes, rebuses and word-plays, makes the socialisation of the individual appear almost miraculous. The 'miracle' of socialisation — that feudal society produces persons adapted to the roles of Lord and Serf, that capitalism produces the capitalist and the worker — cannot be explained by suggesting that external reality imposes its law by force; the psychotic is there to testify that force can be resisted, that the unconscious may call for 'liberty or death'. When Freud confronts this problem, he tends to make the representations of the unconscious derive from a lack or deficit created by the withdrawal of the first satisfaction, the breast. The world would thus come to signify for the individual — who, then, by taking seriously its significations, would adapt to the society's structures of meaning — insofar as it is assimilated to the lost object. Yet Freud himself had shown that this first satisfaction is itself representational or phantasmatic; that the phantasy of the breast, and indeed phantasy-life in general, can provide the longed-for satisfaction. Freud commits the double error which we saw to vitiate Marx's work as well: he takes the real as somehow pre-given and knowable by an outside observer; and he begins from a supposed division of subject and object (*infans* and breast) rather than deriving this division. Castoriadis' point is that for the subject to feel a need or lack, and thus to act, that need or lack must make sense for it. Stripped of its metapsychological apparatus, Freud's analysis of dreams shows that they are *not* so much wish-fulfilments as they are *fulfilled wishes*. The unconscious in its originary state is always-already-satisfied; it is all-powerful, the unity 'Ich bin die Brust'. Absence or desire must make sense for the *psyche*; and they can do so only with regard to the original matrix of sense as the non-lacking, the fulfilled desire. Thus, writes Castoriadis, 'The great enigma here, as throughout, and which will always remain an enigma, is the emergence of separation.'[42] The enigma of separation will remain because it is the enigma of the institution!

To the *imaginaire radical* of the social-historical corresponds an *imagination radicale* of the individual. Equally irreducible in their radicality, both exist as materialised in manifestations which never exhaust their sense but are expressions of their creativity. The analogue of the problem of the creativity of the social-historical emerges as well in the case of the individual. In the ontogenesis of the individual, the first stage is dominated by the all-powerful phantasy of the *infans*; everything and anything has significance as the realisation of the phantasised fulfilment. This is not the manifestation of a primal desire, nor the reply to a perceived absence; for desire supposes that the desired or the absence be invested with a sense. Moreover, we know that at different stages, and socially, in different societies, different objects are invested. It does no good to try to find a 'real' basis for the investment of specific objects: while mouth-breast and penis-vagina must have significance if any society is to continue, there is no such necessity for the psychical investment of anus-faeces instead, for example, of breathing or some other physical function. Castoriadis argues that the unity and fulfil-ment which is the first stage *is* the *imagination radicale*, the matrix of sense which can never be represented as such but through which a world of sense finds its shape. The movement of ontogenesis depends on a rupture which opens the *psyche* towards a potentially senseful world. The encounter with the world as object is at first dominated by the phantasy of omnipotence, with that of the *infans* being replaced by the

projected omnipotence of the parent(s). This second omnipotence must also be overcome; and can only be overcome
through its own self-destitution. This is 'Oedipus'. That is, the
phantasy of the parent's omnipotence gives way once the parent
is recognised as a parent-among-others, as playing a socially
instituted role. Only then can the individual person emerge into
a social world.

> Only the institution of society, proceding from the *imagin-
> aire social*, can limit the *imagination radicale* of the psyche
> and create for it a reality by creating a society. Only the
> institution of society can permit the psyche to emerge from
> its originary monadic madness. . .[43]

This is not to say that society imposes itself on the individual;
rather, that which is instituted in the social-historical presents
the individual with a sense which satisfies the criterion of
meaningfulness established by the nature of the originary unity
that is the *imagination radicale*. The result of ontogenesis, seen
from this point of view, is a return to the originary: the
originary was unity, the always-already-fulfilled phantasm
which is the matrix of sense; for the matured person in the
instituted setting of social signification this same structure is
present; and thus an idea, a word or sign, is the satisfying
meaning. This is the paradox, the result of 'sublimation'.
Commenting on Freud, Castoriadis elaborates:

> To say that sublimation has been imposed on the drives by
> civilization when it is evident that 'civilization' — that is, no
> matter what form of instituted society, even language — can
> only exist if and only if there is sublimation shows the
> irreducibility of the social-historical to the psychic and at the
> same time shows the inverse irreducibility.[44]

More concretely,

> The 'sublimation of homosexuality' in social relations be-
> tween individuals does not mean only or especially that one
> renounces the sexual satisfaction which the others could
> offer, but that these others are not simply sexual 'objects'
> but social individuals.[45]

Society presents the individual with significations which,
although it can live with them and act in terms of them, the
psyche alone could never pose. Each needs the other, yet their

mode of being is radically different. The congruence of social roles that exists in every form of societal organisation cannot be explained by privileging one or the other, the social-historical or the individual. Rather, to explain the congruence, a different ontological premise and a different type of theory is necessary.

Common to the social-historical and the individual is the irreducibility of the originary. The *imaginaire radical* and the *imagination radicale* exist in their manifestations but are never explained or exhausted by them. Castoriadis introduces the notion of a *magma* at this point: 'A magma is that from which one can extract (or in which one can construct) an indefinite number of ensemblist organisations, but which can never be reconstituted (ideally) by an ensemblist composition (finite or infinite) of these organizations.'[46] The notion of a *magma* replaces the traditional ontological Being:

> We assert that everything that can be effectively given — representations, nature, signification — exists in the mode of a *magma*; that the social-historical institution of the world, things and individuals, insofar as it is the institution of the *Legein* and the *Teukhein*, is always also the institution of identitary logic and thus the imposition of an ensemblist organization on a first stratum of givenness which lends itself interminably to this operation. But also, that it is never and can never be *only* that — that it is also always and necessarily the institution of a magma of imaginary social significations. And finally, that the relation between the *Legein* and the *Teukhein* and the magma of imaginary social significations is not thinkable within the identitary-ensemblist frame of reference — no more than are the relations between *Legein* and representation, *Legein* and nature, or between representation and signification, representation and world, or 'consciousness' and 'unconscious'[47]

From this perspective, the contribution of Freud to a radical critique is not his unveiling of traditional morality, but rather the demonstration of the multivalency of representation and the function of phantasy which throw into question the ontological basis of that tradition. The 'fetishism of reality' is shown to be the product of a specific social-historical institution.[48] With this, the perceptual metaphor must fall: 'A subject which would have *only* perception would have *no* perception; it would be totally caught up in the "things," flattened into them, crushed against the world, incapable of turning away from it, and thus incapable of fixating on it'.[49] The standpoint of the outside observer, for whom there is subject/object, signifier/ signified, thought/being, is destroyed. 'All expression', writes Castoriadis, 'is essentially a trope'.[50] There is never a single, cardinal referent, existing separately and singularly, waiting to be taken up by thought. The ontology of the *magma* shows that while the identitary-ensemblist thought of Being-as-determined is necessary for the functioning of a society, it does not exhaust and cannot exhaust the significations that are society as *magma*. The originary and radical nature of the *magma* is what accounts for the possibility of historical creation, just as it explains the creativity of the individual.

V What is Revolution?

In this manner, Castoriadis' ontological reformulation rejoins the political problematic. He had showed Marxism's imbrication in the traditional philosophy to be that which vitiates its project.

> What escapes [the traditional view] is nothing other than the enigma of the world which remains behind the common social world. It is the to-be [*á-être*] that is the inexhaustable provision of alterity; and it is the irreducible challenge to all established signification. What escapes it is also the being itself of society as instituting society, that is, finally, as source and origin of alterity, or as perpetual self-alteration.[51]

Instituted society is only apparently a dead product, a set of fixed matrices; in fact, as *magma*, it is inherently historical. The theoretical project and the practical one come together: the structure of both is axed around the awakening of the instituting nature of society through the theoretical and practical critique of its reified self-understanding. This perspective was already implicit in the redefinition of alienation in institutional terms. Castoriadis spells it out in an important passage:

> In what measure and by what means can individuals accept themselves as mortal without any imaginary instituted compensation; in what measure can thought hold together the demands of the identitary logic which are rooted in the *Legein* and the exigencies of what is (which is surely not identitary without becoming for that reason incoherent); in what measure, finally and especially, can society truly

recognize in its institution its own self-creation, recognize itself as instituting, auto-institute itself explicitly, and surmount the self-perpetuation of the instituted by showing itself capable of taking it up and transforming it according to its own exigencies and not according to the inertia of the instituted, to recognize itself as the source of its own alterity? These are the questions, *the* question of revolution, which not only go beyond the frontier of the theorizable but situate themselves right away on another terrain ... the terrain of the creativity of history.[52]

The theory can offer no reason to expect that this revolution will occur, no material or logical grounds can be produced to argue for it. Rather:

we aim at it *because we want it* and because we know that other people want it — not because these are the laws of history, the interest of the proletariat, or the destiny of being. The instauration of a history where society not only knows itself but *makes itself* as instituting itself explicitly implies a radical destruction of the known forms of institution of society.[53]

'Tu fais la révolution pour toi', was one of the themes of May 1968; 'participation in the decisions which concern our lives' was the slogan of the American New Left. While the bogeyman of 'existentialism' again raises its head here, one can only suggest, after working through the evolution of Castoriadis' position, that it may scare the tenants of the old order more than the revolutionaries!

Castoriadis offers no recipe for revolution; indeed, he shows the inherent impossibility on which the thought which called itself 'revolutionary' was built. But at the same time that he shows how traditional theory is built on the occlusion of the social-historical, he also shows why that alienation was necessary and how it remains as an always-present threat. The ontology of the *magma* does *not* mean that the identitary-ensemblist organisation of the world can somehow be avoided. The *Legein* and the *Teukhein* exist in all societies. What differs are the central *imaginaires* of different societies, which manifest themselves in the different social significations that are instituted. What is aimed at by revolutionaries is the changed *relation* of society to its institution, rendering conscious and open to discussion what had been occluded or repressed. It is because of his recognition of the necessity of the institutions of the *Legein* and *Teukhein* that Castoriadis still insists that a revolutionary organisation is necessary; while his definition of the goal of revolution implies that the inherent danger of bureaucratisation can be fought. The task of the organisation would not be to lead so much as to open reflection. If the organisation puts forth a specific set of demands, these are calculated not as a governmental programme but rather for their interrogatory effect. Thus, for example, the demand that the revolution establish immediately equal pay for all members of the society is not formulated out of considerations of justice, morality or the 'labour theory of value'. The point is that such equality puts into question one of the central forms of the capitalist *imaginaire*, the productivism of its logic. Similar considerations would affect other points in an organisation's programme, such as the elimination of hierarchy.

From the stance of his new ontology, Castoriadis can explain more fully the reasons for his rejection of Marxism as 'the flesh of the world we combat'. One example will suffice to illustrate the further distance travelled. When Marx speaks of the relations of production as relations between persons mediated by things, it appears that the persons and things exist independently, and are then combined into specific relations, which become the target of revolutionary action. Such a stance was already criticised in 'The Relations of Production in Russia'. To that critique, he adds now a further remark:

Society does not, in a 'first time', pose goals and significations in terms of which it could deliberate on the most appropriate technology to serve and incarnate them. Goals and significations are posed from the outset in and by the technology and the *Teukhein* — just as the significations are posed in and by the *Legein*. In a sense, the tools and instruments *are* significations; they are the 'materialization' in the identitary and functional dimension of the imaginary significations of the given society. A production line *is* (and can only be as) a 'materialization' of a manifold of central imaginary significations of capitalism.[54]

Marx of course knew that a machine is not capital because of its properties, any more than gold is automatically money. But he tended to take the things as 'things', as neutral — which they clearly are not. Here, it is Marx who is the 'philosopher' and Castoriadis who recognises the full role of social determinations.

Castoriadis' ontology of the *magma* is still not fully elaborated; a volume on *L'élément imaginaire* has been promised, as has further concrete analysis of contemporary capitalism. The results which have thus far been published already suffice for us to take up these new developments along with him. Castoriadis pushes us to rethink the theory on which our political activity has been built. He gives us a means of conceptualising a New Left praxis. And, ridding us finally of the traditional ontological prejudice which forced the separation of theory from practice, he opens a vista of research problems that claim our attention. Despite the critique by Lefort of his attempt to define the 'content' of socialism, both Castoriadis and Lefort have opened up the dimension of the political which had for too long been taken for granted by revolutionaries. It is to the structure and suppositions of this political project that attention must now be turned.

Notes

CHAPTER 1

1. There have, to be sure, been beginnings. They have been quashed in blood, either by the left bureaucrats (Kronstadt, etc.) or by those of the right (Berlin, Turin, Budapest, etc.). My intention here is not to answer this question, but to look at the nature and role of a theory which might have its place in the analysis of the actual forces at play.

2. Inadequate both as a reading of Marx, and more generally as an interpretation of the relation of theory and practice in the revolutionary process, for its character as an *option* denies any role to theory or to rational choice. In earlier drafts of this paper, I found myself continually sidetracked into polemics with various 'heresies' — which seemed to add little to the positive discussion. I have tried here to avoid them. The theory-praxis problem in its different concrete forms cuts across the polemical history of the working-class movement, from the famous Marx-Weitling quarrel in 1846, on through to the present. Whatever one thinks about Marx's resolution, or that of Lenin, Luxemburg or Lukács, the significant issue for theory is that the problem returns continually — suggesting perhaps that there is no univocal solution but rather that revolutionary *experience* is that which demands theorization, precisely in order to go beyond traditional theory. If this is so, the self-conception of theory and its role would have to be redefined. In the present context, this would mean that the 'heresies' against which I found myself in polemic consisted simply in the breaking down of this interchange: separated one from the other, theory and praxis, the political and the economic, are meaningless. This negative judgement still leaves the positive problem: how to conceive their unity.

3. Hegel had already observed that the notion of thought as a re-presentation or picturing of reality was an inadequate and incomplete approach which isolates its objects in an atomistic dance of juxtaposed, but essentially unrelated, parts. The persistence of the visual mode (Hegel's term is *vorstellendes Denken*) entails the static or contemplative attitude towards oneself and the world. It encourages a dualism of subject-object, and hence the rigid separation of theory and praxis. On the problems of the visual metaphor, the work of Merleau-Ponty should also be brought

into the examination.

4. This is the error of the Althusserians' notion of 'theoretical practice', or of the 'production of knowledge', which, if not just a redundancy, is the attempt to analyze theory as simply another form of production governed by analogous laws. The result of this conflation, despite its claim to structural specificity, is monistic and idealistic. The 'structuralist' claim that we need to go beyond the idealist notion of the transcendental or constitutive subject is an important theoretical innovation. However, the 'death of the subject' which it heralds can also be seen as the historical process of capitalist reification and alienation. Useful as an analytical tool, the structuralist position cannot be taken as a satisfactory theoretical whole.

5. This is not the place for a critique of Engels' materialism. Among many others, Lukács' *History and Class Consciousness* presents an adequate refutation of the 'dialectics of nature'. Interesting attempts to go beyond this have been made by Ernst Bloch on the one hand, and those using the insights of quantum physics on the other (e.g. M. Kosok, P. Heelan, C. Castoriadis). Bloch recalls that nature has not always been conceived as a static Other, but in the case, for example, of the 'Left Aristotleans', is itself a dynamic and utopian principle. Heelan and Kosok attempt to use quantum physics to confront the traditional error of the non-situated or transcendental observer. Castoriadis' ontological reformulations will be discussed below, without, however, making explicit reference to his use of modern mathematics and physics, which appear especially in 'Le monde morcelé' (*Textures*, 72/4—5) and 'Science moderne et interrogation philosophique' (*Encyclopédia Universalis*, Organon, Vol. 23).

6. Henri Lefèbvre, *Everyday Life in the Modern World*, tr. S. Rabinovitch (New York: Harper Torchbook, 1971). Too Little of Lefèbvre is available in English. For a general introduction, see Alfred Schmidt's essay in *The Unknown Dimension*, Howard and Klare, eds. (New York: Basic Books, 1972). On the theory of bureaucratic society see also the discussions below of Lefort and Castoriadis.

7. On another level, the same process is involved in the work situation. The worker must submit passively to hierarchy and authority, must be drilled in the art of self-deprecation and self-hatred so as not to be rebellious and a threat to the control exercised in the most minute aspects of his/her life; but at the same time, the individual worker and the team often find themselves using and inventing all sorts of tricks, not just time-savers but ways to actually make production work, since the rules themselves are often either vague or too constricting. The 'rule book strike', in which rules are followed to the letter, screwing up the production process, is a sign of the contradictory demands placed on the workers: to obey and to be inventive. Cf., for example, Daniel Mothé, *Militant chez Renault* (Paris: Editions du Seuil, 1965), and the theory developed by 'Socialisme ou Barbarie'. It is in this sense that the class struggle is fought every day, and is constitutive of the capitalist system as such. But, as will be seen in the criticism addressed by Castoriadis to the Marxists, this means that the labour theory of value loses its applicability,

for the input of labour-power does not produce a constant output in the quantity of labour, which depends on intensity etc. As all capitalists know, the 'falling rate of profit' can be compensated by increased 'productivity' — i.e. by increased intensity of labour through methods of controlling the work force.

8. On the implications of this for the radical project, particularly as concerns the impact of the mass media on the birth of the 'New Left', see my article 'Les communications de masse et la naissance d'une nouvelle gauche', in *Actes du XVe Congrès des SPLF*, 1971, where I argue that the dialectic of Otherness, in which, as all alike the receptors of the media, we become all the same, and hence are open to the acceptance of a common project. This explains in part the success of the 'exemplary action' technique, and the spread of the student revolt of May 1968. More generally, this is the 'socialization of society' whose results, according to Marx, make possible a revolution which would be universal, ending all class domination.

9. Moreover, as Marcuse notes in his critique of M. Weber (in *Negations*), the bureaucratic rationalization of the world into manipulable quanta makes it impossible to consider the ends for which the System functions. Weber finds himself forced to introduce the dubious notion of charisma here, and the leader gives way to the Führer, above and directing the bureaucracy. Lukács' 'reification' essay in *History and Class Consciousness* posed this as the problem of the 'thing-in-itself' which haunted German Idealism, and whose solution can only be the end of a contemplative stance taken by a subject standing over against its object. The proletariat, as the subject-object identical, becomes the incarnate philosopher. Though Lukács' political translation of this solution runs into problems, for our purpose here what is important is the relativization of the subject-object dualism which is necessary if theory is to be able to confront the ambiguity of a non-positive, opaque reality.

10. This same analysis could be carried out in other domains, most obviously in that of language, where the system of signifiers which we use as a code, establishing their referentiality, is constantly revivified, altered and rendered human by the act of speaking on the part of the subject. In our everyday situation, we *practice* language; yet it often comes to pass that this practice becomes a *praxis*, as we mould the language, shape and possess it. In de Saussure's terms, we have the opposition of *langue* (language, the given system in its systematicity) and *parole* (the act of speaking, which is diachronic or historical). Praxis is thus historical, while practice reproduces the given system. The importance of this argument and its implications are developed in detail in Castoriadis' *L'institution imaginaire de la société* (Paris: Editions du Seuil, 1975).

11. The historical specificity must be stressed, as the fate of Marx's theory of the proletarian revolution shows. 'The' proletariat doesn't exist transhistorically but is constantly formed and reformed in struggles that are a reaction to developments in capitalist production, themselves partially determined by the class struggle. Hence, the importance of the 'new working class' theory, on which cf. my article in *The Unknown Dimension*, op. cit., and S. Mallet, *Essays on the New Working Class.*

12. For an interpretation of the teleology in concrete political practice, there is no better example than Rosa Luxemburg. See my Introduction to *Selected Political Writings* (Monthly Review Press, 1971). On the antinomies to which this position leads, see Chapter 3 below.

13. It is a necessary but not sufficient condition. A well-nuanced, but ultimately unsatisfactory — because incapable of dealing with social praxis — account of the logic here is found in Georg Henrik von Wright, *Explanation and Understanding*, (Cornell University Press, 1971).

14. Thus, despite the remarks about the 'mystifying side' of Hegel's dialectic, of which Marx speaks in the 'Afterword' to the of Political Economy', he distinguishes between the method of presentation and that of investigation. On the dialectical structure of Marx's *Capital*, see the important work of R. Rosdolsky, *Zur Entstehungsgeschichte des Marxschen Kapitals* (Europaische Verlagsanstalt, 1968) The problems of such a position are developed most lucidly by Castoriadis.

15. It is important to stress that the first volume of *Capital* cannot be read alone for this reason. Stopping there would lead not just to theoretical error, but to political messianism and unwarranted hope.

16. For example, the limits on absolute surplus value are overcome through the production of relative surplus-value; after introducing the 'law' of the tendency of the rate of profit to fall, Marx follows with a chapter listing various reasons why the fall may not take place, etc.

17. See the critique by C. Castoriadis, which is developed in detail below.

18. The attempts to realize Marxism in practice have tended towards this direction, not only in Russia but even — however disguised by Mao's pragmatism and the rhetoric of the 'cultural' revolution — in China. (The only systematic and informed critique of China from this point of view is Simon Leys, *Ombres Chinoises* (Paris: UGE, 1974).) I will suggest in the last section of this book that this result is inherent in the *rationalism* that underlies Marx's project, making it the last *avatar* of traditional Western metaphysics — though it would be ludicrous to see the theory as the only cause of this degeneration: would that the bureaucrats took theory even that seriously!

19. Mediation is a central concept. Here, it implies the rejection of any reductionism which would criticise social forms purely and simply because they impose themselves on the individual. Autonomy is not law-lessness or caprice (*Willkür*) as both Hegel and Marx show. We do not want to reject social formations which fall into the realm of plural subjectivity that Hegel calls Objective Spirit — the State and its institutions, language, family, etc. — simply because they are supra-individual. If we refer to a social institution as alienating and therefore inhuman and to be eliminated, this is not because of its nature as the result of plural social praxis, but rather because it is a product which for specific historical reasons has become a tyrannical and one-sided producer of false or non-autonomous human activity. Immediacy is not the goal of autonomous individual; rather, the goal is to be the most mediated, the most diverse, having the most tensile strength. Cf., for example, Marx's criticisms of 'crude' communism in the

3rd of the *1844 Manuscripts.*

20. On this, cf. the style of analysis used by Herbert Marcuse, for example, in 'On Hedonism' or 'On the Affirmative Character of Culture'. The lesson is important, particularly for those stuck in bourgeois institutions created for the accumulation and passing-on of tradition; as well as for judging the concrete forms that present-day social disorganisation is taking.

21. It's an interesting thought-experiment to ask yourself: as 'socialist' Commissar of Research Policy, what would I fund, and why?

22. Cf. Chapter 6 below on Jürgen Habermas' development of this point.

CHAPTER 2

1. For example, the early SDS leaders, and their present-day heirs, engaged in detailed rereadings of Marx. See, e.g. Michael Mauke, *Die Klassentheorie von Marx und Engels* (Frankfurt, 1970); Oskar Negt, particularly the essay 'Marxismus als Legitimationswissonschaft', introducing Leborin, Bucharin, *Kontroversen über dialcktischen u mechanistischen Materialismus* (Frankfurt, 1969), and Hans-Jurgen Krahl's work on the *Grundrisse*, in *Konstitution und Klassenkampf* (Frankfurt, 1971). Recent work in Germany has concentrated itself around what amounts sometimes to a 'Marx philology with revolutionary intent', reinterpreting the 'logic' and the 'dialectic' of *Capital.*

2. On Marx's attitude to the utopians, see the fundamental re-examination by Miguel Abensour, 'L'histoire de l'utopie et le destin de sa critique', in *Textures*, 73/6—7, and 74/8—9. Abensour stresses a *'nouvel esprit utopique'*, which breaks both with the rationalist-technocratic schemas and with the empty and pious eschatology of utopia as an abstract universal.

3. An example is found in a 1912 sociological survey: a 29-year-old metalworker states, 'I am not without hope, for one who is so filled with socialism as myself believes in a liberation like a new Evangel'. Or a 39-year-old metalworker, who states that 'It was the political and trade-union movement which first gave a goal to my being, a content to my life'. (Citations from Grebing, *Geschichte der deutschen Arbeiterbewegung.*) One could cite Dietzgen, Engels, Gramsci and so many others to a similar effect.

4. Cf. Lefort's analysis discussed below Chapter 9.

5. A possible third reason for concentrating on the United States — its position as leader of the capitalist world, where presumably the contradictions, cooptations, etc., are most advanced — is questionable. Particularly as concerns the role of the state, one could look to the examples of France, Britain or Scandinavia as models. This is not the place to debate which country is the 'vanguard of capitalism'.

6. As Jürgen Habermas has pointed out, our very moralistic natural law tradition, defended with the eloquence of a Tom Paine and the passion of Everyman, follows a Lockean notion of natural reason incarnating itself through the labour of the individual. Where the French tradition of Rousseau or the Physiocrats saw natural law rationalistically, as what

not since Machiavelli

ought to be — and what had to be imposed on society — the Anglo-American tradition saw it as already existing, lived in the everyday but deformed and deviated by the intervention of the state. Ours is a tradition of anarchic capitalism, of existentialists carving out their world from day to day. But it is not possible to hark back explicitly to that tradition; it was smothered under its natural results: the monopolies, the consumer society, the interventionist state. Natural law anarchism was not enough.

7. This is not to propose a psychologising interpretation, or to suggest the correlative reductionism. The argument is sociological, posed in terms of social structure and the nature of sociality, as will be seen. It helps to explain the mess in which the remnants of the New Left find themselves — from Jesus freaks to gurus, to the resurging 'Leninist' sects, to the withdrawal into drugs and/or communal ventures.

8. Cf. the lucid analysis by Claude Lefort, 'Le totalitarisme sans Staline', first in *Socialisme ou Barbarie*, 14, 1956; now in *Eléments d'une critique de la bureaucratie* (Geneva-Paris, 1971).

9. See the analyses of Correlius Castoriadis in *Socialisme ou Barbarie* at the time, as well as those of Serge Mallet in *Le Gaullisme et la gauche* (Paris, 1965).

10. The term is taken from the title of Herbert Stein's useful work (Chicago, 1971). The analysis, of course, differs from his.

11. I omit reference to the Chinese Revolution and its aftermath, or to the succession of ex-colonies assuming independence in one or another manner. Not that these are unimportant: simply that their symbolic dimension can only be understood in the mirror of the productivist, bureaucratic capitalist countries.

12. On the 'new working class' theory and its implications, see the translation of Serge Mallet's writings, *The New Working Class: A Socialist Perspective*, edited and translated by Dick Howard and Dean Savage (St. Louis: Telos Press, 1976).

13. Marx predicts this in the form of state capitalism. Simply, Marx didn't see its implications for the structure of the wage-labour/capital relation, and expected the old contradictions to persist in an unchanged manner. This is not the case, and explains the error of 'state capitalism' theses which propose to explain Russia through a kind of Marx-reading. Cf. the discussion of this problem by C. Castoriadis, below, Chapter 10.

14. The references from Claude Lefort are to his article, 'Esquisse d'une genèse de l'idéologie dans les sociétés modernes', in *Textures*, 74/8—9, a slightly altered version of which appeared in the *Encyclopédie Universalis* under the title 'L'ère de l'idéologie'. On Lefort, to whom this interpretation is deeply indebted, see Chapter 9.

In the context of this argument, it is worth referring also to the former colleague of Lukács, Belá Fogarasi, whose article on the function of a communist newspaper was translated in *Radical America* some years back. Fogarasi points out that it is not so much in giving us false news or hiding the news from us that the capitalist press exercises its ideological and mystificatory function — on the contrary, we have perhaps too much of it! What is missing is the context, the sense and meaning of the news that we get.

15. For the critique of Marx, see the works of Claude Lefort, Cornelius Castoriadis and Jürgen Habermas.

CHAPTER 3

1. Pages in parenthesis, followed by the title of an article or phamphlet, refer to the English translation of *Selected Political Writings of Rosa Luxemburg*, edited by Dick Howard, (New York: Monthly Review Press, 1971).

2. Comparison with Hegel, and with Marx, is interesting here. Hegel insists that 'the subject matter is not exhausted in its *goal*, but in its *being carried out*; nor is the *result* the *actual* whole, but rather the result along with its becoming'. (Preface to *Phänomenologie des Geistes*, Felix Meiner Verlag, 1952, p. 11.) Marx's political translation of this, in the *Communist Manifesto*, is that 'in the various phases of evolution through which the struggle between the proletariat and the bourgeoisie passes', the communists must 'always advocate the interests of the movement as a whole'. This 'translation' by Marx is more 'idealist' than the Hegelian position, for it implies that the Party can know the whole even before the carrying out brings it to fruition.

3. See especially pp. 36—7, and 117 of the original edition of the *Antikritik*.

CHAPTER 4

1. See, for example, Hellmuth G. Bütow, *Philosophie und Gesellschaft im Denken Ernst Blochs* (Berlin: Ost-Europa Institut, 1963), which offers an unsympathetic account, as well as the *Festschrift* for Bloch's ninetieth birthday, *Ernst Blochs Wirkung*, which contains a useful historical documentation as well as helpful commentaries. In English, see David Gross, 'Ernst Bloch: The Dialectics of Hope', in Howard and Klare (eds), *The Unknown Dimension: European Marxism since Lenin* (New York: Basic Books, 1972), which contains references to most of the important secondary materials.

2. Lukács' heirs have recently discovered over a hundred letters which Bloch wrote to him during that period. These will soon be published in a German edition. (Bloch says that he has surely lost those which Lukács wrote to him.)
One should note here that, after having criticised Lukács in this review, Bloch nonetheless writes that: '*The foundational metaphysical theme of History* is discovered in another manner, but substantially in agreement, as in *The Spirit of Utopia*.' (Citation from 'Aktualitaet und Utopie. Zu Lukács' "Geschichte und Klassenbewusstsein"', in *Philosophische Aufsätze* (Frankfurt am Main: Suhrkamp Verlag, 1969), p. 619.

3. Ibid., p. 601.
4. Ibid.
5. Ibid., p. 600.
6. Ibid., p. 614.
7. Ibid.
8. Ibid., p. 618.
9. Ibid., p. 619.

10. Ibid., p. 618.

11. Ibid., p. 619. (Bloch's stress)

12. Ibid.

13. Ibid., p. 620.

14. Ibid., p. 621.

15. Ernst Bloch, *Subjekt-Objekt. Erlaeuterungen zu Hegel* (Frankfurt am Main: Suhrkamp Verlag, erweiterte Edition, 1962), p. 503.

16. Ibid., p. 502.

17. Ibid., p. 508.

18. Ernst Bloch, 'Errinnerungen', in *Ueber Walter Benjamin* (Frankfurt am Main: Suhrkamp Verlag, 1968), p. 17.

19. Ernst Bloch, *Erbschaft dieser Zeit* (Frankfurt am Main: Suhrkamp Verlag, 1973), p. 110. (The first edition of this book appeared in 1935, in Zürich, at the Verlag Opling und Helbling.)

20. Ibid., p. 112.

21. Ibid., pp. 116—17.

22. Ibid., p. 117.

23. Ibid., p. 119.

24. Ibid., p. 121.

25. Ernst Bloch, 'Bemerkungen zur "Erbschaft dieser Zeit" ', in *Vom Hasard zur Katastrophe. Politische Aufsätze aus den Jahren 1934—1939* (Frankfurt am Main: Suhrkamp Verlag, 1972), p. 49. (The article dates from June 1936.)

26. *Erbschaft dieser Zeit*, op. cit., p. 122.

27. This phenomenon is analysed in *Subjekt-Objekt* under the title 'Hegel und die Anamnesis. Contra Bann des Anamnesis', where Bloch stresses first of all the two senses of temporality in Hegel as well as the role of formation (*Gestaltung*) and re-membrance (*Er-innerung*) in order to conclude that without this basis the future becomes an abstraction with no foundation, and that for this reason an anamnesis of a very specific type is necessary: 'Precisely without an anamnesis of an archaic or historical-stationary type; for in their essence the work-formations (*Werk-Gestalten*) of the process border not on the return but rather on the Not-Yet, the what-has-never-so-become (*noch nie so Gewesenes*) of utopia.' (Op. cit., p. 488.)

28. Throughout Bloch's works one finds beautifully articulated and important studies of nearly forgotten thinkers from every field of endeavour. Bloch is working at present on the edition of his Leipzig lectures on the history of philosophy. This aspect of his work is more than simply an exercise or a demonstration, as should be clear from the above.

29. Ernst Bloch, *Das Prinzip Hoffnung* (Frankfurt am Main: Suhrkamp Verlag, 1959), p. 326. (This book was written between 1938 and 1947 in the United States, and was revised in 1953 when it was first published, and again in 1959. The first edition appeared in the GDR in three volumes in 1954, 1955, and 1956.)

30. Ibid., p. 327.

31. Ibid., p. 318.

32. Oskar Negt, 'Ernst Bloch — der deutsche Philosoph der Oktober-revolution', published as the Postface to *Vom Hasard zur Katastrophe*,

op. cit.

33. Jürgen Habermas, *Theorie und Praxis* (Neuwied: Luchterhand Verlag, 1963), p. 350.

34. Jürgen Habermas, *Theorie und Praxis* (Frankfurt am Main: Suhrkamp Verlag, 1971, fourth revised edition), p. 349.

35. Ibid., p. 268.

CHAPTER 5

1. On the history of the institute for Social Research, one should consult Martin Jay's extraordinarily well-documented book, *The Dialectical Imagination* (Boston: Little, Brown & Company, 1973). For a devastating critique, see Russell Jacoby, 'Marxism and the Critical School', in *Theory and Society* 1 (1974), as well as the politic between James Schmidt and Martin Jay, in *Telos*, nos 21 and 22.

2. I will be concentrating on Horkheimer's earlier writings, and using as illustrative a programmatic statement by Herbert Marcuse during the same period, during which he was certainly the most skilful and creative exponent of Horkheimer's views. Although the Institute for Research was certainly no one-man show, this choice seems to me justifiable, for not only did the director exercise his 'dictatorship', but also the contribution of the other two most creative spirits associated with the Institute, Walter Benjamin and T. W. Adorno, does not seem to me to fit — save, perhaps with great difficulty — into the perspectives outlined by Horkheimer. Though Adorno and Horkheimer remained collaborators until their deaths, any comparison of their work after the return to Germany would show the enormous difference in their published work: it was Adorno who was the innovative dynamo, with Horkheimer in the background as the administrator. If the assertions that I make in the concluding section of this essay are accepted, it would then, but only then, be possible to integrate Adorno's later work into this perspective of Critical Theory as Horkheimer develops it.

3. 'Kritische Theorie gestern und heute', in *Gesellschaft im Uebergang* (Fischer Taschenbuch Verlag: Frankfurt am Main, 1972). p. 168.

4. 'Bermerkungen über Wissenschaft und Krise', in *Zeitschrift für Sozialforschung*, Band 1, 1932, p. 3. (Future references to this journal will be indicated with the sign, *ZfS*.)

5. 'Zum Problem der Voraussage in den Sozialwissenschaften', in *ZfS*, Band 2, 1933, p. 412.

6. Ibid.

7. 'Die gegenwaertige Lage der Sozialphilosophie und die Aufgaben eines Instituts für Sozialforschung', originally in *Frankfurter Universitaetsreden*, Heft xxxvii, 1931, pages 3—16; reprinted in Max Horkheimer, *Sozialphilosophische Studien* (Fischer Taschenbuchverlag: Frankfurt am Main, 1972), p. 34.

8. See the discussion below of the role of mediation in Critical Theory's own self-understanding.

9. 'Die gegenwaertige Lage. . .', op. cit., p. 38.

10. Ibid., p. 41.

11. Ibid., p. 43.

12. Ibid., p. 46.
13. 'Vorwort', in *ZfS*, Band 1, 1932, pp. 2–3.
14. Ibid., p. 3.
15. Ibid., p. 1.
16. It should be parenthetically noted that Horkheimer is aware that this assertion does not hold for nature, which will always exist and always demand a traditional approach, though modified still, as the results of quantum mechanics indicate. We cannot deal here with Horkheimer's notion of inner and outer nature and his theory of mimesis, which are fully developed only in the *Dialectic of Enlightenment.*
17. *ZfS*, Band 6, 1937, p. 625.
18. Ibid., p. 629.
19. Ibid., p. 279.
20. The implications of this aspect of Critical Theory have been pushed further by two important German New Left thinkers, Oskar Negt and the late Hans-Jürgen Krahl. Negt's most important application of the notion of construction is in his essay on Korsch, 'Theorie, Empirie und Klassen-kampf. Zur Konstitutionsproblematik bei Karl Korsch', in *Arbeiter-bewegung. Theorie und Geschichte*, Jahrbuch 1 (Fischer Taschen-buchverlag: Frankfurt am Main, 1973). Krahl's work was collected together after his death under the title *Konstitution und Klassenkampf* (Verlag Neue Kritik: Frankfurt am Main, 1971).
21. *ZfS*, Band 6, 1937, p. 263.
22. Ibid., p. 268.
23. Ibid.
24. Ibid., pp. 291–2.
25. Ibid., p. 630.
26. Ibid., p. 292.
27. Marcuse, ibid., p. 632.
28. Ibid.
29. This situation is analysed in detail in Marcuse's splendid essay 'On the Affirmative Character of Culture', in the same issue of the *Zeitschrift.*
30. Herbert Marcuse, 'Zum Begriff des Wesens', in *ZfS*, Band 5, 1936, p. 1.
31. *ZfS*, Band 6, 1937, p. 643.
32. 'Authoritaerer Staat', in Max Horkheimer, *Gesellschaft im Ueber-gang*, op. cit., 13.
33. Ibid., p. 19.
34. Ibid.
35. Ibid., p. 18.
36. Ibid.
37. Not the cause! Horkheimer is still working with traditional Marxian categories here, despite the critique of Marxism developed later in the essay. This fidelity to the Marxian theory as having given the essential laws of capital, no matter how much its changed structure and effects is recognised, has already been noted. It is one of the reasons that, by the end of the War, Horkheimer would give up entirely on Marxism and the possibility of revolution. We shall see how thus fidelity to Marxian economics also affects the theory of the 'second generation' of Critical

Theory when we turn to the work of Jürgen Habermas.

38. 'Authoritaerer Staat', op. cit., p. 15.

39. Ibid.

40. Ibid., p. 17.

41. Ibid., p. 20.

42. Ibid., p. 27.

43. Ibid., p. 22.

44. Ibid., p. 28.

45. This is argued in detail in Horkheimer's critique of Mannheim, 'Ein neuer Ideologiebegriff', reprinted in *Sozialphilosophische Studien*, op. cit.

46. 'Authoritaerer Staat', op. cit., p. 23.

47. Ibid., p. 23.

48. Ibid.

49. Ibid., p. 24.

50. Ibid., p. 22.

51. Ibid., p. 20.

52. Ibid., p. 25.

53. Ibid., p. 30.

54. Ibid.

55. Ibid., p. 34.

56. Ibid.

57. This theoretical argument needs to be stressed against those who would date the decline of the Critical Theory from their stay in America, the adoption of 'American' empirical research methods, or even from Horkheimer's own 'bourgeois' character which showed itself so susceptible to the rewards and honours heaped upon him on his return to Germany after the war.

58. Marcuse's case is somewhat more complex if one recalls, for example, the early, Heidegger-influenced essay on 'The Philosophical Foundations of the Concept of Labor in Economics' (1933), translated recently into English in *Telos* no. 16 (summer 1973). Marcuse's politics also represent an independent problem into which we cannot go here.

59. See below, the discussion of Sartre, and especially the analysis of Merleau-Ponty.

60. I have of course 'linearised' Horkheimer's exposition here. Much of his work appears at first glance even confused, until one gets an understanding of the kind of theory Horkheimer is attempting to do.

CHAPTER 6

1. For this reason, I will make use of materials that have come out of the work of the Max Planck Institute for the Life Sciences at Starnberg as well. Particularly important for me have been the works of Claus Offe, the group Offe, Funke and Ronge, Rainer Döbert, Döbert-Nunner, U. Rödel, and the group Kalmbach, Müller, Neuendorff, Rödel and Vogt. The paper by Albrecht Wellmer, to which reference is made below, was not produced directly for the Institute of which he was a member, but shows its influence.

2. Cf. the discussion of Claude Lefort where this analysis is more fully developed. I will return to this problem below. From a Habermasian

standpoint, see the excellent study by R. Döbert, *Systemtheorie und die Entwicklung religiöser Deutungssysteme. Zur Logik des sozialwissenschaftlichen Funktionalismus* (Suhrkamp Verlag: Frankfurt am Main, 1973), esp. pp. 66—71 and 140—54. Beginning with a discussion of the relation of functionalism and systems theory, Döbert demonstrates in his first section the superiority of the latter, in order then to show through an analysis of N. Luhmann (particularly on the notion of causality) the problems of the systems theoretical approach. This is concretized in the second part of the book through an analysis of religious consciousness and belief systems, set off particularly against the systems theoretical account of R. N. Bellah. The conclusion states the need for a further criterion, namely that which a theory of evolution alone could provide. Cf. also Döbert's essay 'Zur Logik des Uebergangs von archaischen zu hochkulturellen Relgions-system', in the volume, *Seminar: Die Entstehung von Klassengesellschaften*, ed. Klaus Eder (Suhrkamp Verlag: Frankfurt am Main, 1973) and his 'Die evolutionäre Bedeutung der Reformation', in *Seminar: Religion und gesellschaftliche Entwicklung* (Suhrkamp Verlag, Frankfurt am Main, 1973), as well as the empirical application of this in Döbert-Nunner, 'Konflikt und Rückzugspotentiale im spätkapitalistischen Gesellschaften'.

3. Jürgen Habermas, *Theorie und Praxis*, 'Einleitung zur Neuausgabe', (Suhrkamp Verlag: Frankfurt am Main, 1971), p. 14. (Note that all references to *Theorie und Praxis*, unless otherwise specified, refer to the 1971 Introduction.)

4. Cf. Ernest Mandel, *Der Spätkapitalismus* (Suhrkamp Verlag, Frankfurt am Main, 1972), who insists that the term does not mean to imply the existence of a 'new essence' of capitalism that would antiquate Marx's *Capital* and Lenin's *Imperialism*. Rather, just as the latter was based on the former, the analysis of late capitalism depends on both as the theoretical base from which to analyse the new forms of appearance. Though the concept late capitalism is only chronological and not synthetic in *his* usage — not in Habermas', as we shall see — Mandel prefers it to e.g. neo-capitalism, for it makes clear that there is no discontinuity, that both forms are still capitalist. Habermas' position on the question of discontinuity is more ambiguous; and indeed, it is hard to see how the fundaments of the analysis of *Capital* apply to the new stage, save on the most undifferentiated level, i.e., that classes still exist and compete. But of course class societies existed before capitalism! Habermas' position on the question is discussed in Section II, and the question of the applicability of the theory of *Capital* recurs in note 6.

5. Pages in parenthesis refer to *Legitimationsprobleme im Spätkapitalismus* (Suhrkamp Verlag, Frankfurt am Main, 1973).

6. That Habermas can base himself on this 'law' seems to me highly questionable. Even in *Theory und Praxis* he had criticized its theoretical formulation, suggesting that historical factors such as that the productivity of science serves to increase the surplus-value produced and thus fights the falling profit rate had to be considered. (Cf. the 1963 edition, pp. 192—4.) In that critique, Habermas still wanted to maintain the labour theory of value. Here in *Legitimation Problems* the demonstration of the changed

nature of late capitalism because of the role of the state, increased monopolies and the end of the free market which leads to the politial determination of wages — all point to an *invalidation of the presuppositions for the labour theory of value*! These arguments are set out in detail by U. Rödel, 'Zusammenfassung kritischer Argumente zum Status der Werttheorie und zur Möglichkeit einer werttheoretisch formulierten Krisentheorie', (Starnberg, 1973). Yet, like Habermas, Rödel bases his later crisis analysis on the 'law' of the tendency of the rate of profit to fall (cf. pp. 17, 19, 20). The only general thrust of this argument that seems to me theoretically consistent is that both Habermas and Rödel see that despite its changed structures, late capitalism is still capitalist insofar as it is still a form of production for accumulation and profit (Marx's M-C-M'). A different analytical approach is taken by another group at Starnberg, R. Funke, C. Offe, and V. Ronge, in 'Formwandel der Politikformulierung und die legitimatorische Prozesse'. The argument sets out from the fact that capitalist society is a class-divided structure. It then asks how the political sphere acts to 'legitimate' this division. In liberal capitalism it was possible for the state to operate through a 'disjunctive' politics, either renewing its legitimation (and that of capitalism) or aiding the capitalists in need (constructing infrastructures, granting privileges, etc.). In late capitalism this disjunctive politics has been replaced by a 'simultaneous politics' which must perform both tasks at once. The structure of state activity can thus be looked at in terms of its 'organic composition' (p. 14n), and its results are seen as a series of contradictions which are then illustrated in detail in the paper. Despite the problems of its economic premises, Habermas' theory seems superior to that of Funke, Offe and Ronge in at least one respect, as we shall see: he can argue not only for the existence of a crisis but, in a sense that will be open to criticism, for its overcoming through social change and political activity guided by a theory.

The problem of an economically imposed capitalist crisis theory runs throughout the Marxian legacy, as we have seen, creating both theoretical and practical antinomies. Rather than deal with this economic theory in its own, economic, terms, it is more useful to ask the *quid juris*: why have Marxists found it necessary to assert this theory? The most obvious answer is that there needs to be a *material* base for social change, otherwise the revolutionary would be an 'idealist' or 'utopian' (or a revisionist/opportunist, like Bernstein, whose rejection of the crisis was accompanied by an explicit Kantianism of the moral Will). Yet, the implications of the position are not so clear as they at first seem. To the Horkheimerian pessimism already discussed, we could add mention here of the gradualist opportunism of the pre-World War I German Social Democrats, typified in Kautsky's *Der Weg zur Macht*, with its idea that since revolution is inscribed in the material facts, revolutionaries must be cautious, build their organisation, and wait! (In general, on the 'Politics of the Crisis Theory', see Russell Jacoby's discussion in *Telos*, No. 23, Spring 1975.) Theoretically, as we will see in detail when we discuss the evolution of C. Castoriadis, this materialism is the last avatar of the traditional ontology of domination; it is a bourgeois ideology. Psychologically, for the militant, the material basis offers a security and even a moral guarantee of the rightness of his/her actions which is but the identical opposite of the 'idealism' that is rejected as bourgeois.

7. Claus Offe, *Strukturprobleme des kapitalistischen Staates* (Suhrkamp Verlag: Frankfurt am Main, 1972), 'Spätkapitalismus — Versuch einer Begriffsbestimmung', p. 24.

8. Theoretical clarification. It is not possible here to follow the detail of Habermas' discussion of each level of crisis laid out in a welter of allusion to the specialised literature of the various fields. It is not this that is new in Habermas' attempt, but rather his mode of integrating the material.

9. Cf. *Legitimationsprobleme*, pp. 19, 99, 117, 123, etc. The reason for this is to avoid the contingency of an empirical analysis of legitimation crises. Motivation will be accounted for through the theory of social evolution, as will soon be clear. See also Habermas' elaboration of this in 'Moral Development and Ego Identity', in *Telos*, No. 24 (1975).

10. Cf. Döbert-Nunner, 'Rückzugspotential . . .', op. cit.

11. Cf. J. Habermas, *Technik und Wissenschaft als 'Ideologie'* (Suhrkamp Verlag: Frankfurt am Main, 1968), esp. pp. 75ff.

12. *Theorie und Praxis*, op. cit., p. 9.

13. In the last analysis, Habermas' theory of evolution as the groundwork for renewed Historical Materialism is based on an analysis of the forms of legitimation. Early in the book he defines the notion of a 'social organisational principle' which is to replace and make more precise the Marxian notion of a 'social formation'. By the end of the book, this notion falls away to be replaced by the forms of legitimation as first, but unsatisfactorily, articulated by Max Weber. Habermas wants to go beyond Weber, for whom legitimation was in the final analysis based either on empirical-psychological grounds or on an unquestionable value-choice — i.e., in neither case could the legitimation be subject to rational discussion. Habermas attempts to base legitimation on a reference to truth *via* communicative action and the theory of evolution. The problem is that in the very definition of a 'social organizational principle' the primary status of legitimation crises is already built in by means of the stress on identity and social integration.

Despite Habermas' vagueness, there is a theoretical argument being presented here whose importance must be stressed. The notion of legitimation or identity crises is necessary to the systems theoretical approach if it is to differentiate systems crisis from learning processes. Legitimation crises perform this function because they are *discursively* founded. They occur when allegiance can no longer be bought; but their foundation cannot be simply left to empirical and contingent facts. This is where the theory of evolution enters, itself based on the truth-related logic of a 'universal pragmatics'. Habermas insists that this is the central thrust of the book: without a theory of evolution he is reduced to guesswork (p. 31); and without a demonstration of the truth-capacity of practical questions, his entire argument goes down the drain (pp. 139—40).

14. Cf. for a summary, Albrecht Wellmer, 'Communication and Emancipation. Reflections on the Linguistic Turn in Critical Theory', in *Stony Brook Studies in Philosophy*, ed. P. Byrne, C. Evans and D. Howard,

(Stony Brook, New York, 1974), 1.

15. Cf. Habermas' essay 'Arbeit und Interaktion. Bemerkungen zu Hegels Jenenser "Philosophie des Geistes",' in *Technik und Wissenschaft als Ideologie*, op. cit.

16. Note that there has been much confusion about the legitimacy of these categories. Habermas writes:

> I do not mind at all *calling* both phenomena praxis. Nor do I deny that normally instrumental action is embedded in communicative action (productive activity is socially organized, in general). But I see no reason why we should not adequately *analyze* a complex, i.e., dissect it into its parts. (Postscript to *Knowledge and Human Interests*, Eng. translation in *Philosophy of the Social Sciences*, 3, 1973; p. 18 n. 27. Hereafter referred to as 'Postscript'.)

These two forms provide the basis for the meta-theoretical reconstruction of a social formation. They are not conceived of as empirical (save in the context of the 'empirical' theory of social evolution, on which cf. id., p. 181, and *Theorie und Praxis*, pp. 26ff., esp. n. 31). We will return to them when we discuss Habermas' theory of social evolution and its role.

17. Cf. Jürgen Habermas/Niklas Luhmann, *Theorie der Gesellschaft oder Sozialtechnologie* (Suhrkamp Verlag: Frankfurt am Main, 1971), especially pp. 114—22, and 202—20. (Hereafter referred to as 'Habermas/Luhmann'.)

18. Cf. Jürgen Habermas, 'Wahrheitstheorien', in *Festschrift für Walter Schultz*, (Neske Verlag, 1973). Habermas writes here:

> The ideal speech situation is neither an empirical phenomenon nor a mere construct but rather an unavoidable assumption that is reciprocally presupposed in all discourses. Though this assumption can be counterfactual it need not be; but even when it is made counterfactually it is an operatively effective function in the communication procedure. I thus speak preferably of an anticipation, a forehold on an ideal speech situation. (p. 258)

And further on, Habermas notes that this ideal speech situation is not like a regulative principle in Kant's sense — it is a factual anticipation of which speech is in need; nor is it an existent, concrete concept in Hegel's sense — for there is no historical social form which perfectly accords with it. Rather, the ideal speech situation would be best compared with a transcendental illusion (*Schein*) if this illusion did not depend on an unsatisfactory transfer (as in the use of the categories of the understanding without reference to experience) but were at the same time constitutive of rational discussion (p. 259).

19. On this, cf. *Legitimationsprobleme*, op. cit., pp. 155—8, and Habermas/Luhmann, op. cit., p. 281.

20. Cf. M. Theunissen, 'Die Gefährdung des Staates durch die Kultur', a review of *Legitimationsprobleme*, in the *Frankfurter Allgemeine Zeitung*, 9 October 1973.

21. The vagueness of Habermas' position here is seen in the following:

... God becomes the name for a communicative structure which forces men under the penalty of the loss of their humanity to go beyond their accidental empirical nature by encountering one another *mediately*, namely through the mediation of an Objective Thing which they themselves are not. (*Legitimationsprobleme*, p. 167.)

To talk about an 'Objective Thing' which we are not, as making possible social relations and personal individuation, is so indeterminate as to help only to make us aware of a necessary component in the argument; more is necessary, and the fact that ultimately Habermas doesn't give that 'more' will be the grounds for criticism below.

22. 'Wahrheitstheorien', op. cit., p. 251.

23. Taken from Offe, *Strukturprobleme*, op. cit., pp. 85ff.

24. The question whether *interests*, by definition, are not particular is taken up below in the discussion of Habermas' theory of 'cognitive interests'.

25. Cf. for example, *Theorie und Praxis*, op. cit., p. 25, for a clear illustration.

26. Rödel, 'Zusammenfassung . . .', op. cit., p. 10.

27. Offe, *Strukturprobleme*, op. cit., p. 90.

28. Habermas/Luhmann, op. cit., p. 281.

29. On this, besides the Habermas/Luhmann debate, and the book by R. Döbert already mentioned, cf. the two *Theorie-Diskussion* volumes published by Suhrkamp after the Habermas/Luhmann debate. See also, R. Bubner, 'Wissenschaftstheorie und Systembegriff', in R. Bubner, *Dialektik und Wissenschaft*, and the provocative, Hegelian-inspired essay by Klaus Hartmann, 'Systemtheoretische Soziologie und kategoriale Sozialphilosophie', in *Philosophische Perspektiven*, Band 5, 1973.

30. Cf. H. Baier, 'Soziologie und Geschichte', in *Archiv. für Rechts- und Sozialphilosophie*, 1966, LII, 1, pp. 67–89; reprinted in *Kritik und Interpretation der kritischen Theorie* (The Hague, 1971). The citation is from p. 377 of the latter.

31. This does not mean, as M. Theunissen suggests (op. cit.), that Habermas must give up the principle that epistemology is based on social theory; it means only that he recognises the need to provide grounds for that assertion.

32. Or of Döbert, op. cit., or of Döbert-Nunner on child development. More recently, see Habermas' 'Moral Development and Ego Identity', and my notes on it in *Telos*, No. 27, 1976.)

33. *Theorie und Praxis*, op. cit., pp. 22–3. The point is made again below in the discussion of the difference between a critical and a reconstructive theory.

34. Wellmer, op. cit., p. 97.

35. Hegel, *Wissenschaft der Logik* (Meiner: Hamburg, 1963), p. 19.

36. Ibid., p. 18.

37. 'Postscript', op. cit., p. 175.

38. *Theorie und Praxis*, op. cit., p. 16.

39. Ibid., p. 26.
40. Ibid., p. 27.
41. Ibid., note 31.
42. 'Postscript', op. cit., p. 181.
43. *Theorie und Praxis*, op. cit., p. 16. Also, 'Postscript', op. cit., p. 177, where Habermas writes: 'The *universality* of cognitive interests implies that the constitution of object domains is determined by conditions governing the reproduction of the species, i.e., by the socio-cultural form of life *as such*.'
44. Ibid., p. 44.
45. Wellmer, op. cit., p. 92.
46. *Theorie und Praxis*, op. cit., p. 45.
47. Cf. *Legitimationsprobleme*, pp. 27—30, especially p. 28 on the role of learning mechanisms.
48. Here, however, one must be careful. Such a claim is the obverse of the worst in the tradition of the Frankfurt School. That is: it is easy — and in the last analysis theoretically useless — to say that any theory of the 'social' or of institutions, i.e., any theory of plural subjectivity, is wrong, ideological or reifying insofar as it denies the particular and/or hypostatises the social. The claim of the particular can always be maintained . . . at the expense of having nothing but particulars, and ultimately being unable to account for them, as Habermas himself realises. The question for social and political theory is that of *mediation*, of the articulation of the universal in the particular and the affirmative relations of the particular to the universal.
49. Habermas recognises that the strict analogy doesn't hold, or that it at best makes sense in the case of the traditional view of the relation of the party to the masses. Cf. *Theorie und Praxis*, op. cit., pp. 35—7, and 'Der Universalitätsanspruch der Hermeneutik', in *Hermeneutik und Ideologiekritik* (Suhrkamp Verlag: Frankfurt am Main, 1971), as well as the critiques of Geigel and Gadamer in that volume.
50. It has since taken a somewhat different turn. Cf. Oskar Negt/Alexander Kluge, *Öffentlichkeit und Erfahrung. Zur Organisationsanalyse von bürgerlicher und proletarischer Öffentlichkeit* (Suhrkamp Verlag: Frankfurt am Main, 1972).
51. *Theorie und Praxis*, op. cit., p. 33. On the problem of institutions, see the discussion below, as well as the chapters on Merleau-Ponty, Lefort, and Castoriadis.
52. Ibid., p. 39.
53. Cf. the excellent and provocative Introduction by Oskar Negt to N. Bucharin, A. Deborin, *Kontroversen über dialektischen und mechanistischen Materialismus* (Suhrkamp Verlag: Frankfurt am Main, 1969), where this term is defined in detail.
54. Habermas adds here the peculiar argument that 'Such attempts are precisely also tests; they test the limits of the changeability of human nature, above all of the historically variable structure of motivations or drives (*Antriebsstruktur*) — limits about which we do not have, and in my opinion for fundamental reasons of principle cannot have theoretical knowledge' (*Theorie und Praxis*, op. cit., p. 42). I take it that Habermas is

either thinking theoretically in terms of his theory of evolutionary stages, or concretely in terms of the psychic stress placed on people in the Movement, for example, by 'smash monogamy' campaigns, or experiments in child-rearing, etc.

55. 'Wahrheitstheorien', op. cit., p. 257.
56. Offe, *Strukturprobleme*, op. cit., p. 74.
57. Ibid., p. 173.
58. Ibid., p. 130.
59. Paragraphs 230—56.
60. Bernard Willms, *Kritik und Politik. Jürgen Habermas oder das politische Defizit der "Kritischen Theorie,"* (Surhkamp Verlag: Frankfurt am Main, 1973). In the following references to Willms, I will not give page references: his arguments are often repeated in different forms in the course of the book.
61. *Theorie und Praxis*, op. cit., pp. 31—2.
62. 'Der Universalitätsanspruch der Hermeneutik', op. cit., p. 158.
63. An interesting attempt in this direction is Negt/Kluge, op. cit., which is rich in illustrative material.
64. Habermas knows that there are concrete political problems that must be dealt with here. In 'Technik und Wissenschaft als "Ideologie",' he follows Offe in posing the question of the 'conflict capacity' of each of these groups. (Cf. for example, pp. 100—2, and Offe's article 'Politische Herrschaft und Klassenstrukturen. Zur Analyse spätkapitalistischer Gesellschaftssysteme', in Kress/Senghaas, eds., *Politikwissenschaft* (Europäische Verlagsanstalt: Frankfurt am Main, 1969.) But the solutions Habermas proposes are so general as to be politically useless. Theoretically the question remains open in Habermas' work. A rapprochement with Lefort and Castoriadis could begin with this problem.
65. *Theorie und Praxis*, op. cit., p. 37.

CHAPTER 7

1. Jean-Paul Sartre, Pierre Victor, Philippe Gavi, *On a raison de se révolter* (Paris: Gallimard, 1974), p. 17. Epistémon, *Ces idées qui ont ébranlé la France* (Paris: Fayard, 1968).
2. Jean-Paul Sartre, *Situations X* (Paris: Gallimard, 1976). Citation from the interview with Michel Contat, 'Autoportrait à soixante-dix ans', p. 217. (Hereafter, 'Interview'.)
3. Jean-Paul Sartre, *L'Etre et le Néant* (Paris: Gallimard, 1943), p. 370.
4. *On a raison*, p. 139.
5. Ibid., p. 101.
6. Ibid., p. 142.
7. Ibid., p. 344.
8. 'Interview', p. 216.
9. *On a raison*, pp. 47—8.
10. 'Interview', p. 144.
11. Replying to Michel Contat's question whether his theory of freedom is not too abstract, Sartre admits: 'I think that in effect a theory of freedom which does not explain at the same time what are alienations,

to what degree freedom can let itself be manipulated, deviated, turned against itself, can very cruelly deceive someone who doesn't understand what it implies, and who thinks that freedom is everywhere.' ('Interview', p. 223.)

12. The reading of Kant as an ontologist, not an epistemologist, is of course open to disagreement. This is not the place to argue about Kant. Suffice it that, for the Sartrean project, ontology is the condition of the possibility of epistemology.

13. All citations, unless otherwise noted, are from Jean-Paul Sartre, *Critique de la raison dialectique* (Gallimard, 1960). This volume includes a preliminary essay, 'Question de méthode', which is translated into English as 'Search for a Method'. An English translation of the entire book is due to appear, published by New Left Books. Here, all translations are my own.

14. 'Question de méthode,' is *not* integral to the theory of the *Critique*. Nor is it the methodological 'key' to Sartre's theory, as Lichtheim argues in his typically urbane, and chatty manner (in 'Sartre, Marxism and History', in *The Concept of Ideology*, p. 294). The *Critique* stands quite well alone, and must be examined in its pretention to ontological foundation to Marxism.

15. I will follow Sartre's usage throughout, italicizing the term *praxis* to show its ontological usage in the *Critique*.

16. Cf. *Critique*, pp. 214–24. The problem of the origin of negativity is present in *Capital* as well. The final section of Volume I, the 'So-Called Primitive Accumulation', was tacked on to meet this problem. The original manuscript version of the final chapter of Volume I, recently published as *Resultate des unmittelbaren Produktionsprozesses*, shows clearly that Marx did not need Primitive Accumulation and added it only as an afterthought.

17. 'Abstract' in the sense that Hegel uses the term, that is, least complex, most immediate moments which are therefore false in isolation but constitutive as moments of the totality. 'Abstract' means the same thing as 'immediate', as opposed to mediated structures which are, for Sartre and Hegel, the most concrete.

18. In interview with M. Contat and M. Rybalka (*Le Monde*, 14 May 1971), Sartre indicates that the promised second volume will not appear. This is not, he insists, for theoretical reasons but simply because he 'will not have time ... before [his] death'. In Contat and Rybalka's monumental *Les écrits de Sartre* (Gallimard, 1970), it is indicated that Sartre had written two chapters for volume II, one on boxing, the other on Stalin (p. 340).

19. In fact, Sartre does not follow through on this, and the grounds for the criticism to be given below are in part based on this inconsistency.

20. 'Marxists' have not always seen this important notion, as witnesses the East German Introduction to Rosa Luxemburg's *Ausgewählte Schriften* (1953) which, in cataloguing her errors for the naïve readers, indicates this as one of them. Sartre's theory makes this point quite clear. The problem of the definition of scarcity remains. As it stands, Sartre's position does not ever permit the overcoming of scarcity, for if that were

to come about, human *praxis* too would come to an end. If we try to concretise the ontology here, we confront the manifold *new* forms of scarcity — of non-polluted air, frees, free time, etc. — that our social form continually creates anew.

21. Sartre's *Critique* is important because, against the view too often held by 'leftists' and 'new leftists' today, that the working class is 'alienated' and 'sold out' to the point that, as Marcuse puts it in his *Essay on Liberation*, this has become a 'biological' characteristic, the crux of the argument here is that the structures of alienation can only be understood as based on free human *praxis*. As a result of this, many philosophical and practical problems are avoided. It would be interesting, though this is obviously not the place to do so, to compare the Sartrean and Marcusian views on humankind: Marcuse's view errs by making consciousness too 'thick', or 'absorbent' of influences in the material-social-historical world, while Sartre's, as will be seen, errs by making it too 'thin'. The point here, however, is only to stress that Sartre's position is superior to that of Marcuse in that, by accounting for the structures of unfreedom in terms of free action it permits the possibility of self-liberation as opposed to liberation from the outside. The difficulty of this position will be seen below.

22. In his Preface to Antonin Liehm's *Trois Générations* (Gallimard, 1969) Sartre analyses the Czech situation in terms of these categories. Space prohibits the reproduction of this analysis which, suffice it to say, is his most brilliant piece of political writing.

23. The role of the Third has already been prepared in the earlier discussion of individual *praxis*. There Sartre asserted that:

> It is not possible to conceive of a temporal process which would begin with the dyad and conclude with the triad. The binary formation as an immediate relation of man to man is the necessary foundation for any ternary relation; but inversely, the ternary relation as the mediation of man between men is the foundation on the basis of which reciprocity recognises itself as reciprocal liason. If the idealistic dialectic made an abusive usage of the triad, it is first of all because the *real* relation of men among themselves is necessarily ternary. But that trinity is not an ideal signification or characteristic of human relations: it is inscribed *in being*, that is, in the materiality of individuals. In this sense, reciprocity is not the thesis, nor is the trinity the synthesis (or inversely); it is a question of lived relations whose content is determined in an already existing society, and which are conditioned by the materiality, and which one can only modify by action. (p. 189)

The parallel between the two levels of categorial analysis is striking, and points once again to the schema of dialectical intelligibility on the basis of a structure of reflexion. The role of the Third will be taken up in more detail below.

24. Whereas for the individual *praxis* the Third was a menace, threatening to make it into an Excess Third, in the group-in-fusion each is made Other (hence, by analogy, excess) by the menace of an Other outside the

group; and hence each is the Same.

25. The rumour need not be true. This is the technique used by states, for example, which maintain their ideological cohesion by installing a permanent fear of the 'red' or 'capitalist' menace.

26. I will return to the implications of this point below.

27. Cf. pp. 417. 431. 507. 667. etc.

28. For example, the Spanish gold was used to illustrate the counter-finality of the practico-inert. Yet it brought into consideration social structures which were more complex, those of series, groups, institutions etc. For a critique of Sartre on this point, cf. Klaus Hartmann, *Sartre's Sozialphilosophie* (Berlin: de Gruyter, 1966). Interestingly, Hartmann finds the same problem in Marx's *Capital*; cf. *Die Marxsche Theorie*, De Gruyter, Berlin, 1970.

29. It is significant that Sartre moves, in mid-paragraph, from this discussion to a consideration of the Hearst press as a manipulator of public opinion (pp. 605—6).

30. In *Situations V* (Gallimard, 1964) p. 213.

31. Reprinted in *Situations X*, op. cit.; the following citations are from pp. 42f.

32. *On a raison*, op. cit., p. 166.

33. Ibid., p. 171.

34. Jean Paul Sartre, in *Situations II*, p. 254 and p. 7. Cited by Simone de Beauvoir in 'Merleau-Ponty et le pseudo-Sartrisme', (*Les Temps Modernes*, 10, II, 1955), pp. 2075, 2082. De Beauvoir's attempt to reply to Merleau-Ponty's critique of Sartre in *Les aventures de la dialectique* is based on her total misunderstanding of the point of Merleau-Ponty's essay, and is not worth discussing here.

35. *On a raison*, op. cit., p. 126.

36. Ibid., p. 45.

37. Ibid., pp. 144—5. Merleau-Ponty emphasises a similar point (AD, p. 275) when he insists that intersubjective action is impossible for Sartre because his transcendental freedom has no history, springing forth a new and full blown in every moment.

38. Ibid., p. 342.

CHAPTER 8

1. The point was in fact made in Sartre's 'Merleau-Ponty vivant', in *Les Temps Modernes*, Oct 1961 (reprinted in Sartre, *Situations IV* (Paris: Gallimard, 1964), p. 243), but with reference to Merleau-Ponty's influence in an earlier period. Cf. Hugh J. Silverman's introductory essay to his translation of 'Philosophy and Non-Philosophy since Hegel', in *Telos*, No. 29, Fall, 1976, where the claim is made as concerns developments in France since the death of Merleau-Ponty.

2. James Edie, 'Introduction', in *The Primacy of Perception and Other Essays* (Northwestern University Press: Evanston, Ill., 1964), p. xiv. Since this statement was made, both volumes have been translated, though *Humanism and Terror* did not appear in the series directed by Mr Edie. I suppose that, in the end, we have to thank the 'blind forces of the market' for doing what the philosopher could not!

3. Dick Howard, 'Ambiguous Radicalism: Merleau-Ponty's Interrogation of Political Thought', in Garth Gillan, ed., *The Horizons of the Flesh* (Carbondale: Southern Illinois University Press, 1973).

4. Claude Lefort, 'La politique et la pensée de la politique', in *Lettres Nouvelles*, lle année, nouvelle série, no. 32, p. 58.

5. Compare the statement in *HT*: 'The decline of proletarian humanism is not a critical experiment which would annul marxism entirely. As a critique of the existing world and of the other humanisms, it remains valid. At least in this sense, *it can not be surpassed*' (p. 165), with the statement printed over a decade later (but written in 1955, at the time of *AD*): 'The decadence of Russian communism does not mean that the class struggle is a myth, that "free enterprise" is either possible or desirable, nor in general that the marxist critique is void' (*S*, p. 338).

6. In an earlier formulation (*PhP*, p. 456), Merleau-Ponty writes: 'To say with Marx that man poses only those problems that he can resolve is to renew the theological optimism and to postulate the explosion of the world'. The implications of this position are crucial to the argument that I am putting forth in this book.

7. Compare the following passage on Trotsky: 'On the plane of the individual, this type of person is sublime. But we must ask whether they are the type who make history. They believe so strongly in the rationality of history that, if for a time history ceases to be rational, they throw themselves toward the wished-for future rather than pass any compromises with the incoherent present' (*HT*, p. 85).

8. As I did in op. cit.

9. *Mésaventures de l'anti-Marxisme, Les Malheurs de M. Merleau-Ponty* (Paris: Editions Sociales, 1956), p. 102. This collective volume published by the political-theoretical 'heavies' of the French Communist Party shows how seriously the critical effort of Merleau-Ponty was taken at the time. The volume is interesting as an antiquity; from the point of view of theory, it is strictly and simply empty and vain verbiage.

10. Insofar as one tries to interpret the theory of the proletariat as an account of the praxis of a plural subject, one escapes the dilemma posed here only to fall into its inverse opposite: the proletariat is treated as an absolute subject constituting the world. The transcendental subjectivity rejected by Marx is therewith placed in an object within the world. The result, as we have seen, is a justification of the voluntarism of the Party, or a mystical view of praxis as the achieved unity of subject and object. That the two sides are but of one coin is shown in Merleau-Ponty's attack on Sartre in *AD*.

11. On this problematic, the work of Claude Lefort is clearly the development of Merleau-Ponty's fundamental insight — although it could be argued that Lefort's contribution to Merleau-Ponty's own development makes him the 'co-founder' so to speak of this position.

CHAPTER 9

1. The work of Jürgen Habermas seems to avoid this reproach. In fact, however, the problems that plague his undifferentiated political theory were seen to depend at least in part on his continued acceptance of

the Marxian analysis of infrastructural contradiction. This same acceptance might also explain the fact that while Habermas' concern is precisely the elaboration of an empirically testable and practically useful Marxian sociology, he finds himself forced to adapt the modes of theory developed by 'bourgeois' sociology to this end.

2. On the group 'Socialisme ou Barbarie', see also the discussion in Chapter 10 of Cornelius Castoriadis. It would demand a separate monograph to trace the nuances of the group's history, or to try to separate the contributions of the individual members. By treating Lefort and Castoriadis separately, I hope to make clear both what unites them and at least the basis, if not the substantial details, of their differences.

3. On the quarrel, cf. Sartre's 'Merleau-Ponty', published in the commemorative issue of *Les Temps Modernes*, and reprinted in *Situations IV* (especially pp. 257ff.). It is hard to avoid adding in reference to this article that Sartre seems never to have understood the radical novelty of Merleau-Ponty's philosophy. His continual categorisation of Merleau-Ponty in terms of a longing for that primal happiness he lived in his youth may be interesting psychology — but it tells us little about Merleau-Ponty . . . though much about Sartre!

4. 'Entretien avec C. Lefort', in *L'Anti-mythes*, No. 14, p. 10. (The interview dates from 19 April 1975, and is now translated in *Telos* No. 30, Winter, 1977. The *Anti-mythes* has also published interviews with P. Clastres, Henri Simon and C. Castoriadis, the latter having been translated in *Telos* No. 23, Spring 1975.)

5. Ibid., pp. 12—13.

6. Ibid., p. 27.

7. This argument is developed particularly in 'Le prolétariat et sa direction', and 'L'expérience prolétarienne', both of which are reprinted in *Eléments d'une théorie de la bureaucratie* (Droz, 1971). In the latter article, Lefort attempts to develop a concrete methodology for the sociological analysis of what the experience and hence the consciousness of the proletariat in fact is, how it changes, etc.

8. The term will be defined more precisely below. It might be noted that this definition of the specificty of the social against Sartre's idealism points to the importance of recognising that the properly sociological deals with '2 plus *n* persons', as Benjamin Nelson points out. Recognising this would have important implications for vogue styles like symbolic interactionism, phenomenological or ethnomethodological sociology.

9. In *Eléments d'une théorie de la bureaucratie* (hereafter *Eléments*), op. cit., p. 65.

10. For example, *Les Temps Modernes'* support for Gomulka as the only choice in the post-1956 situation, even though he was not helping to extend — quite the contrary — the movement that brought him to power. At least by saving the party, and acting cautiously to prevent another Russian invasion, he appeared to be giving History another chance. Or, to take another example, Lefort shows that applying the same 'method' or presuppositions, transforms Sartre's apparently critical 'The Ghost of Stalin' into a surface critique which doesn't go to the foundations of Stalinism but sees a series of errors and contingencies at the root of

Russian political behaviour. In the preceding discussion of Sartre, I pointed to the contradiction of his transcendental position when after an *éloge* to the universality of freedom, he finds himself condemning Solzhenitsyn in the name of Historical Progress.

11. Aside from some nasty polemical remarks, Sartre's major point against Lefort is that Lefort denies mediation, seeing the proletariat in a crypto-Hegelian fashion. Sartre takes Lefort's notion of the accumulation of proletarian experience as following the image of the evolution from the seed to the flower to the fruit. Lefort would thus have a proletariat modelled on Wilhelm Meister or Marivaux's Marianne: through adversity it earns its education. Since Lefort insists that the existence of Stalinism cannot be the result of Pure Will nor of History acting, but rather that it must be accounted for through an analysis of the actual experience of the class, Sartre portrays his attitude as one of the pure intellectual consciousness standing outside the fray.

Sartre does effectively point to a problem in Lefort's position, though he neglects the nuances for polemical purposes. Now that Lefort has seen the problems with his understanding of the proletariat, Sartre's criticisms stand only as a warning — whereas Lefort's attack on Sartre remains valid despite the modifications that Sartre's *politics* seem to have undergone since then. Lefort is correct in pointing out that, though it stresses ambiguity, the Sartrean ambiguity is always *for consciousness*, subjective; and it can be cleared up once one chooses the path of History. For Lefort, Sartre leaves even Hegel, returning to Kant: 'Where the best of Hegel is in his attempt to describe the becoming of Spirit, to show how activity develops within passivity itself, you reintroduce the abstraction of moral consciousness — not the least sure of itself, certainly, nor clear to itself, but transcendent in relation to all its determinations, pure activity permitting neither deliberation nor critique inasmuch as it coincides with its project of revolution' (in *Eléments*, p. 92). And, later, Lefort continues: 'That the proletariat is already a class at the level of the production process, but not in the least a completed synthesis, that there is a dialectic but not a finalism, that the activity of the vanguard organizations must be put within the dynamic of the whole [*ensemble*] while this does not in the least mean that there is an undifferentiated totality nor a miraculous spontaneity — it is clear that all this, which upsets the relation subject-object is for you a "magical thought" ' (id., p. 100). In effect, Sartre's position is nothing but a 'social' exemplification of the dialectic of Self and Other; but already *Being and Nothingness* showed that such a dialectic, even in love, turns out to be antagonistic. Lefort's alternative will be discussed below.

12. 'L'échange et la lutte des hommes', p. 1400. I am citing from an offprint of this article given me by Lefort; unfortunately, I can't find the exact date of publication. The article was written in 1951. All citations from this article in this part of the text are given as 'id.', followed by a page number.

13. 'Sociétés sans historie et Historicité', p. 92. Again, I am citing from an offprint, and have not found the original text. The article was written in 1952. Citations in the text follow the form indicated in n. 12.

14. See Lefort's two discussions of the work of Abram Kardiner, 'Notes critiques sur les méthodes de Kardiner', in *Cahiers internationaux de sociologie*, No. 10, 1951, and the 'Introduction à l'oeuvre d'Abram Kardiner', in the French translation of *L'individu dans sa société* (Paris: Gallimard, 1969). Lefort's use of Freud, mediated in part by some contributions of Jacques Lacan, will be clear below when his notion of *l'imaginaire* of a society is discussed. He does not believe that concepts can be taken over from one domain of explanation to another, nor does he believe in an applied psychoanalysis. However, the *experience* confronted in the psychoanalytic cure, and its metapsychological reflection, show interesting parallels to the problematic Lefort is confronting. Thus, in the Interview with the *Anti-mythes*, he notes that 'whether it is a question of the critique of the myth of revolution, of the myth of the 'good society', of the critique of the contradictions of power, the idea of social division as the original division and hence of the permanence of conflict, of the idea that societies order themselves as a function of the demand and the impossibility of thinking their origins, or again of the idea that the discourse which a society maintains about itself is constitutive of its institution, or of the relation that I attempt to establish between the figures of knowledge and power — in all these cases, the borrowing from Freud is felt.' (op. cit., p. 27.)

15. Later, Lefort will identify the emergence of History with that of a Power, the political, separated from the society and claiming to incarnate its unity. He will return to this. From the point of view of anthropology, cf. Pierre Clastres, *La société contre l'état* (Paris: Minuit, 1974).

16. 'Rapport de Recherches', p. 16. This essay was submitted to the CNRS, Lefort's employer, as part of the dossier for his yearly evaluation. It has not been published.

17. 'Capitalisme et religion au XVIe Siècle', in *Les Temps Modernes*, 78 (1952). I am again citing from an offprint, following the above procedure; this time, however, the publication data were on the offprint!

18. 'L'aliénation comme concept sociologique', p. 50. Again, I am citing from an offprint, and have not got the publication data. The article dates from 1956. Citations in the text follow the above pattern.

19. 'La politique et la pensée de la politique', in *Letters Nouvelles*, lle année, nouvelle série, no. 32, p. 30. Again, citation is from an offprint; date of the article is 1961 or 1962; citations follow the above practice.

20. Lefort will later call this procedure *interpretation*, in order to indicate that the interrogation follows a logic and method which arise from the imbrication and participation of the subject in the subject-matter. Lefort's most recent work deals at depth with the problem of interpretation, bringing to bear not only phenomenological but also Freudian categories.

21. Citation is from 'Réalité sociale et histoire', p. 68. This is the mimeographed version of the student notes, reread and corrected by the professor. They can usually be purchased by students. Lefort is planning to revise these lectures for eventual book publication.

22. 'Notes sociologiques sur Machiavel et Marx: La politique et le réel', p. 116. Once again, I cite from an offprint — but found the data: *Cahiers*

internationaux de sociologié. Vol. 28, nouvelle série, 7e année, janvier-juin, 1960. References in the text follow the usual format.

23. In 'La naissance de l'idéologie et l'humanisme, Introduction' (*Textures*, 73/6—7, pp. 27—68). Lefort points out that Marx and his followers tended to neglect this fundamental insight in arguing about ideology which they took as a masking of the real. Such an argument supposes that we know the real, i.e., in this case that the real basis of Roman society was its productive system, for example. We will return to this point in a moment.

24. The term is taken from the title of a review of Lefort's *Machiavel*, by Marcel Gauchet (in *Critique*, No. 329, Oct 1974). The suggestion of such a logic, however, is already contained in the article we are discussing.

25. '*Rapport de Recherches*', op. cit., p. 12.

26. The similarity with the effort of Jürgen Habermas is remarkable. The major difference in the two approaches emerges from Habermas' stubborn acceptance of the heritage of Marxism — and the traditional theory structure which leads Habermas to his distinction of reconstructive and critical theory. The lack of a satisfactory theory of ideology in Habermas is due to the constitutive or transcendental-ontological position that he adopts from German Idealism. Lefort's theory of ideology *as* the structure of capitalism itself permits him to move toward a logic of the political which remains still an undifferentiated project in Habermas' work.

27. In *Textures*, 71/2—3, pp. 7—79; and *Machiavel: Le travail de l'oeuvre* (Paris: Gallimard, 1973).

28. 'Esquisse d'une genése de l'idéologie dans les sociétés modernes', in *Textures*, 74/8—9, pp. 3—54. A slightly revised version appears in the *Encyclopedia Universalis* (Organon) under the title, 'L'ère de l'idéologie'. A further elaboration of these themes is found in Lefort's 'Le nom de l'Un', in E. de la Boétie, *Discours de la servitude volontaire* (Paris: Payot, 1976).

29. *L'ère de l'idéologie*, op. cit., p. 78.

30. 'La naissance . . .', op. cit., p. 48.

31. 'Esquisse . . .', op. cit., p. 31.

32. Ibid., p. 36.

33. Lefort's recent study of Solzhenitsyn's *Gulag Archipelago*, *Un homme en trop* (Paris: Seuil, 1976) elaborates this theory brilliantly.

34. Piera Aulagnier, a psychoanalyst who was one of the leaders of the Quatrième group's split from the Lacanian Ecole Freudianne, is the author of the recent volume, *La violence de l'intérprétation* (Paris: PUF, 1975), which develops the notion to which Lefort is referring here.

35. 'Rapport de Recherches', op. cit., p. 12.

36. Lefort is preparing a study of 'La naissance de la psychanalyse'. Pursuing this line of criticism, Lefort's collaborator, Marcel Gauchet, has recently published a remarkable study of the second of the *Three Essays on Sexuality*, in *Textures*, 72/4—5, pp. 115—56, and 73/6—7, pp. 69—112.

37. Gauchet, in *Critique*, op. cit., p. 926.

38. 'La politique et la pensée de la politique', op. cit., p. 69.

CHAPTER 10

1. Biographical material cited throughout is taken from 'Introduction générale', in *La société bureaucratique, 1* (Paris: UGE, 1973), from the 1974 Interview with Castoriadis by the Agence Presse Libération de Caen (translated into English in Telos, no. 23, 1975), and from the Interview with Claude Lefort by the *Anti-Mythes* (Paris and Caen) in 1975. I have also relied on long discussions with Castoriadis and Lefort, as well as with former members of the group, such as Mothé, A. and J-F Lyotard, A. and D. Guilléme, and H. Simon. Where there are several versions of an event — such as the splits in the group — I have tried to present a balanced argument of the alternatives presented. I should add here that I have relied on my memory of these conversations, and apologise in advance if I misrepresent any of the positions.

2. Jean-Marc Coudray (C. Castoriadis), in *Mai 1968: la Bréche* (Paris: Fayard, 1968), p. 92. The programmatic past of this essay was distributed as a mimeographed leaflet during May by some of the ex-members; a further discussion was added for the book's publication.

3. This was published, along with the first five instalments, as *L'institution imaginaire de la société* (Paris: Editions du Seuil, 1975).

4. On Trotsky, cf. Claude Lefort, 'La contradiction de Trotsky', originally in *Les Temps Modernes*, no. 39, déc—jan 1948—9, now in Lefort, *Elements d'une critique de la bureaucratie* (Genève-Paris: Librairie Droz, 1971). In the Interview with the *Anti-Mythes*, Lefort stresses his debt to Castoriadis for the economic part of his analysis.

5. 'Les rapports de production en Russie', reprinted in *La société bureaucratique, 1*.

6. Ibid., p. 179.

7. An American splinter from the IVth International, in many ways similar to Socialisme ou Barbarie, did take this direction. The 'Forrest-Johnson' (Dunayevskaya-James) tendency was in close relation with Socialisme ou Barbarie, which translated some of their articles into French. This is not the place to enter into the differences between them, or the split of James and Dunayevskaya, save to indicate that by the mid-1950s, the distance had become radical.

8. Cf. Lefort's 'What Is Bureaucracy?' *Telos* 22 (Winter 1974—5). In his 'Le totalitarisme sans Staline', Lefort insists that the transformation effected cannot be called 'primitive socialist accumulation', as Deutscher suggests, for primitive accumulation in Marx's sense brings about precisely the establishment of relations of domination of Capital over Labour — not socialism. In this sense, Lefort uses the term 'state capitalism', for he believed then that the existence of the proletariat means that Marx's vision of socialism is still possible. Lefort goes on to suggest that the relations between state and civil society in bureaucratic Russia differ from those in bourgeois society, where competition in the latter sphere maintains it separate from the state. He writes: 'Totalitarianism is not a dictatorial regime, as it appears when we speak summarily of it as a type of absolute domination in which the separation of powers is abolished. More precisely, it isn't a political regime: it is a type of society — that form in which all activities are immediately tied to each other, deliberately presented as modalities of a single universe in which a system of values predominates

absolutely, such that all individual and collective activities must necessarily find in that system their coefficient of reality; in which, finally, the dominant model exercises a total constraint at once physical and spiritual on the behaviour of the particular individuals. In this sense, totalitarianism makes the pretence of negating the separation characteristic of bourgeois capitalism among the various domains of social life, the political, the economic, the juridical, the ideological, etc. It effectuates a permanent identification of all. Thus it is not so much a monstrous growth of the political power within society as a metamorphosis of society itself by which the political ceases to exist as a separate sphere' (*Eléments*, p. 156).

Crucial is the role of the party, which 'is the agent of a complete penetration of civil society by the state. More precisely, it is the milieu in which the state changes itself into society, or the society into the state' (ibid., p. 157). Individual action is transformed, given a collective meaning. The party claims to be a mediator; but since the society remains divided, in reality the party is just another particular among the particular interest groups, though it pretends that its decisions have universal social validity. Lefort's interpretation of the 20th Congress of the Russian Bolsheviks is that it marks the self-affirmation of the bureaucracy. During the heroic period, the bureaucracy, like the bourgeoisie of the French Revolution, had to hide its real purpose from itself, draping itself in mythical robes. A quarter of a century, and the industrialisation of Russia, call for a calming of the passions, ending the violence. Where the rising bureaucracy needed the Terror and the myth to forge its own unity, its base once established, it must find forms of a legitimate control. This is all the more necessary as, in the same quarter of a century, a working class has also arisen, forged from the ex-peasantry, and working in conditions of modern industry. Their needs too must be addressed, at least partially. The limits of what the bureaucray can do in this context are — in Lefort's interpretation of the time — those of the proletariat's need for self-management, as well as the fact that, to maintain itself, the bureaucracy establishes, politically, wage and work hierarchies which have as their effect the impossibility of making the Plan, since in such conditions it is not possible to calculate the cost of socially necessary labour power. The inefficiency of the Plan, and the new social needs of an industrial proletariat, force the bureaucracy to assert its hold through new measures of 'liberalisation', aimed at increasing participation in production and thus raising productivity.

9. The analyses of the events of 1953 and 1956 in Eastern Europe which were published in *Socialisme ou Barbarie* remain refreshingly actual. Their implications for the revised view of capitalism were drawn later, as the 'bureaucratic string' was pulled even further. See also 'Sur le contenu du socialisme', in *Socialisme ou Barbarie* (hereinafter *SB*), nos 17, 22, 23. Both Castoriadis and Lefort have recently published new essays on the 1956 Revolution in Hungary, in *Telos*, No. 29, Fall, 1976.

10. The relation betweeen Merleau-Ponty and the Socialisme ou Barbarie group would bear further study, as the essays on Lefort and Merleau-Ponty in this volume already suggest. From the circumstantial — Merleau-Ponty's use of Benno Sarel's still manuscript study of East Germany, his indebtedness to Lefort particularly as concerns the discussion of Trotsky, or the (unacknowledged) citation from Castoriadis in *Les*

aventures (pp. 312—13) or Castoriadis' citation of Merleau-Ponty's definition of praxis (*SB*, no. 38, p. 62), his use of Merleau-Ponty's adaptation of
Malreaux's 'deformation coherente' to describe the *imaginaire radical*
(ibid., no. 40, p. 45), or the return to the ontological problematic of the
institution — to the more substantial, the debt and interaction is immense.
This is not to say that Merleau-Ponty participated in the group's actions,
or that he played any practical role whatsoever. But the evolution of
Lefort and Castoriadis, and the problems elaborated by the revue *Textures*
of whose editorial committee they are members, point to a prolongation
of the Merleau-Pontean interrogation. Also worth mentioning for the
record here is the edition of the journal, *L'Arc* (no. 46, 1971), directed by
Lefort, to which most of the editors of *Textures*, including Castoriadis,
contributed.

11. This problem is concretely elaborated in 'Sur la dynamique du
capitalism' (*SB*, 12—13, 1953—4), and in 'Le mouvement révolutionnaire
sous le capitalisme moderne', *SB*, no. 31, 32, 33, 1960—1). A further
critique of Marx's naturalistic presupposition has been recently elaborated
in 'Justice, valeur et égalité: d'Aristote à Marx et de Marx à nous' in *Textures*,
1976. Here Castoriadis develops his political argument ontologically
by showing the a-historical, naturalist representation that Marx has of
human laboring activity, which either contradicts the determination of
the law of value or renders it trivial. Marx's image of humans as labour is
shown to be precisely that of the capitalist mentality.

12. Introduction générale, op. cit., p. 38.

13. *SB*, no. 38, p. 85; now in *L'institution imaginaire de la société*
(henceforth *L'institution*) p. 129.

14. This analysis is suggested in numerous places by Castoriadis, most
recently in 'La question de l'histoire du mouvement ouvrier', which is the
Introduction to the volume, *L'expérience du mouvement ouvrier, 1* (Paris:
UGE, 1974). (Henceforth 'La question.') The debates between Lefort and
Castoriadis from the early 1950s, and again from the 1950s, have been
reprinted in collections of their work, and each has returned to the
problem in recent interviews with the *Anti-mythes*. It would take us too
far afield to treat the debate in detail, or to discuss the practical problems
that emerged in Socialism ou Barbarie's history. The crucial point in our
context is that both Castoriadis and Lefort recognise that insofar as their
positions were still determined by the problematic of the proletarian
revolution, the debate was deformed. The further issues that emerge have
been dealt with in Chapter 9 and, here, in the concluding discussion of
Castoriadis' reformulation of the notion of revolution.

15. 'La question', op. cit., p. 78.

16. Castoriadis makes use of E. P. Thompson's important *The Making
of the English Working Class* in stressing this point. But where Thompson
avoids drawing the theoretical conclusions from his own work, Castoriadis
brings them to the fore. In effect, Thompson recognises the creative role
of the working class in shaping itself as revolutionary subject, but he
refuses to draw the implications as concerns the Marxism to which he
doggedly holds. Thompson combines the most acute historiographical
methods with an ultimately dogmatic and unthinking hold to what he

takes to be (humanist) Marxism. This was clearly manifest in a recent talk he presented to a group of radical historians in New York City in 1976.

17. 'La question', op. cit., p. 113.

18. Ibid., p. 112.

19. It is obvious that human need is a fundamental factor in history; a starving society can establish no social formation. But we will see in Section IV how Castoriadis deals with this 'natural stratum'. For now, it suffices to add only the observation that the same natural needs have given rise to a dizzying multiplicity of forms of satisfaction, such that their explanation in terms of need is either trivial or practically useless.

20. Thus, the *Communist Manifesto*'s beginning sections read like a hymn of praise to capitalism — one can hardly think of a better justification than the one offered by Marx. The development which culminates in Stalin and the mentality 'sacrifice yourself for the sake of your children('s children?)' is nothing but the logical conclusion of this perspective on history . . . and reads like the moralising of a second-generation American suburban family-father.

21. *SB*, no. 37, p. 45; *L'institution*, p. 75.

22. *SB*, no. 38, p. 50; *L'institution*, p. 90.

23. *SB*, no. 35, p. 10 (article, 'Recommencer la révolution').

24. 'Introduction générale', op. cit., p. 14.

25. Ibid., p. 32.

26. *SB*, no. 35, p. 25 (article, 'Recommencer la révolution').

27. Claude Lefort's comments on this attempt are worth citing here. He argues that: 'It is already a fiction to suppose that men could decide "en connaissance de cause" the general objectives of production if only they were put in the position of being able to evaluate (thanks to the Plan-producing factory) the comparative costs of investments in all sectors, of being able to appreciate the consequences of their choices and to hierarchize those choices. The implication is, in effect, that once it is freed from the false representations and artificial constraints engendered by capitalism, 'desire' relates directly to the real and modulates itself with the aid of a slide-rule'. (In Interview with the *Anti-mythes*, p. 13) This remark is worth noting, even though we shall see that Castoriadis' developed ontology of the *magma* does not make the assumption that in socialism (or anywhere else for that matter) an individual could relate directly to a 'really-real' object.

28. *SB*, no. 37, p. 32; *L'institution*, p. 61.

29. *SB*, no. 39, p. 63n; *L'institution*, p. 187n.

30. *SB*, no. 38, p. 67; *L'institution*, p. 109.

31. In *Les Aventures*, Merleau-Ponty works through the implications of these *identical* assertions in his lengthy critique of Sartre, the reading of which cannot be too highly recommended in the context of today.

32. *SB*, no. 39, p. 28; *L'institution*, p. 143.

33. *SB*, no. 39, p. 37; *L'institution*, pp. 153–4.

34. Introduction générale, op. cit., p. 54. Comparing this assertion with Lefort's 'logic of the political', one sees that what for Lefort is constitutive of the *experience* of the political is here taken ontologically.

35. *SB*, no. 40, p. 63; *L'institution*, p. 222.

36. *L'institution*, p. 486.

37. In this manner, and in a detail which we cannot present here, Castoriadis avoids the reproach of 'existentialism'. A cow can be instituted as all sorts of things, from totem to tool; but it can never write a poem or invent the windmill. 'On ne peut pas dire n'importe quoi', repeats Castoriadis again and again.

38. *SB*, no. 40, p. 44; *L'institution*, p. 200.

39. Through mathematics and philosophy, Castoriadis illustrates this point in detail. The relation instituted by the *Legein* gives a set of significations in terms of which the world is presented; it thus constitutes what Castoriadis calls 'identitary-ensemblist logic'. The operators of the *Legein* — relations of separation/identification, with regard to/insofar as, validity as/validity for — can be indefinitely interated and combined. Once the specificity of the *Teukhein* — that it gives the relation of finality or instrumentality, referring what is to what is not yet could be — is added, the tradition of practical philosophy can be derived as well.

40. *L'institution*, p. 341.

41. One might observe here a reformulation of Marx's insights. Each society has a different finality which is instituted by its *Teukhein* and *imaginaire central*. Revolution properly speaking would be the institution of a new social finality, such that revolution would be based on 'labour' as instituted. In fact, however, we shall see that the revolution for which Castoriadis calls is not simply a change in the finality of production, although it includes that; it is something more and other. To call for a change in productive finality is to remain within the instituted thought of the *Legein* and the *Teukhein*. While recognising the impossibility of doing without these, Castoriadis wants to change our relation to them. Reform would be a change in social finality; revolution implies a change in social relations.

42. *L'institution*, p. 406.

43. Ibid., p. 417.

44. Ibid., p. 420.

45. Ibid., p. 422.

46. Ibid., p. 461.

47. Ibid., pp. 462–3.

48. Ibid., p. 446.

49. Ibid., pp. 450–1.

50. Ibid., p. 476.

51. Ibid., p. 495.

52. Ibid., pp. 295–6. Lefort's criticism on this point should be noted: 'The idea of auto-institution partakes of the most profound illusion of modern societies, i.e. of those societies in which (as Marx observed) little by little the relations of man to the earth, and relations of personal dependence are dissolved; of those societies in which there is no longer the possibility of inscribing the human order, the established hierarchies, in a natural or supernatural order — or better, the two at once — for the visible disequilibria there always pointed to an invisible order ... modern societies (and I am obviously not thinking only of the work of theorists, but of the discourse implied in social practice) are busy seeking in

themselves the foundation of their institution'. (Interview with *Anti-mythes*, p. 18.) Lefort sees Castoriadis giving in to the illusion of a total theory, in spite of his awareness of the danger. Castoriadis' reply would no doubt be to point out that Lefort's phenomenological ontology of experience leaves no room for a political project at all, and hence that he denies the possibility of revolution. He would further point out, as with reference to Lefort's critique of his analysis of the content of socialism (see n. 27), that while Lefort's description of modern societies is accurate, their search for their own foundation still takes the form of a traditional ontology based in a rationalism. His own notion of auto-institution does not follow the common-sense image of the consumer consciously choosing guns or butter, nor is it a version of the 'knowledge is power' theme. Despite their verbal differences, the two positions seem to me closer to one another than either would admit.

53. *L'institution*, p. 498.
54. Ibid., p. 483.

Index*

---

*Compiled by Charles Haeckling